A HISTORICAL INTRODUCTION TO
THE LAW OF OBLIGATIONS

A Historical Introduction
to the Law of Obligations

D. J. IBBETSON

OXFORD
UNIVERSITY PRESS

OXFORD
UNIVERSITY PRESS

Great Clarendon Street, Oxford OX2 6DP

Oxford University Press is a department of the University of Oxford.
It furthers the University's objective of excellence in research, scholarship,
and education by publishing worldwide in

Oxford New York

Athens Auckland Bangkok Bogotá Buenos Aires Calcutta
Cape Town Chennai Dar es Salaam Delhi Florence Hong Kong Istanbul
Karachi Kuala Lumpur Madrid Melbourne Mexico City Mumbai
Nairobi Paris São Paulo Singapore Taipei Tokyo Toronto Warsaw
and associated companies in Berlin Ibadan

Oxford in a registered trade mark of Oxford University Press
in the UK and certain other countries

Published in the United States
by Oxford University Press Inc., New York

British Library Cataloguing in Publication Data
Data available

Library of Congress Cataloging in Publication Data
Data available

ISBN 0-19-876412-X

1 3 5 7 9 10 8 6 4 2

Typeset in Times by
J&L Composition Ltd, Filey, North Yorkshire
Printed in Great Britain
on acid-free paper by
Biddles Ltd, Guildford and King's Lynn

Preface

Legal history takes many forms. This book is a history of legal categories, concepts and doctrines; the mechanisms used by lawyers to organize their thoughts. Such a work is of necessity both speculative and constructive. Legal ideas are not natural facts waiting to be uncovered, and even the lawyers who use them rarely take the trouble to formulate them explicitly. On the contrary, they are indeterminate and flexible, always at least potentially in a state of flux. Lawyers, if they put their mind to the matter at all, will commonly disagree about them. Even if there is a sufficient consensus among lawyers at any given time to enable us to identify a fairly solid core, there will always be forward-looking individuals proposing different models and structures.

However slippery it is to grasp, it does not follow that legal doctrine has no history. Quite the reverse. The fact that it is in its nature fluid and dynamic enables us to describe its history with more certainty than we can describe its state at any single point in time. It might still be argued that it is not worthwhile to do so. Only in the most uncontroversial cases will legal doctrine itself directly determine the outcome of actual litigation; judges have always had a sufficiently wide range of techniques available to them to ensure that they can reach a desired decision should they want to do so strongly enough. None the less, it is not irrelevant; even a sceptic will admit that the way in which a question is put and the form in which legal argument is couched will have some effect on the answer that is given. It operates as a restraint on judicial flights of fancy, it can be used to legitimate decisions. More importantly, so long as our conception of justice requires that like cases should be treated alike it provides the framework enabling lawyers to identify relevant similarities and differences between one case and another.

I hope that I have addressed at least some of the questions that historians of English law have traditionally found important. Inevitable limitations of space and time have meant that I have glossed over many points of detail and have simplified complex stories. Nor has it been possible even to touch on the full range of arguments put forward by others. The closer the work approached the twentieth century, the stronger the feeling of helplessness in the face of the huge mass of material. All I can hope to have done is to waymark a path through the thickets, pointing out a few of the more interesting sights along the route.

Legal history is too important to remain within the domain of specialist legal historians. The structure of modern law is too heavily dependent on the legacy of the past for it to be marginalized as something of purely antiquarian interest. If we are to make sense of today's law we have to understand its history, and it is only when we can make sense of it that we can confidently begin to reform it. Equally importantly, English legal history cannot remain the exclusive property of English legal historians. The moves towards an increasing harmonization of European private law have been accompanied by an increasing concern with European legal history on the part of continental scholars. If Europe is not to begin at Calais, English legal historians have to speak the same language as their continental counterparts or allow it to be assumed by default that the development of English law was not significantly different from the pre-codification development of continental legal systems, that the Common law was part of the European *ius commune*. I hope this book contributes to these debates.

The book has been long in the making. In the course of the research and writing of it I have contracted debts of gratitude to many friends and colleagues for references, corrections, inconvenient questions and timely hints. Thanks in particular are due to Paul Brand, Mindy Chen-Wishart, Robert Feenstra, Jeffrey Hackney, Henry Horwitz, Neil Jones, Jeroen Kortmann, Mike Macnair, Mark McGaw, Christopher McNall, Hector MacQueen, Paul Mitchell, Ben Parker, Bernard Rudden, Roger Smith, Jane Stapleton and Warren Swain. I am especially grateful to Mindy Chen-Wishart for reading the chapters on modern contract law and unjust enrichment and gently pointing out where I had gone astray. Over the years I have had the enormous advantage of near-daily conversation with my colleagues at Magdalen College: John Feltham, Katharine Grevling, Roger Smith, Colin Tapper and Guenter Treitel. I have gained no less from the comments and criticisms of generations of students; there can be no better testing ground for ideas than an Oxford tutorial, and no better way of winnowing wheat from intellectual chaff. Above all, I have benefited from the learning, generous advice and commitment to scholarship of John Baker and Peter Birks; to each of them I owe a great deal. Needless to say, all faults which remain are my responsibility alone.

It is the happy privilege of the historian to be able to choose a convenient cut-off point at which to end a study. I have made no attempt to take account of any changes in the law taking effect after 25 April 1999.

Contents

Table of Cases

CASES IN LOCAL COURTS

ANONYMOUS CASES

Abbreviations

AF	Ames Foundation
B&M	J. H. Baker and S. F. C. Milsom, *Sources of English Legal History* (London, 1986)
Bac Abr	M. Bacon, *New Abridgement of the Law* (1736)
BL	British Library
BNB	F. W. Maitland (ed.), *Bracton's Note Book* (London, 1887)
Bodl	Bodleian Library, Oxford
Br Abr	R. Brooke, *Abridgement* (1573)
Bracton	*De Legibus et Consuetudinibus Angliae* (S. E. Thorne (trans.), *Bracton on the Laws and Customs of England* (Cambridge, Mass., 1968–77))
Britton	F. M. Nichols, *Britton* (Oxford, 1865)
C1	Public Record Office, Petitions in Chancery (fifteenth century, otherwise undated, unless stated)
C2/Eliz1	Public Record Office, Petitions in Chancery, reign of Elizabeth I
CEMCR	A. H. Thomas, *Calendar of Early Mayor's Court Rolls* (Cambridge, 1924)
CPMR	A. H. Thomas, *Calendar of Plea and Memoranda Rolls* (Cambridge, 1926–61)
CP 40	Public Record Office, Plea Rolls, Court of Common Pleas
CRO	County Record Office
CRR	Curia Regis Rolls
CUL	Cambridge University Library
ELABD	R. C. Palmer, *English Law in the Age of the Black Death* (Chapel Hill, NY, 1993)
E127	Public Record Office, Exchequer Decrees and Orders
F Abr	A. Fitzherbert, *La Graunde Abridgement* (1516)
Glanvill	*Tractatus de Legibus et Consuetudinibus regni Anglie qui Glanvilla vocatur* (G. D. G. Hall (ed.), *The Treatise on the laws and Customs of the Realm of England commonly called Glanvill* (London, 1965))
HLS	Harvard Law School
HMC	Historical Manuscripts Commission

IT	Inner Temple
JUST 1	Public Record Office, Plea Rolls, Justices in Eyre
KB 27	Public Record Office, Plea Rolls, Court of King's Bench
Kiralfy, *Source Book*	A. K. R. Kiralfy, *A Source Book of English Law* (London, 1957)
LI	Lincoln's Inn
MT	Middle Temple
PP	Parliamentary Papers
PRO	Public Record Office
Ro Abr	H. Rolle, *Abridgment des Plusiers Cases* (1668)
RS	Rolls Series
SC2	Public Record Office, Court Rolls
SS	Selden Society
Stath Abr	N. Statham, *Epitome Annalium Librorum tempore Henrici Sexti* (1490)
Vin Abr	C. Viner, *General Abridgment of Law and Equity* (1741–58)

Table of Regnal Years

William I	1066–1087
William II	1087–1100
Henry I	1100–1135
Stephen	1135–1154
Henry II	1154–1189
Richard I	1189–1199
John	1199–1216
Henry III	1216–1272
Edward I	1272–1307
Edward II	1307–1327
Edward III	1327–1377
Richard II	1377–1399
Henry IV	1399–1413
Henry V	1413–1422
Henry VI	1422–1461 and 1470–1471
Edward IV	1461–1483
Edward V	1483
Richard III	1483–1485
Henry VII	1485–1509
Henry VIII	1509–1547
Edward VI	1547–1553
Mary	1553–1558
Elizabeth I	1558–1603
James I	1603–1625
Charles I	1625–1649
Interregnum	1649–1660
Charles II	(1649) 1660–1685
James II	1685–1688
William III	1689–1702
Anne	1702–1714

George I	1714–1727
George II	1727–1760
George III	1760–1820
George IV	1820–1830
William IV	1830–1837
Victoria	1837–1901
Edward VII	1901–1910
George V	1910–1936
Edward VIII	1936
George VI	1936–1952
Elizabeth II	1952–

Prologue: The Prehistory of the English Law of Obligations

The Common law of obligations grew out of the intermingling of native ideas and sophisticated Roman learning. The friction between them was a prime force for legal change, and has remained so right up to the present day. The present chapter is an attempt to identify these basic building blocks.

PERVASIVE IDEAS

Few if any modern-day historians would want to go to the extremes of nineteenth-century German historiography in postulating the existence of a unitary Germanic legal system extending throughout northern Europe in the early Middle Ages.[1] Even if we were minded to do so, there are hardly sufficient data from which to draw substantial conclusions. But this is not to say that we have to ignore traditional social values completely; there is sufficient evidence for us to be able to sketch out a few very basic ideas, which seem to have been widely spread throughout early medieval Europe. The evidence is widely diffused and the observations based on it have to be treated with great caution. They may all be wrong. Nevertheless, the attempt has to be made, for it is only on the basis of the existence of such a belief system that we can begin to make sense of the contours of the later medieval law of obligations.

Penalties and Entitlements

Early medieval systems had a clear conception of the penalization of wrongdoing. Texts frequently refer to the infliction of a fixed penalty for relatively minor infractions[2] or to the payment to the injured party of double the value of the loss caused.[3] This early idea of wrongdoing does not allow a clear division between crime and tort, between public and

---

[1] J. Q. Whitman, *The Legacy of Roman Law in the German Romantic Era* (Princeton, 1990), esp. 66–91; W. Davies and P. Fouracre, *The Settlement of Disputes in Early Medieval Europe* (Cambridge, 1986), 2–3.

[2] J. Grimm, *Deutsche Rechtsaltertümer* (4th edn., Leipzig, 1899), 2.210–54; F. Liebermann, *Die Gesetze der Angelsachsen* (Halle, 1906), 2.336–8.

[3] E. Mayer, 'Das altspanische Obligationenrecht in seinen Grundzügen' (1920) 38 Zeitschrift für Vergleichende Rechtswissenschaft 31, 52–66.

private wrongs: legal redress for wrongs would invariably be activated by the victim or the victim's family, but the penalty might go either to the victim or to some personification of the state. Juxtaposed with this idea of penalizing wrongdoing is a broad idea of claims based on entitlements. The central core of this idea is the familiar proprietary one postulating a relationship between a person and a specific thing, but it extended far beyond this to cover claims to generic goods or money. A claim to recover goods that had been stolen, a claim to receive goods that had been bought, and a claim to wages that had been earned would have been typologically equivalent.

The central division here is between the nature of claims rather than between the circumstances giving rise to those claims. The modern category of torts would map easily into the medieval principles relating to the penalizing of wrongdoing and the modern category of property would map into the medieval entitlement-based claims; neither would exhaust them. More importantly, there was no room for a separate category equivalent to our contractual liability. A contract[4] might generate an entitlement-based claim, as where the seller of goods demanded the price or the buyer of goods demanded the thing; or it might generate a wrong-based claim. Medieval Iceland and Norway, for example, imposed a penalty for 'breach of handshake', which clearly had a 'contractual' dimension,[5] and early Spanish and French texts similarly penalized the failure to carry out a sale that had been the subject of a binding agreement.[6]

Wrongs: Dishonour and Loss

While it would be pointless to try to define what constituted wrongdoing, since this is inevitably specific to particular cultures, it is noteworthy that medieval culture seems to have been concerned more with dishonour than with loss. This has the effect of skewing the sources towards deliberate rather than accidental injury, for it is transparently more dishonouring to hit a person deliberately than to do the same amount of harm accidentally. None the less, beneath the surface there may lurk ideas of a duty to compensate for unintentionally caused harm: in Iceland, for example, accidental injury was not in itself the subject of legal redress, but the failure

[4] For what constituted a contract at this time, cf. below, p.4.
[5] A. Heusler (ed.), *Isländisches Recht: Die Graugans* (Weimar, 1937), 298; *Den ældre Gulathings-Lov*, 72, 78, in R. Keyser and P. A. Munch (eds.), *Norges Gamle Love* (Christiania, 1846–95), 1.37, 39.
[6] A. Otero Varela, 'Las Arras en el Derecho Español Medieval' (1955) 25 Anuario de Historia del Derecho Español 189, 197–8; A. Esmein, *Études sur les Contrats dans le Très-Ancien Droit Français* (Paris, 1883), 28. Later English sources show the same idea at work: M. Bateson, *Borough Customs, i* (18 SS), 217–19.

to pay compensation within two weeks was regarded as dishonourable and (hence) brought it within the purview of the law.[7]

Early legal sources place considerable emphasis on breaches of peace.[8] This carried no necessary implication of violence, and might have included any breach of the law. More importantly, wrongs were characterized not simply as breaches of the peace, but as breaches of a particular person's (or group's) peace. Favoured places or persons could be placed under the king's peace—under the king's protection—so that wrongs done there or against them fell within the king's jurisdiction. The notion of the king's peace had considerable elasticity; it could be exploited by Anglo-Norman monarchs extending the boundaries of royal power, and it could be exploited by Anglo-Norman litigants wanting to take advantage of the processes of the kings' courts.

The Economy of Exchange

In the modern world the circulation of goods is achieved largely through contracts, most obviously the contract of sale. The early medieval European world was very different, for, although sales did occur, the transfer of property by way of gift was of far greater importance. It was, in this respect, typical of relatively undeveloped economic systems.[9] These gifts were not simple acts of altruism: on the contrary, the giving of a gift created a tension between the parties that could be resolved only by the original recipient making a counter-gift.

This obligation of reciprocity was forcefully articulated in northern European literary sources. Its starkest expression is found in the Icelandic *Havamal*, repeated in the earliest written laws of Norway and Sweden, in the form 'A gift demands a gift'.[10] The impetus towards reciprocity might have been very strong, but we must not lose sight of the fact that the stimulus to make the counter-gift came from the original recipient, not the donor: to request a counter-gift would undermine the voluntariness of the original gift and so dissolve the whole transaction. It follows from this

[7] W. I. Miller, *Bloodtaking and Peacemaking* (Chicago, 1990), 62.

[8] J. Goebel, *Felony and Misdemeanor* (Pennsylvania, 1937), 1–61; F. Pollock and F. W. Maitland, *History of English Law* (2nd edn. reissued, Cambridge, 1968), 2.453, 463.

[9] M. Mauss, *The Gift* (trans. I. Cunnison, London, 1954), remains the foundation for analysis of the gift economy; the best theoretical explanation is P. Bourdieu, *Outline of a Theory of Practice* (trans. R. Nice, Cambridge, 1977), esp. at 3–15. Subsequent work is discussed and criticized in D. Cheal, *The Gift Economy* (London, 1988). For medieval Europe, see A. Gurevich, *Categories of Medieval Culture* (London, 1985), 221–39; Miller, *Bloodtaking and Peacemaking*, 77–109. Specifically with reference to Anglo-Saxon England, see N. L. Surber-Meyer, *Gift and Exchange in the Anglo-Saxon Poetic Corpus* (Geneva, 1994).

[10] *Havamal* §146; cf. §§40–6 (in W. H. Auden and P. B. Taylor, *Norse Poems* (London, 1981), 165, 152); K. von Amira, *Nordgermanisches Obligationenrecht* (Leipzig, 1882), 1.506 ff. For the meaning of 'obligation' in this context, see Bourdieu, *Outline of a Theory of Practice*, 6, 16–22.

that the true difference between a gift and a contract was not that the one was gratuitous and the other reciprocal. Both involved reciprocity, but in a gift the nature and extent of the reciprocation was determined by the recipient, whereas in a contract it was a matter for negotiation.[11]

Oaths: Threats and Promises

In early medieval Europe, an individual who wished to take on a solemn obligation as to future behaviour would do so by means of an oath.[12] This would normally involve the recitation of words in a set form accompanied by some form of ritual gesture—for example placing one's (right) hand on a weapon, on a cross, on the Bible, on a reliquary or on the bones of an ancestor, or simply holding up the right hand with the thumb and first two fingers extended.[13] The overtones of these symbolic acts were complex and wide-ranging, but the essential core of oath-taking was relatively stable. In its typical form, it presupposed an external power, normally a god, by whom the swearer swore the oath; should the oath be broken, the god was called upon to impose punishment. Though oath-breaking ranked alongside murder in the hierarchy of wrongdoing,[14] it attracted no human sanction. Nor was there any sense in which the beneficiary of an oath was entitled to take steps to secure its performance. It followed from the fact that the oath created a relationship between the swearer and the god by whose name it was sworn, obliging the swearer to perform, that it could be used not merely to strengthen undertakings of beneficence but also to strengthen maledictions. In this context there was no difference between threats and promises: in neither was there any room for second thoughts if the swearer came to regret the oath.

Contracts and Personal Bonds

In addition to the oath, we may see a variety of other practices designed to engender relationships that would not be broken. These may be divided into two types: the handing-over of a pledge or some other token from

[11] Miller, *Bloodtaking and Peacemaking*, 85–6. For an argument, on philological grounds, that exchange was the whole basis of Indo-Iranian contractual thinking, see M. A. Meillet, 'Le Dieu Indo-Iranien Mitra' (1907) 10 Journal Asiatique 143.

[12] For the oath, see in general R. Verdier (ed.), *Le Serment* (Paris, 1991). For its use in medieval Europe, centring on Germany, see L. Kolmer, *Promissorische Eide im Mittelalter* (Kallmünz, 1989), esp. chs. 3 and 4.

[13] F. Billacois, 'Rituels du serment: Des personnages en quête d'une "voix off"', in Verdier, *Le Serment*, 1.23–33; J.-C. Schmitt, *La Raison des gestes* (Paris, 1990), 16–17, 296.

[14] J. Gaudemet, 'Le Serment dans le droit canonique médiéval', in Verdier, *Le Serment*, 63, 66–8.

debtor to creditor; and the mimicry of the creation of family or purely personal ties.

A thing handed from debtor to creditor might be something of substantial worth, or something more or less purely symbolic. Although on the surface these represent identical situations, in fact they seem to have functioned in very different ways. The substantial pledge is the easier to comprehend. Behind it lay the plausible assumption that the giver would want to perform the stipulated act in order to obtain the return of the pledge. So long as the value of the pledge was sufficiently high, and so long as its value could be realized in some way by the pledgee, there would be no real need for further means of putting pressure on the pledgor to perform.[15] On the contrary, the problematical situation would be where performance had been duly accomplished but the pledge had not been returned: such a case might have needed legal intervention to force the return of the property. Where the pledge was a worthless trifle—Frankish law referred to the handing-over of a twig or small stick[16]—the inducement for performance was something more complex than simple economic pressure. Here we need to look to the analogy of the oath. Just as the oath was a conditional self-curse, bringing about vengeance if the oath was broken, so the handing-over of the symbolic stick (or other token) effected a similar conditional self-curse, but in this case the power to activate the vengeance was in the hands of the pledgee.[17]

The handing-over of coins or rings was also commonly associated with the creation of personal ties, most obviously by marriage. Other rituals primarily associated with the creation of personal bonds might equally be translated from here into a more commercial context. Just as individuals making peace with each other or marrying each other might kiss or join, slap, or shake hands, so too might individuals making what we would regard as commercial contracts. The twelfth-century lawyer Azo went so far as to postulate an etymology of the Latin *pactum*, agreement, from the handslap, *percussio palmarum*;[18] however spurious his etymology, it does give a strong indication of the centrality of the handshake and related

---

[15] H. D. Hazeltine, *Die Geschichte des englischen Pfandrechts* (Breslau, 1907), 141–4.

[16] F. Pollock and F. W. Maitland, *History of English Law* (2nd edn. reissued, Cambridge, 1968), 2.186–7; P. Ourliac and J. de Malafosse, *Droit romain et ancien droit* (Paris, 1957), 1.51–2, 62–3.

[17] P. Huvelin, 'Magie et droit individuel' (1905) 10 Année Sociologique 1, 26–34 (perhaps too extreme). For the symbolism associated with sticks, see K. von Amira, *Der Stab in der germanischen Rechtssymbolik* (1909) 25 Abhandlungen der Königlich Bayerisschen Akademie der Wissenschaften, Philosophisch-philologische und Historische Klasse 1; note esp. p.150 n.8; other types of token are dealt with briefly in Ibbetson, 'From Property to Contract: the Transformation of Sale in the Middle Ages' (1992) 13 Jnl Leg Hist 1, 6–7. [18] Azo, *Summa Codicis*, 2.3.

gestures in European practice.[19] Equally potent was the sharing of wine in the creation of family ties and in their analogues, the making of treaties of peace, or the symbolizing of the community of the faithful in the mass. The same symbolic value could be retained by the use of these practices in the creation of more profane relationships.[20] All of these were well established by the twelfth century (and all survive today), providing a practical vocabulary for the expression of the creation of contractual relationships.

OBLIGATIONS IN ROMAN LAW

Fundamental to the Roman law[21] was a rigid cleavage between property and personal obligations, between rights *in rem* and rights *in personam*. The law of property governed the relations between persons and things; the law of obligations governed the relations between persons and persons. It was against this background that Justinian's *Institutes* gave the classic definition of an obligation: 'An obligation is a tie of law, by which we are so constrained that of necessity we must render something according to the laws of our state.'[22]

By the middle of the second century AD, the basic division between obligations arising out of delict (wrongdoing) and obligations arising out of contract had been clearly established, though it was recognized that there was a miscellaneous body of obligations that did not fit into either of these groups.[23] In contrast to the Germanic claim-based division between penalties and entitlements, Roman law divided actions by reference to their source. By the time of the Emperor Justinian four centuries later two further source-based categories had been added, quasi-contract and quasi-delict.

Delict

Justinian's *Institutes* identified four specific delicts: theft; robbery; causing wrongful loss; and *iniuria*, best translated as 'outrageous behaviour'. The first two of these played no part in the later law and can safely be ignored, but the last pair were of considerable importance. 'Causing wrongful

---

[19] Manuscripts of the thirteenth-century German *Sachsenspiegel* illustrate some thirty different forms of hand gestures: K. von Amira, *Die Handgebärden in den Bilderhandschriften des Sachsenspiegels* (1905) 23(2) Abhandlungen der Königlich Bayerisschen Akademie der Wissenschaften, Philosophisch-philologische und Historische Klasse, 161.

[20] See, with a wealth of examples, H. C. Trumbull, *The Blood Covenant* (New York, 1885).

[21] For the Roman law, see most comprehensively W. W. Buckland, *Textbook of Roman Law* (3rd edn., by P. G. Stein; Cambridge, 1963). On the law of obligations in particular, see R. Zimmermann, *The Law of Obligations* (Cape Town, 1990).

[22] Justinian, *Institutes*, 3.13.pr.   [23] Gaius, *Institutes*, 3.88.

loss',[24] based on a *lex Aquilia* traditionally (but no doubt inaccurately) dated to 287–286 BC, was concerned with damage to property. Strictly speaking it applied only to cases where the damage had been directly caused by the wrongdoer; supplementary remedies (*actiones utiles* or *in factum*) were supplied where the damage had been caused indirectly, and by the time of Justinian it is likely that these remedies went so far as to cover situations where economic loss had been caused wrongfully even where there had been no property damage. By this time wrongfulness was anchored to the idea of blameworthiness, *culpa*, but it was never further defined. It was wide enough to encompass something akin to the modern idea of negligence, but never co-extensive with this; in reality it was simply the reflection of the community's perception of what was wrongful. The fourth delict, *iniuria*,[25] covered all those situations where the wrongdoer's deliberate conduct constituted an affront to the honour of the victim. The conduct might take any form: common examples would be physical attacks, offensive language, or breaking into someone's home. In particular, it was, for the Romans, the appropriate action to cover injuries to free people.

Contract

Just as Justinian's *Institutes* divided delictal liability into four principal heads, so too was contract divided into four—verbal, written, consensual, and real—though the specific category of written contracts was obsolete by Justinian's time and had no part to play in the subsequent history. All were underpinned by the idea of agreement, *consensus*, though this functioned in different ways in the different categories of contracts.

The verbal contract, typified by the form known as the *stipulatio*, is given the most detailed treatment in the *Institutes*, and it is here that we find the most substantial treatment of the general principles of contractual liability.[26] This was a formal agreement, constituted by an exactly matching question and answer, which produced a unilateral obligation binding only the promisor. The precise details of the *stipulatio* are of no interest in the present context, but the general principles are important. First of all, the parties had to be acting voluntarily, with their words governed by their minds. There were rules of capacity excluding infants and lunatics from being parties to a *stipulatio*; and an apparently valid *stipulatio* might be vitiated by fraud or duress, though this had to be expressly pleaded. Secondly, there had to be an agreement and not simply a promise. Despite the unilateral nature of the liability created, it was essential that there should be a corresponding question and answer. A simple promise without

---

[24] Justinian, *Institutes*, 4.3.   [25] Ibid. 4.4.   [26] Ibid. 3.15–3.20.

a preceding question was a nullity, as was a promise to do something different from what had been demanded in the question. Moreover, it was essential not merely that the parties' words matched each other, but also that their intentions matched. If one thing was meant by the questioner and another thing by the promisor, then the *stipulatio* was a nullity: an apparent agreement might be undermined by error. Thirdly, the *stipulatio* created rights and duties only between the parties to it. It could have no effects whatsoever on third parties, making them neither creditor nor debtor. Fourthly, the action lay to give to the creditor the agreed performance. It did not matter whether any act had been done in reliance on the promise or any actual loss suffered: the creditor was entitled to performance or its value.

While the verbal contract was defined by its form, the consensual contracts were defined by their substance. They were divided into four heads, covering the most significant economic transactions: *emptio venditio*, or sale; *locatio conductio*, which covered a range of transactions from hire of goods to employment, held together rather loosely by the common feature that one person put property or services at the disposal of another in exchange for money; *societas*, or partnership; and mandate, where one person agreed to do something for another gratuitously.[27] Legal rules determined which category any particular transaction fell into, and the parties had no power to designate it as something else. On the other hand, they did have considerable freedom to fix their own terms; the law provided only a standard set of rights and duties, which applied in the absence of the parties' agreement to the contrary.

All four types of consensual contract were underpinned by the general principles of contracts dealt with above: voluntariness; agreement; lack of effect on third parties; and enforcement of contractual entitlements independent of reliance or actual loss suffered. With the exception of mandate, all of the consensual contracts were reciprocal, in the sense that each of the parties was to gain something from the agreement. In all four types it was the simple agreement of the parties that created the contract, without any necessary formality and without any need for either party to have begun to perform, though mandate (being gratuitous) was slightly anomalous in giving either party fairly wide powers to withdraw from the contract without liability. All were circumscribed by a requirement of good faith.

Outside the four consensual contracts, simple agreements—pacts—were in principle unenforceable. By the time of Justinian, though, it was just becoming established that in other forms of exchange agreements (goods for goods, goods for services, services for services) a party who had fully

---

[27] Justinian, *Institutes*, 3.23–3.26.

performed one side of the agreement might have an action to force the other party to perform the other side. Such agreements were known as innominate contracts; as relative latecomers on the scene of Roman law they do not play a significant part in Justinian's *Institutes*, but the general idea of reciprocal agreement that they embodied was to have a full part to play in the legal developments throughout Europe in and after the Middle Ages. Another latecomer that was to have a part to play in later developments was the *pollicitatio*, an informal promise of a gift to a municipality.[28] It was here that lawyers of the seventeenth century and afterwards found the legal basis for their rule that a promise did not create legal obligations until it had been accepted.

The juxtaposition of the *stipulatio* and the consensual contracts, especially as expanded by the innominate contracts, brings out the underlying duality of the Roman contractual system. On the one hand, there was a mechanism enabling individuals to frame their arrangements in such a way that they would be enforced by the law; on the other, there was a set of rights and duties deemed to apply to the common types of transactions unless the parties agreed otherwise.

The final category of contracts, the real contracts, stands apart from this duality. These were all species of loan, where liability arose not from the simple agreement but from the actual handing-over of the property.[29] Most primitive was *mutuum*, the loan of money or other consumable property; the borrower was obliged to return to the lender not the original property but the equivalent value of that which had been lent. By the side of this there were several forms of loans of things where the borrower was required to return the actual thing lent: *commodatum*, the loan for use; *depositum*, the loan for safe-keeping; and *pignus*, the handing-over of a pledge. Each of these had its own rules, though there were general principles governing the care that the borrower was required to take of the thing.[30] The three latter types approximated to the modern bailments, and the lender's claim for the return of the thing might easily have been classified as a proprietary claim rather than one arising out of contract, a property right rather than a personal obligation. For Roman law, though, property rights were so rigid as to create potential difficulties if the lender were limited to proprietary remedies—there would have been great difficulties, for example, if the lender brought a proprietary action for the return of the goods lent and the borrower asserted that they in fact belonged to a third party—hence it adopted the more precise analysis that the obligation to return the thing stemmed from the fact of the loan, not from any supposed property right on the part of the lender. The way was clear for all varieties of loan,

---

[28] Zimmermann, *Obligations*, 496 n.115. [29] Justinian, *Institutes*, 3.14.
[30] Ibid. 3.14.2.

whether for consumption or not, to be classified together as a distinct species of contract.

Quasi-Contract

The third head of personal obligation, as its name suggests, was seen as in some way related to contract. It included such situations as the recovery of money paid by mistake, which could be regarded as analogous to the loan of money; and the performance of some service for the benefit of another, analogous to the contract of mandate.[31] What separated these situations from straightforward contracts was that there was no genuine agreement between the parties. There was perhaps a dimly perceived idea that quasi-contractual obligations were based on a principle of unjust enrichment,[32] but this was never adequately formalized by the Roman jurists and there is no trace of it in the *Institutes*. The equation of these non-contractual situations with genuine contractual liability had a thoroughly baleful effect on later Common-law developments.

Quasi-Delict

Finally, the Romans completed their fourfold division of personal obligations with a category that seems to have had no doctrinal coherence. It consisted of two situations of strict liability imposed on the occupiers of buildings, the liability of a judge to take over the liability of a defendant when his procedural error had led to the premature termination of a lawsuit before judgment had been given, and the strict liability of an innkeeper for the loss of a guest's goods. The last of these heads of liability crept into English law in the Middle Ages, possibly by direct borrowing from Roman law; but in the absence of any doctrinal unity the category of quasi-delict has had no part to play in the development of English law. It can safely be ignored.

---

[31] Justinian, *Institutes*, 3.27.

[32] D.50.17.206: 'Jure naturae aequum est, neminem cum alterius detrimento et injuria fieri locupletiorem', repeated in substantially the same form in D.12.6.14.

Part One. Form and Substance in Medieval Law

The medieval Common law was a law of actions and procedure. The structure of the law was provided by the forms of action. Legal expertise consisted in the knowledge of the way in which claims should be framed and the ways in which the legal process could be manipulated in order to get the better of one's opponent. It was highly technical, sometimes arcane, likened to a complex game of chess. This formalism tends to conceal substantive principles, but there is no reason to doubt that medieval law was undershot by substantive ideas. The problem is to identify what they were.

By the thirteenth century, the forms of actions themselves allow us to identify the broad conceptual categories of tort and contract, trespass and covenant. Indeed, one of the most potent forces for change in the medieval law seems to have been the exploitation of the uncertain boundary between the two. We may without too much imagination sketch the main outlines of these concepts. Glimmers of light escape from the cracks between the forms of action; hints are dropped in the course of legal argument. Records of litigation in local courts, where people tended to say what they meant more readily than in the royal courts, add to the picture; though we have to take some care not to be misled by what might turn out to be atypical local practices. Further insight can be gained from the medieval equivalents of academic works: Glanvill towards the end of the twelfth century, Bracton in the second quarter of the thirteenth, Britton and Fleta in the 1290s. Finally there are what are coming to be seen as basic teaching materials, from the law school of medieval London and the business school of medieval Oxford.

The picture sketched out is necessarily a distortion. Legal categories are not real entities; different people might legitimately see things in different ways; abstract words can have a shifting range of meaning. Medieval law, though, was no worse in this respect than that of the twentieth century. On the contrary, where the whole focus of the law was on forensic practice rather than academic speculation, there was far less scope for individual theorizing about fundamental principles, and where legal culture was largely oral rather than printed there was far less opportunity for ideas that diverged from the mainstream to gain any measure of acceptance.

It is far less easy to speak with any degree of assurance about more detailed rules of 'the law of tort' or 'the law of contract'. This is not simply a problem of interpreting the surviving evidence. The nature of the trial process inevitably allowed a fuzziness around the edges of the law: issues of a high level of generality were commonly left to the jury, defendants might swear away liability by the 'irrational' process of wager of law. Even when we do see very specific determinations of cases, we must take care not to assume too easily that these represented the application of rules in the modern sense. Before the explosion of widely circulating printed law reports in the seventeenth century there was less opportunity for rules to become fixed, with the result that there was an inevitable indeterminacy on the outer boundary of legal liability.

1. *Structural Foundations*

LIABILITY FOR WRONGDOING: DAMAGE AND DISHONOUR

The twelfth-century royal courts seem to have been little concerned with personal obligations. The stress of Glanvill's *Treatise* is almost entirely on personal status and the law of real property; one of its fourteen books, the tenth, looks in the direction of contractual liability,[1] but there is little thought of the provision of redress for wrongdoing. There is one short section dealing with criminal wrongs—*placita criminalia*—but the focus of this is on the punishment of those guilty of the most serious forms of antisocial behaviour—treason (and the fraudulent concealment of treasure trove), homicide, arson, robbery, rape, forgery, and theft—rather than on the compensation of their victims.[2] Some types of wrongful conduct, most obviously dispossession of freehold land and the closely related situation of nuisance (interference with the enjoyment of freehold land), would have fallen within the range of the real actions that formed the mainstay of the royal courts' work; but it was their association with freehold property rather than simply wrongful behaviour on the part of the defendant that activated the royal courts.[3] The earliest plea rolls tell the same story. In addition, from the beginning of the thirteenth century we begin to find a small number of more general 'trespass' actions, commonly alleging that the wrong complained of was done in breach of the king's peace; these actions were not freely available, but writs would be granted to magnates or other favoured individuals who would and could pay for the king's intervention. Such complaints become increasingly common by the middle of the thirteenth century: more litigants were willing to pay for the king's justice, and more litigants were manipulating the form of criminal process known as the 'appeal' in order to bring complaints of more trivial wrongdoing to the royal courts.[4] Some time, perhaps in the late 1250s, the writ of trespass became

---

[1] Below, p.17.   [2] Glanvill XIV (ed. Hall, 171–7).
[3] R. van Caenegem, *Royal Writs in England from the Conquest to Glanvill* (77 SS), 283–90; D. W. Sutherland, *The Assize of Novel Disseisin* (Oxford, 1973); S. F. C. Milsom, *Historical Foundations of the Common Law* (2nd edn., London, 1981), 137–43. These writers differ profoundly in their analyses of the early history of the action, but none (I think) would dissent from my very general formulation. For the assize of nuisance, see J. S. Loengard, 'The Assize of Nuisance' [1978] CLJ 144. Glanvill XIII. 33–7 (ed. Hall, 167–9) makes it abundantly clear that at first nuisance was no more than an alternative aspect of novel disseisin.
[4] C. A. F. Meekings, *Crown Pleas of the Wiltshire Eyre 1249* (Devizes, 1961), 81–8. For the relationship between the appeal process and the writ of trespass, see A. Harding, *Roll of the*

a 'writ of course' and was routinely available to anybody who asked for it. Writs of trespass (*brevia de transgressione*) make their appearance in the Registers of Writs, and they become an increasingly common feature in the plea rolls of the royal courts.[5] This does not mean that the vast majority of wrongdoing went unredressed before the late thirteenth century. Glanvill himself directs us to the ecclesiastical courts,[6] and actions of trespass are plentiful in the earliest manorial and borough court records; through these it is possible to obtain some idea of the contours of liability.

We should beware of attempting to impose any rigid structure on the early action of trespass. The word 'trespass' meant no more than 'wrong', and its legal use had no predetermined boundaries.[7] It is, however, possible to identify from the early records two ideas at work: affronts to honour, and the causation of loss. If we are to understand the idea of wrongdoing in the twelfth and thirteenth centuries, we cannot afford to ignore either of these elements.[8]

By the middle of the thirteenth century, when the local courts' records begin, the causation of loss appears to be the predominant feature of trespassory liability: in every case the plaintiff alleges that loss has been caused by the defendant's conduct. It should be noted that 'loss' here is a very broad concept. Cases in the Wallingford Burghmote—the court with some of the earliest surviving records—give some indication of this.[9] At its simplest, unsurprisingly, it included genuine out-of-pocket loss, as where the plaintiff's property had been stolen, destroyed, or damaged.[10] Less simply, it could represent an attempt to put a value on a loss that was essentially unquantifiable, as in the case where the plaintiff alleged some

---

Shropshire Eyre of 1256 (96 SS), pp.xxxii–lviii. Harding rightly stresses that we must be careful not to draw too firm a line between criminal and civil wrongs at this time; but in broad terms we may say that the appeal process was aimed at securing the punishment of the wrongdoer (although the complainant might hope to recover some compensation along the way), while the writ of trespass was aimed at the securing of compensation (although the wrongdoer might incidentally suffer imprisonment and have to pay a fine to the king).

[5] G. D. G. Hall, 'Some Early Writs of Trespass' (1957) 73 LQR 65.

[6] Glanvill, X.12 (ed. Hall, 126): 'Any breach of faith [or trespass] involved may be sued upon in an ecclesiastical court.' Hall's translation (inexplicably) omits 'or trespass'.

[7] G. L. Williams, *Liability for Animals* (Cambridge, 1939), 128, developed by S. F. C. Milsom, 'Trespass from Henry III to Edward III' (1958) 74 LQR 195, 407, 561; cf. Milsom, *Historical Foundations*, 285.

[8] J. S. Beckerman, 'Affronts to Honor and the Origins of Trespass', in M. S. Arnold *et al.*, *On the Laws and Customs of England: Essays in Honour of Samuel E. Thorne* (Chapel Hill, NY, 1981), 159, 165 n.35.

[9] See HMC, 6th Report, Appendix, 572 ff. Cases referred to are transcribed in this volume (referred to below as HMC), or remain in manuscript in the Berkshire CRO, ref. W/JBa.

[10] e.g. *Sotewelle* v. *Pain* (1233; HMC 573); *de Wodecote* v. *Holle* (1245; HMC 574); *le Cuver* v. *Verder* (1275; W/JBa 25 m.3d).

physical injury[11] or verbal insult.[12] It was wide enough to include a loss of expectations, covering situations where the defendant had failed to carry out a covenant or contract made with the plaintiff.[13] It would even perhaps include situations where the defendant's wrongful act prevented the plaintiff receiving the benefit of some contract from a third party.[14]

It is less easy to put down any markers as to what made conduct wrongful. All too frequently the courts' records conceal the specific fact situations behind a general *iniuste*, leaving the historian none the wiser. It clearly covered unjustified physical interference with the person, land, or goods, and it seems likely that this interference did not have to be deliberate.[15] It clearly covered unjustifiably opprobrious words.[16] It clearly covered the breach of a contract or covenant,[17] though as the thirteenth century progressed cases of pure non-performance, as opposed to mis-performance, become very uncommon. There is little point in trying to be more specific than this: wrongfulness was at its heart an open-ended concept, which could be moulded to shifting social perceptions of acceptable and unacceptable behaviour.

Cutting across this unspecific nature of wrongdoing, to some extent overlaid upon it, was the older idea of the affront to honour.[18] As has been seen, the concern with dishonour was a central feature of the Germanic (including Anglo-Saxon) notion of wrongdoing, reflecting the importance of honour and status within Germanic society.[19] It is an idea still close to the surface in the *Leges Henrici Primi* (*c*.1114);[20] its traces are

---

[11] e.g. *Alixa* v. *Pani* (1238; HMC 574); *Perderel* v. *Poter* (1245; HMC 574).

[12] e.g. *de Ros* v. *de Stalles* (1232; HMC 573); *Alice* v. *Walter* (1233; HMC 573).

[13] e.g. *Cocus* v. *Pewman* (1261; W/JBa 14 m.1). See too the cases cited below, n.17.

[14] The most obvious situation in which this arose was where a servant was enticed away into another's employment: Britton, 1.131. A good early example is *de Chalkeleye* v. *Cocus* in the Ruthin court in 1300 (SC2/215/68 m.1; summarized in R. A. Roberts (ed.), *Court Rolls of the Lordship of Ruthin* (London,1893), 47), an action supplementary to the primary suit against the servant. See further E. Clark, 'Medieval Labor Law and English Local Courts' (1983) 27 Am Jnl Leg Hist 330, 335 n.18. Another situation where loss of the benefit of a contract with a third party might be alleged was where the defendant had defamed the plaintiff (e.g. *Geyst* v. *Dunwich* (1292; 101 SS 30), *Wakefield* v. *Brownsmith* (1306–8; 101 SS 31)) or his goods (*Engham* v. *Burton* (1287; 101 SS 29), *Curteys* v. *Poyfoy* (1289; 101 SS 30)).

[15] Cf. M. S. Arnold, *Select Cases of Trespass from the King's Courts 1307–1399* (100 SS), pp.xlii–xliii; below, p.58.

[16] R. H. Helmholz, *Select Cases of Defamation to 1600* (101 SS), pp.xlviii–lxv. In the ecclesiastical courts liability was anchored to the making of untrue allegations of criminal behaviour, but secular courts did not always observe such a limitation: below, p.113.

[17] *le Hainere* v. *le Saltere* (1277; Andover In and Out Hundred (Hampshire CRO) 2/HC/4, m.18 (non-delivery of goods sold)); *le Riche* v. *de Appelsawe* (1282; Andover In and Out Hundred (Hampshire CRO) 2/HC/8 m.5d (breach of warranty of quality)); *de Bocland* v. *de Abbehale* (1298; London Mayor's Court, *CEMCR*, 9) (non-delivery of goods sold)); *Glover* v. *Kyng* (1308; Shrewsbury Borough Court (Shropshire CRO) SRR 3365/758 m.6) (retention of hired goods after end of term). Below, n.69.

[18] For what follows I draw heavily on Beckerman, 'Affronts to Honor'.

[19] Above, p.2.   [20] Beckerman, 'Affronts to Honor', 165–72.

easily discernible in the form of pleadings in the thirteenth-century manorial and borough courts, and present in a shadowy form in the records of the royal courts.[21] Commonly the plaintiff alleged not simply that the defendant had caused loss (*dampnum*), but also shame (*huntagium*, *pudor*).[22] Indeed, the way in which the claim for damages was framed might put considerable emphasis on this element.[23] It should be stressed that this idea of dishonour is a structural feature of trespassory liability, albeit one that is increasingly overshadowed by the unbounded notion of wrongfully causing loss, and not simply an element associated with certain forms of wrongdoing. The records of the Wallingford burghmote again show its range. It is, of course, found in claims based on offensive words,[24] but is by no means limited to these; it is no less present in claims based on injury to the person,[25] injury to property,[26] or the failure to perform a covenant.[27]

A concern with dishonour is a clear feature of Bracton's rather loose treatment of liability for wrongs in the second quarter of the century. Trespass was not at this stage a significant feature in the regular jurisdiction of the king's courts, and it was perhaps for this reason that his treatment is heavily dependent on the Roman law: it is a rather ragged attempt to bring together the Romans' liability on the *lex Aquilia*, wrongfully causing loss by damaging property, and the delict *iniuria*, focusing on dishonour and deliberate injuries to the person.[28] The element of dishonour in *iniuria* may seem to echo the element of dishonour found in the local courts' action of trespass. It is, however, a disharmonious echo, for two different conceptions of dishonour are in issue. The Roman idea, repeated by Bracton, was essentially upward looking; it was concerned primarily with insolence from an inferior to a superior, if only a self-styled superior. Bringing the action emphasized the plaintiff's superiority. The Germanic conception presupposed a relationship between near-equals, if not actually a downward-looking one. Offensiveness to a superior should be met with physical retribution; to complain of such behaviour, let alone to make it the

---

[21] For the royal courts, see H. G. Richardson and G. O. Sayles, *Select Cases of Procedure without Writ under Henry III* (60 SS), pp.cviii–cxiv. Their account, written largely in ignorance of the local court records, overstresses the parallel with canon law.

[22] Beckerman, 'Affronts to Honor', 172–6.   [23] Ibid. 175.

[24] e.g. *de Ros* v. *de Stalles* (1232; HMC, 6th Report, Appendix (hereafter HMC), 573); *Alice* v. *Walter* (1233; HMC 573); *Witer* v. *Scat* (1238; HMC 573); *Hurur* v. *Ysabel de Hundestrate* (1238; HMC 573); *Painter* v. *Eldret* (1238; HMC 574); *de Rom* v. *Eustace* (1238; HMC 574).

[25] e.g. *le Mercer* v. *fitz Aumor* (1238?; HMC 574); *Alixa* v. *Pani* (1238; HMC 574); *Perderel* v. *Poter* (1245; HMC 574).

[26] e.g. *Stanford* v. *Wike* (1232; HMC 573); *Sotewelle* v. *Pain* (1233; HMC 573); *de Wodecote* v. *Holle* (1245; HMC 574).

[27] e.g. *Aurifaber* v. *de Stalles* (1252; Berkshire CRO, W/JBa 11) (pleaded as an action of covenant); *Cocus* v. *Pewman* (1261; W/JBa 14 m.1) (pleaded as an action of trespass). Note too its presence elsewhere in actions of covenant and debt: below, nn.45, 70.

[28] Bracton f.155–155b (ed. Thorne, 2.437–8). For the Roman law, see above, p.7.

subject of a lawsuit, was in itself demeaning and served merely to underline the lower status of the complainant.[29] The falseness of Bracton's echo suggests that he was merely using the vocabulary of his Roman sources, and that the concept of dishonour was no longer for him a substantial feature of liability for wrongs. Whatever weight we put on his language, it is clear that dishonour was in the process of disappearing from the legal register; it plays no part in the pleading of actions of trespass in the royal courts in the second half of the thirteenth century.[30]

As the language of dishonour disappeared, liability for wrongdoing was exclusively focused on the causation of loss. This became the central feature of the action of trespass, and it has remained the central feature of the English law of tort. Far more difficult was the question whether trespass would be left in this essentially unbounded form or whether it would crystallize around particular sorts of loss-causing wrongdoing.

GLANVILL AND THE LAW OF DEBT

By comparison with the murkiness of the history of trespass in the twelfth and early thirteenth centuries, we are relatively well provided for in attempting to penetrate the scope of contractual liability; but it is only relative. Book X of Glanvill's *Treatise* deals with the writ of debt. It is coloured by an untypical degree of hesitancy, and probably owes more than the rest of the work to Roman law.[31] Its focus is narrow, and it is possible to extract from it only the most veiled hint as to any underlying ideas of contractual liability that might have existed. Nevertheless, despite these limitations, it brings out a number of features fundamental to much of the later Common law.

This tenth book bears the title 'Pleas concerning the debts of laymen'.[32] It begins with an uncompromising claim of jurisdiction—'Pleas concerning the debts of laymen also belong to the crown and dignity of the lord king'[33]—and continues by giving the form of the appropriate writ to summon the debtor to court.[34] By contrast, at two points in the book, the author is at pains to point out that 'private agreements'—*privatae conventiones*—are not customarily dealt with by the king's courts.[35] Such

---

[29] Not only in the Middle Ages: D. Herzog, *Happy Slaves* (Chicago, 1989), 132.

[30] The latest examples of this form of pleading that I have noticed are in the Exeter Mayor's Court in the reign of Edward II, although there are undoubtedly later examples that I have not found; it is fair to say, though, that the pleading form is very uncommon even in local courts after 1300. [31] Below, n.47.

[32] Glanvill, X (ed. Hall, 116). [33] Glanvill X.1 (ed. Hall, 116).

[34] Glanvill X.2 (ed. Hall, 116–17).

[35] Glanvill X.8, X.18 (ed. Hall, 124, 132). For the meaning of *privatae conventiones*, see P. Hyams, 'The Charter as a Source for the Early Common Law' (1991) 12 Jnl Leg Hist 173, 180–1.

claims might be allowed as a matter of special royal grace, which would presumably have to be paid for, but Glanvill's text is clear that they were not seen as forming part of the regular jurisdiction of the king's courts.[36] For him, then, there is a clearly demarcated (if not clearly defined) distinction between actions to recover debts and actions to enforce agreements. Alongside this is a hint of recognition that there might be a distinction between 'contracts' and 'agreements', *contractus* and *conventiones* in the Latin, though the precise nature of this distinction is shadowy in the extreme.[37]

The specimen writ of debt provided by Glanvill involves a claim for money: 'Command N. to render to R., justly and without delay, one hundred marks which he alleges that he owes him and which, he complains, he is unjustly withholding from him.'[38]

The plea rolls show that it was wider than this, extending also to claims for both specific and generic goods.[39] It was based on the plaintiff's entitlement to the money or the goods;[40] the reason for the entitlement, the *causa*, nowhere appears on the face of the writ. This *causa* might well be a contract—Glanvill specifically lists five such contractual *causae*[41]—but it did not have to be. It would be an anachronistic mistake to try to categorize the action of debt as a 'contractual' action. The plaintiff is claiming something as his due, his right; the form of the writ is close to the strongly proprietary writ of right (the fundamental action used to claim real property);[42] and in one of its aspects, the action *de re adirata*, it could be used to formulate what we can only regard as a proprietary claim, the claim of the 'owner' of goods against an innocent purchaser of them.[43] Just as

---

[36] R. van Caenegem, *Royal Writs in England from the Conquest to Glanvill* (77 SS), 256 n.1, 493 no.154. Hall, *Glanvill*, 189, seems far too hesitant.

[37] Glanvill X.18 (ed. Hall, 132).

[38] Glanvill X.2 (ed. Hall, 116): 'Precipe N. quod iuste et sine dilatione reddat R. centum marcas quas ei debet ut dicit, et unde queritur quod ipse ei iniuste deforciat.'

[39] The early Registers of Writs hardly distinguish between the various types: G. D. G. Hall, *Early Registers of Writs* (87 SS), 76–7. For discussion, see S. F. C. Milsom, 'Law and Fact in Legal Development' (1967) 17 Univ Tor L J 1, 6.

[40] Some historians, Maitland among them, have gone further than this and argued that the whole basis of the writ of debt is proprietary; but the use of this language is anachronistic, importing too many of our own preconceptions about the nature of property. See A. W. B. Simpson, *A History of the Common Law of Contract* (Oxford, 1975), 75–80.

[41] 'The cause of the debt may be loan for consumption, or sale, or loan for use, or letting, or deposit or any other just cause of indebtedness' (Glanvill X.3 (ed. Hall, 117)).

[42] van Caenegem, *Royal Writs in England from the Conquest to Glanvill* (77 SS), 254: 'The writ . . . was literally drafted after the wording of the classic *praecipe* for land, so literally in fact that certain expressions . . . were taken over, in spite of being inappropriate in a personal action for debt, although appropriate enough in a real action for tenure.'

[43] S. F. C. Milsom, *Novae Narrationes* (80 SS), pp.clxxviii–clxxix; J. M. Kaye, 'Res Addiratae and the Recovery of Stolen Goods' (1970) 86 LQR 379. The action is found only in local courts, but it is common there and its proprietary dimension is explicit. A good example is *Tatenale v. Aquam* (1312; Chester Pentice Court (Chester CRO) SR 9 m.13); in *Bynon v. Hope* in the Chester Pentice Court in 1320 (SR 27 m.2d) it was said that the plaintiff '*clamat proprietatem*'.

occurs in the writ of right, there is as well sometimes a hint of an association with wrongdoing in the writ of debt. In the admittedly crude classification of the mid-thirteenth-century *Fet Asaver*—where pleas in the king's
courts are divided into pleas of trespass and pleas of land—the writ of debt
is treated as a plea of wrong (trespass);[44] in local courts it is occasionally
infected by the language of shame and dishonour that was one aspect of
wrongdoing;[45] and ideas of fault normally associated with wrongdoing
might sometimes have come into play.[46]

Much of Glanvill's terminology is borrowed from Roman law, and in
places there are superficial similarities to the rules of Roman law.[47] Whether
Glanvill's model is Justinian's *Institutes* or some version of the vulgar law of
the western Roman empire is not easy to determine: his treatment of
purchase and sale, for example, bears a far greater resemblance to the
Visigothic code or its derivatives than it does to Justinian.[48] Whichever
is Glanvill's model, the Roman leanings of his text are confined to its
surface; its substance is a long way from Roman law. For Glanvill the
contract was only the *causa* of an entitlement, and the entitlement was the
basis of the plaintiff's claim; in Roman law the contract itself was the basis
of the action. Glanvill is concerned with the liability of sureties in a way
that is wholly different from Justinian's law.[49] Much of Glanvill's treatment
assumes that the debtor will have given to the creditor a gage or pledge and
that the creditor's primary protection is to be found in its sale; there is no
such assumption in Roman law.[50] The Romans' consensual contracts
(including sale) were completed by the simple agreement of the parties;
but when Glanvill alludes to such a principle in sale he immediately falsifies
it: 'A purchase and sale is effectively complete when the contracting parties
have agreed on the price, *provided that* this is followed by delivery of the
thing purchased and sold, or by payment of the whole or part of the price,
or at least by the giving and receipt of earnest.'[51]

The essentially Germanic idea of entitlement behind the action of debt,

---

[44] G. E. Woodbine, *Four Thirteenth Century Law Tracts* (London, 1910), 53, 112.
[45] e.g. *de Stallis* v. *de Vik* (1261; Wallingford Burghmote (Berkshire CRO) W/JBa 14 m.1d);
Tabernarius v. *Gilk* (1272; Ipswich Great Court (Suffolk CRO) C5/2/2 m.10d).
[46] e.g. *Bydeford* v. *Aunfrey* (1291; CP 40/90 m.53). Below, p.90.
[47] van Caenegem, *Royal Writs in England from the Conquest to Glanvill* (77 SS), 379–82.
[48] Glanvill X.14 (ed. Hall, 129–30). For the vulgar law, see E. Levy, *West Roman Vulgar
Law: The Law of Property* (Philadelphia, 1951), 156–64, and P. Merêa, 'Sobre a Compra e
Venda na Legislação Visigótica', in *Estudos de Direito Visigótico* (Coimbra, 1948), 83; for
Justinian's law, see *Institutes*, 3.23. The treatment of earnest money—*arra*—is especially
suggestive. Glanvill (X.14; ed. Hall, 130) leaves open the question of whether a person who
has given or received earnest may withdraw; this reflects the hesitancy of the *lex Romana
Visigothorum* 5.4.4 and its derivatives, rather than the certainty of Justinian's *Institutes* 3.23.pr.
[49] Glanvill X.3–5 (ed. Hall, 118–20); Justinian, *Institutes*, 3.20.
[50] Glanvill X.6–11 (ed. Hall, 120–6).
[51] Glanvill X.14 (ed. Hall, 129 (emphasis added)).

with its near-proprietary overtones, and the division between actions to obtain the payment of debts and actions to enforce agreements, are fundamental to Glanvill's treatment of the liability arising out of contracts. They were to become two of the principal distinctive features of the Common law, and their long-term consequences remain in the Common law of contract to the present day.

Glanvill's writ of debt was sufficiently flexible to encompass claims to specific chattels as well as generic goods and money. As far as actions for chattels (but not land) were concerned, there was no difference between owning something and being owed it. Hence there existed a stark division, even in the early Common law, between claims to land and claims to chattels.[52] There was no division corresponding to the Roman split between rights *in rem* and rights *in personam*. The Common law never overcame this cleavage; it never developed a proprietary action analogous to the Romans' *vindicatio* that might have united the rules of real property to those of personal property.

The features of Glanvill's treatment of the action of debt that have been discussed so far had long-term effects on the structure of the Common law. A further feature, no less potent in its long-term implications, affected the internal workings of liability arising out of contracts. Glanvill lists two forms of proof available to a plaintiff: proof by witnesses and proof by sealed charter.[53] In the former case there was room for some investigation, but in the latter case the document was conclusive: 'Where he acknowledges the seal publicly in court, he is bound to warrant the charter exactly and to observe without question the agreement set out in the charter as it is contained therein; and he should blame his own poor custody if he suffers damage because the seal was poorly kept.'[54] So long as his seal was on the deed, the defendant was liable; the only defences were to deny that the seal was his or to deny that the document was a deed at all—*non est factum suum*—because it was formally defective, because it had not been properly

---

[52] Note the division between pleas of land and pleas of wrongdoing in *Fet Asaver* (above, n.44).

[53] I take this to be the sense of Glanvill X.12: 'Per teste siquidem idoneum potest fieri inde disrationatio et per duellum; per cartam quoque' (ed. Hall, 126). Hall's translation, 'Proof of the debt may be made by suitable witnesses, or by battle, or by a charter', gives the impression that battle is a third form of proof. This seems wrong. At a later point in X.12 Glanvill sees battle as appropriate when reliance is placed on witnesses (ed. Hall, 127); I know of nothing to suggest that the plaintiff who failed to produce witnesses or charter could force the defendant to battle. For further discussion, see G. E. Woodbine, *Glanvill* (New Haven, 1932), 256.

[54] Glanvill X.12 (ed. Hall, 127). I have departed slightly from Hall's translation, 'he is strictly bound to warrant the charter'. In the Latin the adverb *prescise* governs *warantizare* rather than *tenetur*: it describes the way in which the debtor should warrant rather than the way in which he is bound. By the end of the thirteenth century this might have been watered down to the extent that it might have been necessary that the defendant had put the seal on the document: *Hamilton* v. *Seton* (1282; CP 40/45 m.38d): 'numquam fecit ei predictum scriptum nec sigillum suum apposuit.'

executed by delivery to the creditor, or because it was conditional.[55] The former was hazardous; if the jury found that the plea had been falsely made, the defendant would be imprisoned.[56] It was no plea that the obligation had been performed, unless the defendant could produce a sealed acquittance;[57] hence the defendant could not plead that the sum due had been paid, nor that the deed had been returned to the defendant for cancellation but that it had subsequently been snatched back by the plaintiff.[58] This stern rule would effectively have short-circuited any discussion of the underlying nature of the liability whenever the agreement had been embodied in a sealed charter. The point is succinctly stated in an early fourteenth-century notebook: if words of obligation are used in the writing, then the writing itself is the cause of the obligation.[59]

COVENANT AND A LAW OF CONTRACT

In its earliest form, the action of trespass had the capacity to deal with breaches of contract. The disappointed contractor who could not, or preferred not to, enforce performance by the action of debt might none the less receive a measure of compensation by making a claim based on the defendant's wrong in breaking the covenant.

In the course of the thirteenth century there emerged out of this wrong-based remedy an explicitly contractual action, the action of covenant. It first appeared in the royal courts right at the end of the twelfth century, and by the 1220s it was very common.[60] Within the royal courts it was concerned especially with real property, most notably leases,[61] though it was not confined to such situations. In 1200, for example, an action is

[55] Formally defective, e.g. 6 CRR 177; not delivered, e.g. *de la Lude* v. *Norwolde* (Eyre of Somerset, 1280; L. Landon (ed.), *Somerset Pleas 8 Edw I* (Somerset Record Society, 44, 1929), 66); conditional, e.g. *de Wilvingham* v. *de Penburgh* (Eyre of Dorset, 1268; JUST 1/202 m.7). See generally Britton, 1.162–71.
[56] YB 20 & 21 Edw I (RS) 40; YB 20 & 21 Edw I (RS) 110; *Neville* v. *Botereux* (Eyre of Northamptonshire, 1329; 97 SS 498); YB H.12 Ric II (AF) 118. cf. *de Bentel* v. *de Knyveton* (Eyre of Derbyshire, 1269: C. E. Lugard (ed.), *Calendar of the Cases for Derbyshire from Eyre and Assize Rolls* (Barnston, 1938), 121 (imprisonment for wrongful denial of charter raised as defence). Imprisonment might follow if the validity of a charter was impugned for some other cause, such as a false plea of infancy: *Saddock* v. *le Taillur* (Eyre of Staffordshire, 1227; G. Wrottesley (ed.), *Plea Rolls, temp. Henry III* (William Salt Archaeological Society, 4, 1883), 55). [57] Bracton, f.101 (ed. Thorne, 2.289).
[58] *Glaston* v. *Abbot of Crowland* (Eyre of Northamptonshire, 1329; 98 SS 665, 678).
[59] *Casus Placitorum* (69 SS), p.lxxxvii no.35: 'Ista verba in scripto, obligatum esse, faciunt scriptum esse pro causa rei obligate.'
[60] Simpson, *History of Contract*, 9; Ibbetson, 'Words and Deeds: The Action of Covenant in the Reign of Edward I' (1986) 4 Law & Hist Rev 71, 71–5.
[61] Pollock and Maitland, *History of English Law*, 2.217. A late version of the thirteenth-century *Brevia Placitata* deals with covenant specifically as an action concerned with leases: 66 SS 204.

referred to in one place as a plea of covenant, in another as a plea of chattels.[62] In 1226 an action of covenant was brought against one Adam the Carpenter concerning a bell tower; perhaps he was selling or leasing it, but it is altogether more probable that he was building or repairing it.[63] Given the strong emphasis of the royal courts at this time on actions concerning land, it is hardly surprising that the early action of covenant displays the same leanings; but 'covenant' meant no more than 'agreement', just as 'trespass' meant no more than 'wrong', and there is no good reason for imposing any predetermined limitations on the sort of agreements that might be actionable.[64] Certainly there were no such limitations in local courts; so far as the royal courts are concerned, the Registers of Writs—precedent books or formularies of model writs—mention no such limitation, and the Statute of Wales (1284) could say, without any hint of awkwardness, that there were as many forms of writ of covenant as there were types of agreement. For an anonymous lecturer of the early fourteenth century the ideas of covenant and contract were essentially indistinguishable.[65]

The new action of covenant occupied an ambiguous niche between the entitlement-based action of debt and the loss-based action of trespass. The idea of contract that it embodied was the same as lay behind Glanvill's action of debt; and the predominant form of the writ—by the fourteenth century the only form of the writ—was similar to that of debt in that its primary clause commanded the defendant to perform the agreement: 'Command B. that justly etc. he keep with A. the covenant made between them about one messuage with appurtenances in N.'[66]

It looked to the fulfilment of the plaintiff's expectations, his entitlement. At the same time it had strong trespassory dimensions, which from time to time, both in the royal courts and in the relatively unformulaic records of local courts, might seep through to the surface. It was, in form and in substance, an action for damages. Plaintiffs might complain of the breach of the agreement rather than begging for its enforcement: a common form of entry in the plea rolls of the middle of the thirteenth century shows that the defendant was required to explain why the agreement was being breached, using a form of language more appropriate to trespass than to debt—*quare non tenet conventionem inter eos factam*[67]—and sometimes the action is explicitly described as a plea of trespass, a plea of trespass and

[62] 1 CRR 357, 401.   [63] 12 CRR 1915.
[64] S. F. C. Milsom, 'Reason in the Development of the Common Law' (1965) 81 LQR 496, 500.   [65] CUL MS Dd 7.6(2) f.12: 'Conventio enim oritur ex contractu.'
[66] 87 SS 79 (writ CC 153c); cf. the writ of debt, above, n.38.
[67] See e.g. 11 CRR 140, 237, 2536; 12 CRR 300, 404, 508, 559, 663, 911, 1139, 1197, 1298, 1557, 1607, 1915, 2126, 2252, 2373, 2398; 14 CRR 2190; 15 CRR 437, 553, 854, 1662, 1695; 16 CRR 1408, 1571. cf. 16 CRR 2361: 'quare detinet unam carucatam terre . . . contra conventionem'.

broken covenant, or a plea of *iniuria*.[68] An action of covenant might be referred to in argument as based on a *tort*;[69] the language of shame and dishonour might continue to be used;[70] and even in the royal courts it was underpinned by ideas of fault and blame.[71]

This ambiguity was never quite resolved. One pervasive theme of the next seven centuries of legal history was the friction on the boundaries of the action for breach of contract—on the one hand, between it and the action to give effect to a contractual entitlement and, on the other, between it and a straightforward action in tort. The scars are plainly visible in the Common law of the end of the twentieth century.

[68] e.g. *de Kemesie* v. *de Kemesie* (Eyre of Oxford, 1241; J. Cooper (ed.), *The Oxfordshire Eyre 1241* (Oxfordshire Record Society, 56, 1989), 25 pl.260, 35 pl.317; 16 CRR 2119); *Cocus* v. *Pewman* (Wallingford Burghmote, 1261; (Berkshire CRO) W/JBa 14 m.1d ('*de magna iniuria*'); *Charite* v. *Sichrich* (1273; W. O. Ault, *Court Rolls of the Abbey of Ramsey*, 267) ('*iniuriabat . . . de quoddam pacto unius vacce inter eos convento*'); *Bothelbras* v. *Drake* (1307; Bridport Borough Court (Dorset CRO) C4 m.1) ('trespass and broken covenant'). Both the *quare* form of pleading and the description of the action as 'trespass' continue to be found in local courts through the fourteenth century.

[69] YB 20 & 21 Edw I (RS) 278; YB 30 & 31 Edw I (RS) 142.

[70] *Aurifaber* v. *de Stalles* (1252; Wallingford Burghmote (Berkshire CRO) W/JBa 11 m.1; *Houhil* v. *Dodeman* (1253; Leicester Merchant Gild; M. Bateson, *Records of the Borough of Leicester* (London, 1899), 1.66); *Cocus* v. *Pewman* (1261; Wallingford Burghmote (Berkshire CRO) W/JBa 14 m.1d); *de Tiddolvesid* v. *Walerand* (1261; Steeple Ashton Manor Court, SC2 208/1 m.1); *Le Flemang* v. *Pyrneys* (1275; W. P. Baildon (ed.), *Court Rolls of the Manor of Wakefield* (Yorkshire Archaeological Society, 29; 1901), 138–9; *Harald* v. *Harald* (1282; J. Amphlett (ed.), *Court Rolls of the Manor of Hales, 1272–1307* (Oxford, 1910), part 1, 212).

[71] Below, p.88.

2. Unity and Fragmentation of the Medieval Law of Contract

With the emergence of the action of covenant as a specifically—and exclusively—contractual remedy, the stage was set for the Common law of obligations to align itself with Roman law. If events had been allowed to run their course, trespass would have become the equivalent of the Romans' delictal liability and covenant the equivalent of their contract, leaving the entitlement-based action of debt-detinue to cover the proprietary ground of the Romans' *vindicatio*. That this did not occur was almost wholly the result of a tiny procedural tightening in the rules of proof applicable to the action of covenant but not to trespass or debt, as a result of which it became significantly less attractive to plaintiffs. Like a plant shooting up too enthusiastically at the start of spring only to be faced with a late frost, it did not have the resources to protect itself against this setback and it rapidly withered away.

THE FORMALIZATION OF COVENANT

Around the beginning of the fourteenth century there appeared in the royal courts a rule that an action of covenant could be brought only if the parties' agreement had been embodied in a document under seal. Exactly how or why this rule developed is a matter of controversy; a number of explanations have been suggested, but no measure of scholarly consensus has emerged.[1] In practice actions of covenant in the royal courts had very commonly been based on such sealed agreements, since the sort of agreements important enough to litigate in the royal courts were the sort of agreements important enough to put in writing, and in the thirteenth century putting an agreement in writing inevitably meant putting it under seal. It may well be that the rule was no more than a loose generalization from past practice: if something (nearly) always does happen, it is easy to shift almost imperceptibly to the proposition that it must happen. Whatever the true explanation, it seems likely that the rule was more the result of an accident than the product of a piece of conscious law-making.

---

[1] Ibbetson, 'Words and Deeds: The Action of Covenant in the Reign of Edward I' (1986) 4 Law & Hist Rev 71; R. C. Palmer, 'Covenant, Justices Writs, and Reasonable Showings' (1987) 31 Am Jnl Leg Hist 97; Note, 'Proving the Will of Another: The Specialty Requirement in Covenant' (1992) 105 Harv L R 2001.

The first clear statement of the requirement of a deed occurs in a Year Book case of 1292.[2] The plaintiff had lent his horse to the defendant for use in a jousting tournament, agreeing that the defendant would pay to him thirty marks (£20) if the horse was maimed or killed. The horse was killed, and the plaintiff claimed the thirty marks. His action was brought not by writ but by bill, a mode of initiating proceedings that did not require the complainant to use any particular form, so that it was indeterminate whether the action was properly described as debt (claiming the thirty marks) or covenant (complaining of the breach of the agreement).[3] The defendant argued that it should not matter, and that the action was not well brought in either event. If it was properly described as debt, then it fell foul of a rule stipulating that only debts below forty shillings could be claimed by bill; above that sum a writ was necessary.[4] If, on the other hand, it was properly described as covenant, then it fell foul of the rule requiring a deed: 'We pray judgment whether we need answer his suit, in the absence of writing.'[5]

The rule seems to have been well established by the end of the thirteenth century, and so far as we can see there was no dispute about its application to straightforward cases of non-performance of agreements. What was not clear were its boundaries. Was it a rule of form, applicable to all actions of covenant, or a rule of substance about the types of agreement whose non-performance would be actionable?

A good example of the friction that might occur is in the *Waltham Carrier Case* in the Eyre of London in 1321.[6] The defendant had agreed to carry the plaintiff's hay to London. The agreement was made in London, but the hay was delivered to the defendant at Waltham in Essex. It never arrived in London, and the plaintiff brought his action. As in *Corbet* v. *Scurye* the proceedings were by bill, so that the precise nature of the claim did not have to be formulated. The normal action for non-delivery of goods would have been detinue, where the plaintiff would have had to show no more than that the hay had been handed over but not redelivered. But if the action was properly one of detinue, there was a procedural problem. Justices in Eyre had jurisdiction to hear actions begun

---

[2] *Corbet* v. *Scurye* YB 20 & 21 Edw I (RS) 223, 487 (B&M 282).

[3] For the bill jurisdiction, see G. O. Sayles, *Select Cases in the court of King's Bench*, iv (74 SS), pp.lxvii–lxxxvi. There is more detail in H. G. Richardson and G. O. Sayles, *Select Case of Procedure without Writ* (60 SS). For examples of bills in eyre, see W. C. Bolland, *Select Bills in Eyre* (30 SS).

[4] YB 20 & 21 Edw I (RS) 487. Cf. Britton, 1.155. The argument in the case ascribes the rule to statute. This may be an erroneous reference to the Statute of Gloucester, 1278, c.8; but this is about trespass rather than debt, and assumes the rule rather than imposing it; the only statutory provision of the rule is in the Statute of Wales 1284, cap. 9. See generally J. S. Beckerman, 'The Forty-Shilling Jurisdictional Limit in Medieval English Personal Actions', in D. Jenkins (ed.), *Legal History Studies 1972* (Cardiff, 1975), 110.

[5] YB 20 & 21 Edw I (RS) 223, per Louther.   [6] 86 SS 286 (B&M 285).

by bill only if the cause of action had arisen in the county where the eyre was sitting, in this case London; in detinue the fact of the delivery was the cause of the action,[7] and here that had occurred in Essex. Hence a writ would have been necessary.[8] To counter this the plaintiff might argue that the action was properly covenant, shifting his focus away from the hay that had been detained to the agreement that had been breached. It was here that the objection that there need be a deed began to bite:

Gregory. Every covenant depends upon specialty, and you show none. We ask judgment.

Fastolf. You do not have to have specialty for a cartload of hay.

HERLE, J. And for a cartload of hay we shall not undo the law. Covenant is none other than the assent of the parties, which lies in specialty.[9]

As in *Corbet* v. *Scurye*, the plaintiff lost either way.

The essence of the defendant's argument in the *Waltham Carrier Case* seems to have been that, although the action should be treated as formally one of covenant, in substance the claim was based on the failure to deliver the hay. The same line of reasoning might be used when the complaint was of what we may broadly call contractual mis-performance. It is well illustrated by a simple case of 1304.[10] The plaintiff had leased land to the defendant for a period of two years. The defendant had gone into occupation, but had failed to vacate the land at the end of the term. Assuming that the facts as alleged were true, there was no doubt that the defendant was liable for wrongful occupation of the land and should be forced to return it to the plaintiff. A perfectly good writ was available for this purpose, the writ of entry *ad terminum qui preteriit* (for a term that had ended). The plaintiff here chose to bring a writ of covenant, counting on the agreement and its breach, instead of the writ of entry. The defendant objected that the action should not lie in the absence of a deed under seal, but Bereford J. overruled it. In substance, liability was based on the wrongful occupation of the land, and this was the true cause of the plaintiff's action: it was a matter of indifference whether the plaintiff chose to bring a writ of entry or a writ of covenant, for the claim was the same in either case. The forms of action, we might say, were simply the shells into which the substance of liability was fitted.

Another example of the same phenomenon arose in cases where there had been a lease and a sublease. *X* leases land to *Y*; *Y* subleases it to *Z*; *Z*

---

[7] J. B. Ames, *Lectures on Legal History* (Cambridge, Mass., 1913), 72.

[8] Cf. the similar situation in *Bruges* v. *Colkyrk* (86 SS 276), where the plaintiff had lent a tent to the defendant. The court here rejected the argument that the action should not lie in the absence of a deed: the receipt of the tent in London was the cause of action.

[9] Similarly, in *Adam* v. *B* (86 SS 352): 'A covenant expresses the will of another, and the will of another can only be averred by a deed.'

[10] YB 32 & 33 Edw I (RS) 198; BL MS Harg 375 f.10ᵛ (B&M 284).

wrongfully cuts down trees. This constituted waste, and X was entitled to compensation.[11] His action lay against his immediate lessee, Y; even though he had not personally chopped down the trees, he was liable because the waste had been committed. Y in his turn would seek compensation from Z, and there could have been little doubt that he should be liable. A wrong had been committed—waste—and he had committed it. The difficulty was to find an appropriate form of action. The writ of waste would not lie; there was a technical rule that it could only be brought at the suit of a person holding in fee, and here the plaintiff, Y, would only have held a lease. A writ of trespass would be awkward, for Y could not plausibly have asserted that Z, as his lessee, had acted by force of arms in breach of the king's peace.[12] The only real possibility was a writ of covenant. This situation arose in a case of 1304.[13] The defendant made the predictable objection that the action should not lie in the absence of a deed under seal, but the objection was overruled. As in the case of the wrongful holding-over of land at the end of a lease, the substance of the plaintiff's claim was the defendant's wrong; the action of covenant was merely the shell within which the claim was formulated. Bereford C.J. made the point quite explicitly in a similar case in 1312:

If a man lease tenements to another for a term of years without specialty, do you think that he can make waste? (*implying*, No); and as she offers to aver the lease which you do not deny, it seems that this averment is sufficient. Besides waste is a thing which implies something against the law. Therefore it lies with you [i.e. the defendant] to show specialty to cover your wrong . . .[14]

As late as the 1320s the courts might still have been willing to allow actions of covenant to be brought for the mis-performance of oral agreements, for causing loss by doing the job badly rather than for not doing it at all. In an action in the Eyre of London of 1321 against a surgeon who had promised to cure a wound but had done so so badly that the plaintiff's hand was lost, the defendant objected that the action would not lie in the absence of a deed, and the court adjourned the case for further consideration;[15] and in the Bedford Eyre of 1330 a plaintiff successfully brought an action of covenant in a similar situation where there may not have been a deed.[16] By

---

[11] For the writ of waste, see Milsom, *Novae Narrationes* (80 SS), pp.cxc–cxcviii.
[12] Below, p.39.   [13] YB 32 & 33 Edw I (RS) 296.
[14] YB 4 Edw II (42 SS) 171, 173; 192 (variant text in B&M 285). Here the plaintiff was a dowager, who, like the leaseholder, did not have an estate in fee.
[15] *Anon* (86 SS 353). Contrast the certainty of the *Waltham Carrier Case* and *Adam* v. *B* (above, nn.6, 9) in the same eyre.
[16] *Warner* v. *Leech* (Kiralfy, *Source Book*, 184). In another case in the same eyre (*Anon* (LI MS Hale 137 f.172), below, p.45) covenant was brought against a defendant who had hired four cows to the plaintiff and subsequently driven them out of the plaintiff's control; the report reveals no objection to the use of covenant, though it is a reasonable inference that the agreement was purely oral.

this time, though, the rule was hardening into one of form rather than substance, and by the 1340s it was clear beyond doubt that an action of covenant could be brought only where the agreement was contained in a sealed document whatever the underlying substance of the plaintiff's claim.[17]

The effects of the introduction of what no doubt appeared to be a minor procedural rule were enormous. Most obviously it nipped in the bud any possibility there might have been that the action of covenant would blossom into a general remedy for breach of contract. There is a stark contrast with the development of the law of real property, where first the assize of novel disseisin and then the action of trespass were massaged into a generally available remedy for the establishment of title to land, largely superseding the myriad remedies of the thirteenth century.[18] In contract, instead of integration, the ossification of the action of covenant brought about an even greater fragmentation of the remedies available for breaches of contracts, and, although we may piece together what might appear to us to be regularities beneath the surface of the various forms of action used in contractual contexts, we can normally only guess whether contemporaries saw them as clearly as we might think we do. It is a telling fact that the first abstract treatise on property law, Littleton's *Tenures*, was written in the middle of the fifteenth century, whereas it was not until the eighteenth century that we begin to find any parallel treatment of contractual liability.[19]

COVENANT AND THE CONDITIONAL BOND

The introduction of the requirement of a sealed deed in the action of covenant meant that it could no longer be used for informal contracts. On the face of it it should still have retained considerable vitality, given that most serious agreements—most agreements serious enough to litigate in the royal courts—were in fact embodied in sealed documents. However, a practical shift in the mode of drafting contracts that occurred in the first half of the fourteenth century had the effect of cutting so far into this remaining area of the business of the action of covenant that by the end of the fourteenth century it had essentially fallen into disuse.

It has already been seen that a document under seal granting money from one person to another would be strictly enforced by an action of debt.[20] In the fourteenth century draftsmen adapted this device to agree-

---

[17] *de Wetenhale* v. *Arden*, YB 20 Edw III (RS part II) 148 (Kiralfy, *Source Book*, 181).
[18] Sutherland, *Assize of Novel Disseisin*, 126–68, esp. 148–50.   [19] Below, p.218.
[20] Above, p.20.

ments generally, whether or not they were concerned with the payment of money.[21] This required some chicanery, but it was immensely effective. Suppose, for example, that John was to build a house for Robert. The obvious way to draft the agreement would be to say simply that John covenanted to build a house of such dimensions by such a day. If the house was not duly built, Robert would have an action of covenant to obtain damages from John for his breach of the agreement. Alternatively, John could make a bond for a sum of money—say £20—subject to a condition that the bond should be void if the house was duly built by a certain day. This condition might be contained in a separate document, but it was more convenient to write it on the back of the bond—literally, endorsed on it— and by the middle of the century this was the commoner form. Now, if John failed to build the house on time, Robert's action would not be covenant for unliquidated damages to be assessed by a jury but rather debt for the £20. If John wanted to claim that he had in fact built the house, he had to plead by way of defence that the condition had been performed and that the bond had therefore lost all its force.[22]

From the point of view of the creditor, who would be invariably in the stronger bargaining position, the conditional bond had many advantages over a simple covenant. To begin with, the sum specified as being due for non-performance would normally be in excess of the plaintiff's loss. So long as the courts were not worried by the possibility that they might be enforcing penalties[23] or sanctioning usury, it would operate as a very strong inducement on the defendant to perform the condition punctiliously. In the same way, if the agreement ever did come to be litigated, all the advantages rested with the creditor. Pleading in debt was slightly easier for the plaintiff than pleading in covenant, and process was slightly more advantageous.[24]

---

[21] For the detailed development of the various devices, see R. C. Palmer, *English Law in the Age of the Black Death* (Chapel Hill, NY, 1993), 62–91. It may be that the impetus for change came from the increasing sophistication of education in business practice in the fourteenth century, particularly at Oxford. Formularies emanating from these business schools were widely copied, and were obviously used as precedent books. This is not to deny, of course, Palmer's thesis that the Chancery (and the judges) were sympathetic to these practical changes, and that they may have gone out of their way to encourage their use and facilitate their effectiveness.

[22] For a more detailed analysis of the working of the conditional bond, see Simpson, *History of Contract*, 88–135.

[23] Bereford C. J. had doubts on this score in *Umfraville* v. *Lonstede* (YB 2 & 3 Edw II (19 SS) 58), though in *Scott* v. *Beracre* in the Eyre of Kent 1313–1314 (27 SS 23 25, 27) documents in this form were treated as acceptable. Such doubts as there must have been soon quelled: YB M.21 Edw III f.29 pl.9. It was not until around 1500 that relief began to be granted: below, p.213. Local courts might have been less willing to enforce penal clauses (e.g. in London: *Liber Albus*, trans. H. T. Riley (London, 1861), 186–7).

[24] In covenant the plaintiff had to plead that the defendant was in breach, whereas in debt on a conditional bond the defendant had to plead performance. If the defendant defaulted in appearance, for example, the plaintiff in debt would be entitled to immediate judgment in the

The sum due was fixed in advance and was hence not subject to the potential vagaries of jury assessment. In covenant damages were at the discretion of the jury, so that if the defendant had substantially performed it might have been expected that the damages would be reduced to take account of this; in debt on a conditional bond, the penalty was due in full unless the condition had been performed to the letter.[25] Furthermore, in covenant the risk of performance becoming impossible lay with the plaintiff, but in debt on a conditional bond it lay with the defendant.[26]

The combination of all these advantages operated rapidly to cause contracting parties to make use of the conditional bond rather than the direct covenant form. As a consequence, litigation was irreversibly transferred away from the action of covenant and into the action of debt.

The utility of the conditional bond was not limited to situations where the parties might have made a simple covenant. In addition it could be used as a way of strengthening the hand of creditors of ordinary money debts. A person owed £10, for example, might take a bond for this amount; alternatively, and more attractively, the bond might be made for £20 subject to a defeasant condition of the payment of £10 by a certain date. In the latter case, if the debtor did not pay the £10 by the due date, the creditor would have an action of debt for the £20. In the first half of the fourteenth century there was considerable doubt whether the action should be allowed, for the double sum was clearly a penalty and possibly usurious,[27] but by the early 1350s these doubts had been set aside[28] and the way was open for the conditional bond—in both its forms—to take its place as the principal device for the framing of substantial contracts, a place it was to maintain until the eighteenth century.[29]

THE FRAGMENTATION OF REMEDIES FOR INFORMAL CONTRACTS

Litigants who wished to sue on unsealed agreements in the royal courts were not able to use the action of covenant and were therefore forced to

amount of the debt; in covenant a jury would still have to be empanelled to assess the damages. In addition, the improvements in process introduced into personal actions in 1352 (25 Edw III Stat 5 c.17) did not apply to covenant, which was by this stage moribund.

[25] YB P.20 Hen VI f.23 pl.2.   [26] Below, p.91.

[27] Though already in the twelfth century the civilians Huguccio and Bernard of Pavia had argued that such instruments were not in principle usurious: J. P. Noonan, *The Scholastic Analysis of Usury* (Cambridge, Mass., 1957), 107–9.

[28] In *Scott* v. *Beracre* (Eyre of Kent 1313–1314; 27 SS 23 25, 27) it seems to have been held that where the condition and the obligation were 'of the same nature' (i.e. where the condition on which the debt became payable was itself the payment of a sum of money) the instrument would be regarded as usurious and the doubled debt as a penalty. This position was reversed in 1352: YB M.26 Edw III f.17 pl.9. See Palmer, *Black Death*, 79–82.

[29] For its later history, see below, p.150.

frame their claims within some other form of action. Most obviously available were the actions of debt and detinue, now clearly separating from each other, so long as the claim was for a specific sum of money or for goods; a cluster of remedies existed to protect lessees of land; and most employment contracts came to be regulated by the Ordinance and Statute of Labourers passed in the wake of the Black Death.[30] Beyond these, litigants resorted to the action of trespass, whose boundaries were repeatedly tested through the fourteenth and fifteenth centuries by the efforts of plaintiffs and their lawyers to apply it to contractual situations.[31] Some common features of contractual liability may have existed,[32] but each remedy had its own rules, each had its own conceptual underpinning. The technicalities of each form of action reflected back onto the situations in which they applied, progressively remoulding the way in which common situations were analysed.

The writ of debt provided a wholly serviceable remedy for the very common situation where the outstanding obligation from a transaction was to pay money, though litigants had to be sure-footed in order to avoid procedural pitfalls.[33] Its principal potential disadvantage was that its foundation on near-proprietary ideas of entitlement meant that the action could be brought only if the claim was for a sum certain.[34] This seems to have been less of a problem in practice than it might appear in theory. It was obviously sufficient if the sum due had been explicitly fixed by the contract or could be unequivocally identified by reference to the contract, as where a ship's cargo was bought at so much per ton. It was equally sufficient if it was fixed by some regulation extrinsic to the contract—for example where labourers' wages had been laid down by guild or municipal regulation or (after 1349) by the justices of labourers, or the price of food and drink in a tavern determined by the clerk of the market.[35] Nor was there a problem if it could be determined by custom: it was settled practice, 'common right', that a serjeant at law could charge 3s. 4d. and an attorney 1s. 8d. as a retainer, and he could sue for this sum even if the fee had not been expressly agreed with the client in advance.[36] More awkward was the case where the price had been left to be settled later, or where an agreement was made to do a job of work for a reasonable sum; in these situations the action of debt should not in theory have been available, but in practice it is

---

[30] W. McGovern, 'The Enforcement of Oral Covenants prior to Assumpsit' (1970) 65 Northwestern U L R 576; 'The Enforcement of Informal Contracts in the Later Middle Ages' (1971) 55 Cal L R 1145.   [31] Below, p.127.
[32] Below, ch.5.
[33] See in particular W. McGovern, 'Contract in Medieval England: The Necessity for Quid pro Quo and a Sum Certain' (1969) 13 Am Jnl Leg Hist 173, 189–90.   [34] Above, p.18.
[35] B. Putnam, *The Enforcement of the Statutes of Labourers, 1349–1359* (New York, 1908), 72, 76, 154–6; YB P.12 Edw IV f.8 pl.22 at f.9.
[36] YB M.30 Hen VI f.8 pl.1 at f.9, per Moile.

probable that a plaintiff who claimed an amount that was in fact a reasonable sum would succeed notwithstanding the technical impropriety.[37]

Another procedural problem of the writ of debt was that in most cases of actions based on contracts defendants were permitted to wage their law.[38] This meant that a defendant who was willing to deny under oath that the sum claimed was due, and who could find eleven 'oath helpers' to swear in support of the principal oath, would leave court without the facts ever being investigated.[39] It was, inevitably, easy for a debtor to avoid liability. In practice, though, wager of law came to be relatively little used.[40] Oaths were taken seriously in the Middle Ages, and defendants who wished to wage their law might seek advice from the judges as to whether they might in conscience do so;[41] and, as oaths began to be treated more cavalierly, social pressures told against wager of law if this was seen as a dishonourable way of not paying one's debts.[42] Alternatively, more negatively, it is possible that the risk of defendants waging their law discouraged creditors from bringing suits in the first place. The availability of wager of law did not only affect the procedure of the writ of debt, but came also to influence the substantive law. The most obvious context was where actions were brought against executors after the death of the original debtor. Wager of law was not available to executors, for they could not normally swear that the debt was not due: they could not know. But it was unfair that the executors should be put in a worse position than the testator, so early in the fourteenth century it began to be held that they could avoid liability if they denied any knowledge of the contract.[43] By the sixteenth century it had become a rule that executors should not be liable, whether or not they

---

[37] Simpson, *History of Contract*, 65.

[38] It was excluded in a small number of situations: Simpson, *History of Contract*, 140–4.

[39] For wager of law, see J. H. Baker, *Introduction to English Legal History* (3rd edn., London, 1990), 87–8, and, for a comparative perspective, H. C. Lea, *Superstition and Force* (Philadelphia, 1878), 13–91. There is a good description of the detailed operation of wager of law in HLS MS 162 ff.178ᵛ–180ᵛ and Bodl MS Rawl C 459 ff.202–4; J. S. Beckerman, 'Procedural Innovation and Institutional Change in Medieval English Manorial Courts' (1992) 10 Law & Hist Rev 197, 204–12.

[40] S. F. C. Milsom, 'Sale of Goods in the Fifteenth Century' (1961) 77 LQR 257, 266.

[41] YB P.22 Edw IV f.2 pl.8. A sufficiently high proportion of defendants who waged their law failed subsequently to make it that we may be sure that it was not just a cynical formality.

[42] Ibbetson, 'Sixteenth Century Contract Law: *Slade's Case* in Context' (1984) 4 Ox Jnl Leg Stud 295, 313 n.100.

[43] *Anon* (Eyre of London, 1321; 86 SS 346); YB T.41 Edw III f.13 pl.3; YB P.46 Edw III f.10 pl.7; YB M.10 Hen VI 24 pl.84. For earlier discussions, see YB 21 & 22 Edw I (RS) 457; YB 3 & 4 Edw II (22 SS) 21. See generally W. McGovern, 'Medieval Contract Law: Wager of Law and the Effect of Death' (1968) 54 Iowa L R 19, 42–3; Simpson, *History of Contract*, 143–4. In theory this meant that creditors on simple contracts were deprived of a remedy unless they could find one in a local court; in practice, though, such testamentary debts were frequently litigated in ecclesiastical courts: R. H. Helmholz, 'Debt Claims and Probate Jurisdiction in Historical Perspective' (1979) 23 Am Jnl Leg Hist 68.

specifically raised the issue themselves;[44] it was a maxim of the Common law, a principle so basic that it was not susceptible to proof or argument,[45] and not simply as an inconvenient consequence of the procedural rules of the action of debt. It was as if the right to wager of law had become divorced from the form of action and attached to the indebtedness itself. It was not only outsiders to the contract whose position might be affected by this attachment of wager of law to the indebtedness; creditors who manœuvred to reformulate their claims within a form of action where wager of law was not available could be met by the objection that it was not possible to do so in such a way that defendants were deprived of their rights.[46]

The writ of debt was easily employable in contractual contexts, and its use did not involve any serious wrench to the conceptual structure of the law. The writ of detinue, on the other hand, applied in a wide range of non-contractual situations, and its contractual applications were infected by ideas that had been generated in wholly different contexts.[47] The twisting and turning associated with these ideas produced a number of odd doctrines in medieval law, several of which continue to exist in the modern legal system. The action of detinue had had proprietary overtones in the thirteenth century, though these were perhaps more visible in local courts than in the royal courts.[48] Local courts dealt with claims against defendants allegedly in possession of the plaintiff's chattels—the action *de re adirata*—whereas, as far as the royal courts were concerned, at this time the action of detinue normally arose out of an essentially contractual relationship, most commonly a bailment or the sale of goods; the only situation in which ideas of property might routinely be brought into play was where the plaintiff complained that the defendant detained the charters that evidenced title to land.[49] In the course of the fourteenth century, as the royal courts came to deal more frequently with claims to chattels analogous to the local courts' *de re adirata*, this proprietary dimension came more to the

---

[44] The older view, that the executors would not avoid liability if at any stage in the pleadings they admitted the contract, is still found in YB P.15 Edw IV f.25 pl.7; but in his abridgement of the case (before 1558) Brooke adds a rider to the effect that the non-liability of the executors was something that the judges could apply of their own motion: Br Abr, *Executors*, 80.

[45] Below, p.134. For the idea of a maxim as a proposition so basic that its validity could not be questioned, see C. St German, *Doctor and Student*, 1.8 (91 SS 57).

[46] Thus a Statute of 1403 (Stat 5 Hen IV cap.8) attempted to prevent creditors avoiding wager of law by falsely alleging that the sum due had been determined by the parties' accounting before auditors (where wager of law was not permissible) rather than by simple contract (where it was). In the sixteenth century the development of the action of assumpsit was slowed down by the apparent need to protect defendants' rights to wage their law: below, p.138.

[47] For the developments of the writ of detinue in the fourteenth and fifteenth centuries, see Milsom, *Historical Foundations*, 262–75. [48] Above, p.18.

[49] YB 30 & 31 Edw I (RS) 407; YB 32 & 33 Edw I (RS) 207; *Lindseye v. Suthe*, YB 6 Edw II (34 SS) 167; Milsom, *Novae Narrationes* (80 SS), pp.clxxvii–clxxix.

surface and by the middle of the century it could be stated as a general principle that 'Detinue supposes possession precedent'.[50] The most immediate victim of this maxim was the anomalous form of detinue known as *de racionabili parte bonorum*, a claim by a widow or children against the executors of a deceased husband or father for a reasonable share of the estate. This type of claim had originated in a common writ of detinue,[51] but it could not be sustained in the face of the objection that the widow had never had 'possession precedent' in the goods, and the action came be to recharacterized as an action in its own right wholly distinct from detinue.[52]

The increasingly proprietary character of the writ of detinue inevitably came to affect the perception of those contractual situations where it was commonly employed. Bailment was the most obvious case. There was no doubt that the bailor could have a writ of detinue against a bailee who failed to redeliver the bailed goods. This was sufficiently obvious that there was no real need to theorize about whether the basis of the action was contractual or proprietary, and we can hardly imagine that it was a matter of any great concern to the lawyers of the thirteenth century. Sometimes, though, the issue did arise in circumstances where the answer might make a difference. In a case at the end of the thirteenth century, for example, the bailee lacked contractual capacity, and it was argued that she should not be liable in detinue; this would make sense if the action was contractual in its nature but not if it was proprietary. Unfortunately the report of the case is inconclusive,[53] but when the point arose tangentially in the mid-fifteenth century it was assumed that an infant would not be liable in detinue counting expressly on a bailment.[54] Where there were two joint bailees, the ordinary contractual rule would dictate that an action of detinue should be brought against them jointly,[55] but a property rationale would push in the direction of allowing it to be brought against any one bailee who was in possession; the point was argued in 1406, the majority of the court eventually favouring the 'contractual' view that the co-bailee had to be joined.[56] The same issue could arise where property belonging to several co-owners was bailed by one of them; here, according to fourteenth-century authority, the action should properly be brought only by the bailor.[57] On the other hand, the proprietary

---

[50] YB M.30 Edw III f.25. Cf. YB T.50 Edw III f.16 pl.8, where it was argued that detinue would lie only where the plaintiff had an antecedent 'property' in the goods. The increasingly clear division between property and obligation perhaps points to a civil-law influence: C. Donahue, 'Ius Commune in England' (1992) 66 Tul L R 1745, 1760–4.

[51] YB 1 & 2 Edw II (17 SS) 39.

[52] Milsom, *Novae Narrationes* (80 SS), p.clxxvii n.5.

[53] *Mortimer* v. *Mortimer,*YB 20 & 21 Edw I (RS) 189 (B&M 264).

[54] YB T.11 Hen VI f.40 pl.35. The infant would be liable, though, if the action made no express mention of the bailment, alleging simply that the goods had been found.

[55] Below, p.76.   [56] YB H.7 Hen IV f.6 pl.37.

[57] *Luke* v. *Lanum*, YB 8 Edw II (41 SS) 98 at 100; YB P.49 Edw III f.13 pl.6, per Belknap C.J.

aspect of the bailment might come to the fore when goods were delivered by one person to another to be delivered over to a third party: here the third party might bring detinue.[58]

The point at which the conflict between proprietary and contractual reasoning would arise most sharply was where the bailee wanted to allege that the goods did not in fact belong to the bailor, but to a third party. It was clear that the bailee should not be allowed to keep them, though less clear why not. When this had arisen in Roman law, it had led to the characterization of the relationship in terms of contract: the bailor had a right to the return of the goods because they had been lent, not because they were his property.[59] By the time that the question arose in England, in the middle of the fifteenth century, the proprietary dimension of detinue was sufficiently strong to avoid this form of recharacterization. The action was indeed founded on a claim to property in the goods, but, it was said, the bailee was estopped from denying the bailor's title.[60] Roman law and English law reached the same result—once the bailment relationship had been established, the bailor could recover the goods from the bailee—but the conceptual frameworks of the two systems were radically different. This, in its turn, had secondary effects, as, for example, when the bailee wanted to explain that the failure to return the goods was the result of *force majeure*.[61]

Similar twists are visible in the other principal contractual situation where detinue was used, the sale of goods. The buyer who wanted to sue for the non-delivery of generic (i.e. non-specific) goods would be open to the same objection as the widow claiming a reasonable provision from her deceased husband's estate, that no identifiable thing was claimed, and no antecedent possession—or property—could be alleged. It followed from this that the action could not properly be detinue, and it came to be categorized in lawyers' minds as debt—though, to general confusion, the wording of the plaintiff's claim followed the wording of the action of detinue.[62] On the face of it, the same objection (perhaps in muted form) could have been raised against a claim in detinue for specific goods: the buyer was claiming that he had bought the goods, not that he had formerly owned or possessed them. Quite early in the fourteenth century, by about 1330, the courts sidestepped this difficulty by saying that the sale of goods

[58] YB 12 & 13 Edw III (RS) 245. For further references, see Ames, *Lectures on Legal History*, 73 n.1; but these are all cases of detinue of charters, where different rules may have applied.   [59] Above, p.9.
[60] YB P.7 Hen VI f.22 pl.3. As Baker points out (*Spelman's Reports*, ii (94 SS), 248) the question could in practice be avoided because of the availability of wager of law; the defendant bailee would simply plead *non detinet*, denying that the goods were detained, and that would be the end of the matter.   [61] Below, p.94.
[62] i.e. the plaintiff should allege that the defendant *detinet* the thing, not *debet et detinet*. See Milsom, *Historical Foundations*, 262–3.

itself operated as a transfer of title to the buyer, whose claim was therefore not simply for the non-delivery of goods sold but for the wrongful retention of goods owned.[63] This was not quite so outrageous an invention as it appears, for in Germanic systems the sale of goods had traditionally been analysed as a means of transferring ownership;[64] though the assumption in these systems was that sale was a cash transaction rather than one based on credit. The adoption of this doctrine of the automatic transfer of property effectively prevented the Common law formulating the simple contractual analysis of sale found in Roman law and adopted throughout continental Europe.[65] It was partly responsible for Blackstone's apparently curious and incoherent treatment of the law of contract, uncomfortably split between the law of property and the law of wrongs;[66] and even in the later twentieth century the proprietary dimension of the sale of goods is frequently stressed at the expense of the contractual.

The writs of debt and detinue were able to fill in many of the gaps left by the formalization of the action of covenant, especially in situations involving money or chattels, although in doing so they forced some fairly typical transactions into a rather ill-fitting strait-jacket. The problem here, from a conceptual point of view, was that attention was shifted from the transaction itself to the proprietary (or near-proprietary) effects of the transaction. This inevitably masked the underlying contractual base of such common transactions as sale and bailment. In addition, peripheral remedies had a part to play, further destroying the unity of simple legal institutions. A question whether goods sold were of the quality demanded by the contract could be raised in three wholly distinct ways, for example: in a trespassory action for breach of warranty by the buyer (from the 1380s); as a defence to an action of debt brought by the seller, when the buyer claimed that some particular quality was a condition of the validity of the contract; or, again where it was a condition of the contract, in an action of debt by the buyer for the return of the purchase price.[67] Unsurprisingly, it was a long time before the Common law could begin to generate any coherent theory about the nature of contractual terms.[68]

In other situations too the problem was not so much that the remedies used shifted the focus of the transaction, but that they were so fragmented

---

[63] Ibbetson, 'Sale of Goods in the Fourteenth Century' (1991) 107 LQR 480, 490–6. Well into the fifteenth century, to add to the confusion, it appears that actions against defaulting sellers might masquerade as actions against bailees, concealing the fact that there had ever been a sale: Milsom, 'Sale of Goods in the Fifteenth Century' (1961) 77 LQR 257, 274.

[64] Levy, *West Roman Vulgar Law*, 131–4, 156–64. It should be noted that Bracton's treatment of sale (ff.61b-62; ed. Thorne, 2.181–3) is dealt with under the general rubric 'Of Acquiring the Dominion of Things'.

[65] Ibbetson, 'From Property to Contract: The Transformation of Sale in the Middle Ages' (1992) 13 Jnl Leg Hist 1, 12–13.   [66] Blackstone, *Commentaries*, 2.442–70, 3.153–66.

[67] Below, pp.83 ff.   [68] Below, p.223.

that the unity of the underlying relationship forever slipped out of view; plaintiffs were forced to use a range of remedies, each with its own particular function. Nowhere is this more visible than in the case of leases. In the thirteenth century, actions based on leases were very commonly framed within covenant, though a range of other remedies was available; in the fourteenth century these other remedies took over.[69] Looking first from the point of view of the lessee, the most obvious situation requiring a remedy was that of ejection from the land before the end of the term. If the ejection were done by the lessor, or someone claiming through the lessor (typically a purchaser), the thirteenth-century plaintiff had a choice of two actions: covenant, and the trespassory *quare ejecit infra terminum*.[70] By the end of the century covenant was clearly seen as the predominant remedy; writing in the 1290s, Britton treats it simply as the lessee's action to recover the land, equivalent to the freeholder's novel disseisin, making no reference at all to the availability of *quare ejecit*.[71] Early in the fourteenth century *quare ejecit* reappeared, retaking the ground that had been lost to covenant. Moreover, at the same time as the judges might have been becoming reluctant to give orders for specific recovery of the land in actions of covenant,[72] they reversed their earlier position on *quare ejecit*, moving towards a willingness to grant it.[73] For Britton, if the lessee was ejected by a stranger, the only remedy was covenant against the lessor, essentially requiring him to defend the lessee's rights.[74] Early in the fourteenth century this was replaced by a trespassory action directly against the ejector, the so-called *ejectio firme*.[75] The same fragmentation can be seen if we turn our attention to the remedies available to the lessor. Where covenant might have been used for a range of situations in the late thirteenth century, soon in the fourteenth these were covered by a variety of remedies. If the lessee failed to pay the rent due, the lessor's proper remedy was the writ of customs and services, annuity, or debt; no longer was there the option of bringing covenant, as there had been in the thirteenth century. The lessee who cut down trees or similarly misused the land would be liable to a writ of waste or, later in the century, a straightforwardly trespassory remedy.[76] A writ of entry *ad terminum qui preteriit* would lie against the lessee who did not vacate the land at the

---

[69] This was not simply the direct result of the requirement of a deed in covenant, for leases would very frequently be made under seal. Rather, the formalization of covenant had dislodged it from its conceptually central position as a remedy for breach of contracts, with the consequence that it lacked the weight to hold together the multifarious situations that might arise when leases went wrong.

[70] For the early history of *quare ejecit*, see Milsom, 'Trespass from Henry III to Edward III' (1958) 74 LQR 195, 199–200.   [71] Britton, 1.416–18.

[72] Below, p.88.   [73] YB 4 Edw II (42 SS) 181.   [74] Britton, 1.418.

[75] *Goldynton v. Hardy*, YB 6 Edw II (34 SS) 226.

[76] For the use of covenant in this situation, see above, n.10.

end of the term, rather than covenant.[77] Whatever tendency there might
have been to bring cases within the action of covenant at the end of the
thirteenth century, it was rapidly reversed in the fourteenth.

A final example of the fragmentation of contractual remedies is provided
by contracts to perform services. Debt was always available to the worker
whose fee was not paid, but there was no single remedy in the reverse
situation. Contractual misperformance was, at first in disguise, brought
within the action of trespass, but it was not until around 1500 that it was
finally accepted that contractual non-performance could constitute a trespass too.[78] The Ordinance and Statute of Labourers of 1349–1351[79] made
it an offence for a worker retained for a fixed period to depart from service
without good cause within that period, and this was almost immediately
interpreted as entitling the employer to bring a civil remedy for damages;[80]
and, although the action was trespassory in form and substance, it is worth
noting that sometimes the mask slipped and a reporter referred to it as an
action of covenant.[81] Furthermore, departing from service was treated as
including not turning up for work after having been retained to do so.[82]
Not all contracts of employment were within the Ordinance and Statute,
however: they applied only to those who had been retained for a fixed
period of six months or more[83] and excluded, for example, chaplains, who
were servants of God rather than man.[84] Some of these excluded cases
might have been mopped up elsewhere: the courts with some considerable
hesitation allowed actions to be brought against defaulting attorneys, for
example.[85] Outside these situations, though, a plaintiff had to try des-
perately to argue that a case of non-performance was in reality a case of
mis-performance and that trespass was therefore an appropriate remedy.
Unless this could be done, so far as the Common law was concerned, the
plaintiff would be remediless.[86]

---

[77] For the use of covenant in this situation, see above, nn.15, 16.

[78] Below, pp.48–56, 129.   [79] Stat 23 Edw III, Stat 25 Edw III stat 2.

[80] Putnam, *Enforcement of the Statute of Labourers*, 165–214; cf. T. J. André, 'The Implied
Remedies Doctrine and the Statute of Westminster II' (1980) 54 Tul L R 589, 604–13.

[81] YB M.45 Edw III f.15 pl.15; Putnam, *Enforcement of the Statute of Labourers*, 162–3.
Other contractual ideas might have been at work too: McGovern, 'Enforcement of Oral
Contracts' (1971) 59 Cal LR 1145, 1155.   [82] Below, p.75.

[83] YB M.28 Edw III f.21 pl.18; YB P.29 Edw III f.27 (argument that Statute applied only to
retainers for customary terms of six months or one year); Putnam, *Enforcement of the Statute
of Labourers*, 191–2. Even in the case of agricultural labour there seems to have been a
preference for shorter-term hirings: S. A. C. Penn and C. Dyer, 'Wages and Earnings in
Late medieval England' (1990) 43 Ec Hist Rev (2nd ser.) 356, 366–9.

[84] YB T.50 Edw III f.13 pl.3. The courts might have wavered: Putnam, *Enforcement of the
Statute of Labourers*, 187–9.

[85] *Somerton's Case*, YB T.11 Hen VI f.55 pl.26, YB H.11 Hen VI f.18 pl.10, YB P.11 Hen VI
f.24 pl.1 (B&M 385); below, p.127. Cf. *Robert fitz Gilbert v. John of Thornhill* (1291; 57 SS 40).

[86] Below, p.127.

3. Trespass, Trespass on the Case, and the Medieval Law of Tort

THE CORE OF TRESPASS: FORCIBLE WRONGDOING

The appearance of the action of covenant enables us to give some shape to the underlying features of contractual liability. Paralleling this, the recognition of the action of trespass as an ordinary feature of the jurisdiction of the royal courts gives some shape to an emergent law of tort.[1] At one level 'trespass' continued to mean no more than 'wrong'—in popular usage and in non-technical legal usage[2]—but by the 1270s it had developed by the side of this a more sharply focused legal meaning.[3] This shift took place primarily in the royal courts; the rapidity with which the newer ideas spread into the local courts would have varied according to individual circumstances, but it is easy to demonstrate the continuing resilience of the older general idea of trespass as undefined wrongdoing in local courts' records well into the fourteenth century.[4]

One feature of the action of trespass in the royal courts was its concern with breaches of the king's peace.[5] This was a jurisdictional concept rather than a definitional one: it said nothing about what a trespass was, but looked rather to which trespasses would be actionable in the royal courts.[6] The early twelfth-century *Leges Henrici Primi* had given a definition of the king's peace, but one so fanciful as to be useless: 'The king's peace shall extend thus far from his gate, where he is in residence, in all four directions from that place, that is to say, three miles, three furlongs, the breadth of three acres, nine feet, the breadth of nine hands and of nine grains of barley.'[7] It did presumably have some function, for individuals or whole localities could be put under the king's peace,[8] but in truth it was so

---

[1] On this see esp. Milsom, 'Trespass from Henry III to Edward III' (1958) 74 LQR 195.

[2] Cf. the general meaning in Statute Westminster I (1275), chs.1, 13, 15, 16, 17, 22 and 29 with the specific meaning in ch.8 of the Statute of Gloucester (1278). The general meaning has survived in the 'Forgive us our Trespasses' of the Lord's Prayer.   [3] Above, p.17.

[4] e.g. *le Seler* v. *Musse* (1312; Essex CRO, CR2 m.6 (I. H. Jeayes (ed.), *Court Rolls of the Borough of Colchester* (Colchester, 1921–41), 1.62); *Wylemot* v. *Webbe* (1360; Essex CRO, CR12 m.8 (Jeayes (ed.), *Court Rolls of the Borough of Colchester*, 2.97)).

[5] For the earlier background to this, see above, p.3.

[6] Milsom, 'Trespass from Henry III to Edward III' (1958) 74 LQR at 576. Cf. *Fet Asaver*, in G. E. Woodbine (ed.), *Four Thirteenth Century Law Tracts* (London, 1910), 112.

[7] L. J. Downer (ed.), *Leges Henrici Primi* (Oxford, 1972), 121, para.16.1

[8] Individuals: 87 SS 65, 170 (Writs CC 107, R 253–4); boroughs: A. Ballard, *British Borough Charters* (Cambridge, 1913), 1.80.

malleable a concept as to be easily manipulable by litigants who wanted to bring their cases before the royal courts, and even for Glanvill and Bracton it was an allegation that the complainant might add, not something that had to exist in reality.[9] There may well have been some idea that only wrongs involving an interference with a royal interest or wrongs involving the invasion of land properly belonged to the king's courts,[10] and in this way the allegation of a breach of the king's peace could serve as a ticket enabling the plaintiff to bring the action in the royal court.[11] But it was a very flimsy ticket, either given freely to those who asked for it or easily and undiscoverably forged. In reality, to say that something had been done 'against the king's peace' meant very little more than that it was within the king's jurisdiction; in the thirteenth century it had none of the overtones of public disorder that would later be associated with 'breach of the peace'.[12]

Of far greater importance in moulding the royal courts' action of trespass was the idea of force. Allegations that the wrong had been done *vi et armis*, by force of arms, are found early on and become very common by the end of the thirteenth century,[13] and some sources specifically refer to trespass writs as *brevia de quare vi et armis*.[14] In Registers of Writs dating from around 1300 we begin to find the rule that trespass writs alleging force of arms can be heard only in the king's courts.[15] It may be that by this time the words were coming to have a jurisdictional function equivalent to the allegation that the king's peace had been broken, but even if this is so we must be careful not to make too much of it.

To begin with, local courts may not have taken much notice of the exclusion—allegations of wrongs done *vi et armis* are fairly common in the fourteenth century—and even if they expunged the offending words it does not seem to have made a great deal of difference to their conception of what constituted an offending act. When John de Brus complained in the Oxford borough court in 1292 that Henry of Tywe had slapped him across the head and face with a fish (the result of a dispute about the quality of the

---

[9] Meekings, *Crown Pleas of the Wiltshire Eyre 1249* (Devizes, 1961), 69–70. Glanvill I.2 (ed. Hall, 4); Bracton f.154b (ed. Thorne, 2.436).

[10] Though the category of 'trespass' was broad enough to include non-payment of a debt: *Fet Asaver* (G. E. Woodbine (ed.), *Four Thirteenth Century Law Tracts* (London, 1910)), 112; above, p.19.

[11] The image is Milsom's: 'Trespass from Henry III to Edward III' (1958) 74 LQR 195, 223.

[12] In local courts, too, it was common to allege a 'breach of the peace', but here it might be the lord's peace, the mayor's peace, or the sheriff's peace that was broken.

[13] Milsom, 'Trespass from Henry III to Edward III' (1958) 74 LQR 195, 201, 206, 208, 212.

[14] This is the rubric under which writs of trespass are treated in most versions of *Brevia Placitata* (66 SS 36, 120 ('le bref de trespas que est apelee Quare vi et armis'), 221).

[15] G. J. Turner, *Brevia Placitata* (66 SS), p.lxiv n.1; Hall, *Early Registers of Writs* (87 SS), p.cxxxii. The version of the rule in Bodl MS Rawl C 310 f.66ᵛ (*c*.1310) adds breach of the (king's?) peace to the list of prohibited allegations. Cf. the slightly different formulation in BL MS Add 31826 f.231ᵛ (*c*.1300), excluding cases of wounding and bloodshed from subordinate courts.

plaintiff's wares),[16] he could as easily have sued in the king's court, complaining that Henry had acted *vi et armis*.

Secondly, the rule (if rule it was) excluded cases only from subordinate courts. It did not say that writs not alleging force of arms should not go to the king's courts. In practice writs of trespass not uncommonly omit the allegation. Actions are found, for example, complaining of the non-repair of sea walls (a public duty imposed on landowners whose property adjoined the sea) or of the interference with a market that was the subject of a royal franchise.[17]

Thirdly, even when force was alleged, it does not seem to have meant a great deal. It has been accurately described as a low threshold test, connoting very little more than an invasive interference with the plaintiff's land, goods, or person;[18] certainly the blood-chilling lists of weaponry—sticks, swords, bows and arrows—that regularly typify plaintiffs' complaints bear no relation whatsoever to reality. At the beginning of the fourteenth century even this low threshold did not actually have to be crossed: a jury verdict that the defendant had done the acts complained of, but that his conduct had not been forcible, was held by Bereford J. in 1304 to justify the entry of judgment for the plaintiff,[19] and in 1310 the words were dismissed by the same judge as being merely form.[20]

The allegation of force of arms, like the allegation of the breach of the king's peace, could not in itself serve as the defining characteristic of the jurisdiction of the royal courts. In combination, though, the two allegations did exert a strong gravitational force on the way in which the action of trespass was perceived and the way in which it developed. It is not difficult to appreciate why lawyers might have wanted to identify some core feature: without it, if 'trespass' meant 'wrong', then the writ of trespass was standing as a residuary category defined solely by the wrongs that were excluded from it, those wrongs that had otherwise well-defined scopes such as the writs of waste or ravishment of ward. The gravitational force of the allegations of *vi et armis* and the breach of the king's peace seems to have stemmed from the collocation of three factors. First was the minimal amount of force inherent in the allegation of *vi et armis*. If all that was needed was an unwanted tap on the shoulder or toe on the doorstep, then practically any physical interference could be brought within the scope of the action. Second was that the largest category of what might

[16] Oxford Borough Court (Oxford City Library), D.7.1a. [17] Below, pp.42, 67–8.
[18] Palmer, *Black Death*, 159. [19] YB 32 & 33 Edw I (RS) 258.
[20] *Petstede* v. *Marreys*, YB M.4 Edw II (22 SS) 29. It would probably be wrong to explain away these cases as aberrant decisions of the notoriously radical Bereford C.J. Exactly the same thing occurred in the Chester Pentice Court in 1318: *Eccleshale* v. *Swon* (A. Hopkins (ed.), *Selected Rolls of the Chester City Courts* (Chetham Society, 3rd ser., 11; Manchester, 1950), 78).

have been regarded as non-forcible actionable wrongs—defamatory words—had already been conceded to the ecclesiastical courts, and it was not until the sixteenth century that the royal courts began to assert jurisdiction over them.[21] Such cases could hardly have been described as forcible, however minimal the threshold, and had they been present in the royal courts they would have provided an obstacle to any generalization of trespassory liability in terms of forcible wrongdoing. The third factor was the availability of the action of covenant. The allegations of *vi et armis* and the breach of the king's peace were thought to be inappropriate where the defendant had acted with the consent of the plaintiff,[22] and they would consequently have been inappropriate in actions based on contractual mis-performance, a fairly common form of trespassory liability (broadly defined) in the earlier thirteenth century. But, once the action of covenant had been established, the exclusion of such situations from the royal courts' action of trespass did not entail their exclusion from the royal courts, merely their recasting in a different form of action.[23]

With defamation hived off into the ecclesiastical courts and breach of contract rerouted into the action of covenant, the action of trespass could easily be identified by reference to its core feature, the wrongful use of a minimal degree of force. Still, though, not every situation could be squeezed into such a straitjacket. The rare cases of wrongful interference with purely economic interests—erecting a rival market in competition with an established franchise, for example—would normally not be describable as forcible at all; nor would cases based on omissions, such as the failure to repair a sea wall or a bridge. It might have been possible to characterize such situations as involving an interference with a royal interest, since the right to hold a market without competition would be based on a royal franchise, and the obligation to repair a sea wall or bridge was a public duty, but if this was relevant it would only explain why the royal courts might hear the action and not why it was a trespass in the first place. Other situations treated as 'trespass' outside the royal courts might have been more problematic, though not necessarily excluded from the royal courts: the liability of innkeepers for the loss of a guest's goods;[24] the liability of a sheriff who had allowed a sequestration to lapse causing the

---

[21] Below, p.114.

[22] *Taumbes* v. *Skegness*, YB 5 Edw II (31 SS) 215; YB P.11 Edw II (61 SS) 290; *Toteshalle* v. *Orfevre* (Eyre of London, 1321; 86 SS 149).

[23] Ibbetson, 'Words and Deeds: The Action of Covenant in the Reign of Edward I' (1986) 4 Law and History Review 71, 75.

[24] *de Hoo* v. *Maynard* (1311; Jeayes (ed.), *Court Rolls of the Borough of Colchester*, 1.17, 20); *Beaubek* v. *de Waltham* (1345; London *CPMR 1323–1364*, 220). Cases are not found in the royal courts until 1368: below, n.80.

plaintiff to lose a right of action;[25] the liability of a householder for the escape of fire;[26] the liability of the seller of goods for breach of a warranty of quality;[27] inducing breach of contract by telling lies about the plaintiff.[28] Such cases hovered uncertainly around the edges of the writ of trespass: they did not fit within the core of minimally forcible wrongdoing, but they could not easily be channelled into any other form of writ.

CONTRACTUAL MIS-PERFORMANCE AND NON-FORCIBLE WRONGS

By the beginning of the fourteenth century, then, the action of trespass had become established around a core of (minimally) forcible wrongdoing, wrongs characterized as having been committed *vi et armis* against the king's peace. Some situations could not easily be brought within this core, and partly because of them there remained a tension between the narrow identification of trespass with forcible wrongs and the older generic notion of trespass as wrong. The tension was particularly marked in cases of contractual mis-performance, which had been frozen out of the writ of covenant after the introduction of the requirement of a sealed deed. In such cases litigants who for one reason or another wanted to sue in the royal courts rather than in a local court increasingly looked to the action of trespass for a remedy. As a result there was a significant rise in the pressure to bring within the scope of the writ of trespass a range of situations that on the face of it could not be fitted within the core of *vi et armis* wrongdoing.

There are a number of cases in the second decade of the fourteenth century that show this relocation at work. In 1313, for example, an action of trespass was brought claiming that the defendant had sold three sacks of wool to the plaintiff and then, fraudulently and against the agreement (*contra conventionem*), and in breach of the king's peace, had put an immense quantity of salt in with the fleeces in order to increase their weight.[29] The action failed, explicitly on the grounds that it was founded

[25] *Sely* v. *Barber* (1305; London *CEMCR*, 179). A similar case in the royal courts is *Lambyn* v. *Mereworth and Welford* (1313) 49 SS 28, where an action was brought against the sheriffs of London for allowing an imprisoned debtor to be released before the debt had been paid.
[26] *de Basinge* v. *le Lou* (1302; London *CEMCR*, 139). For examples in the royal courts, see *de Brainton* v. *de Pyn* (1290; 55 SS 181; B&M 320); *de Shorne* v. *de Langton* (1320; 103 SS 400, case 35.2).
[27] *de Shorisdich* v. *Lane* (1300; London *CEMCR*, 68); *de Loveyne* v. *de Burgo* (1305; London *CEMCR*, 216); *de Mauncestre* v. *Bolam* (1305; London *CEMCR*, 262). The first successful action in the royal courts was in 1382: *Aylesbury* v. *Wattes* (YB 6 Ric II (AF) 119) (below, p.84).
[28] F. W. Maitland and W. P. Baildon, *The Court Baron* (4 SS) 40 (not explicitly 'trespass').
[29] *Kemp* v. *de Oxford* (103 SS 447, case 42.1). This may be the anonymous case reported in YB 7 Edw II (39 SS) 14.

on a breach of covenant rather than on a wrong against the king's peace. Similar cases involved bailments. In 1312 and 1318, actions were brought against defendants who had, *vi et armis* in breach of the king's peace, taken away or destroyed charters that had been handed over to them to inspect.[30] In two actions in the Eyre of London in 1321, one by bill and one by writ, actions were brought against the bailees of coffers who had (*vi et armis* in breach of the king's peace) broken them open and removed some of the contents.[31] In all of these cases the defendants objected that the action should not lie because the allegation of the forcible breach of the king's peace was inconsistent with the allegation of the bailment. Except in the case of 1318, where the judge was the radical Bereford C.J., these objections were upheld and the plaintiffs' claims failed.[32]

The obvious practical solution for plaintiffs who wanted to get their cases into the king's courts would have been to attempt to formulate them in terms of general trespass writs, expunging any reference to the contract or bailment. The resulting writ would appear perfectly good: that the defendant by force of arms in breach of the king's peace damaged the plaintiff's property. The only formal question would be whether it misrepresented the plaintiff's claim so drastically that the action would fail on the facts.

In the nature of things it is not easy to demonstrate that this actually occurred: it was in the plaintiff's interest to ensure that the true basis of the claim was concealed, and, so long as this was done successfully, the records will reveal to us nothing but writs in the standard form alleging forcible wrongdoing. Sometimes, though, the facts alleged look so improbable that our suspicions are inevitably aroused. An indication of what might happen is the relatively early case of *Rattlesdene* v. *Grunestone* (1317);[33] here there is enough transparency in the pleadings to give us a clue as to the reality underlying the action. The plaintiff alleged that the defendants had sold to him a barrel of wine, which remained in their possession. Before it had been delivered, they by force of arms, with swords bows and arrows etc, drew off a great part of the wine from the barrel and replaced the wine they had extracted with salt water, as a result of which the whole of the wine was spoiled and completely ruined, to their great damage and in breach of the king's peace etc. It is hard not to suspect that the true basis of the claim was a shipping accident.[34] Similar writs alleging the forcible extraction and

---

[30] *Taumbes* v. *Skegness* (YB 5 Edw II (31 SS) 215); YB 11 Edw II (61 SS) 290.
[31] *Toteshalle* v. *Orfevre* (86 SS 149); *Burton* v. *Polet* (86 SS 150); see too the note, perhaps of *Burton* v. *Polet*, at 149.
[32] In *Burton* v. *Polet* (86 SS 150) all we are told is that the defendant withdrew from his writ before the defendant entered any plea; given the background of the other cases, it is reasonable to infer that the reason for the nonsuit was the repugnance between the allegations of bailment and breach of the king's peace.   [33] YB 10 Edw II (54 SS) 140.
[34] One wonders whether something similar might have lain behind *Kemp* v. *de Oxford* (above, n.29).

adulteration of wine, all looking suspiciously like shipping accidents, are found throughout the fourteenth century.[35]

Even this degree of transparency diminishes after about 1320; almost all we see are opaque standard-form writs, but we may be confident that some of these conceal situations of contractual mis-performance. The use of general writs in these situations is clearly visible in the later fourteenth century without being treated as objectionable,[36] and it is an attractive assumption that this reflects the practice of the earlier part of the century. There are, for example, a suspiciously large number of general writs for injuring or killing horses where the defendant was described as a smith,[37] in one of which the writ actually alleges that the plaintiff's horse had been killed by sticking nails into its hoof.[38] Similarly, laming by a smith or farrier could be encapsulated within a general writ alleging a forcible wrong in breach of the king's peace; again, these cannot plausibly be anything other than cases of contractual mis-performance.[39] A case, brought by bill, in the Eyre of Nottingham in 1329 points to the same conclusion that general trespass writs might conceal cases of badly performed contracts. The plaintiff brought an action claiming that his doctor had undertaken to cure his eye but had acted so unskilfully that the eye had been lost.[40] The defendant objected to the form—arguing that the claim sounded in covenant rather than trespass—but the court seems to have been concerned rather with the substantive issue of whether the doctor, as a 'man of occupation', could be liable at all.[41] In a case that was the mirror image of this a year later in the Bedfordshire Eyre, where the plaintiff's bill complained of the breach of covenant and the defendant argued that the case was properly one of trespass, the better view seems clearly to have been that there was no reason why the plaintiff should not be able to elect whether to bring covenant or trespass.[42]

---

[35] *ELABD* 161 n.29. Another example printed by Palmer is *Bokenham* v. *Shraggere* (1362; *ELABD*, 329, case A3h).

[36] *de Wenden* v. *Ferrer* (1363; 103 SS 261, case 21.5); *Fitzsimon* v. *Ferrer* (1371; 103 SS 262, case 21.7); *Rankin* v. *Ferrer* (1377; 103 SS 262, case 21.8); *de Stapleton* v. *Marshall* (1380; 103 SS 264, case 21.10).

[37] Milsom, 'Trespass from Henry III to Edward III' (1958) 74 LQR 195, 220–1; A. K. R. Kiralfy, *The Action on the Case* (London, 1951), 142. Palmer's more intensive study of the plea rolls in the second half of the fourteenth century has brought to light more than fifty such cases involving killings: *Black Death*, 364–5.

[38] *de Rook* v. *de Hauleye* (1352; *ELABD* 365, case A14a).

[39] Palmer, *Black Death*, 225. Other situations might equally raise our suspicions that the writ is not telling the whole story: Milsom, 'Trespass from Henry III to Edward III' (1958) 74 LQR 561, 566–7.

[40] *The Oculist's Case* (B&M 340). No record of the case in the relevant eyre roll has been traced. [41] See below, p.64.

[42] LI MS Hale 137 f.172 (I have not been able to identify the case in the rolls of the eyre; it is possible that the action was in fact discontinued). The plaintiff brought what is described as a bill of covenant alleging that it had been agreed that he would look after the defendant's cattle

It was not only in cases of contractual mis-performance that we may strongly suspect that general allegations of forcible wrongdoing are concealing more complex fact situations. Tempting a servant away from an employer might be characterized as a forcible abduction in breach of the king's peace;[43] a writ claiming that the defendant had forcibly abducted the plaintiff's wife (in breach of the king's peace) might be brought where the wife had gone wholly voluntarily, concealing situations of elopement or seduction behind the language of abduction and ravishment.[44] Writs alleging that the defendants incited their dogs to bite neighbours' sheep may perhaps conceal situations where the owner had simply failed to control a dog that was known to have a propensity to bite.[45]

The fact that the standard-form language of the general trespass writ could be stretched by imaginative litigants to include a range of situations that should on the face of it have been excluded shows no more than that plaintiffs wanted to get their cases into the royal courts and that the general trespass writ was one of their chosen vehicles; it does not in itself show that such subterfuge was acceptable. Litigants might have been prepared to hoodwink judges, but judges might not have been prepared to be hoodwinked. Sometimes, though, the veil is lifted slightly further, and we may be certain that the true fact situation was as clear to the judges as it is to us. This is best seen in actions begun by bill, which were not afflicted by the rigid formalism of actions begun by writ.[46]

The best, and best-studied, example of this is the well-known Humber Ferry case of 1348, *Bukton* v. *Townsend*.[47] The defendant was a ferryman, who had received the plaintiff's horse to carry across the river Humber. Through the defendant's fault the horse died, and the plaintiff

---

for a year, and that within the year the defendant with force of arms had taken the cattle away from him. It was objected that covenant was appropriate only in cases of complete non-performance, and that here an action of trespass ought to have been brought. To this John de la Rokele replied that the only difference between total non-performance and partial non-performance was that in the former case the damages would be greater; and Shareshull Sjt argued by analogy with cases of ejection from leases that there was no reason why covenant and trespass should not arise on the same facts.

[43] Arnold, *Select Cases of Trespass from the King's Courts 1307–1399* (100 SS), p.xliv. Enticement away from service had been made unlawful by the Ordinance of Labourers of 1349 (Putnam, *The Enforcement of the Statute of Labourers 1349–1359*, 175–6, 181–4), and Arnold's examples of the use of the *vi et armis* writ date from after this time.

[44] Arnold, *Select Cases of Trespass* (100 SS), pp.xlv–xlviii.

[45] Milsom, *Historical Foundations*, 215–18; Arnold, *Select Cases of Trespass* (100 SS), p.lxii. Milsom and Arnold rely heavily on *Moygne* v. *Ganet* (1365; 103 SS 409, case 37.1), which Palmer (*Black Death*, 234–8) rightly points out did in fact involve an incitement, albeit an incitement by the defendant's servants rather than the defendant himself.

[46] The bill jurisdiction was heavily circumscribed, restricted principally to cases arising in the county in which the court was sitting.

[47] YB 22 Lib Ass pl.41, corrected in B&M 358; for variant readings of the manuscripts, see A. K. R. Kiralfy, 'The Humber Ferryman and the Action on the Case' [1953] CLJ 421.

brought his action by bill, seemingly drafted in an essentially trespassory form:

that the same Nicholas [the defendant] . . . received a certain mare from John [the plaintiff] to carry safely across the River Humber in Nicholas's boat, and the same Nicholas so loaded the boat against John's will that he lost the aforesaid mare through Nicholas's fault, in the way that the same John complains by his bill, to John's damage of 40s.[48]

Defendant's counsel argued that the claim sounded in 'covenant' rather than 'trespass', no doubt leading on towards the predictable objection that in the absence of a document under seal the covenant would not have been actionable in the royal courts. The court rejected this argument: 'It seems that you did him a trespass when you overloaded his boat so that his mare perished.' Judgment was given for the plaintiff.

In the Humber Ferry case there is no possibility that the judges were not aware of the true basis of the plaintiff's claim: it was laid out in the bill for all to see. That they allowed the claim to succeed strongly suggests that they saw no impropriety in the use of a trespassory action to recover damages for contractual mis-performance. It is possible that the way in which the bill was formulated helped in this: the plaintiff seems to have sidestepped the potential objection that the action could not be characterized as trespass because the defendant had been acting with his consent by explicitly shifting attention to the mode of performance, the overloading, and to the fact that this had been done against his will.[49]

Had the Humber Ferry case been brought by writ the claim could—and no doubt would—have been formulated as a simple case of *vi et armis* killing,[50] but in some cases successfully brought by bill the plaintiff would have been hard-pressed to squeeze the case into the form demanded by a writ. A good example is the extraordinary case of *Trote* v. *Lynet*.[51] The plaintiff brought an action claiming that the defendant had inveigled him into bed naked, and when he was asleep had introduced into the bed one Alice, the defendant's sister. Two witnesses were then brought in and told that the plaintiff had promised to marry Alice and requested to note that they were lying together naked. Later, at the defendant's instigation, Alice

---

[48] B&M 358; the quotation is from the jury's verdict. Cf. Palmer, *Black Death*, 173–6.

[49] Cf. above, nn.31, 32. Cf. the relatively cruder formulation in the case from the Eyre of Nottingham of 1329, above n.40, where it was apparently alleged simply that the defendant had undertaken to cure the plaintiff and had put out his eye in so doing, without any explicit statement that the defendant had done anything against the will of the plaintiff.

[50] In *Laneham* v. *Botild* (1346; *ELABD* 174) a very similar fact situation was formulated within a straightforward *vi et armis contra pacem* writ, but was not pleaded to issue. See too YB 27 Lib Ass f.143 pl.64 (1353), another bill case, though on different facts, where the plaintiff with the full knowledge of the court reformulated his claim in a bland general form to escape a self-contradiction in the original bill.   [51] 1358; *ELABD* 389, case A23e.

initiated a suit in the consistory court (presumably to establish the validity of the marriage), and the two witnesses were called to testify. As a result of this fraud and deception, the plaintiff claimed that he had suffered loss of £300. Perhaps surprisingly, the jury believed the story; the plaintiff was awarded damages of 40 marks, and the defendant was imprisoned. In another case a year later a bailiff who had arrested the defendant in a lawsuit and wrongly allowed him to go free was held liable to compensate the original plaintiff for his loss.[52] A carrier who had been hired to carry peat but failed to do so within the time specified for performance was held liable in 1362.[53] None of these cases could easily have been described in terms of forcible wrongdoing; but all fell within the extensive range of trespass.

THE ORIGINS OF TRESPASS ON THE CASE

Plaintiffs bringing their actions by writ, therefore, suffered two disadvantages by comparison with those able to proceed by bill.[54] In cases of contractual mis-performance and the like they were forced to use general forms, and hence to a greater or lesser extent to misdescribe the nature of their claims; and, secondly, in the most extreme cases, they might not have been able plausibly to formulate their claims in terms of forcible wrongdoing, and so have been prevented from bringing them in the royal courts at all.

The latter of these was obviously problematical. Cases involving sellers fraudulently tampering with goods in breach of agreement could not even masquerade behind an allegation of force of arms; an attempt to bring trespass in such a situation had failed in 1313.[55] Breach of warranty of

---

[52] *de Northcote* v. *de Aston* (1359; *ELABD* 383, case A21b). The case was determined in the same eyre as the original order to arrest the defendant was made.

[53] *de Athelingflet* v. *de Maydeston* (*ELABD* 329, case A3i).

[54] For what follows, traditionally discussed in terms of the origins of the action of trespass on the case, see Milsom, 'Trespass from Henry III to Edward III' (1958) 74 LQR 407, 561; 'Reason in the Development of the Common Law' (1965) 81 LQR 496, 501–4. The pre-Milsom theories are best described by C. H. S. Fifoot, *History and Sources of the Common Law* (London, 1949), 66–74. Perhaps the last statement of the conservative position (relating the development of trespass on the case to cap. 24 of the Statute of Westminster II (1285)) is T. G. Watkin, 'The Significance of In Consimili Casu' (1979) 24 Am Jnl Leg Hist 283. More radically, and with a wealth of supporting evidence, in *English Law in the Age of the Black Death* Palmer has forcefully argued that the changes of the third quarter of the fourteenth century were changes in substantive law brought about as deliberate responses to the massive social upheaval caused by the Black Death; a full discussion of the richness of his theory is beyond the scope of the present work. The concerns of this chapter are with the form in which claims were couched rather than their substance, and, although in places my interpretation of the evidence will inevitably differ from Palmer's, most of what follows is more or less consistent with the thrust of his analysis.

[55] *Kemp* v. *de Oxford* (103 SS 447, case 42.1) (above n.29).

quality was treated as a wrong; but it could hardly be pretended that it was forcible, and such cases were apparently excluded from the royal courts.[56] Cases involving the failure to act would inevitably raise problems: the failure to repair a sea wall or millpond, or to scour a ditch, might be treated as wrongs, but they could not be characterized as forcible breaches of the king's peace. Should they be excluded from the king's courts? The language of forcible wrongdoing might extend to misperformance of a contract; but it could hardly comprehend non-performance or late performance.[57] Were these to be excluded from trespass? Could an action be brought against an innkeeper whose guest's goods disappeared? Could an action be brought against a landowner from whose land a fire escaped? Could an action be brought against a defaulting sheriff? All of these would have been treated as actionable wrongs in local courts;[58] none could plausibly have been concealed behind a *vi et armis* trespass writ.

It is less easy to see why litigants should have been disadvantaged by the former problem.These cases would not have been excluded from the royal courts, and the only real difficulty would have been that the claims would have to be stated in a way that treated the truth rather elastically.[59] On the face of it, this does not seem too serious a problem, given that there was no judicial objection to the degree of stretching involved. In practice, however, there may have been real difficulties for plaintiffs in these cases too.

To see the difficulty it is necessary to sketch out fourteenth-century civil procedure. The first step was the obtaining of the writ and its service on the defendant; this was designed to do no more than ensure that the defendant turned up in court. Once the parties were before the judges in Westminster, they would plead the case to issue: the plaintiff would formulate the claim (in the 'count') and the defendant would enter a defence (in trespass this was normally a simple 'not guilty', the general issue). The plaintiff's count might be more elaborate than the stark form of the writ, but it could not say anything at variance with it. If the writ had specified that the defendant came with force of arms, for example, the count should not reveal any facts

---

[56] An action succeeded in 1307, but there might have been a royal interest in the case: *Ferrers* v. *Dodford* (58 SS 179). Cf. Kiralfy, *Action on the Case*, 83–4.

[57] An attempt was made to bring a non-perfomance claim within trespass, without alleging *vi et armis* or *contra pacem*, in 1303: *ELABD* 181 n.1. [58] Above, nn.24–8.

[59] It has been argued (e.g. by Milsom, 'Trespass from Henry III to Edward III' (1958) 74 LQR 561, 575) that an additional disadvantage might have been that the defendant could be subjected to the more stringent process by *capias*—arrest without an initial summons—which was technically only appropriate in trespass writs where a breach of the king's peace was involved. If there were any doubts about the propriety of this, they can hardly have survived the statute of 1352 (Stat 25 Edw III Stat 5 c.17), which extended the process of *capias* to all personal actions except covenant (which by this time was primarily used as a means of initiating the conveyance of land by fine).

inconsistent with this.[60] Once issue had been joined, the case was adjourned to the county in which the dispute had arisen. What this meant was that a writ *venire facias*, containing a summary of the issue reached by the parties on the pleadings, was sent to the sheriff of the county requiring him to summon a jury to appear before the judges when they next visited the county (on their twice-yearly assize circuit).[61] This jury would not be a jury in the modern sense, a group of disinterested individuals expected to listen to evidence in court and to make a judgment on the basis of that and that alone. On the contrary, they were specifically selected with a view to taking advantage of their knowledge of the case: at the least they should come from the neighbourhood in which the dispute arose; and, if anything hinged on the validity of a document, for example, it would be quite normal to summon those who were alleged to have witnessed it,[62] either as jurors or in addition to the jurors. When the judges arrived on their assize circuit, the parties would undoubtedly have had an opportunity to explain the truth of their cases.[63] Before this, though, the sheriff would have outlined the nature of the case (necessarily on the basis of the summary of the case in the *venire facias* writ) to the jurors who had been summoned,[64] and they would have been expected to make some investigation as to the truth of the plaintiff's claim.[65] It was here that the difficulty arose. The greater the disparity between the way in which the claim had been formulated in the pleadings and the true base of the plaintiff's claim, the greater the risk that the jurors would investigate the wrong issues. If the pleadings talked of the defendant's attacking the plaintiff's horse with an axe, the jurors might not think to investigate whether he had incompetently stuck a nail into the horse's hoof while shoeing it. If the pleadings talked of the violent replacement of wine with sea water, they might not think to investigate the circumstances of a shipping accident. Of course the true basis of the claim would have an opportunity to come out at the assize hearing, perhaps several months later; but the jury might have been left in doubt as to the relevance of such a story, and in any event we might well suspect that

---

[60] Though inevitably this might happen in practice, however improper it was in theory; see e.g. *ELABD* 386, cases A22d and A22e.

[61] For an excellent example of the way in which the pleadings were condensed in writs of *venire facias*, see that in *Stratton* v. *Swanlond* extracted in *ELABD* 346–7, case A7w.

[62] J. B. Thayer, *Preliminary Treatise on Evidence at the Common Law* (London, 1898), 94–104, esp. 97–102.

[63] M. S. Arnold, 'Law and Fact in the Medieval Jury Trial: Out of Sight, Out of Mind' (1974) 18 Am Jnl Leg Hist 267, 275. It was probably not until the fifteenth century that witnesses in the modern sense began to appear: Thayer, *Preliminary Treatise on Evidence*, 125–9.

[64] G. O. Sayles, *Select Cases in the Court of King's Bench, ii* (57 SS), p.cv.

[65] This was still the case in the mid-fifteenth century: YB P.28 Hen VI 6 pl.1.

they would not then be in a particularly good position to give an answer to a question that they had not previously considered.[66]

Focusing the writ of trespass on forcible wrongdoing, therefore, produced two distinct difficulties. Most obviously, some cases of acknowledged wrongdoing were excluded entirely from the royal courts, since they could not plausibly be designated as forcible. Less obviously, but more significant numerically, plaintiffs with claims that could be forced into the standard-form language of the trespass writ were being required to misrepresent their claims in such a way that there was a real risk that the jury would be misled as to the true basis of the action, with a consequent risk that they would come to court ill-equipped to give a proper verdict.

In the middle decades of the fourteenth century these problems were explored, and by about 1370 a workable solution had been found to them. It is, however, not at all easy to unpick all the issues that were at stake or to give a neat description of the main lines of the story: the Year Books shed only a little light before the mid-1360s, and the plea rolls give an impression more of anarchic—or hesitant—experimentation than of a quiet linear development of legal ideas. At heart there were two issues. Should plaintiffs be allowed to use writs in non-standard forms in order to get the details of their stories into the formal pleadings, and hence into the writ *venire facias*? Should they be allowed to use such non-standard writs if the story told revealed that the wrong alleged did not constitute a forcible breach of the king's peace? Subsidiary to this was a third question: could they use such non-standard writs to bring cases that would formerly have been effectively excluded from the scope of trespass?

Trespass writs in which plaintiffs gave background information to their claims (usually in a subordinate clause beginning 'whereas', *cum*) are found from the first half of the thirteenth century.[67] There was, therefore, nothing new about attempts to use them in the middle of the fourteenth century. Nor was there anything improper about doing so. The only real brake on their use was that the judges were perhaps reluctant to sanction them unless there was a risk that the jury might be misled if the claim was formulated in a bland general writ. The point is well illustrated by the discussion in *The Miller's Case* in 1367.[68] The plaintiff had taken his corn to the defendant miller to be ground into flour. The defendant had ground it and delivered it to the plaintiff, keeping for himself two bushels. On the face of it there was

---

[66] This problem is normally looked at from the standpoint of the defendant and considered in terms of the propriety of special pleas, but plaintiffs would have been no less affected by it. Pleading the general issue, the simplest and least risky formal response to the plaintiff's count, could have had disastrous results if it prevented the jury from focusing their minds on the precise question in dispute. The difficulties are well analysed by Arnold, *Select Cases of Trespass* (100 SS), pp.x-xxvi.

[67] Milsom, 'Trespass from Henry III to Edward III' (1958) 74 LQR 407.

[68] YB M.41 Edw III f.24 pl.17.

nothing wrong with the retention of the two bushels; this was the ordinary
way in which millers were paid for their labour. The present plaintiff,
however, claimed that he had a prescriptive right that his corn be ground
free, and he brought an action of trespass against the defendant complaining of the wrongful retention: 'Whereas the aforesaid John [the plaintiff]
and his predecessors from the time beyond which memory does not run
ought to have ground without payment of toll etc the aforesaid defendant
etc by force of arms prevented the aforesaid plaintiff from grinding without
payment of toll etc.' Defendant's counsel objected to the presence of the
'whereas' clause in which the plaintiff had set out his claim to the prescriptive right. He should be forced to use a standard general writ, alleging
simply that the defendant miller had forcibly taken two bushels of his
corn. Plaintiff's counsel argued that the 'whereas' clause was appropriate,
but Witchingham J. was against him and the plaintiff was forced to withdraw his action, no doubt to begin afresh with a bland general writ.[69] It is
not difficult to see what was at stake here. The plaintiff wanted to tell his
story to ensure that the jury focused on the precise question in dispute,
whether he had a prescriptive right to have his corn ground without paying
the customary toll, rather than asking themselves more generally whether
the defendant had wrongfully retained the two bushels of corn. In reject-
ing the writ in its original form, the court seems to be actuated by a belief
that the jury would not be misled into considering the wrong question if
the writ were in the standard form.[70]

A plaintiff who was able to surmount this hurdle and tell the background
story would be in no difficulty if the pleaded facts were not inconsistent
with the allegation of forcible wrongdoing. There are many actions where
the plaintiff first lays a special right, such as the right to take for himself
animals found wandering on his land (known as waif), and continues by
claiming in standard form that the defendant forcibly took such animals.[71]
In other less clear cases it might have been arguable that the facts were
consistent with the allegation of force, and it is possible that around 1360
the courts may have begun to allow a greater degree of flexibility than
would have been the case in the second quarter of the fourteenth century.
Thus, in 1360, issue was reached in the King's Bench in a case where a
bailee was alleged to have *vi et armis* in breach of the king's peace destroyed
cloth that had been delivered to him to be fulled.[72] Sometimes the allega-

[69] But cf. YB T.44 Edw III f.20 pl.16, where a writ in substantially the same form was
upheld.
[70] Cf. the mirror principle at work with special pleas: Arnold, *Select Cases of Trespass* (100
SS), pp.xvi-xx.   [71] For examples, see Palmer, *Black Death*, 407–15.
[72] *le Blake* v. *le Fullere* (*ELABD* 359, case A11c). As early as 1355, perhaps, a case involving
wrongful acts by a bailee described as *vi et armis* and in breach of the king's peace was allowed
to go to issue: *de Harewode* v. *de Bukyngham* (*ELABD* 328, case A3d). The plaintiff alleged

tions of force were transparently inappropriate. Actions are found, for example, where the defendant was alleged to have *vi et armis* kept a dog that he knew to be dangerous and that had subsequently attacked the plaintiff's animals or done other damage,[73] and, despite the obvious meaninglessness of the allegation that the dogs were kept with swords, bows, and arrows, at least one case in this form was pleaded to issue in the Common Pleas in 1361.[74] More commonly, as the boundaries of trespass were pushed back, plaintiffs omitted the allegation of force and limited themselves to characterizing the wrong as a breach of the king's peace. The 'non-forcible' keeping of dangerous animals was often so described, for example.[75] In a case pleaded to issue in the Common Pleas in 1360 the plaintiff alleged that he had bailed cloth to the defendant to be fulled and that the defendant had torn it into pieces in breach of the king's peace.[76] The defendant took the general issue, and the case was (twice) sent to the county for the verdict of a jury. In 1366–7, still in the Common Pleas, an owner of sheep recovered damages against a shepherd who had guarded them inadequately, again in breach of the king's peace.[77] These were situations that could probably have been hidden behind general trespass writs if the plaintiffs had wished to do so; it seems that the judges were allowing a return to the breadth of meaning—or lack of meaning—given to the allegations of the breach of the king's peace in the thirteenth century.[78] But with such a reduced meaning the phrase could be slotted into situations where it looked particularly out of place, perhaps situations in which no action could formerly have been brought. As early as 1349 the King's Bench had allowed proceedings on a bill where the defendant was said to have forged a bond and sued on it in breach of the king's peace;[79] and in 1368 judgment was given against an innkeeper whose guest's goods had been stolen by thieves in breach of the king's peace, a situation implicitly stated not to have been litigated beforehand in the royal courts.[80] In the

---

that the defendant shipowner had *vi et armis* uncovered wool fells that had been loaded in his boat, with the result that they had become impregnated with sea water and rotted. At first sight this looks as if it might be another fanciful embellishment of a shipping accident, but the presence of a second count claiming that the defendant had attacked the plaintiff's servant probably points to it as a genuinely forcible scuffle.

[73] *ELABD* 368–77 (cases A15e, A15h, A15j, A15p, A15q, A16c, A16e, A16g, A16p, A16q, A16u, A16y, A16z, A16bb, A16ee, A16ff, A16gg, A16mm, A17a).

[74] *Eynsford* v. *de Hempton* (*ELABD* 372, case A16c).

[75] *ELABD* 368–77 (cases A15a, A15b, A15d, A15k, A15l, A15m, A15n, A16a, A16f, A16h, A16k, A16l, A16n, A16r, A16aa, A16dd, A16jj, A17c, A17d).

[76] *Cleseby* v. *de Willingham* (*ELABD* 359, case A11b). Cf. *le Blake* v. *le Fullere* (above, n.72).

[77] *de Northwood* v. *Couper* (*ELABD* 351, case A9h).   [78] Above, p.40.

[79] *de Hapham* v. *Cok* (*ELABD* 391, case A23l).

[80] *Navenby* v. *Lassels* YB 42 Lib Ass pl.17 (trans. in Kiralfy, *Source Book*, 202 and (abbreviated) in B&M 552). Knyvet C.J. refers to the fact that a similar action had been brought in the King's Council, and in the report of the case in BL MS Eg 748 f.123ᵛ the reporter appends a reference to the existence of liability in London (for which see Kiralfy,

1370s, Milsom observes, allegations of the breach of the king's peace seem to have been inserted into writs almost indiscriminately; although this was rapidly held to be improper, it gives some indication of the degree to which the phrase had become denuded of meaning.[81]

Most radically of all, the plaintiff might simply recite the story and assert that loss had been caused by the defendant's wrong without any allegation of force or breach of the king's peace. An excellent early example of this is *Childerhouse* v. *Laverok* in 1352–4:[82] whereas the plaintiff had bailed his ship to the defendant, the defendant allowed it to float free, with the result that the ship and its contents were lost. The case was not pleaded to issue in the Common Pleas; it was claimed by the bailiffs of the borough of Great Yarmouth as properly belonging to that court. Here the defendant pleaded not guilty, but there was obviously some problem; after three adjournments without taking a verdict, the plaintiff withdrew his action.[83] There are many other such unpleaded writs in the plea rolls of the 1340s and 1350s,[84] but we can merely guess how the judges would have reacted if any of these, with no pretence of being a forcible breach of the king's peace, had reached them.[85] Perhaps they would have been accepted, perhaps not. In the mid-1360s, though, we begin to find such cases in which plaintiffs win judgments.

The first of these, *Broadmeadow* v. *Rushenden*,[86] began by writ in December 1363. An action was brought against a London doctor who had promised to cure an injured woman's arm, claiming that he had carried out the treatment so carelessly, negligently, or maliciously that her hand had been lost. The case was pleaded to issue in Easter term 1364, and a writ sent to the sheriff of London to empanel a jury. The jury found a verdict for the defendant, and in Michaelmas term 1365 judgment was entered accordingly. It may well be that this marks the real watershed in the expansion of trespassory liability. Although the other forms with the intrusive, seemingly

---

Action on the Case, 151). The plaintiff here was a king's messenger and the allegation of the breach of the king's peace might not have been so far-fetched—indeed, the plaintiff is said to be suing on the king's behalf as well as his own—but there are similar cases pleaded to issue with the same allegation where there was not any colour of a royal interest: e.g. *Bolton* v. *Ede* (1373; 103 SS case 41.2), *Pound* v. *Folksworth* (1374; 103 SS case 41.3). For other examples of the form, see Palmer, *Black Death*, 378–82.

[81] Milsom, 'Trespass from Henry III to Edward III' (1958) 74 LQR 407, 433.

[82] 103 SS 417, case 39.2.

[83] Great Yarmouth borough court (Norfolk CRO) Y/C4/74 m.5d. The records of the court show a considerable degree of legal sophistication and Common-law knowledge on the part of Yarmouth litigants or their lawyers, so it is possible that there was objection to the form of the writ. There is, though, no suggestion of this in the record, and it seems to have been the practice of the clerks at Yarmouth to note unsuccessful formal challenges as well as successful ones.   [84] Palmer, *Black Death*, cites several dozen examples.

[85] It has always to be borne in mind that judicial involvement began only when the defendant responded to the writ.   [86] 103 SS 422, case 40.1; *ELABD* 343, case A7e.

inappropriate, allegations of the breach of the king's peace (with or without an allegation of force) continue to be found, the *Broadmeadow* v. *Rushenden* form without any such allegation soon came to predominate. In 1369, in *Waldon* v. *Mareschal*, it was held improper to include an allegation of a breach of the king's peace in an action brought against a horse doctor who, it was claimed, had killed a horse by negligent treatment.[87] Two years later, in 1371, a plaintiff fell foul of this rule: the flooding of the plaintiff's land as a result of the defendant's failure to repair river walls was described as being in breach of the king's peace, and the writ abated in consequence.[88] By 1375 the *Broadmeadow* form of writ, which came to be known as trespass on the case, was the appropriate one to be used by plaintiffs who wanted to get the details of their story into the pleadings. Within only a few years the boundary between general trespass and trespass on the case was beginning to harden. In *Berden v Burton*, in 1382, a general action of trespass was brought alleging that the defendant had burned down the plaintiff's house. When the plaintiff elaborated the story by saying that the defendant's men had threatened his servants, causing them to leave their fire unattended with the result that his manor burned down, the defendant immediately demanded judgment on the grounds that on these facts the action should have been case rather than trespass. Belknap C.J. was sympathetic to this objection. As a result the plaintiff changed his story, alleging that the fire had been caused by sparks from the defendant's men's torches. Belknap C.J. was happy with this: such facts were consistent with a general allegation that the defendant had forcibly burned down the plaintiff's house.[89] It is not easy to discern from *Berden* v. *Burton* exactly what the boundary between the two forms of action was; it might have been between direct and indirect causation, or between intentional and non-intentional acts. By the end of the century, though, it had become established as a rule of thumb that it was improper for plaintiffs to use general writs in circumstances where the facts demanded a special writ.[90] No longer should actions against negligent blacksmiths be concealed behind writs alleging blankly that the defendant had *vi et armis* in breach of the king's peace killed or injured the plaintiff's horse.

This establishment of the action of trespass on the case had three very

---

[87] YB M.43 Edw III f.33 pl.38 (B&M 359). On more careful examination of the writ it was found that the offensive words had not in fact been included, so the action was able to proceed. See too *Stratton* v. *Swanlond*, YB H.48 Edw III f.6 pl.11 (B&M 360).

[88] YB T.45 Edw III 17 pl.6. Cases including the uneasy reference to the breach of the king's peace continue to be found (e.g. *ELABD* 404–6, cases A24fff (1375), A24jjj (1376), A24sss (1379)), though none of these is pleaded to issue. See, generally, Milsom, 'Trespass from Henry III to Edward III' (1958) 74 LQR 407, 433–4.

[89] YB T.6 Ric II (AF) 19. The case was eventually settled.

[90] YB H.13 Ric II (AF) 103.

important consequences for the structure of the English law of obligations. First of all, it introduced an artificial distinction into the law of torts between the general action of trespass *vi et armis* in breach of the king's peace and the action of trespass on the case in which the plaintiff's story was told and the allegations of force and breach of the king's peace omitted. No differences of substance hung on this distinction, and such procedural differences as there were were of minimal importance.[91] None the less, the two actions developed independently of each other, causing friction on the (artificial) boundary between them. Right up to the nineteenth century litigants had to be sure that they used the correct form of action for their claim, and some features of twentieth-century law continue to bear the marks of this history.[92] Secondly, loosed from the core of forcible wrongdoing, trespass on the case was left with no inbuilt boundaries and had an almost unlimited potential to expand into other areas, both providing remedies in situations that had formerly been remediless and offering an alternative form of action where an existing remedy was thought to be inadequate. It was not until the end of the fifteenth century that this potential began to be seriously exploited, but from then onwards trespass on the case relentlessly gained ground. Thirdly, the placing of situations of contractual mis-performance within trespass on the case— the most significant feature of the fragmentation of remedies for broken contracts in the fourteenth century—marked the planting of the seed around which contractual liability was to recrystallize in the sixteenth century and later.

---

[91] The availability of *capias* in trespass *vi et armis* (above, n.59) was the only significant difference, and, although this was extended by statute to the action on the case in 1504 (Stat 19 Hen VII c.9), even in the eighteenth and nineteenth centuries lawyers were still trying to point to the differences between the two forms of actions: M. J. Prichard, 'Trespass, Case and the Rule in *Williams* v. *Holland*' [1964] CLJ 234, 240.   [92] Below, pp.163, 302.

4. *The Substantive Law of Torts*

The substantive law of torts in the Middle Ages was inherently messy, though perhaps no more messy than its twentieth-century counterpart. The fundamental reason for this is not difficult to discern. Unlike the law of property or the law of contract, both of which (at least in part) have to formulate guidelines within which individuals can arrange their affairs, the law of torts always has to respond retrospectively to alleged wrongdoings. The medieval law, like that of the twentieth century, provided a mould within which issues could be raised but in itself provided few answers to the substantive questions that might have been asked.

A second difficulty is more specific to the medieval law. The main core of the law of torts was to be found within the unforthcoming general action of trespass, in which plaintiffs monotonously alleged simply that they had been injured in their person, land, or goods by the forcible act of the defendant. The effective boundaries of liability are practically concealed from us by the uniformity of this form of pleading. Whenever issues arose that we might want to characterize as questions of law—when an employer should be liable for the wrongs of an employee, for example—these would largely have been determined by the jury, with a minimum of judicial control. The same is true of the proper criteria for the award of damages.[1] This meant that the law was able to respond with maximal flexibility to social perceptions of where liability should lie in individual cases; the principal losers are the legal historians who seek for clear answers to questions that were never explicitly asked. There are, however, stray remarks in the Year Books that give some guidance as to the way in which cases were approached; and large-scale trawls through the huge mass of entries in the plea rolls has cast some light on the substantive law. We are, paradoxically, better provided for in trying to discern the imposition of liability in situations away from the mainstream, for, once the action of trespass on the case had established itself in the middle of the fourteenth century, plaintiffs were able to formulate their claims with a degree of transparency that enables us to penetrate beneath the forms of pleading to the underlying facts.

---

[1] For a rare case where the court significantly increased an award of damages, see *de Billesleye* v. *Holt* (1304) BL MS Add 31826 f.353, CP 40/145 m.238. The fact that the defendant (who had thoroughly beaten up the plaintiff) was poor was not a factor to justify a reduction in the plaintiff's damages.

STRICT LIABILITY AND THE ROLE OF FAULT

On the face of it, liability in trespass was strict rather than fault-based.[2] The defendant who had caused harm to the plaintiff's person, land, or goods should be forced to compensate for this. Throughout the medieval and early modern periods there is a strong focus on the loss suffered by the plaintiff rather than on the wrongful conduct of the defendant: 'If a man suffers damage it is right that he be compensated'; 'When someone does something he is bound to do it in such a way that no prejudice or damage is done to others by his action.'[3] It is, of course, possible that the apparent rigours of this approach might have been mitigated by the jury in cases where its application led to a perceived unfairness, and it has been argued that the rule of strict liability existed only on the surface, concealing the jury's invariable consideration of the question of fault.[4] The opaqueness of jury verdicts—a simple guilty or not guilty—means that we cannot conclusively demonstrate or disprove this. No doubt the jury did from time to time depart from the strict application of whatever rules did exist, but the balance of arguments is against the conclusion that it occurred in any systematic way. The few chance remarks of judges and counsel in the Year Books, and in reports as late as the seventeenth century, point to an analysis in terms of strict liability without any hint that a completely different analysis applied in practice;[5] the mass of cases in the plea rolls show that plaintiffs in trespass did not in fact allege fault on the part of defendants, and defendants hardly ever pleaded that the injury had been caused without their fault;[6] and the evidence of the Year Books strongly suggests that they were not attempting to do so. Approaching the question without the preconception that liability must have been fault-based, it is hard to avoid the conclusion that liability in the writ of trespass was prima facie strict.

This is not to say that liability in trespass was absolute. There clearly existed a number of defences that allowed defendants to admit that they had caused the injury and to explain that their behaviour was justified. No doubt there was no closed list of such defences, but its main outlines are unsurprising. Trespass to the person, for example, might be justified by

---

[2] M. S. Arnold, 'Accident, Mistake, and Rules of Liability in the Fourteenth-Century Law of Torts' (1979) 128 U Penn L R 361; *Select Cases of Trespass* (100 SS), pp.xlii-xliii.

[3] *Hulle* v. *Orynge* (*The Case of Thorns*) YB M.6 Edw IV f.7 pl.18 (B&M 327), per Littleton J. and Bryan Sjt. respectively.   [4] Milsom, *Historical Foundations*, 296–7.

[5] *Hulle* v. *Orynge* (*The Case of Thorns*) YB M.6 Edw IV f.7 pl.18 (B&M 327); YB T.13 Hen VIII f.16 pl.1; *Weaver* v. *Ward* (1616) Hob 134 (B&M 331); *Dickinson* v. *Watson* (1682) T. Jones 205 (B&M 334). See Baker, *Spelman's Reports, ii* (94 SS) 222–4.

[6] There are, however, a few cases where this did happen: e.g. *de Wenden* v. *Ferrer* (1363; 103 SS 261, case 21.5); *Fitzsimon* v. *Ferrer* (1371; 103 SS 262, case 21.7); *Rankin* v. *Ferrer* (1377; 103 SS 262, case 21.8); *de Stapleton* v. *Marshall* (1380; 103 SS 264, case 21.10).

self-defence or defence of others (though probably not defence of property); by a plea that the defendant had lawfully arrested the plaintiff; or by lawful chastisement.[7] Similar justifications might negative liability for an apparent trespass to goods, most commonly that the defendant had some sort of right to take the goods.[8] Trespass to land was slightly different, but there were many situations in which one person might claim to have a right to enter the property of another.[9] Justificatory defences such as these had their application almost exclusively where the defendant's act was deliberate. They did nothing to undermine the main core of strict liability, that the defendant who had accidentally caused harm to the plaintiff would still be liable.

It would, however, be a bad mistake to exaggerate the contrast between this regime of strict liability (qualified by justificatory defences) and a regime of fault liability. Essentially the same issues of the ascription of responsibility arise in each method of analysis; in the latter method they are discussed openly in terms of fault, while under a regime of strict liability they are largely concealed behind the language of causation. Such questions of causation would rarely, if ever, be explicitly pleaded; they were fundamental to the central question of trespassory liability, whether the defendant caused the harm to the plaintiff, and would have been considered behind the general issue of not guilty.

The most obvious of these arguments based on causation was that the injury had been caused by the injured party rather than by the defendant.[10] There is a world of difference, intuitively clear, between the man running under the cart and the cart running over the man. Both formulations may refer to the same brute facts—the collision between the man and the cart—but the difference between them is none the less significant: in the former case responsibility for the injury is ascribed to the man, in the latter case to the cart and (presumably) its driver. Or, to put it loosely in the ordinary language of the twentieth century, in the former case it was the man's own fault.[11] Thus, around 1300, a man who brought an action complaining of a battery lost his case when it was shown that he had first hit an innkeeper's

---

[7] Arnold, *Select Cases of Trespass* (100 SS), pp.xxxiv–xli. [8] Ibid., pp.l–lx.
[9] Ibid., pp.lxx–lxxxiii.
[10] Ibid., pp.xli–xlii; Baker, *Spelman's Reports, ii* (94 SS), *223* n.5. Arnold is, however, dangerously misleading in treating this as a 'defence of contributory negligence', which carries too many overtones that the defendant is enabled to avoid liability despite having satisfied the ordinary criteria of guilt. For medieval lawyers, the basic criterion of liability—that the defendant had caused harm to the plaintiff—had not been met. W. S. Holdsworth, *History of English Law*, 3.378–9, is more accurate.
[11] Medieval lawyers might use similar language too: e.g. *atte Hall* v. *atte Hall* (1374; 100 SS 16, case 2.16) ('*in defectum et de facto proprio*'); *Wade* v. *Spragg* (1374; 100 SS 21, case 2.21) ('*de necligencia, stultitia, et facto suo proprio*'); *Goodson* v. *Walklin* (1376; 100 SS 18, case 2.18) ('*ex stultitia et defectu*'); *Reygnesbury* v. *Croyle* (1397; 100 SS 30, case 2.31) ('*ex stultitia et defectu*').

wife over a dispute about a tavern bill, as a result of which the hue and cry had been raised against him: it was his own folly and he was the cause of the battery.[12]

Alternatively, the defendant might argue that the injury was caused by a third person. Such a defence would not necessarily point to a simple case of mistaken identity. The Marshal of the King's Bench, for example, when sued for permitting the escape of prisoners in his custody, defended himself by claiming that their escape was the result of the act of the king's enemies without the connivance of the marshal; their act, it was argued, was on a par with a sudden tempest or other act of God.[13] Again, in the ordinary language of the twentieth century, the plaintiff was not injured through the defendant's fault.

Not far from this was the situation where the immediate cause of the injury was the defendant's animal rather than the defendant in person. Again, the language of causation might mask basic issues of fault and responsibility. From the mid-fourteenth century the owner of cattle was in theory strictly liable if they wandered into a neighbour's field, but such cases normally hinged around whether it was the responsibility of the plaintiff or the defendant to keep the fence between their properties in repair.[14] The owner of a domestic animal acting against its nature, such as a dog biting sheep, would not be liable; unless, of course, it had been incited or, at least from the mid-fourteenth century, the owner had known of its dangerous propensity.[15] Liability would in principle attach to the owner of a bull that was known to be dangerous and gored some other person;[16] unless, perhaps, the plaintiff was wrongfully crossing the defendant's field or the defendant had a private right entitling his bull to wander freely around the village (the so-called right of free bull).[17] Whatever the language used by contemporaries, it is difficult in the twentieth century not to think of these situations in terms of questions of fault.

The medieval law came closest to allowing a defence of accident when defendants shifted causal responsibility away from themselves onto God. If the wind blew the defendant's thorns onto the plaintiff's land, there would

---

[12] *Curteys* v. *Crepping* (1300) BL MS Add 37657 f.47, CP 40/122 m.82d. See too the dismissive remarks of Bereford J. in *John of Lancaster* v. *Culy* (1307?) BL MS Add 31826 f.26: if the defendant had used the amount of force allowed by custom, then the plaintiff's injury was '*sa folie demeyne*'.

[13] YB H.33 Hen VI f.1 pl.3; cf. YB M.9 Hen VI f.53 pl.37 (servant selling bad wine without connivance of defendant). Baker, *Spelman's Reports, ii* (94 SS), *223* nn.2, 3.

[14] YB 27 Lib Ass f.141 pl.56: a straightforward trespass action (by bill) complaining of the escape of the cattle; defendant liable because the escape was the result of 'default of keeping'. YB H.21 Hen VI f.33 pl.20; YB M.22 Hen VI f.7 pl.12. See generally G. L. Williams, *Liability for Animals* (Cambridge, 1939), 218–24.   [15] Palmer, *Black Death*, 228–51.

[16] *Ichelesbourne* v. *Lok* (1377; *ELABD* 374, case A16v).

[17] See the discussion of Lord Kenyon C.J. in *Brock* v. *Copeland* (1794) 1 Esp 203. For free bull, W. C. Bolland, *Year Book 5 Edward II* (31 SS), pp.xxxii–xxxv.

be no liability, since the wind rather than the defendant had caused the intrusion.[18] The gaoler would not be liable for the escape of his prisoners if the gaol had been broken open by a sudden tempest;[19] nor, apparently, would the carrier of goods be liable if the ship in which they were being carried was blown on to a sandbank in a storm.[20] But, of course, not all natural phenomena could be treated as acts of God sufficient to exculpate the defendant: the gaoler excused by a sudden tempest could not expect to be similarly relieved in the case of a short sharp shower. Yet again, the apparently value-neutral language of causation can be seen to disguise value-loaded issues of responsibility.

The medieval action of trespass, then, was built on a theory of strict liability, subject to a range of justificatory defences. The operation of ideas of causation, however, meant that this strict liability was suffused through and through with ideas of fault. Normally it would not be necessary to scratch the surface of the language of causation and to expose its sub-structure,[21] though this might occur in the most awkward peripheral cases.[22] The man who clipped the thorn hedge between his land and the land of his neighbour could hardly argue that God had done the clipping if the thorns fell over the boundary (though he might easily argue that God had blown them there if there had been a wind); he might, however, argue that he should not be liable if he could not have cut the hedge in any other way.[23] In the same way, the man who cut down a tree on his own land in such a way that it fell over his neighbour's boundary would be liable—he could hardly argue that he had not done the chopping—unless he could show that he could not have acted in any other way.[24] Analogous problems later arose with guns, whose sensitive mechanisms might be triggered all too easily by a clumsy user. However unintentional the act, it would have been difficult to say that it had been committed by God. In such a case, the

---

[18] *Hulle v. Orynge (The Case of Thorns)* YB M.6 Edw IV f.7 pl.18 (B&M 327), per Choke J.

[19] YB H.33 Hen VI f.1 pl.3.

[20] *Rogerstun v. de Northcotes* (1366; 103 SS 423, case 40.2).

[21] Cf. classical and post-classical Roman law, for example, where causal tests and fault-based tests seem to have been treated as effectively interchangeable for at least half a millennium: e.g. Justinian, *Institutes*, 4.3.5.

[22] Cf. *Stapelton v. Snayth* YB P.29 Edw III f.32 (Kiralfy, *Action on the Case*, 210; *ELABD* 398 case A24n), where an action for damage caused by the failure to repair a river wall comes very close to depending on the question of the defendant's fault: the pleadings show issue being taken on whether the damage was caused by the defendant's default (*defectus, defaut*) in repairing; but the Year Book reporter twists the meaning of *defaut*, adding a query (at f.33) whether the defendant ought not to have demurred on the question whether he could be liable without his *defaut*. In context, this last word can only be translated as 'fault'.

[23] *Hulle v. Orynge (The Case of Thorns)* YB M.6 Edw IV f.7 pl.18 (B&M 327), per Choke J. The actual case involved the defendant's entry into the plaintiff's land to gather up the thorns; it was assumed that this would have been justifiable if the entry of the thorns was not in itself a wrongful act. It is possible that the case, in reality, conceals a boundary dispute.

[24] YB T.13 Hen VIII f.16 pl.1, per Browne Sjt.

defendant would not be liable if the shot was 'utterly without his fault' or the result of 'unavoidable necessity'.[25]

More straightforwardly, the language of fault came to the surface in those relatively unusual situations where individuals could be liable for situations that were not the result of their own acts. Waste is a good example: the lessee of land was liable not specifically for committing waste (as where trees were wrongfully cut down or the house had fallen down), but for waste being committed.[26] The lessor had merely to show that the trees had been cut down, and not that it was the lessee who had done it. The real question, therefore, was not whether the defendant had cut down the trees but whether he or she was responsible for their cutting, not whether the defendant had pulled the house down but whether he or she was responsible for its falling, questions that could not be framed within the language of causation. In such cases the focus on fault was explicit.[27] Exactly the same problem arose when fire spread from one person's property to another's. The clear rule, described by the end of the fourteenth century as 'the custom of the realm', was that the defendant would be liable for the spread of 'his fire' even if the immediate cause of the spread had been a high wind, the paradigm case of an act of God.[28] In this context, just as in the action of waste, the language of fault was brought explicitly to the surface, since the straightforward language of causation failed to address the right issues.[29] The same was true of the liability of the inn-keeper when a guest's goods were stolen.[30]

The language of fault came to the surface too in cases of contractual mis-performance, at least once these could be formulated transparently as actions of trespass on the case after the middle of the fourteenth century.[31] To say that the defendant had undertaken to do something and then done it causing loss to the plaintiff would on the face of it not have disclosed any cause of action. In order to provide a basis for the action, therefore, the plaintiff had to shift the focus from the fact of the defendant's act to the

---

[25] *Weaver* v. *Ward* (1616) Hob 134 (B&M 331); *Dickinson* v. *Watson* (1682) T. Jones 205 (B&M 334). Below, p.158.   [26] Milsom, *Novae Narrationes* (80 SS), pp.cxc–cxcviii.
[27] YB 21 & 22 Edw I (RS) 29; *Abbot of Fountains* v. *la Chapele*, YB 9 Edw II (45 SS) 76. S. S. Walker, 'The Action of Waste in the Early Common Law', in J. H. Baker (ed.), *Legal Records and the Historian* (London, 1978), 185, 198–9.
[28] Milsom, 'Trespass from Henry III to Edward III' (1958) 74 LQR 195, 213–15; Arnold, *Select Cases of Trespass* (100 SS), pp.lxviii–lxx.
[29] *de Brainton* v. *de Pyn* (1290; 55 SS 181; B&M 320); *de Shorne* v. *de Langton* (1320; 103 SS 400, case 35.2); YB M.48 Edw III f.25 pl.8 (B&M 304); *Cook* v. *Hasard* (1387; 103 SS 404, case 35.6).
[30] It is transparent in the common form of the writ, where the innkeeper's duty is to guard guests' goods 'such that by the default of the said innkeepers or their servants' no damage to or loss of the goods should occur. On the liability of innkeepers, see below, n.68.
[31] Above, pp.48–56. The same approach is visible earlier when not masked by the problematic language of the forms of action.

mode of performance of the job: 'whereas the same Stephen [the defendant] undertook at Bedford well and faithfully to cure a horse belonging to the same John [the plaintiff] worth forty shillings which was accidentally wounded, the aforesaid Stephen so negligently and unduly applied his cure to the aforesaid horse that the aforesaid horse perished.'[32] The language of causation is inadequate to the task of pointing to the basis of liability, and the language of fault immediately takes over.

Liability in tort in the Middle Ages, therefore, was suffused by some idea of fault.[33] This is not to say that there was anything akin to the modern notion of negligence, an external standard according to which the wrongfulness of conduct could be assessed.[34] On the contrary, acceptance of the idea that medieval liability was fault-based involves no more than the recognition that the incidence of liability depended on societal perceptions of where the blame ought to be laid in any individual case. The law made little attempt to dictate to juries the answer to the question who was responsible, nor even to provide any further definition of the circumstances in which responsibility should be inferred. It made no difference whether it was formulated in terms of the language of causation, fault, blame, guilt, or responsibility; ultimately it was for the jury to determine where liability for an allegedly wrongful injury should lie.

THE SCOPE OF TRESPASSORY LIABILITY

Just as the nature of legal responsibility reflected societal values, these same values largely permeated the scope of legal liability. The general action of trespass gave little scope for judicial control,[35] and—so far as we can penetrate beneath the monotonous standard-form pleading—it seems that in practice it would normally be for the jury to determine whether the circumstances were such that liability might be imposed. In anachronistically modern terms, that is to say, the jury would have decided both whether a duty was owed and whether that duty had been breached. Where the plaintiff's story was visible on the face of the record—in actions of

[32] *Swanton* v. *Smith* (1378, 103 SS 424, case 40.3).
[33] English law, therefore, reflected the Canon Law principle enshrined in X.5.36.9: 'If loss is caused by your fault . . . it is necessary that you make amends for it' (*Si culpa tua datum est damnum . . . iure super his satisfacere te oportet*). There is, in addition, a very strong element of fault-based reasoning in contractual actions at this time: below, p.90.
[34] Cf. Arnold, *Select Cases of Trespass* (100 SS), pp.xlii–xliii, where 'fault' and 'negligence' are treated as identical.
[35] It is possible that the judges at the trial did give the jury some guidance, but the nature of the surviving reports and their concentration on purely legal arguments in Westminster Hall means that there would be no report of this and it would be hidden from the gaze of the historian: M. S. Arnold, 'Law and Fact in the Medieval Jury Trial: Out of Sight, Out of Mind' (1974) 18 Am Jnl Leg Hist 267, 276–7.

trespass on the case, and generally in actions brought by bill—the powers of the jury were circumscribed; in these situations the judges were able to wield control over the imposition of liability.[36] From these cases, and from occasional general actions of trespass in which we are permitted to glimpse beneath the surface of the pleadings, it is possible to discern something of the principles and practices that were at work.

The medieval law of torts was primarily concerned with the granting of redress for physical injury, or for such interferences as the entry into another's land or the taking of another's chattels. Indeed, it could be said that there was a general principle that an individual who had unjustifiably caused physical injury to another's person or property (with all the overtones of fault contained in the ideas of unjustifiability and causation), or had interfered with it, should be liable.[37] It did not matter whether the injury was caused directly or indirectly, though the more indirect the connection between the defendant and the injury the more likely it was that causal responsibility would be placed elsewhere; in practice, too, because of the relative inappropriateness of the simple assertion that the defendant had caused the injury, there was a tendency for such actions to be formulated as trespass on the case rather than as general trespass *vi et armis.*[38]

There may have been some situations in which the courts were unwilling to impose liability even where physical injury had been prima facie wrongfully caused. In a case in 1329, for example, Denum J. expressed considerable reluctance to hold liable doctors or other 'men of occupation'—'men of mystery'—accused of professional incompetence.[39] It may be that there was a perceived difficulty in leaving the assessment of whether the defendant had in fact acted incompetently to a jury of laymen,[40] and as yet the trial process was not sufficiently sophisticated to allow for the receipt of

<hr/>

[36] See too Palmer, *Black Death*, for a sustained argument that the Chancery deliberately manipulated the range of circumstances in which writs would be granted and so would have exercised effective control over the scope of liability in the second half of the fourteenth century.   [37] Above, p.58.

[38] Palmer, *Black Death*, 388–91.

[39] *The Oculist's Case* (Eyre of Nottingham, 1329; B&M 340).

[40] The problem was sidestepped in local courts, where a jury of the appropriate professionals could be used. In London, for example, the sheriff might summon a jury of merchants, surgeons, sailors, or the like (A. H. Thomas, *Calendar of Early Mayor's Court Rolls* (Cambridge, 1924), pp.xlii–xliii); in a case in Chester, a jury of tailors was impanelled to say whether work had been properly done (*de Standun* v. *Assor* (1302); Hopkins (ed.), *Selected Rolls of the Chester City Courts*, 122). Alternatively, the parties might put themselves on the arbitration of appropriate professionals: *Forest* v. *Harwe* ((1424) London *CPMR* 4.174), where a panel of surgeons and barbers held that the patient's failure to respond to treatment was the patient's own fault or the result of the Moon's being in Aquarius rather than the consequence of the ineptitude of the doctor. Merchants were sometimes used in the royal courts on *ad hoc* commissions or where the custom of merchants was in question: e.g. Plac. Abb. 201 (1281); *Dederic* v. *Abbot of Ramsey* (1315) 46 SS 86.

any form of expert evidence as to the defendant's ability. Whatever the reason for the doubts, they were soon allayed, and from the second half of the fourteenth century such actions against professionals were a staple part of the action of trespass on the case. This may have been just one facet of a wide-ranging and strenuous movement to hold individuals to their obligations in the wake of the demographic crisis caused by the Black Death, though the evidence for such a general programme is susceptible to different interpretations.[41] Another example of unwillingness to allow actions notwithstanding the fact that loss had been caused by prima-facie wrongful conduct was the principle that some types of public officials should not be discouraged from the execution of their offices by the fear of legal liability: it was open to question whether gaolers and the like should enjoy immunity from actions for wrongful arrest or false imprisonment if they were acting in pursuance of what appeared to be a valid warrant; and nightwatchmen arresting suspicious strangers had a statutory immunity under chapter 4 of the Statute of Winchester, 1285, though the precise scope of this immunity was a matter of debate.[42] A fortiori, no civil action could be brought in respect of alleged wrongdoing in a trial: not against indictors acting under oath, against jurors for a false verdict, against a judge or justice of the peace who had presided over the trial, nor against defendants who had falsely waged their law by swearing a false oath.[43] Officials who acted wrongfully outside the immediate context of the trial, though, were not exempt from liability.[44]

The concept of physical injury was sufficiently elastic to allow for the imposition of liability for threats of physical injury where these had caused fear to the plaintiff.[45] It was but a small step from this to hold that liability should be imposed for lying in wait to claim someone as one's villein, for such a threat to a person's status was tantamount to a threat of imprisonment.[46] It was argued that allegations that a person was a villein, or a thief or a murderer, created a similar risk, but it was not until the end of the fifteenth century that the royal courts were willing to extend liability in this direction; until that time defamatory words were the standard example of *damnum absque iniuria*, loss without wrong.[47]

---

[41] Palmer, *Black Death*, esp. 186–96.
[42] Arnold, *Select Cases of Trespass* (100 SS), pp.xxxvi–xxxix.
[43] P. H. Winfield, *History of Conspiracy and Abuse of Legal Procedure* (Cambridge, 1921), 66–81; C. St. German, *Doctor and Student* (91 SS), 232. Nor would the ecclesiastical courts intervene in cases of the alleged swearing of false oaths in judicial proceedings, despite the obvious perjury involved. Some disappointed litigants sought their remedy in Chancery, though it is unclear how successfully: W. T. Barbour, *History of Contract in Early English Equity* (Oxford, 1914), 99, 197; *Alcok* v. *Adys* (C1/67/185).
[44] Arnold, *Select Cases of Trespass* (100 SS), pp.xxxiii, xxxvi–xxxvii.
[45] Ibid., pp.xxxii–xxxiii. [46] Baker, *Spelman's Reports*, ii (94 SS), *190* n.4.
[47] *Haukyns* v. *Broune*, YB T.17 Edw IV f.3 pl.2 (B&M 629). There were a few very exceptional situations in which liability was imposed for wrongs with a defamatory tinge, but the

The medieval law of tort was almost exclusively concerned with the compensation of those who had suffered physical injury to the person or property. In a few situations, though, plaintiffs who had suffered purely economic loss were able to recover damages. These crystallized into a small number of discrete agglomerations of cases, and were not formulated in terms of any general principle.[48]

The main body of cases related to interference with servants.[49] An employer had a clear right of action if his servants were forcibly abducted. This might originally have been thought of in terms of the mainstream of liability for physical injury, with the quirk that the action was brought at the suit of someone other than the injured party,[50] but it extended to cases of enticement where no independent wrong had been done to the servant. This liability for enticement was consolidated by the Ordinance and Statute of Labourers of 1349–51,[51] and it was by this time clearly based on the interference with the master's economic interests. Masters might have been thought to have some sort of near-property right over their servants, so that such an enticement was not significantly different from the obviously trespassory leading-away of a donkey by dangling a carrot in front of its nose. In the same way, lords could be seen to have a proprietary right over their tenants, so that they could recover damages for losses suffered as a result of the tenants being intimidated by the defendants.[52] The liability was extended yet further by the establishment of a rule that masters could recover damages not only when their servants were abducted or enticed away, but also when they were injured by the wrongful act of the defendants.[53]

A similar body of cases centred around the abduction of feudal wards. Wardships were valuable economic assets and openly bought and sold as such, and a trespassory action, the writ of ravishment of ward, lay whenever the ward was abducted to the loss of the guardian. As in the case of abduction of servants, the real focus of the action was on the loss suffered by the guardian rather than on the wrong done to the ward. Indeed, in a

only one that lay explicitly for injurious language was the slander of magnates (*scandalum magnatum*), based on chapter 34 of the Statute of Westminster I (1275): Helmholz, *Select Defamation Cases* (101 SS), p.lxviii. Below, p.114.

[48] For a modern parallel, talking of 'pockets of liability', see B. J. Stapleton, 'Duty of Care and Economic Loss' (1991) 107 LQR 249.

[49] G. H. Jones, 'Per Quod Servitium Amisit' (1958) 74 LQR 39.

[50] As happened in the case of the rape and abduction of women, where the appeal of rape (which had to be brought by the injured woman, and which aimed at punishment rather than compensation) was supplemented and then superseded by a trespassory action for damages for 'ravishment' brought by the husband, founded on chapter 34 of the Statute of Westminster II (1285): J. B. Post, 'Ravishment of Women and the Statutes of Westminster', in Baker (ed.), *Legal Records and the Historian*, 150.   [51] Above, p.31.

[52] *Terry* v. *Beverley* (1384; 100 SS 2, case 1.11); Kiralfy, *Action on the Case*, 105.

[53] Even where the servant was acting wholly voluntarily: YB M.21 Hen VI f.9 pl.19.

fair number of cases there is a strong suggestion that the ward was a willing participant rather than an innocent victim, and, although juries were more sympathetic to the defendants in such cases than in cases of forcible kidnapping, it is not difficult to find cases in which judgments were given against defendants who had simply helped wards to abscond[54]—though the fact that such wards were by definition minors perhaps meant that it was not altogether easy to distinguish between situations of abduction and enticement. The same analysis lay behind the granting of an action of trespass to a father whose daughter had been abducted and married off, with no mention of whether or not the daughter had consented; what was important was that it had been done against the will of the father, and that he had thereby lost the value of arranging her marriage.[55] As in the case of interference with servants and tenants, the action of the guardian or father had a proprietary underpinning: selling the marriage of a ward or daughter was tantamount to selling the child,[56] and the abduction or enticement away of the child was not simply an interference with the power to arrange a valuable marriage but more tangibly the deprivation of a valuable economic asset.

The only other context in which liability was regularly imposed for the wrongful interference with a purely economic interest was where the defendant hindered the plaintiff's franchise; again, this could easily be conceptualized as interference with a property right. A typical situation would be where the plaintiff had received a royal grant of the right to hold a market in a particular place. Now, if the defendant impeded customers on their way to the market or prevented the franchisee's representative from collecting tolls due from merchants selling their goods there, an action of trespass would lie.[57] These cases would invariably have involved independent wrongs to the persons primarily affected and may thus be seen as analogous to the actions based on the forcible abduction of wives and servants, but, as in these situations, the franchisee's right to sue did not depend on there having been such an independent wrong: an action would lie against a

---

[54] S. S. Walker, 'Common Law Juries and Feudal Marriage Customs in Medieval England: The Pleas of Ravishment' [1984] Illinois L R 705, 710–11, 717. As late as 1356, though, a special verdict that the ward had willingly eloped with the defendant left the King's Bench in doubt as to whether this justified giving judgment for the plaintiff, though the case was anomalous for other reasons and we should probably not read too much into it: *Galeys* v. *Mott* (1356; 100 SS 94, case 9.1); Arnold, *Select Cases of Trespass* (100 SS), p.xlv.
[55] *Tolymer* v. *Mounpynzoun*, YB 9 Edw II (45 SS) 28; *Lincoln* v. *Simond* (1391; 100 SS 96, case 9.2).
[56] S. S. Walker, 'Widow and Ward: The Feudal Law of Child Custody in Medieval England' (1976) 3 Feminist Studies 104, 106.
[57] YB 17 & 18 Edw III (RS) 213. Arnold, *Select Cases of Trespass* (100 SS), pp.xlviii–l; Milsom, 'Trespass from Henry III to Edward III' (1958) 74 LQR 407, 418–21.

person who set up a rival market in order to entice away merchants[58] or against a merchant who sold goods outside the market and hence avoided the tolls that would otherwise have been due,[59] and some might even have thought to frame an action of trespass against a person who refused to pay the toll that was properly due.[60]

Outside these situations the courts showed no inclination to impose a widespread liability for interference with economic interests. Occasional entries are found on the plea rolls where plaintiffs alleged that the defendants had committed a forcible wrong to another person, indirectly causing purely economic loss to the plaintiffs themselves,[61] but these cases peter out after the preliminary stages of process and we have no way of knowing for certain how the judges would have reacted if the proceedings had gone further. A more radical attempt to obtain compensation for interference with a purely economic interest arose in 1410, when the schoolmasters of the Grammar School at Gloucester sought to recover compensation when a rival school was set up in the town, causing them to have to reduce their fees. This was treated with short shrift: it was loss without wrong, *damnum sine iniuria*.[62] No doubt the same fate occurred to a Chancery suit around 1440, where the petitioners complained that the respondents had cut into their expected profits from exhibiting an ostrich to the paying public by abducting the bird and parading it around the streets with the result that anybody who wanted to see it could do so for nothing.[63] It was not until the efflorescence of actions in the sixteenth century that we begin to see any more general attempt to impose liability for the tortious interference with economic interests.

The action of trespass was strongly focused on the liability of those who had wrongly caused harm to another. A corollary of this was that liability was very rarely imposed for simple omissions. The medieval Common law rarely imposed positive duties to act independent of contract, and throughout the fourteenth and fifteenth centuries the courts set their faces firmly and consistently against the use of the action of trespass to recover

---

[58] *Huse* v. *Cogan*, YB 5 Edw II (31 SS) 100; Arnold, *Select Cases of Trespass* (100 SS), p.xlviii n.293. The action was framed as a nuisance rather than as a straightforward trespass writ, presumably because the plaintiff wanted to get an injunction as well as damages.

[59] *Prior of Coventry* v. *Grauntpie*, YB 2 & 3 Edw II (19 SS) 71.

[60] Milsom, 'Trespass from Henry III to Edward III' (1958) 74 LQR 407, 421.

[61] e.g. *Aylmer* v. *de Humberstone* (1366, CP 40/425 m.297; *ELABD* 165 n.49) (trampling sand); *de Grantham* v. *de Chesham* (1367, CP 40/427 m.335d; (100 SS), p.xxxii n.151) (attacking oath-helpers, frightening them away).

[62] *Hamlyn* v. *More*, YB H.11 Hen IV f.47 pl.2 (B&M 126). Cf. *Kellet* v. *Harpham* (C1/67/169), where the petitioner complained about the respondent's behaviour in attempting to prevent him from setting up in competition.

[63] *Charles and Lynde* v. *Prior of Royston* (C1/11/227–30). The petitioners did not own the bird (it was the property of the king), and so they could presumably not maintain a simple action of trespass to goods.

damages for contractual non-performance.[64] The only important exception to this was that positive duties to repair walls or roads, or to keep ditches scoured, were commonly imposed; here the plaintiff had to be careful to show how the defendant's duty had arisen, either by virtue of the tenure of land or by prescription. From their inception these writs stood aloof from the main stem of liability in trespass; they were securely tied to the plaintiffs' property rights and the defendants' obligations arising out of their tenure of property.[65] Like the action of nuisance, they were conceptually as much a part of the nascent law of property as of the nascent law of torts.[66]

Normally liability for a wrong lay with the person who had committed it, but in some situations the liability was transferred onto a person other than the immediate wrongdoer. Thus an innkeeper was liable to his or her guests if their goods were stolen, whether or not the innkeeper was personally implicated in the theft,[67] and the occupant of land was liable for the escape of fire that had been started by a servant or guest.[68] Whether there was a more general vicarious liability, imposing liability on masters for the wrongs of their servants, is largely a matter of semantics. A statute of 1354 assumed a fairly wide liability, providing that merchants and others should not forfeit their goods because of the wrongs of their servants, unless the servants had acted by the command or procurement of the master or were in the course of performing some task entrusted to them by the master.[69] A similar general principle was articulated in London in a case of 1376, where it was said that the master should be liable even if the servant had acted against his will[70]—though a defendant in Colchester in 1360 presumably thought that he was not admitting liability when he claimed that his failure to weave cloth within an agreed time was not his fault but that of his servants.[71] Evidence from the royal courts seems to point to a more restrictive approach, that the specific acts of the servants must have been commanded or at least assented to by the master.[72]

---

[64] Below, p.127.   [65] Palmer, *Black Death*, 284–8.   [66] Below, pp.98–106.

[67] The innkeeper was liable even if the theft was the work of malefactors wholly unconnected with the inn: *Navenby* v. *Lassels*, 42 Lib Ass f.260 pl.17 (B&M 552); *Neulond* v. *Ruddock* (1378; *ELABD* 380, case A19x). On innkeepers' liability generally, see Kiralfy, *Action on the Case*, 150–3; Palmer, *Black Death*, 253–60.

[68] BL MS Add 5925 f.86, cited by Palmer, *Black Death*, 157 n.14 (where it was held that only the occupant was liable); *Beaulieu* v. *Finglam*, YB P.2 Hen IV f.18 pl.6 (B&M 557). For the development of liability for fire, see Palmer, *Black Death*, 275–8.

[69] Stat 27 Edw III stat 2 cap.19.

[70] *Multon's Case* (1376; *CPMR* 2.227) (= Corporation of London Record Office, Roll A21 m.12d: 'licet hoc ex sua voluntate non fuit factum'). The case was complicated by the fact that the wrongdoer was a child who was not personally amenable to legal process.

[71] *Wylemot* v. *Webbe* (1360; Essex CRO, CR12 m.8 (Jeayes (ed.), *Court Rolls of the Borough of Colchester*, 2.97)).

[72] Pollock and Maitland, *History of English Law*, 2.533–4; J. H. Wigmore, 'Responsibility for Tortious Acts' (1894) 7 Harv L R 383, 384–92; Palmer, *Black Death*, 157–8. Cf. *Lampen* v. *atte Ford* (1320; 103 SS 416, case 39.2); YB M.9 Hen VI f.53 pl.37.

'Command', though, was susceptible of a sufficiently wide definition to enable the courts to impose liability on masters for servants' incompetent performance of their jobs: a master who undertook to shoe a horse and then entrusted the task to a servant, it was said in 1471, would be liable if the servant did it carelessly.[73] Behind this lies a theory of representation: the masters were liable because they were acting through their servants, not because of the operation of some legal rule that imposed liability on masters for their servants' wrongs; and the servants were not themselves liable to compensate the injured party at all.[74]

[73] YB T.11 Edw IV f.6 pl.10, per Choke J. Cf. E. Clark, 'Medieval Labor Law and English Local Courts' (1983) 27 Am Jnl Leg Hist 330, 346 n.70.

[74] BL MS Add 31826 f.70, cited by Palmer, *Black Death*, 157 n.13. Cf. too BL MS Add 5925 f.86 (above, n.68), where the occupant of land rather than his guests was liable for the escape of fire caused by the guests.

5. The Substantive Law of Contract

The underlying structure of contractual liability was laid down by the end of the thirteenth century and remained fundamentally the same through the fourteenth and fifteenth centuries, though the fragmentation of remedies in the wake of the formalization of the action of covenant means that the picture has to be pieced together from the different forms of action. Liability depended on a voluntary agreement; whatever form of action was in issue, only the parties to the agreement were affected by it; whatever the form of action, the purpose of the plaintiff's claim was to obtain the value of the intended performance; and, in informal contracts, the law was concerned only with relationships of reciprocity. Each of these principles was more or less clearly visible by 1300; each of them was honed into a more sophisticated shape in the ensuing two centuries. The basic framework, though we know of no contemporary lawyer who articulated it so simply, was the model of exchange.

VOLUNTARINESS, AGREEMENT, AND THE FORMATION OF CONTRACTS

Underpinning the whole idea of contract was that the parties must have acted voluntarily; it was axiomatic that contractual liability stemmed from the parties' *voluntas*.[1] It was normally only where the transaction was embodied in a sealed document that any question about this would be raised to the surface, for in actions based on oral transactions any dispute about voluntariness would commonly be concealed behind the general denial of liability away from the gaze of the legal historian.[2]

Neither an infant nor a lunatic could act voluntarily, so neither was in principle capable of taking on contractual liability; nor could a person whose will had been overborne by imprisonment.[3] In the latter situation it was the overbearing of the will rather than the fact of imprisonment that

---

[1] This is made abundantly clear by a lecturer at the start of the fourteenth century: 'Contractus vero ex mutuis verbis mera voluntate partis utriusque probatis' (CUL MS Dd 7.6(2) f.12). Cf. f.11ᵛ: '[I]nstrumento sigillum est apponendum in signum federis operis voluntate spontanea completi.'

[2] There are occasional Chancery petitions complaining of actions brought on fraudulent contracts and the like that were formulated in such a way that wager of law was not possible and where defendants were fearful of a corrupt jury: e.g. *White* v. *Martyn* (C1/67/49).

[3] *Casus Placitorum* (69 SS) 33 no.31: 'In how many cases can a man defeat his own deed? In three, [if he is] within age or imprisoned or insane.' For a more wide-ranging treatment of defences to actions of debt on a sealed bond, see Britton, 1.162–71.

mattered, so that a defendant who pleaded that he had been in prison at the time of making the deed could be met with a counter-plea that the deed had been made of his own free will notwithstanding the imprisonment.[4] Neither fraud nor mistake was a defence, except for the anomalous situation where the defendant had sealed the document after it had been misread to him (not necessarily by the beneficiary of the obligation) with the result that he was under a misapprehension as to its contents; here, probably in the fourteenth century, the defence of *non est factum* came to apply.[5]

In the fourteenth and fifteenth centuries attempts were made to take the defence of duress to its logical conclusion by widening it beyond its original restricted scope. There was no difficulty in including threats of serious personal violence, hardly more doubt in extending it to threats of imprisonment as well as actual imprisonment,[6] and there were moves to include within its compass any threats whatsoever that overbore the will of the party.[7] In 1467, for example, it was argued by Serjeants Jenney and Yonge that the defence should be available to a defendant who had sealed an obligation only because the plaintiffs had wrongfully taken his animals and would not release them until he had done so.[8] Danby C.J., Moyle J., and Littleton J. agreed, for a threat to take a man's goods or to burn down his house might sap his will just as much as a threat to his person;[9] Choke J. was less sanguine, recognizing that to extend the defence of duress so far would lead to 'the avoidance of most obligations in England'. In the same way, the defence was held in check by the assumption that threats to harm third parties were not sufficient reason to allow the defendant to avoid his bond.[10]

The Chancery might have been able to mitigate the rigours of the Common law, though there is little to suggest that it did so systematically. Surviving petitions from the fourteenth and fifteenth centuries where it was asked to cause the cancellation of bonds procured by duress suggest that the boundaries of duress were the same here as elsewhere, imprisonment and threats of serious personal injury, though the precise circumstances might not always have provided a defence at Common law. In *Ocle* v.

---

[4] *Pembridge* v. *Mortimer* (1274) 55 SS 4; *Fisher* v. *Newgate*, YB 2 Edw II (17 SS) 155. Cf. YB H.5 Edw III f.7 pl.23 (there is a longer and better version in LI MS Hale 137(2) f.356).

[5] *Prior of Dunstable* v. *Smyth*, YB 1 Hen VI (50 SS) 23 pl.7; YB H.3 Hen VI f.37 pl.35; YB T.3 Hen VI f.52 pl.19; YB H.15 Edw IV f.18 pl.7. Cf. YB T.44 Edw III f.22 pl.28 (illiterate bound by release sealed by him, trusting third party's assurance that would not prejudice him). Petitioners in Chancery similarly sought the cancellation of obligations that had been misread to them: e.g. *Moriana* v. *Syne* (C1/148/67); *Duplage* v. *Capell* (C1/198/23).

[6] YB H.39 Hen VI f.50 pl.16 at f.51, per Moyle and Aysshton JJ.

[7] Simpson, *History of Contract*, 99.   [8] YB M.7 Edw IV f.21 pl.24.

[9] Though Moyle J. was willing to assume the opposite less than a decade earlier: YB H.39 Hen VI f.50 pl.16.   [10] YB H.39 Hen VI f.50 pl.16; YB M.21 Edw IV f.12 pl.4.

Clypesby, for example, the petitioner alleged that he had been imprisoned by the respondent, who was claiming him as his villein, until he had sworn an oath on the gospels that he would arrange for third parties to enter an obligation on his behalf. After his release, believing himself to be bound in conscience by his oath, he procured the obligation; now he sought the help of the Chancellor in obtaining its cancellation.[11] There is some evidence in the petitions that Chancery was invited to take on a wider jurisdiction to relieve generally against mistakes, though we cannot be sure whether the suggestion was acceded to.[12] The only area in which we may be confident that the Chancery would give relief that was denied at Common law was where it was alleged that the deed had been procured by fraud;[13] such petitions are so common that it is hard to suppose that they did not form a regular part of Chancery jurisdiction.

Formal contracts, in essence, took effect unilaterally. The debtor must have acted voluntarily; the debtor must have sealed the document; and the debtor must have delivered the document to the creditor.[14] Informal contracts, by contrast, were bilateral: the law required not simply a voluntary act but an agreement between the parties.[15] 'Covenant' meant 'agreement', a 'coming-together'; it was based on 'the assent of the parties'.[16] 'Contract' has a similar etymological base—a 'bringing-together'—and it too always connoted an agreement rather than a unilateral promise; it could be said to be derived from 'the will of each party as proved by their mutual words'.[17] If we look to what the parties did rather than what the law said, we find the same bilaterality: they shook hands—together; they shared a drink—together; or one gave and one received a coin as a token to bind the

---

[11] C1/5/118. For other examples see *de York* v. *Crop*, 10 SS 127; *Pickering* v. *Tonge*, 1 Cal Ch xliv (imprisonment); *Spark* v. *Rotheley* (C1/4/6). W. T. Barbour, *The History of Contract in Early English Equity* (Oxford, 1914), 84 n.1.

[12] e.g. *Tate* v. *Cheyne* (C1/32/246–51) (sum due expressed in pounds rather than marks); *de Opiciis* v. *Blount* (C1/104/30) (miscalculation of amount due). A second petition in *Duplage* v. *Capell* (above, n.5) alleges that the bond was made 'in sport': C1/198/22.

[13] Barbour, *Contract in Early English Equity*, 84 n.2. Examples are extremely numerous.

[14] The defendant might deny that the document had been delivered at all, or claim that it had been delivered in escrow: *Glaston* v. *Abbot of Crowland* (Eyre of Northamptonshire, 1329; 98 SS 665), per Aldborough, Scrope J. *dubitante*; *Haveryngge* v. *Laurence*, YB M.12 Ric II (AF) 60 pl.12; YB M.4 Hen IV f.3 pl.11; YB H.8 Hen VI f.26 pl.15; YB M.9 Hen VI f.37 pl.12; YB M.10 Hen VI f.25 pl.15.

[15] Cf. the similar stress on *consensus* in Roman law: above, p.7. The English lawyers' formulation of the nature of liability may have been in part influenced by this, though there was a strong earlier medieval tradition of the sanctity of '*convenientiae*': F. Calasso, *Il negozio giuridico* (Milan, 1959), esp. pp.113–68; P. Ourliac, 'La Convenientia', in *Études d'histoire du droit privé offertes à Pierre Pétot* (Paris, 1959), 413–22.

[16] *Waltham Carrier Case* (1321) 86 SS 286 (above, p.25).

[17] CUL MS Dd 7.6(2) f.12 (above, n.1); in this it differed from a gift, which stemmed from the will of the giver alone. Cf. YB P.17 Edw IV f.1 pl.2, per Choke J.

agreement.[18] There is, it is true, some tension in the language used, and occasionally we find the more unilateral 'promise'; but even in these cases the promise is usually characterized as one side of an agreement and not as something standing alone.[19]

The agreement between the parties may have been a necessary condition of the creation of an informal contract, but it may not have been sufficient. On the basis of the discussions in Glanvill and Bracton, it has been suggested that medieval English law had a 'real' theory, according to which there was no contract until one party's side of the agreement had actually been performed.[20] This is, at best, misleading. To begin with, the theory is based exclusively on texts relating to the sale of goods, where it is said that in the absence of earnest money the contract is perfected only by the delivery of the goods or the payment of the price in whole or in part.[21] Sale of goods, though, might have been anomalous; in the thirteenth century it was still hovering uncertainly on the borderline of a property transaction and a contract,[22] and it is not safe to draw general conclusions from it. In addition, the so-called real nature of sale has to be severely qualified by the legal effects of the practice of giving earnest money. This was clearly established by the end of the twelfth century, though Glanvill is hesitant about its precise effects. Bracton is more confident, allowing the buyer to withdraw from the sale on forfeiture of the earnest and the seller to withdraw on repayment of double its value, but this is no more than the Roman law rule of Justinian's *Institutes* transplanted into thirteenth-century England and there is no evidence that it ever applied in practice. Any lack of clarity was resolved by the early years of the fourteenth century, apparently borrowing from the practice of merchants: when earnest, or 'God's penny', was given, the sale was binding on both parties, so

---

[18] Handshake: e.g. M. Bateson, *Borough Customs, ii* (21 SS) 172 (Berwick Guild Statutes, 13th century), 182 (Grimsby Charter, 1259). Sharing a drink: F. W. Maitland, *Select Pleas in Manorial Courts* (2 SS), 139 (Fair Court of St Ives, 1275); *William of Ayshperton* v. *Baldewyn le Tanour* (1288; Exeter Mayor's Court (Devon CRO) CR3 m.34d); Barbour, *Contract in Early English Equity*, 206–7 (fifteenth century, after 1450); YB H.16 Edw IV f.11 pl.11. Giving and receiving a coin: Glanvill X.14 (ed. Hall, 129). See generally Ibbetson, 'Sale of Goods in the Fifteenth Century' (1991) 107 LQR 480, 485–6, and the references there cited. For these formalities in the early medieval period, see above, p.5.

[19] In the royal courts, for example: 15 CRR 481; *de Tostes* v. *de Todeham* (1282; CP 40/44 m.12); *de Ulnesby* v. *de Lancaster* (1283; CP 40/49 m.42d); *de Ingolisma* v. *Abbot of Robert-bridge* (1284; CP 40/53 m.67); *de Essex* v. *Criketot* (1292; CP 40/93 m.114d); *Burewelle* v. *le Waleys* (1292; CP 40/96 m.201d). The language of promising is commoner in local courts, no doubt because the less formulaic character of their pleadings allowed for a greater variation. Promises played a larger part in the language of the ecclesiastical courts: see below, p.136.

[20] e.g. Fifoot, *History and Sources of the Common Law*, 225–8; criticized by Simpson, *History of Contract*, 193–6. The terminology is derived from Roman law: above, p.7.

[21] Glanvill X.14 (ed. Hall, 129), above, p.19; Bracton, f.61b (ed. Thorne, 2.182).

[22] Above, p.36.

that the seller was bound to deliver the goods and the buyer was bound to pay the price.[23]

Other types of contracts cannot be fitted into the 'real' model flimsily anchored in the texts of Glanvill and Bracton. In employment or service relationships, for example, the employee could bring an action of debt for wages without actually having performed the service that was due; all that was necessary was to have been ready and willing to perform it.[24] The same applied in the converse case: an action on the Statute of Labourers would lie against an employee who failed to arrive for work, not merely against one who had begun to work but then left within the contract period.[25] Similarly, and unsurprisingly, a lessee of land for a term of years would be liable to pay the rent for the agreed term whether or not he had in fact chosen actually to occupy the land.

It follows from this that legal consequences might arise before there had been performance on either side. A binding contract might have been created from which neither party could unilaterally withdraw: neither could with impunity reject the other party's tender of performance.[26] English law did not have a 'real' theory of contract.

What we do not know is whether anything more than the simple agreement of the parties was necessary to create a binding contract. If there was any doubt whether the parties had passed beyond the stage of negotiation, it would invariably have been concealed behind a simple plea of the general issue and either the defendant's wager of law or an uninformative jury verdict. As a result it is impossible to formulate any precise rules; all we can do is make some tentative observations. It is clear that the making of many types of contract—not just the sale of goods—was commonly accompanied by the payment of earnest or God's penny, and we learn tangentially of the use of other formalities such as the handshake and the sharing of a drink.[27] The status of these customary formalities remained ambiguous well into the sixteenth century. Probably they were at first regarded as substantive requirements for the creation of a binding

---

[23] Ibbetson, 'Sale of Goods in the Fourteenth Century' (1991) 107 LQR 480, 488–93. The rule is most easily visible in *Novae Narrationes* (80 SS) 289, C261A, and a manuscript of *The Court Baron*, Bodl MS Rawl C 459 f.214ᵛ. The establishment of this meant that the contract was 'real' in a completely different sense: once the agreement accompanied by earnest money had been made, the buyer immediately became owner of the goods.
[24] YB M.21 Hen VI f.6 pl.16, at f.7 per Newton C.J.; YB T.18 Edw IV f.8 pl.12, per Littleton J. The same rule applied in the writ of annuity: YB H.21 Edw III f.7 pl.20; YB H.41 Edw III f.6 pl.14; YB M.41 Edw III f.19 pl.3; YB H.8 Hen VI f.23 pl.9.
[25] YB M.41 Edw III f.20 pl.4; YB H.46 Edw III f.4 pl.10; YB M.47 Edw III f.14 pl.15. Cf. too Putnam, *The Enforcement of the Statute of Labourers 1349–1359*, 192* (presentment of Emma le Wright); E. Clark, 'Medieval Labor Law and English Local Courts' (1983) 27 Am Jnl Leg Hist 330, 344 n.60.   [26] Simpson, *History of Contract*, 193–6.
[27] Above, n.18.

contract,[28] though by the end of the fourteenth century there is more than a hint that an agreement to sell goods on credit would be effective without further formality so long as the parties had agreed on the date at which payment was to be made.[29] In fifteenth-century Scarborough it was said to be a customary rule that wager of law was not open to the defendant where God's penny had been given, and it must follow from this that it was not a necessary form.[30] Of course, even when these customary practices had no substantive function in the making of contracts, so long as they remained general customs they would inevitably have been taken into account in determining whether or not the parties had passed beyond the stage of negotiation. If no coin had been handed over, no hands shaken, or no drink shared, and if the parties had not gone on to act as if a contract had been made (for example, by delivering goods or beginning to work), it would have been very difficult for the jury to hold that a contract had in fact been entered into, and a party against whom an action of debt or detinue was brought could safely have waged his law.[31]

It seems, therefore, that the medieval Common law regarded the contract as made once the parties had reached an agreement; though in practice there might have been some resistance to holding that an agreement had in fact been reached in the absence of God's penny or the like. It is important to recognize that this meant only that neither party was free subsequently to withdraw unilaterally from the arrangement; it might—and usually would—still be necessary to perform or to tender performance of one's own duty in order to activate the liability of the other party.[32]

THE BOUNDARIES OF CONTRACT

Privity

The effect of the contract was to create a relationship between the parties to it, and a corollary of this was that in principle actions had to be brought by and against them all. The disappointed plaintiff could not choose to sue only one of several joint debtors or covenantors,[33] unless they had

---

[28] The God's penny clearly has a crucial function in the formation of a binding contract of sale in the text from *Novae Narrationes* cited above, n.23.

[29] *Staughton* v. *Love* (1397; 100 SS 177, case 13.50). See too YB H.14 Hen VIII f.18 pl.7 at f.19 per Caryll Sjt., at ff.19–20 per Fitzherbert J., at f.20 per Broke J., at f.21 per Pollard J., at f.22 per Brudenell C.J.; BL MS Harg 388 f.30ᵛ.   [30] *Cokke* v. *Helperby* (C1/67/151).

[31] Cf. YB P.17 Edw IV f.1 pl.2, per Choke J.: a contract was constituted by the agreement of the parties, but an agreement would not be inferred if the buyer of goods had not paid any money to the seller.   [32] Below, text at n.110.

[33] 16 CRR 148G: 'Nullus sine altero potest respondere, eo quod debent dictum debitum in commune.' *Prior of Conishead* v. *de Ros* (Eyre of Westmoreland, 1279; JUST 1/983 m.16); *de Bedford* v. *Terr* (1282; CP 40/47 m.81d).

expressly bound themselves jointly and severally.[34] It was perhaps less clear whether an action might be brought at the suit of only one of a number of joint covenantors,[35] and if the plaintiff was successful in such a case it was open to question whether damages could be recovered in respect of the losses of those covenantors who were not parties to the action.[36]

More important was the inverse situation, that persons not party to the agreement could not sue or be sued on it. In the middle of the thirteenth century Bracton states this as a general principle,[37] the slightly later *Natura Brevium* includes it without further comment as an unquestioned feature of the action of covenant,[38] and (most obviously in the case of formal contracts) it was repeatedly stated as axiomatic that only the parties to the document could sue or be sued on it.[39]

Unlike in Roman law,[40] there was no difficulty in allowing third parties to be affected indirectly. This was most easily achieved by the conditional bond, setting out that the debtor should pay a fixed sum of money to the creditor unless he had conferred some benefit on the third party by a certain date. If the debtor failed to satisfy the condition, then the creditor could sue for the full amount of the penalty;[41] since the action aimed at the recovery of the debt to which the creditor was entitled, it was no argument that he had not personally suffered any loss by the creditor's default and that consequently no damages were recoverable.[42] But deeds were relevant only between those who were 'party and privy' to them, so it was important

---

[34] e.g. *Vincent* v. *de la Croyz* (1282; CP 40/45 m.36d); *le Monnor* v. *le Skynnere* (1291; CP 40/90 m.30); *Pessindenne* v. *Potter* (Eyre of Kent, 1313–14; 27 SS 12).

[35] The point was expressly raised by way of defence in *Croppehull* v. *Hermonere* (Eyre of Derbyshire, 1281; JUST 1/148 m.15d), and apparently decided in the defendant's favour. By contrast, the action was allowed, despite objection by the defendant, in YB 32 & 33 Edw I (RS) 454, 529, and in *Galvein de Bec* v. *Abbot of Stanleghe* (1300) CP 40/133 m.155, BL MS Add 37657 f.16. I am grateful to Dr Paul Brand for the latter reference.

[36] YB 32 & 33 Edw I (RS) 454, 529. For the general rule that damages could not be recovered in respect of the loss of a third party, see YB 33–5 Edw I (RS) 140; *Dean of Hereford* v. *La Maudeleyne and Deweswelle*, YB 10 Edw II (54 SS) 4. This was an offshoot of the principle that the action of covenant would not lie if no loss had been suffered: 'ex conventione vero fracta que dampnum non infligit non oritur actio' (CUL MS Dd 7.6(2) f.12).

[37] Bracton, f.18b (ed. Thorne, 2.69): 'an agreement made between certain persons does not bind others, only those between whom it was made.' (The apparent qualification in the passage immediately following (2.69–70) is the result of a mistranslation.) The same principle is found at f.47b (ed. Thorne, 2.145) and f.220 (ed. Thorne, 3.161). Note also f.100 (ed. Thorne, 2.285), but on this occasion the statement of principle is no more than a paraphrase of Justinian's *Institutes*, 3.19.3.

[38] *Natura Brevium* (1566 edn.), f.102ᵛ: 'A writ of covenant does not lie except between those who are parties to the covenant or their heirs or their assigns.' Although parts of the *Natura Brevium* probably date from the fourteenth century, this point is found in copies made before the end of the thirteenth, e.g. Bodl MS Bodl 559 f.83ᵛ.

[39] e.g. YB M.39 Edw III f.22; YB M.3 Hen VI f.18 pl.27; YB H.3 Hen VI f.26 pl.8.

[40] Above, p.8.

[41] YB M.3 Hen VI f.18 pl.27; YB H.3 Hen VI f.26 pl.8; YB P.33 Hen VI f.16 pl.7.

[42] Cf. the position in the action of covenant; above, n.36.

that the condition actually appeared in the deed between creditor and debtor; if it was in a collateral document between the debtor or creditor and the third party, it could not be used by way of defence in an action between creditor and debtor.[43] Nor was there any problem in the reverse situation, where the debt arose in the event of a third party not having conferred some benefit on the creditor by a certain date. So long as a deed was used, the law put no obstacle in the way of a guarantee of another person's debt.[44]

In actions based on informal agreements the stress on the need for privity between the parties was, if anything, more marked than in actions based on formal agreements. Here the rule that only the parties to the agreement could be directly affected by it[45] was complemented by the conception of the contract as a reciprocal relationship, as an exchange. As a result of this, not only was it impossible for third parties to be directly affected by contracts, but it was problematic whether they could even be affected indirectly.[46]

Both formal and informal contracts, then, had at their core a firm requirement of privity. It was soon extended slightly beyond the immediate parties to the contract.[47] For the most part this involved no more than the application of basic Common-law principles such as the liability of executors on a written contract of their testator or the liability of a husband on a contract made by his wife before their marriage. It extended to heirs and assigns so long as they were expressly mentioned in the contract, though even this might have been controversial at the beginning of the fourteenth century when an anonymous lecturer warned his audience that wise men did not much care for such a clause: it was 'inane' to attempt to oblige one's heir, for the obligation was wholly personal and he could not be affected by a *res inter alios acta*.[48] In addition it was held that an action of debt could be brought by a lessor of land against a sublessee despite the fact that there was no direct contractual nexus between them.[49] This extension was clearly regarded as anomalous and a reflection of the well-established rules of warranties included in grants of land; by the sixteenth century it was being treated as a rule specific to real property, and

---

[43] YB M.3 Hen VI f.18 pl.27; YB H.3 Hen VI f.26 pl.8.

[44] YB 18 Edw III (RS) 23; YB T.44 Edw III f.21 pl.23; *Ferriers v. Bottisham*, YB H.6 Ric II (AF) 161; YB P.11 Hen VI f.35 pl.30.

[45] YB H.41 Edw III f.10 pl.5; YB H.6 Hen IV f.7 pl.33; YB M.10 Hen VI f.11 pl.38; YB M.21 Hen VI f.1 pl.1.   [46] Below, p.81.

[47] Cf. YB M.21 Hen VI f.1 pl.1, per Yelverton: 'None shall take advantage of a condition except those who are parties or privy.'

[48] CUL MS Dd 7.6(2) f.13. See W. McGovern, 'Medieval Contract Law: Wager of Law and the Effect of Death' (1968) 54 Iowa L R 19, 41–2.

[49] YB M.39 Edw III f.22; YB M.10 Hen VI f.11 pl.38. The same rule applied in covenant: YB H.42 Edw III f.3 pl.14.

formulated in the language of 'privity of estate' rather than 'privity of contract'.[50]

The rule caused problems where a contract was intended to confer a benefit on a third party, and various mechanisms were developed that in practice mitigated it. The most obvious route to sidestep it was to name the beneficiary as a joint party; individuals named as parties to the agreement, even if they had taken no active part in its confection, would be entitled to sue as joint creditors.[51] In an early case, for example, the Countess of Lincoln brought an action for loss caused to her by breach of an agreement made between the Prior of Spalding and the Abbot of St Nicholas in 1232, which had been afforced on one side by the Earl of Chester and Lincoln, whose heiress the plaintiff was.[52] This gave some power to confer benefits on third parties; and, if the agreement provided that the creditors should be paid jointly or severally, any one of them could bring the action without joining the others.[53]

Secondly, there was a well-developed law of agency that allowed servants to make contracts for their masters, monks to make contracts for their houses, mayors to make contracts for their towns, and the like.[54] There was no conflict between the fact of agency and the rules of privity of contract, for the agent was nothing more than the mouthpiece of the principal and in the eyes of the law the contract was made with the principal personally. Allowing that one person could effectively act on behalf of another in no way entailed that he or she could equally effectively act for the benefit of another. As soon as the boundary of agency had been reached, plaintiffs immediately shifted from the framework of 'contract' to the framework of 'property', where the rules of privity had no part to play. Thus where *A* handed over goods to *B* to be delivered to *C*, *C* could maintain a writ of detinue against *B*.[55] Similarly, where *A* delivered money to *B* to hand over to *C*, it was held that *C* should have a remedy against *B*; the remedy was not the writ of debt, but the writ of account, and the liability was quite explicitly explained in proprietary language rather than contractual.[56] The activation of property concepts, though, meant that the beneficiary had to be able to point to some thing—goods or money—that the intermediary

---

[50] A. W. B. Simpson, *A History of the Land Law* (2nd edn., Oxford, 1986), 116–18.

[51] YB M.3 Hen VI f.26 pl.8, per Babington.

[52] W. Dugdale, *Monasticon*, 3.220; 17 CRR 767. YB 33–5 Edw I (RS) 140 seems to be another example of the same type of agreement.

[53] *Galvein de Bec* v. *Abbot of Stanleghe* (1300) CP 40/133 m.155, BL MS Add 37657 f.16. It was apparently standard form to draft mercantile bonds in this way in the late thirteenth century, but an early fourteenth-century commentator noted that it was no longer the fashion to do so: CUL MS Dd 7.6(2) ff.12ᵛ–13. [54] Simpson, *History of Contract*, 552–5.

[55] YB 12 & 13 Edw III (RS) 245.

[56] YB P.41 Edw III f.10 pl.5; YB H.6 Hen IV f.7 pl.33. See S. J. Stoljar, *Year Books 14 Edward II* (104 SS), pp.xi–xiv, and 'The Transformations of Account' (1964) 80 LQR 203, 209–11.

had received; it was not enough to show simply that there was a right to receive a thing. This route did not permit the wholesale evasion of the rules of privity of contract.

A third possibility was for a contract to be made to the use of a third party. At law, the rule held that the third party could not sue,[57] but in the later Middle Ages the Chancery intervened to protect the beneficiary. Where *A* made a bond with *B* to the use of *C*, an action would be granted to *C* to force *B* to bring an action at Common law,[58] and some examples are found of petitions in Chancery brought at the suit of disappointed beneficiaries.[59] Alternatively, if *C* obtained the bond, he could bring an action on it in *B*'s name.[60] None the less, these mechanisms do not seem to have been widely used as a means to achieve an evasion of the rules of privity. The fact that they were needed at all goes a long way to show the firmness of the underlying rule.[61]

Reciprocity

Glanvill's treatment of contract had drawn the sharp distinction between actions based on informal transactions and actions based on formal documents. So far as the latter were concerned, the courts were not concerned to look behind the document. In the former, though, the nature of the transaction was crucial, and the scope of legal liability was determined by the range of transactions—*causae*—of which the law would take cognizance.[62] In the course of the fourteenth and fifteenth centuries this was articulated in terms of an idea of reciprocity, *quid pro quo*, and the opposition between formal and informal contracts was aligned directly with the opposition between gratuitous and reciprocal agreements.

The division between gratuitous and reciprocal agreements would not have seemed out of place in the twelfth or thirteenth century, though it would not have been expressed in these terms and would have been only an approximate reflection of contemporary practice.[63] Undoubtedly actions

---

[57] For an early example, see *Penketh* v. *Whitefeld* (Eyre of Lancashire, 1292; JUST 1/408 m.26), where an agreement between the parents of prospective marriage partners had provided that land should be conveyed 'to the use of' the couple, but the action for default was brought between the parents. Local courts seemingly took the same line: *de London* v. *Roper* (1359; Jeayes (ed.), *Court Rolls of the Borough of Colchester*, 2.78).

[58] YB P.2 Edw IV f.2 pl.6, per Moile and Danvers JJ.; YB P.7 Hen VII f.10 pl.2 at f.12, per Morton C.

[59] e.g. *Lawe* v. *Haldenby* (C1/60/103) (petition against obligee of bond who had obtained payment of it); *Morgon* v. *Grise* (C1/60/110) (petition against obligor and obligee who had since intermarried); *Wyndowt* v. *Milton* (C1/111/99) (respondent denies that he ever made contract with petitioner or to his use).

[60] YB M.34 Hen VI f.30 pl.15, per Prisot C.J.   [61] See below, pp.140–1, 241–4.

[62] Above, p.18.

[63] The point is well made by Maitland (Pollock and Maitland, *History of English Law*, 2.214): 'Still we think that all along there is a strong feeling that, whatever promises the law

could be brought on agreements under seal that were gratuitous, and most of the transactions that lay behind actions on informal contracts were reciprocal. Not all could be so described, however. Actions could be brought on promises to indemnify against loss that might be suffered or where benefit had been conferred on a third party,[64] on agreements to pay compensation for wrongs committed by the defendant on the plaintiff,[65] where there had been a reckoning between debtor and creditor to fix the amount due on a series of contracts,[66] or on informal agreements where money or other property was promised as a marriage gift by the parents of the prospective bride or groom.[67] Although not strictly reciprocal, none of these situations could properly be described as gratuitous; even the promises of marriage money were not simply acts of generosity motivated by unconstrained goodwill, but often carefully negotiated transfers designed to ensure the economic viability of the new family and the financial security of both partners.[68]

In the course of the fourteenth and fifteenth centuries the requirement of reciprocity or *quid pro quo* in cases of informal contracts became more rigid.[69] This can be seen most obviously in the repeated statements that the simple grant of a debt required a deed under seal.[70] It came to be held that agreements to pay damages did not generate debts,[71] and that a reckoning of debts due would not be actionable in itself (as opposed to each debt-creating contract being actionable individually).[72] An action of debt would not lie against a guarantor, or in any other situation where benefit was conferred on a third party rather than on the defendant personally,[73] unless

may enforce, purely gratuitous promises are not and ought not to be enforceable.' The distinction between contracts and unilateral gifts was made explicitly in the first decade of the fourteenth century: above, p.73.

[64] 15 CRR 481; *de Melebury* v. *de Maundevill* (1293; CP 40/100 m.48).

[65] *de Whaddon* v. *de Heningsham* (1291; CP 40/90 m.26d); *de Ingolisma* v. *Abbot of Robertbridge* (1284; CP 40/53 m.67) (compromising action).

[66] *de la Ford* v. *Collyng* (1284; CP 40/54 m.52d) (accounting for profits made in joint venture); *atte Fen* v. *de Melchbourn* (1346; CP 40/345 m.382d) (*concessit solvere*).

[67] *Burewelle* v. *le Waleys* (1292; CP 40/96 m.201d); YB 22 Lib Ass f.101 pl.70; *Cobyndon* v. *Abbot of St Augustine's* (1380; CP 40/477 m.366d).

[68] For the medieval marriage market, see S. Waugh, *The Lordship of England* (Princeton, 1988), ch. 1. Promises made on marriages continued to plague the Common lawyers for centuries: below, p.142.

[69] Simpson, *History of Contract*, 148–60; S. F. C. Milsom, 'Account Stated in the Action of Debt' (1966) 82 LQR 534, 539.

[70] *Loveday* v. *Ormesby* YB 3 Edw II (20 SS) 191; YB 11 & 12 Edw III (RS) 587; YB P.29 Edw III f.25. Cf. *Anon* (Eyre of Northamptonshire, 1329; 98 SS 743), allowing an action on an oral grant provided that there was a good 'cause' for it.

[71] Milsom, 'Account Stated' (1966) 82 LQR 534, 539–40; cf. YB M.7 Hen VI f.12 pl.17 at f.13.   [72] Milsom, 'Account Stated' (1966) 82 LQR 534.

[73] YB 18 Edw III (RS) 23; YB T.44 Edw III f.21 pl.23; YB M.9 Hen V f.14 pl.23; YB P.11 Hen VI f.35 pl.30 at f.38; YB M.37 Hen VI f.8 pl.18.

it could be inferred that he had benefited indirectly.[74] Promises to pay money on marriage were more problematical, exacerbated by doubts whether they were not in reality properly within the jurisdiction of the ecclesiastical courts, with argument focusing around whether the marriage could count as *quid pro quo*; the wise litigant perhaps preferred to seek a remedy in Chancery.[75] There was less doubt about agreements to pay for past services: the defendant received nothing under the agreement, so there was no *quid pro quo* and consequently no actionable debt.[76] It was probably not essential, however, that the debtor should receive a physical thing for there to be *quid pro quo*; a right of action seemingly sufficed. Thus the seller of goods would have had an action of debt for the price even if the goods had not been delivered, arguably even if it were proved that the goods had never existed.[77] These rules were occasionally expressed by the Romanist maxim *Ex nudo pacto non oritur actio* ('No action lies on a bare pact').[78] In such terms, the Common law recognized two types of clothing for pacts: a document under seal, and a *quid pro quo*.

As well as operating to exclude informal gratuitous arrangements from the domain of the law of contract, the idea of reciprocity behind the language of *quid pro quo* served to generalize the situations within which contractual liability would arise. There was no such general principle in the earlier Common law, typified by Glanvill's treatise, where there was a limited list of named contracts that generated debts. Though other types of agreements might have been actionable as covenants, they did not necessarily create debts.[79] Slowly, the law moved from this causal theory of liability to an abstract general theory. The first reported discussion of the point occurred in 1339, where an attorney brought an action of debt to recover a sum due on a retainer. Despite objections first that this was properly a covenant rather than a contract, and secondly that it amounted to a grant of a debt that required a deed, the court held that the action well lay, since the creditor had *quid pro quo*.[80] By the beginning of the fifteenth

---

[74] YB P.9 Edw IV f.1 pl.1; YB T.17 Edw IV f.4 pl.4.

[75] YB P.29 Edw III f.33; F Abr, *Dette*, 8 (1357); YB T.45 Edw III f.24 pl.30; YB M.7 Hen VI f.1 pl.1; YB M.37 Hen VI f.8 pl.18; YB T.14 Edw IV f.6 pl.3; YB T.15 Edw IV f.32 pl.14; YB T.17 Edw IV f.4 pl.4. For Chancery petitions, see e.g. *Fetiplace* v. *Somerton* (C1/16/334); *Gyffard* v. *Gyrnon* (C1/16/311); *Luyt* v. *Boteler* (C1/60/142); *Taylour* v. *Clerk* (C1/60/143); *Scarlet* v. *Harrys* (C1/108/13).   [76] YB P.29 Edw III f.25.

[77] YB M.37 Hen VI f.8 pl.18, per Prisot C.J.; *Twyvell* v. *Onehand* (C1/11/303–306) (goods taken out of seller's control before time of contract, unknown to either buyer or seller; petitioner in Chancery seeks relief on assumption that liable to pay for them).

[78] e.g. YB M.9 Hen V f.14 pl.23; YB P.11 Hen VI f.35 pl.30 at f.38; YB T.17 Edw IV f.4 pl.4. And in Chancery petitions: *Luyt* v. *Boteler* (C1/60/142); *Grene* v. *Capell* (C1/94/22).

[79] Above, p.18.

[80] YB 11 & 12 Edw III (RS) 587. Despite a series of cases holding that actions of debt could be brought for sums due on retainers, doubts continued to be raised right until the end of the fifteenth century: J. L. Barton, 'The Medieval Contract', in *Towards a General Law of Contract* (Berlin, 1990), 15, 25.

century it seems to have been generally accepted that an action of debt would lie for money due on any reciprocal agreement,[81] and by the sixteenth this could be formulated as a general definition of contract: 'An agreement concerning personal things is a mutual assent of the parties, and ought to be executed with a recompence, or else ought to be so certain and sufficient, as to give an action or other remedy for recompence: and if it is not so, then it shall not be called an agreement, but rather a nude communication without effect.'[82]

Three further observations are pertinent. First, it should be stressed that the present concern is with the identification of the types of transaction of which the law would take cognizance—that is, *whether* there was a contract. The language of *quid pro quo* might also be used, and frequently was used, to define the moment at which a party's obligations to perform the contract were activated—that is, *when* the contract became actionable. This is a very different question, though the use of the same language has tended rather to obscure the distinction.[83] Secondly, it should be noted that the requirement of *quid pro quo* was not simply a feature of the action of debt. In cases in the fifteenth century in which attempts were made to use the action of trespass on the case as a remedy for non-performance of contracts it is stressed in argument that the plaintiff's claim would be well founded (if it could be well founded at all) only if the defendant had received *quid pro quo.*[84] Even in actions on the case based on contractual mis-performance it was common practice to specify that the defendant had received a 'competent salary' or the like in exchange for his service.[85] Despite the trespassory framework of these actions, there was a strong contractual dimension to them, and this was expressed in terms of the idea of *quid pro quo.* Thirdly, this narrowing of the requirement of reciprocity in actions on informal contracts was not as clear a feature of the law of the local courts as of the royal courts; the former might have retained the more generous approach to liability found in the royal courts before the middle of the fourteenth century.[86]

Contractual Terms

The parties' contractual obligations were in principle determined by their agreement. If the contract was based on a written document, then all that

---

[81] YB H.12 Hen IV f.17 pl.13; YB M.37 Hen VI f.8 pl.18.
[82] *Reniger* v. *Fogossa* (1550) Plo 1, 5, per Griffiths Solr. The translation in the English Reports is inaccurate, omitting the second 'not' in the final clause.
[83] Below, n.110. The complexity of the questions discussed is well brought out by Barton, 'The Medieval Contract', in *Towards a General Law of Contract*, 15.
[84] *Watkin's Case*, YB H.3 Hen VI f.36 pl.33 (B&M 380); *Anon* (1440; B&M 389).
[85] W. McGovern, 'The Enforcement of Informal Contracts in the Later Middle Ages' (1971) 59 Cal L R 1145, 1158–9.   [86] Milsom, 'Account Stated' (1966) 82 LQR 534, 537.

was required was to construe the words, applying routine canons of construction, such as that any ambiguities should be resolved against the maker of the document.[87]The Common-law courts would not allow written terms to be varied by a purely oral agreement of the parties,[88] but there is good reason to think that the Chancery might have been willing to go behind the document.[89] So far as unwritten agreements were concerned, there was not a great deal of room for legal rules to determine the content of the contract: difficult questions could invariably be concealed behind the general issue and the defendant's wager of law or a general verdict of the jury.

In some types of contracts, most importantly contracts of sale, there might be terms collateral to the primary obligations arising under the contract, such as undertakings as to the quality of goods sold. Such terms were commonly known as 'warranties'.[90] At first, actions on them might be framed as either covenant or trespass,[91] though in the royal courts the trespassory form was problematic since it was normally impossible to allege that there had been any force or interference with a royal interest.[92] At the end of the fourteenth century it was settled that they were properly litigable under the rubric of trespass on the case, using the language of deceit, despite arguments to the effect that the action properly sounded in covenant.[93] Since the action was trespassory in its nature, the successful plaintiff would recover damages for the loss suffered, in an amount to be assessed by the jury.

The central feature of the action was that the plaintiff had suffered loss by the defendant's deceit. Consequently, there would be no liability if the plaintiff could and should have recognized at the time of the sale that the warranty was in fact false. No action would lie, for example, if the seller sold red cloth with a warranty that it was blue, unless, of course, the buyer could not see;[94] nor on a warranty that a horse was sound if in fact it was blind, unless the buyer did not have the opportunity to inspect it.[95] Equally, the warranty had to be of some fact that it could be in the power of the

---

[87] F. Bacon, *Maxims of the Law*, Reg. 3, and the references there cited.

[88] Ibid., Reg. 25, and the references there cited.

[89] Barbour, *History of Contract in Early English Equity*, 90–2.

[90] See in particular Kiralfy, *Action on the Case*, 83–7, 91–4; Milsom, 'Sale of Goods in the Fifteenth Century' (1961) 77 LQR 257, 278–82; Simpson, *History of Contract*, 240–7.

[91] In London, for example: *de Shorisdich* v. *Lane* (1300; *CEMCR* 68) (trespass); *de Mauncestre* v. *Bolam* (1305; *CEMCR* 262) (covenant); *de Loveyne* v. *de Burgo* (1305; *CEMCR* 216) (trespass).

[92] Cf. *Ferrers* v. *Vicar of Dodford* (1307; 58 SS 179), where issue was joined on a trespassory action in the King's Bench; it was explicitly stated that the plaintiff was acting on the king's business.

[93] *Aylesbury* v. *Watts*, YB M.6 Ric II (AF) 119; *Rempston* v. *Morley*, YB 7 Ric II (AF) 30; *Garrok* v. *Heytesbury*, YB T.11 Ric II (AF) 4 (B&M 507). It followed that initial process might be by attachment rather than summons, and that it was not necessary to join all contracting parties as defendants.   [94] YB T.11 Edw IV f.6 pl.10, per Fairfax Sjt. and Brian C.J.

[95] *Barantine's Case*, YB M.13 Hen IV f.1 pl.4 (B&M 509), per Hankford J. and Thirning C.J.

seller to know:[96] no action would lie if the warranty was that seed would grow, or that a horse would travel thirty leagues in a day.[97] In practice this meant that the warranty must relate to some state of present fact and not be a prediction of the future, which could be known only by God, or a promise as to the future, which would amount to a covenant and con-sequently—according to the orthodox learning of the fifteenth century— have to be embodied in a deed.

The action for breach of warranty would lie only if a warranty had genuinely been given.[98] The strength of this rule is brought out by two anomalous situations in which liability was imposed in the absence of an explicit warranty. First was the case of the sale of food. Statute had forbidden the sale of corrupt food, and it was consequently held that such a seller would automatically be liable to the buyer.[99] Liability here stemmed straightforwardly from the breach of the statute and it was irrelevant whether or not there had been any warranty. The two grounds of liability were treated as wholly distinct, although both were litigable by superficially similar forms of action of trespass on the case; there was no attempt to treat liability for breach of warranty as the central case and then to analogize from it by using any language of implied warranties. Secondly, it was occasionally suggested that liability would lie in the absence of a warranty if the seller actually knew that the goods sold were defective.[100] Again, liability here was treated as wholly distinct from liability for breach of warranty, not an extension of it.

To say that it had to be proved that a warranty had genuinely been given reveals nothing about what would count as a genuine warranty. This would have been a question of fact. It is hard to imagine that a jury would require much to convince them that the hirer of a horse to ride from London to York had received a warranty that it was sound;[101] on the other hand, a warranty that wool or seed came from a particular source might require far stronger evidence.[102]

---

[96] The pleadings always state that the seller positively knew the statement to be false, but issue was never taken on the knowledge: Arnold, *Select Cases of Trespass* (100 SS), p.lxxxiv n.673. But see *Anon* (1452; Stath Abr, *Actions sur le cas*, 25), which points to a view that knowledge was necessary: Simpson, *History of Contract*, 246–7.

[97] YB T.11 Edw IV f.6 pl.10, per Brian C.J. and Choke J.

[98] Issue was frequently taken on the question of whether the warranty had been given: Arnold, *Select Cases of Trespass* (100 SS), p.lxxxiv.

[99] *Fitzwilliam's Case*, YB P.7 Hen IV f.14 pl.19 (B&M 508); YB M.9 Hen VI f.53 pl.37 (B&M 509); YB T.11 Edw IV f.6 pl.10 (B&M 511).

[100] e.g. *Shipton* v. *Dogge*, YB T.20 Hen VI f.34 pl.4, 51 SS 97 (B&M 391), per Paston J.; cf. *le Lacer* v. *de Canterbury* (1304; London *CEMCR* 154). Similarly, in actions alleging that sellers of goods had not had title to them, no warranty need be alleged: Milsom, 'Sale of Goods in the Fifteenth Century' (1961) 77 LQR 257, 282.

[101] *Bernard* v. *Appleby* (1396; 103 SS 451, case 42.7).

[102] *Salman* v. *Wroth* (CP 40/744 m.276 (Milsom, 'Sale of Goods in the Fifteenth Century' (1961) 77 LQR 257, 282 n.66)); YB T.11 Edw IV f.6 pl.10, per Brian C.J.

Cutting across the treatment of terms as actionable warranties, it might be agreed between the parties that some term should operate as a condition of the whole validity of the contract. Evidence of this is easiest to find in local court records, but there is no reason to believe that these were untypical of the law of the royal courts. The sale of a horse might be expressed to be subject to a condition that the bargain be void if the horse was not sound[103] or the sale of a cow might be subject to a condition that it be in milk.[104] Such a claim was functionally different from a claim that there was a warranty. It did not ground an action for damages, but either underpinned a defence that there should be no liability on the contract since it was subject to an unfulfilled condition[105] or entitled those who had performed their side of a putative bargain to reclaim any money paid or property passed.[106] It followed from this difference in function that the restrictive rules about what could constitute a warranty did not apply to conditions. It might be a condition in a contract for the sale of wine not simply that the wine be of good condition at the time of the sale but that it should be so at the time of the delivery; if it were not, the buyer would be entitled to reject it.[107] Nor need the condition purport to be a representation of fact: money might be handed over to a trading partner on condition that he find pledges, with the proviso that the money might be reclaimed should he fail to do so;[108] or goods might be delivered to an intending buyer subject to a condition that they should be returned if not paid for.[109] We must be careful, therefore, not to think that terms could be defined *ab initio* either as conditions or as warranties; some warranties were conditions and some conditions were warranties, and whether a term was described as one or the other depended wholly on the remedy that the party was seeking.

Assuming that the contract itself was admitted, defendants might none the less deny that their own obligations under it had yet become actionable: it might have been agreed that their obligation to perform would arise only on the occurrence of some specified event, which would take effect as a

---

[103] *Houton* v. *Bosele* (1376; London *CPMR* 2.220).

[104] *Sansum* v. *Devenyshe* (1340; Manor of Chalgrove (Oxfordshire), Magdalen College Oxford 121/20 m.1); *Bono* v. *Wychecall* (1391; Manor of Candlesby (Lincolnshire), Magdalen College Oxford 66/1 m.3d).

[105] e.g. *Irland* v. *atte Walle* (1366; London *CPMR* 2.56) (issue on whether covenant to sell land made subject to consent of vendor's wife); *Pyioun* v. *Godwyne* (1375; London *CPMR* 2.198) (issue on whether lease had been made subject to condition that lessor sweet-talk (*pulchre loqui*) current tenant to surrender her term).

[106] e.g. *de Curtenay* v. *de Elilaund* (Eyre of London 1276; M. Weinbaum (ed.), *The London Eyre of 1276* (London Record Society, 12, 1976) 103 pl.488). Ibbetson, 'Unjust Enrichment in England before 1600', in E. J. H. Schrage (ed.), *Unjust Enrichment* (Berlin, 1995), 121, 127 n.29; below, p.268.

[107] *Fitzwilliam's Case*, YB P.7 Hen IV f.14 pl.19 (B&M 508) (a more complex case where the condition was annexed to a warranty).

[108] *Mercer* v. *Muchelmers* (1289; Exeter Mayor's Court (Devonshire CRO) CR4 m.40).

[109] *Tichfelde and Charke* v. *Trendel* (1292; CP 40/92 m.202).

condition precedent. Sometimes this would be external to the parties, such as would be found in typical insurance contract. Probably more commonly, though, the conditioning event would be the performance of the obligations of the other party to the contract. It would frequently be the case, for example, that it would be agreed in a contract of sale that the buyer's obligation to pay the price would be activated only by the seller's delivery of the goods, or in a contract of employment that the employer's obligation to pay wages would be activated only by the employee's doing the work.[110] Normally in such a case, as one would expect, if the condition had not occurred, the defendant's obligation would remain in suspense and the plaintiff would not (yet) be able to bring an action. Sometimes, however, it might be necessary to go further and ask whose responsibility it was that the condition had not occurred. Thus, in a contract for the sale of goods, if the only reason that the goods had not been delivered was that the buyer had not been there to receive them, there was no defence in an action by the seller for the price; similarly, in an action for wages it would be no defence that the work had not been done if the only reason for this was that the employer had prevented it.[111] In the thirteenth century the language of fault might have been used in asking such a question; by the fifteenth century it was formulated more rigidly, asking whether the failure of the condition was the result of the act of the plaintiff or an act of God.[112]

EXPECTATIONS, ENTITLEMENTS, AND LIABILITY FOR BREACH OF CONTRACT

It is one thing to describe the contents of a contract, another to determine the rights of the parties should it not be performed.[113] The early Common law of obligations can be seen in terms of the polarization between the wrong-based action of trespass on the one hand and the right-based actions of debt and detinue on the other. Trespass was an action for damages, assessed by a jury, compensating the plaintiff for loss suffered. In debt, by contrast, plaintiffs sought to obtain something to which they were entitled, and their compensation was assessed accordingly. This is well illustrated by a case in 1319: an action was brought for thirty quarters of barley; the jury, examined by Bereford C.J., said that the market price of barley on the day at which it should have been delivered was 12s. per

---

[110] YB P.40 Edw III f.24 pl.27; YB M.44 Edw III f.27 pl.6; YB M.49 Hen VI f.18 pl.23.
[111] YB M.21 Hen VI f.6 pl.16 (1442), at f.7 per Newton C.J.; YB T.18 Edw IV f.8 pl.12 (1478), per Littleton J. [112] Below, n.135.
[113] This question is discussed at greater length in D. J. Ibbetson, 'Absolute Liability in Contract: The Antecedents of *Paradine* v. *Jayne*', in F. D. Rose (ed.), *Consensus ad Idem* (London, 1996), 1 (abridged in 'Fault and Absolute Liability' (1997) 18 Jnl Leg Hist 1).

quarter, though the contract price was only 3s. per quarter. The debt due was calculated by reference to the market value rather than the contract price.[114]

The action of covenant, as it was developing in the thirteenth century, fitted uncomfortably between these poles. Sometimes, especially in the context of leases, the plaintiff's remedy was specific performance of the contract,[115] and in such cases it is easy to place the action close to the entitlement-based pole of the action of debt. More commonly, the action was for damages,[116] invariably assessed by the jury. We cannot know how damages were assessed. Where the action was for the mis-performance of a contract, we may guess that they were aimed at the compensation of the plaintiff's loss; the doubts about the possibility of recovering damages in contracts for the benefit of third parties suggest that there was a feeling in these cases that the plaintiff was being compensated for loss suffered;[117] more generally, though, we may see a pull in the direction of assessment by reference to the plaintiff's expectations.

The law of obligations underwent a structural realignment in the fourteenth and fifteenth centuries, resolving this ambiguity in the position of the action of covenant. The strong polarity between damage-based remedies and entitlement-based remedies was restored, the former mapping onto the action of trespass (or the law of tort) and the latter onto the action of debt (or the law of contract).

The main impetus for this was the transfer of cases of contractual mis-performance into the domain of the action of trespass in the fourteenth century, particularly after the emergence of trespass on the case in the

---

[114] *Le Hunte's Case*, YB 12 Edw II (70 SS) 93, YB T.12 Edw II (81 SS) 85. The same rule applied with shifting rates of exchange of currencies, or where coinage had been debased: *Staunton* v. *Tylburgh* (C1/32/402); YB H.9 Edw IV f.49 pl.6. At the beginning of the sixteenth century lawyers concerned to downplay the efficacy of debt and detinue briefly asserted the contrary. The courts would not interfere with these calculations, though they might (as in *Le Hunte's Case* itself) interfere with the jury's award of additional damages for the non-delivery. But cf. a case in 1326, for example, where a jury awarded damages of 100s. on top of a debt of 70s.; Herle J. was clearly surprised by the size of the award, but, having ascertained that this was indeed the intention of the jury, judgment was given accordingly: LI MS Hale 141 f.98v.

[115] H. D. Hazeltine, 'Early History of Specific Performance of Contract in English Law', in F. Berolzheimer (ed.), *Rechtswissenschaftliche Beiträge: Juristische Festgabe des Auslandes zu Josef Kohlers 60. Geburtstag* (Berlin, 1909), 67, esp. 68–76. *Casus Placitorum* (69 SS), 42. In 1305 we are told that a plaintiff in covenant had expected to recover the term and had asked for only a small sum by way of damages; when the court refused to award the term, he was disappointed to be awarded only the trivial amount he had claimed: YB 32 & 33 Edw I (RS) 474. It was still normally the case in the mid-fourteenth century that the ousted lessee would recover the land for the balance of the term (YB M.7 Edw III f.65 pl.67), and Fitzherbert (*Natura Brevium*, 145M) suggests that this might still have been the case in the sixteenth century.

[116] YB 21 & 22 Edw I (RS) 182: the action of covenant is 'in its nature given to recover damages'. YB 30 & 31 Edw I (RS) 143.   [117] Above, n.36.

1360s. This was a transparently tortious remedy, and, despite early doubts about the propriety of shifting cases of breach of contract—'covenant'—into such a trespassory matrix,[118] it was soon established that it was the appropriate remedy in such situations. By contrast, until the very end of the fifteenth century, the courts maintained a spirited—if incoherent—defence of the rule that the trespassory remedy could not be used in cases of pure non-performance.[119] As a result of this there was built into the Common law a strong cleavage between not performing agreements, provided with quintessentially contractual remedies, and performing agreements badly, provided with actions in tort. By the middle of the fifteenth century it was strongly arguable that, even where there was a covenant under seal to do something, if the defendant did it badly, the plaintiff's proper remedy was trespass on the case and not an action of covenant.[120] This strength of focus on non-performance as the core of contractual liability went hand-in-hand with an increasingly strong focus on giving effect to expectations rather than compensating for actual loss suffered. At its simplest, the shearing-off of mis-performance cases from the main stream of contractual liability meant that informal contracts were predominantly litigated by means of the action of debt; and, as in the thirteenth century, the action of debt was concerned solely with giving to plaintiffs their entitlements.

Secondly, the replacement of the action of covenant by the action of debt on a conditional bond meant that at the level of formal contracts too the action would be formulated in terms of the plaintiff's entitlement. The claim would always take the form of an action of debt to recover the value of the bond. In analytical terms, the action was always based on non-performance rather than mis-performance; and plaintiffs got what they were entitled to rather than damages.

Thirdly, as the proprietary dimension of the writ of detinue became more marked in the course of the fifteenth century,[121] so too did the stress on the vindication of the plaintiff's entitlement. In the two common situations where the action was based on a contract, bailment and the sale of goods, compensation was invariably assessed by reference to the value of the goods rather than by considering what loss the plaintiff had suffered. In 1449 a bailor brought an action against a bailee who had failed to return the goods to him; it was said that, where the loss suffered was greater than the value of the goods, the additional loss would not be recoverable in the writ of detinue.[122] The same probably applied in the sale of goods: a purchaser of goods who had contracted to sell them on to a third party, subject to a penalty, petitioned for relief in Chancery when the goods were

---

[118] *Waldon* v. *Mareschal*, YB M.43 Edw III f.33 pl.38 (B&M 359).　　[119] Below, p.126.
[120] Milsom, *Historical Foundations*, 252–3, 325–32. The most explicit statement of the argument is in *Shipton* v. *Dogge*, YB T.20 Hen VI f.34, pl.4, 51 SS 97 (B&M 391).
[121] Above, p.34.　　[122] Stath Abr., *Actions sur le cas*, pl.25 (B&M 397).

not delivered on the due date and the penalty consequently forfeited; the Common law, it was said, did not provide a remedy in such a situation.[123] The rule might equally operate to the buyer's advantage; where there had been a rise in the value of the goods sold between the date on which the contract was made and the due date for delivery, the amount to be recovered was assessed by reference to the latter rather than to the contract price. The action lay to compensate for lost expectations rather than out-of-pocket losses.

This structural realignment of the law of obligations into wrong-based actions for damages and right-based actions for entitlements had the further effect of redefining the nature of liability for breach of contract, so that by the end of the fifteenth century there was a clear polarization between liability in tort (typically in trespass), which was essentially fault-based, and liability in contract (typically in debt), which was essentially strict. In the latter situation, instead of looking at what the defendant had done wrong, the law came to concentrate on the plaintiff's entitlement and the listing of those factors that might negative the rights that prima facie arose under the contract.[124]

This would not have been so in the thirteenth century. We may without difficulty discern the fault-based foundation of the action of trespass, though this was largely concealed behind the language of causation,[125] but contractual liability was far more ambiguous. In so far as they were concerned with simple non-performance, debt and detinue might have fitted into a model of strict liability, in the sense that once the contract had been perfected, the plaintiff had a near-proprietary right to the agreed goods or money. But detinue could be brought in cases of mis-performance—for example, where bailed goods had been destroyed or damaged—and here liability was seen in explicitly fault-based terms.[126] This was not merely the speculative law of the treatise writer imbued with ideas culled from Roman law, but the practical law of the courts. In 1291, for example, an action of detinue was brought against the bailee of sheep when he failed to return them alive at the end of the bailment period; the defendant admitted the bailment but claimed that he was not liable since the sheep had perished because of the flooding of the land on which they were being kept, and not because of any fault (*defectus*) on his part; issue was joined on whether or not they had died through the fault and bad custody of the bailee.[127] The

---

[123] *Fabian* v. *Wolfyt* (C1/60/122).

[124] For the terminology, see B. Nicholas, 'Fault and Breach of Contract', in J. Beatson and D. Friedman (eds.), *Good Faith and Fault in Contract Law* (Oxford, 1995), 337.

[125] Above, pp.59–63.   [126] Bracton f.99b (ed. Thorne, 2.284); Britton, 1.157.

[127] *Bydeford* v. *Aunfrey* (1291) CP 40/90 m.53. Similarly in Great Yarmouth in 1353 a careful jury in a writ of detinue found both that the defendant bailee was not detaining the plaintiff's goods and also that they had not been lost through his fault (*defectus*): *Belchere* v. *Lewe* (Great Yarmouth Borough Court (Norfolk CRO) Y/C4/74 m.5).

same focus on fault was found in actions of covenant for mis-performance. At the end of the thirteenth century Fleta makes the point that a shepherd should be liable for the death of sheep only if this had been caused by his fault, *culpa*.[128] In one highly anomalous situation, where a lessee had been ejected by someone other than the lessor and the lessor had recovered the land from the ejector, the defendant lessor would be liable in covenant even though he was not responsible for the ejection. An annotator of Britton, writing around 1300, clearly thought this was noteworthy, observing with more than a hint of a raised eyebrow that it involved the liability in covenant of a defendant who was not at fault: 'qui ne est de rien culpable del engettement'.[129] If the exception proves the rule, we could hardly ask for better proof.

The strong trespassory dimension of the thirteenth-century action of covenant has already been noted,[130] and it is unsurprising, therefore, that the language of fault infected cases of non-performance as well as of mis-performance. The evidence here is more sketchy, for in practice there would be a need to consider the criteria of responsibility only if performance of the obligation had become impossible. Such cases were relatively unusual, but in a very revealing case of 1293 the relevance of fault in this area too is explicit.[131] Simplifying the facts slightly, the defendant had made a covenant to transfer land to the plaintiff by subinfeudation. At the time at which the agreement was made this would have been perfectly possible, but by the time it came to be performed subinfeudation had been abolished by the Statute *Quia Emptores* and the defendant was hence unable to perform. The defendant argued that the non-performance had occurred through no fault of his own,[132] the Court of Common Pleas found in his favour, and in 1293 its judgment was upheld on a writ of error to the King's Bench.

As cases of contractual mis-performance were sheared off into the proper domain of the action of trespass on the case and actions for contractual non-performance came to concentrate on the plaintiff's entitlement rather than the defendant's breach, so any identification of fault as the basis of contractual liability was eaten away. Contractual liability became strict, in that the contract gave to the plaintiff certain entitlements, and it was for the defendant to show some reason why these entitlements

---

[128] Fleta II.72 (72 SS 243): 'ad vim autem maiorem vel ad casus fortuitos non tenetur quis nisi sua culpa interuenerit.'

[129] CUL MS Dd 7.6(3) f.27. We might, of course, retort that, though the defendant was not responsible for the ejection, he was at fault in failing to hand over the land to the lessee after he had recovered it.   [130] Above, p.22.

[131] *Richard of Windsor* v. *Maurice of Membury* (1293; 57 SS 160).

[132] 57 SS at 164: 'nec in ipso Ricardo [the defendant] fuit aliquis defectus de hoc quod dominus rex . . . statuit quod perquirentes tenementa teneant illa de capitalibus dominis feodi de quibus ipsi venditores illa tenuerunt.'

should not be given effect by the court. In reality we should think not so much in terms of contractual liability becoming stricter, but rather in terms of the redefinition of that part of the law of contract within which fault was most obviously the basis of liability as falling properly within the domain of the law of tort.

This shift towards strict liability has to be seen at two levels: liability on formal contracts, and liability on informal contracts.

So far as contracts under seal were concerned, from the middle of the fourteenth century the action of covenant came to be replaced by the action of debt based on a conditional bond. The structure of the conditional bond was that the obligor was bound to pay a fixed sum (a debt) unless some condition was satisfied by a certain date; and, although in strict legal terms the primary obligation was to pay the fixed sum, in substance the intention of the parties was that the obligor should perform the condition.[133] It followed from this that, instead of asking whether the defendant was in breach of his contract (as occurred in the action of covenant in the thirteenth century), liability hinged on whether or not the condition had been fulfilled. At first, it seems, the courts approached this issue by transplanting the fault-based approach of covenant into the action of debt: instead of asking whether defendants had broken the covenant, they asked whether they had broken the condition, using the same language of fault in order to answer the question. This is brought out well, if artificially, in *Ravenser* v. *Middleton* (1383).[134] The defendant entered into a bond to the plaintiff, subject to a defeasant condition that the bond would be void if he stood to the award of arbitrators to be made in a matter in dispute between the parties. In an action of debt on the bond, the defendant pleaded the condition, but said that the arbitrators had made no award. The plaintiff countered this by arguing that the defendant's plea was tantamount to an admission of liability, since he had admitted that the condition had not been performed. The court rejected this: it was not enough to say that the condition had not been performed if this was not the defendant's fault (*defaut*). By the end of the fifteenth century such a fault-based analysis had disappeared. If the condition had not been performed, then the defendant was, prima facie, liable to pay the sum due on the face of the bond. This was subject to two exceptions: if the breach of the condition could be attributed to the plaintiff or someone 'privy' (such as a bailiff or a member of the family), or to an act of God, then the defendant would avoid liability.[135] If, on the other hand, it

---

[133] For the working of the conditional bond, see above, p.29.

[134] YB T.7 Ric II (AF) 26 pl.10.

[135] Act of the plaintiff: YB T.12 Hen IV f.23 pl.6; YB P.7 Edw IV f.4 pl.10; YB M.22 Edw IV f.25 pl.6. Act of God: YB P.2 Edw IV f.2 pl.2, per Choke J.; YB M.8 Edw IV f.9 pl.9 esp. at f.10, per Yelverton J.; YB H.14 Edw IV f.3 pl.6; YB H.4 Hen VII f.3 pl.7 at f.8, per Townsend Sjt *et totam curiam*; YB M.15 Hen VII f.13 pl.24.

was the result of a third party's failure as in *Ravenser* v. *Middleton*, the defendant's liability would remain intact. The shift in theory involved here was significant—it paved the way for the adoption of the theory of absolute liability in contract[136]—though it was rather less important in practice, since few cases would be decided differently under the two approaches. Indeed, beneath the surface, as a background justification for the rules, where liability was imposed on defendants who did not themselves seem to be responsible for the breach of the condition (as, for example, when it was caused by the refusal of an independent third party to cooperate in some arrangement), it could be said that it was their own fault—or folly—to have entered into the agreement in the first place.[137]

This move away from fault liability was not confined to actions brought on conditional bonds; by the end of the fifteenth century it had spread from there to actions brought on straightforward covenants. Reasoning explicitly by analogy with the law of conditional bonds, it was held that the covenantor should be liable for non-performance of the covenant, unless the reason for the non-performance was the act of the plaintiff or an act of God. Thus, a man who had failed to perform a covenant to build a house was not liable if the reason for his failure was that the covenantee had refused to allow him on to the land;[138] nor would executors be liable if the covenantor had died (the most obvious example of an act of God) without having been able to perform the covenant.[139] Moreover, again by analogy with the conditional bond, it was not simply that the covenantor was not (yet) in breach: the refusal of the covenantee or the death of the covenantor operated to discharge the covenant permanently.[140] On the other hand, a man who had agreed with another to marry a certain woman was liable when he failed to do so even though the only reason for the failure was that the woman had refused his suit;[141] in this case, his failure could be attributable neither to the plaintiff nor to God. The thirteenth-century idea that liability in covenant was based on fault was eaten away by the fifteenth-century idea that liability on a conditional bond was not.

There was little room for any consideration of fault in actions based on informal contracts. If the plaintiff's claim was based on mis-performance, where fault might most obviously have been relevant, then it would have been recategorized as tortious, an action of trespass on the case. In claims

---

[136] Below, p.213.
[137] YB P.33 Hen VI f.16 pl.7; YB P.7 Edw IV f.4 pl.10, per Choke J.; YB M.8 Edw IV f.14 pl.15; YB M.22 Edw IV f.25 pl.6 at f.26, per Catesby and Pygot Sjts.
[138] YB T.18 Edw IV f.8 pl.12
[139] YB H.48 Edw III f.1 pl.4; YB P.10 Hen VII f.18 pl.4. It would have been different if the covenant had been breached before the covenantor's death, or if it was not personal to the covenantor and could be performed by somebody else.
[140] According to Choke J. the obligation was discharged 'a touts jours'.
[141] YB P.33 Hen VI f.16 pl.7.

for non-performance, fault would normally have come into play only if the obligation had become impossible; and this could normally occur only in a contract to perform services, not in a contract to deliver goods or pay money. This was the very situation in which the medieval Common law had its principal remedial gap: debt and detinue would not lie, and until 1499 there was no action of trespass on the case in the absence of some positive act of misfeasance. In the nature of things, therefore, where informal contracts are concerned, there is hardly any evidence of a shift from explicitly fault-based liability towards strict liability.

The one situation in which the shift is visible is where the action was for the non-delivery of specific goods and the defendant was claiming that they had been destroyed. In the thirteenth century the issue was framed simply in terms of whether the defendant had been at fault;[142] in the fifteenth the defendant who could not deliver the goods would automatically be liable, unless it could be shown that the reason for non-delivery was an act of the plaintiff (presumably), an act of God, or some other *force majeure*.[143] Evidence from other situations, though more equivocal, is consistent with this. An employee sued for departure from service (under the Statute of Labourers) would be excused if it could be shown that the departure was justified; the factors that counted as justifications all involved wrongdoing on the part of the employer.[144] An employee who had unjustifiably left his employment before the end of the term would have no action for wages, even for the period worked; whereas one who had been improperly dismissed before the end of the agreed term would be entitled to wages for the full contract period.[145] And a lessee of land who had been prevented from enjoying it by the lessor's wrongful ouster or by act of God would be excused the payment of rent.[146]

---

[142] Above, n.127.

[143] YB M.10 Hen VI f.21 pl.69; YB M.2 Edw IV f.15 pl.7; YB T. 8 Edw IV f.6 pl.5; YB M.9 Edw IV f.33 pl.9; YB M.2 Ric III f.14 pl.39. The principle is most clearly seen in the analogical situation of the liability of a gaoler for the escape of his prisoner: YB H.33 Hen VI f.1 pl.3.

[144] Putnam, *Enforcement of the Statute of Labourers*, 192–3.

[145] YB P.40 Edw III f.24 pl.27; YB M.21 Hen VI f.6 pl.16; YB M.49 Hen VI f.18 pl.23; YB T.18 Edw IV f.8 pl.12.

[146] 11 Lib Ass f.30 pl.13; YB M.15 Hen VII f.14 pl.6. These were anomalous, though the principle still holds good: the rent was seen as issuing from the land, so it was prima facie a defence that the lessee had not received any benefit from the land out of which the rent could be paid.

Part Two. The Triumph of Trespass on the Case

The sixteenth century marks a transitional stage between the medieval law, which was very heavily dominated by the forms of action, and the modern law, with its focus on substantive rules and principles.

By the middle of the fifteenth century the Common law was undergoing a crisis. Its rules were bafflingly complex and its procedures so byzantine that even getting one's opponent into court was no simple matter. The lawyers responded to this by a variety of expedients, halting the decline and reviving their fortunes: the early sixteenth century, it has been said, marked the Renaissance of the Common law. One of these expedients was a greater willingness to allow experimentation with the action of trespass on the case.

Trespass on the case had two enormous advantages from the point of view of the plaintiff litigant. As an action of trespass, its focus was on the alleged wrongdoing of the defendant; and it was to all intents and purposes formless, capable of adjustment and adaptation to the facts of any individual case. Given that practically any legal claim could be reformulated in terms of the wrongdoing of the other party, it followed that trespass on the case could be used both to bring into the Common law situations that would formerly have been excluded and to reformulate existing actions in such a way as to shed inconvenient limitations or to bypass cumbersome procedures.

By the early years of the sixteenth century the three principal satellite torts of the Common law had emerged. The action on the case for nuisance had grown up alongside the proprietary assize of nuisance, providing a remedy for those complaining of an interference with their enjoyment of land; the action on the case for conversion had grown up alongside the action of detinue, protecting rights in moveable property; and the action on the case for defamation developed alongside the ecclesiastical remedy to give compensation to those injured by malicious allegations. Each of these had developed rules already; these rules were not abandoned by their ingestion into trespass on the case, but all underwent mutations so as to fit within their new-found trespassory home. By 1600 all were firmly consolidated and had eaten away at the territory of the pre-existing remedies. In the graphic language of the 1590s, trespass on the case was a monstrous child turning on its natural parents.

At the same time trespass on the case, in the form that came to be known as the action of assumpsit, took over the ground of informal contracts; by 1600 it had largely eclipsed the traditional action of debt. Picking up where it had faltered in the early fourteenth century, the Common law was able to develop assumpsit as a general contractual remedy. Ideas that had remained only dimly articulated in the fourteenth and fifteenth centuries were brought up to the surface and exposed to the light. In the process they were given a tortious twist that was to skew the whole of the later law of contract.

Nuisance, conversion, defamation, and assumpsit did not exhaust the capabilities of trespass on the case. Its sixteenth-century potential can be seen from the list of other situations in which it was used (not always successfully) in the sample of cases reported by John Spelman early in the century and by Edward Coke at its end: enclosing common land; enticement of servants; extortion; infringement of franchisal rights; non-payment of a legacy; malicious prosecution; allowing an apprentice to mis-spend his youth; squandering a master's money; wasting bailed goods; the enforcement of uses; suing in another's name without a warrant; misfeasance in public office; slander of title of land; negligence by a bailee burning a house; deceit; forgery of a deed; damage done by a dog; cheating at dice; improper distraint.

The one area of the law of obligations that was wholly unaffected by this was the main core of the law of tort, the ground covered by the medieval action of trespass. There would have been theoretical problems in the expansion of trespass on the case in this direction: there was a resistance to the overlapping of forms of action, and the arguments that had been used to justify the growth of nuisance, conversion, defamation, and assumpsit would not have been easily applicable to an encroachment into the territory of trespass itself. More to the point, perhaps, there was very little pressure to do so. Trespass served the purposes of litigants perfectly adequately, and without any inconvenient procedural limitations that might have prompted plaintiffs to experiment with a different form of action.

6. *Tort, Property, and Reputation:*
The Expansion of the Action on the Case

It may be no more than a linguistic solecism to say that the medieval law of torts was defined by the scope of the writ of trespass, for 'trespass' and 'tort' are no more than French versions of 'wrong'. Just as the action of trespass, in its central core, was divided into trespass to land, trespass to the person, and trespass to goods, so too we should see the medieval law of torts as focused strongly on invasive interferences with land, the person, and chattels. The emergence of the action of trespass on the case in the middle of the fourteenth century provided an alternative, unconstrained, form in which actions of trespass could be brought and hence softened the focus of the law of torts on such invasive interferences. So long as it could be alleged that the plaintiff had suffered some harm as a result of wrongful conduct on the part of the defendant, it could be argued that a remedy should be given, irrespective of the way in which that harm had been brought about. It followed from this that the action on the case had an indefinite and near-infinite potential to expand the scope of tortious liability. At first this potential was slowly realized, and few situations were brought within it that could not have been framed, with a degree of broad-mindedness, within the tripartite structure of the general action of trespass; but around the end of the fifteenth century and the beginning of the sixteenth there was a marked surge in its application to previously unrecognized situations. The effective range of the law of torts was thereby extended, and this extension was consolidated during the sixteenth century.

By the beginning of the seventeenth century we may see the law of torts as having three aspects. First was the core, centred on the general action of trespass but extending into trespass on the case, dealing with invasive interferences. Second was a group of tolerably well-bounded 'nominate' torts, of which nuisance, conversion, and defamation were the most obvious examples. Finally there was a miscellaneous ragbag of situations in which plaintiffs had succeeded in convincing the courts that they had suffered loss for which they ought to be compensated—an open-ended set of 'torticles', as one modern commentator has dubbed them.[1] Of the first of these aspects little need be said at the present juncture, for it was not until the eighteenth or nineteenth century that the courts began to give any explicit structure to this area of liability; of the third little can be said,

---

[1] B. Rudden, 'Torticles' (1991–2) 6/7 Tulane Civil Law Forum 105.

for in its nature it was (and is) inherently unstructured. The present chapter, therefore, will deal only with the second aspect: the developments of nominate torts to protect property interests and reputation.

From its earliest roots the action of trespass protected property rights. So long as there had been an invasive interference, a 'trespass' in the modern non-legal sense of the word, an action would lie against the alleged wrongdoer. The difficulty with the use of these remedies was that in theory they provided the successful plaintiff with damages rather than the land in issue. This was sidestepped in the sixteenth century by the use of the action of ejectment, an action designed to protect the lessee rather than the free-holder, in which specific recovery of the land could be achieved.[2] Encrusted with a byzantine collection of fictions, the action of ejectment became to all intents and purposes a real action in everything but form.[3]

Trespassory remedies came to be used in other proprietary situations too. Two were of particular importance: nuisance and conversion, covering the interference with enjoyment of land and the interference with moveable property respectively. In each of these the rules mimicked those of the property remedies that they superseded, but neither wholly lost its tortious dimension. Unlike ejectment, nuisance and conversion still have their niche in twentieth-century textbooks on the law of torts.

NUISANCE

The assize of novel disseisin was probably introduced in 1166 as a remedy to protect possession of freehold land.[4] Right from the beginning it was interpreted as giving a remedy not simply to the person who had been ejected from the land but also to the person whose enjoyment of the land had been improperly interfered with.[5] In this it replicated the Roman law's possessory interdicts, which had themselves been extended to cover such types of interference.[6] The 'enjoyment' form of the writ, then, was only a specialized variant of the 'dispossession' form: the plaintiff had to allege not simply a dispossession, but the way in which his enjoyment had been compromised, such as by the raising or demolition of a ditch; and it was

---

[2] Baker, *Introduction to English Legal History*, 341–3.
[3] *Anon* (1588) BL MS Harl 4562 f.88: the action is mixed; not merely personal because judgment is given to recover possession, not merely real because technically the action did not concern the freehold.
[4] The date and original purpose of the assize are the subject of controversy. See J. S. Loengard, 'The Assize of Nuisance: Origins of an Action at Common Law' [1978] CLJ 144, 145 n.1; and P. A. Brand, 'The Origins of English Land Law: Milsom and After', in *The Making of the Common Law* (London, 1992), 203.
[5] Loengard, 'Assize of Nuisance' [1978] CLJ 144, 161–3.
[6] D.43.16.3.15; D.43.16.11; D.43.17.3.2.

necessary to allege that it had been done to the harm—nuisance, *nocumentum*—of the plaintiff's free tenement.[7] Without these allegations the claim would have lacked foundation, for it would have involved no more than that someone had done something on his own land. The assize of nuisance, therefore, came to develop alongside the main stream of the assize of novel disseisin.

A number of features stem from the fact that the remedy was in substance directed towards the protection of the freeholder's possession. First, most obviously, since the plaintiff had to be a freeholder, those with lesser interests in land—for example, leaseholders—could not make use of the assize.[8] Secondly, as generally in novel disseisin, the recognitors (jury) had to view the land.[9] Thirdly, since novel disseisin was aimed at the protection of possession, its primary consequence was an order to restore the plaintiff into possession, transplanted into the context of interference with enjoyment as an order to abate the nuisance; in both situations the award of damages was only a secondary remedy.[10] Moreover, just as the plaintiff in novel disseisin had to show that the disseisin had occurred 'recently', since a specified date, so too did the plaintiff if the claim was for an interference with enjoyment.[11]

For most of the first century of its existence there was no attempt to put the assize of nuisance on any theoretical footing, though the Curia Regis Rolls give a good indication of the circumstances within which the action would have lain: mills, dykes, sheepfolds and piggeries, obstruction of bridges and roads, interference with chartered markets and fairs.[12] It was only in the middle of the thirteenth century, in Bracton's *Treatise*, that we find any discussion of the basis of the action.[13] With perhaps more than half an eye to the Roman law, nuisances are treated as disseisins of servitudes, borrowing directly from Justinian's *Institutes* the conclusion that not only the plaintiff but also the defendant in the action had to be a freeholder.[14] The connection with servitudes also had the effect of associating

---

[7] Glanvill XIII.34–6 (ed. Hall, 168–9).

[8] For the protection of leaseholders, see below, n.41.

[9] Sutherland, *Novel Disseisin*, 66. It came to be regarded as sufficient that the view had been made by a majority of the recognitors.

[10] e.g. 3 CRR 132 (1204). It is stated as a rule in Bracton ff.232, 234, 234b (ed. Thorne, 3.190, 196, 197).

[11] Glanvill XIII.35, 36 (ed. Hall, 168); *Early Registers of Writs* (87 SS) 260, R656. In *de Araz* v. *Bosant* (1232; *BNB* 701) the assize went against the plaintiffs when it was shown that the nuisance had occurred before the limitation date, even though it had been exacerbated since that date.   [12] C. T. Flower, *Introduction to the Curia Regis Rolls* (62 SS), 325–34.

[13] Bracton ff.231b, 232–236b (ed. Thorne, 3.189–201). There is a useful discussion in Fifoot, *History and Sources of the Common Law*, 7–9.

[14] Bracton f.234 (ed. Thorne, 3.195) (twice); cf. Justinian, *Institutes*, 2.3.3. Hence in YB 32 Lib Ass f.194 pl.2 it is said that the bringing of an assize of nuisance presupposes that the place where the nuisance originated was the freehold property of the defendant.

the law of nuisance with easements and natural rights in land, an association that was to be retained into the nineteenth century.[15] Secondly, the text stresses the need for a nuisance to be both harmful and wrongful; there must be both *damnum* and *iniuria*. There was nothing radical about either of these elements, for both were clearly present in the original text of the writ, harm in the allegation that the act was to the *nocumentum* of the plaintiff's tenement and wrong in the requirement that the defendant should have acted *iniuste*. What is different about the Bractonian text is that these elements are now elevated almost to the level of an organizing principle. At an abstract level the principle is stated three times, once as a straightforward rule, once as a gloss on the word *nocumentum* in the writ, and once by way of gloss on *iniuste*.[16] A nuisance is not wrongful, and so not actionable, if done with the plaintiff's consent;[17] heirs and successors are not liable, except perhaps as to the restoration of the status quo ante, because they should not be liable to pay the penalty for the delicts of others.[18] In order to determine whether a competing market is actionable, the real question is to ask whether it is harmful and wrongful.[19] More generally, an actionable nuisance can be described simply as an *iniuria*, a word that in Bracton's text is practically equivalent to our 'tort'.[20]

It is with Bracton's analysis that we begin to see a clear division building up between the assize of nuisance and the assize of novel disseisin, though it should be noted that his whole treatment of nuisance does fall under the general heading of novel disseisin. If the defendant's wrongful act takes place partly on his own land and partly on the plaintiff's, should the plaintiff bring an assize of novel disseisin or an assize of nuisance?[21] This division was substantially fixed by the end of the thirteenth century, by which time plaintiffs who had brought an assize of nuisance might lose on the grounds that the proper action should have been novel disseisin.[22] Nuisance was on its way to becoming a tort, though one heavily influenced by its proprietary foundations.

Side by side with the assize of nuisance, there existed a writ of nuisance directed to the county court.[23] Although independent of the assize, its form was closely modelled on it: the defendant must have acted unjustly and

---

[15] Below, p.184.

[16] Bracton, ff.231b, 234 (twice) (ed. Thorne, 3.189, 195, 195–6). The last of these, according to Thorne (1.402), occurs in so few manuscripts that it may well be a later gloss incorporated into the text.   [17] Bracton, f.232 (ed. Thorne, 3.190).

[18] Bracton, f.234 (ed. Thorne, 3.195).

[19] Bracton, ff.235–235b (ed. Thorne, 3.198–9).

[20] Bracton, f.234b (ed. Thorne, 3.197). For the use of *iniuria*, see J. L. Barton, 'Bracton as a Civilian' (1968) 42 Tul L R 555, 561–4.   [21] Bracton, f.234b (ed. Thorne, 3.197).

[22] *de Gonceby* v. *le Power* (1290; Plac Abb 284a)

[23] Milsom, *Novae Narrationes* (80 SS), pp.xcvii–civ. See e.g. 87 SS 261, R658. The jurisdictional boundary between nuisances actionable in royal courts and those actionable in local courts was abolished by statute in 1382: Stat 6 Ric II, stat.1, c.3.

without judgment to the nuisance of the plaintiff's free tenement. Local courts might themselves give remedies closely related to the assize of nuisance where activities on one person's land interfered with a neighbour's enjoyment, as where a cesspit was constructed too close to the neighbour's property or where privacy was interfered with by windows overlooking the plaintiff's land.[24] Like the assize of nuisance proper, the primary (perhaps exclusive) aim of such complaints was to get the nuisance removed.

Distinct from these remedies, though still referred to as relating to nuisances—*nocumenta*—were the criminal presentments that could be made in manorial or other local courts.[25] Here the concern was very much with public inconvenience: the diversion or stopping of watercourses, the raising or razing of dykes or walls or ponds, the blocking or narrowing of roads.[26] In the City of London, the articles of the Wardmote prohibited, *inter alia*, the burning of fuel other than wood or charcoal, the placing of filth in the street or outside other people's doors, and the keeping of swine or cows to the annoyance (*noysaunce*) of neighbours.[27] We might choose to think of these types of nuisance as 'criminal' rather than 'tortious', but we could not cavil at their being described as 'wrongs'; it may well be, in fact, that it was the focus on the wrongfulness of this kind of nuisance that provided the impetus for the Bractonian analysis of the assize of nuisance in terms of wrongs.[28]

The characterization of nuisances as wrongs meant that they had the potential to be actionable by the writ of trespass.[29] This potential was realized in the fourteenth century, though its roots go back into the thirteenth. The most obvious use of trespass was where the defendant's wrong had actually involved an intrusion into the plaintiff's land, for this could trivially be described as a forcible breach of the king's peace. Only slightly more problematically, cases which could be regarded as public wrongs (i.e. those which could have been the subject of criminal presentments) could be brought within the domain of forcible trespass if the

---

[24] H. M. Chew and W. Kellaway (eds.), *The London Assize of Nuisance 1301–1431* (London, 1973), pp.xx–xxvi.

[25] F. J. C. Hearnshaw, *Leet Jurisdiction in England* (Southampton, 1908), 43–64.

[26] See e.g. the articles of the view of frankpledge listed by Fleta, 2.52 (72 SS 176). There are many examples of fines for wrongs of this type, whether or not referred to specifically as *nocumenta*, in W. Hudson, *Leet Jurisdiction in Norwich* (5 SS).

[27] H. T. Riley, *Liber Albus: The White Book of the City of London* (London, 1861), 287–92 (= *Munimenta Gildhallae Londiniensis* (RS) 1.337). Such public nuisances were also remedied, though infrequently, by private complaints: Chew and Kellaway, *The London Assize of Nuisance 1301–1431*, pp.xxvi–xxx.

[28] It is noticeable that many of the distinctly Roman resonances in Bracton's treatment relate to the Roman interdicts concerning the blocking of or interference with public rights of way (D.43.8; D.43.11), rivers and watercourses (D.43.13; D.43.20; D.43.21), and springs (D.43.22), rather than with the interdicts more closely associated with private rights.

[29] See in particular Arnold, *Select Cases of Trespass* (100 SS), pp.lxxxii–lxxxiii.

defendant had acted outside the plaintiff's land, though it would not have
been easy to use this remedy if he had been acting on his own property.
Thus, for example, early fourteenth-century Registers of Writs commonly
contain a precedent for the forcible breaking of a weir;[30] and examples are
found in the plea rolls of the diversion, blocking, or pollution of watercourses.[31] It was objected in 1317 that the proper remedy in these situations
was an assize of nuisance rather than a writ of trespass;[32] we do not know
whether the objection was upheld in this case, but in any event no more was
heard of it and it seems to have been generally accepted afterwards that
trespass was an appropriate remedy. Moreover, in the area of public nuisances it did not matter that the allegation was of an omission (which in its
nature could never be described as a forcible breach of the king's peace)
rather than an act: from the middle of the thirteenth century we find
trespassory remedies for the flooding of land as a result of the failure to
repair sea walls,[33] and there are many examples of writs complaining of the
interference with franchisal markets and fairs.[34] There was seemingly
greater reluctance to allow trespass to extend into the domain of private
nuisance, the stronghold of the assize: trespassory actions for the blocking
of gutters, for example, appear in the records rather later than do actions
for the blocking of streams.[35] Two complementary factors combined to
produce this phenomenon: on the one hand, from the middle of the
thirteenth century there was a willingness on the part of the king's courts
to allow trespassory actions in cases of public wrongs even if these could
not be described as forcible breaches of the king's peace; on the other hand,
as late as the middle of the fourteenth century cases of purely private
nuisances might be excluded from the king's courts unless they could be
so characterized. Since most private-nuisance cases would have involved
defendants acting on their own land, which could not properly be described
as forcible breaches of the king's peace,[36] plaintiffs who did not want to use
the assize (if the nuisance had been abated, for instance, but the plaintiff
had already suffered some loss) would be forced to sue in a local court—we

---

[30] *De gurgite vi et armis fracto*: 87 SS 189, R352; earlier examples are found in MS
Registers, e.g. BL MS Lansd 476 f.157ᵛ. It may have been assumed that the weir was on the
plaintiff's land, though this does not appear from the writs.

[31] *de Lowth* v. *Abbot of Lesnes* (1317; 103 SS 348, case 31.1); *Basset* v. *South* (1335; 103 SS
348, case 31.2); *Abbot of Louth Park* v. *Walter, Parson of Somercotes* (1329; 103 SS 351, case
32.1, KB 27/280 m.82); *Prior of Hatfield Peverel* v. *Roger de Willingale* (1364; 103 SS 352, case
32.2).   [32] *de Lowth* v. *Abbot of Lesnes* (1317; 103 SS 348, case 31.1).

[33] Milsom, 'Trespass from Henry III to Richard III' (1958) 74 LQR 407, 430–4; Palmer,
Black Death, 284–8.

[34] Milsom, 'Trespass from Henry III to Richard III' (1958) 74 LQR 407, 418–23; Palmer,
Black Death, 288–92.

[35] Milsom, 'Trespass from Henry III to Richard III' (1958) 74 LQR 407, 434; Palmer, *Black
Death*, 287–8.

[36] YB 21 Lib Ass f.74 pl.1 at f.75; YB M.48 Edw III f.27 pl.13; Kiralfy, *Action on the Case*, 58.

find viscontiel writs of trespass for blocking ditches and the like in Registers from the 1340s at the latest[37]—or to use a general *vi et armis* writ, concealing the fact that the wrong had been done on the defendant's own land.

With the emergence of trespass on the case in the 1360s there was nothing to prevent plaintiffs bringing trespassory actions for all manner of loss-causing private nuisances, even though the defendant had admittedly acted on his own land.[38] At first there seems to have been no reason why this should not overlap with, and potentially supersede, the assize of nuisance; but, just as the boundary between trespass and case became rigid,[39] so too did the boundary between the action on the case and the assize. Thus, in *Rikhill's Case* in 1400[40] the plaintiffs (who included two judges) failed when they brought an action on the case alleging that they had been hindered in the exercise of a right of way over the defendant's land: the assize was the appropriate remedy. The action on the case, therefore, applied where the assize would not have lain: where one of the parties was not a freeholder;[41] where the nuisance could be described as affecting the person rather than the land (for example, a smelly dungheap);[42] where there was an omission rather than an act;[43] where a right of way was only narrowed or partly blocked.[44]

It was not simply that the action of trespass on the case was allowed to fill the gaps left by the assize of nuisance; the scope of assize of nuisance contracted in order to accommodate an increasingly generous interpretation of the scope of the trespassory remedy, with the result that by the beginning of the sixteenth century the assize of nuisance was coming to be supplanted.[45] Throughout the sixteenth century the conservative Court of Common Pleas held to the theory that the action on the case and the assize of nuisance were mutually exclusive remedies, even if the assize was being allowed an increasingly narrow scope;[46] by contrast, by the end of the century the King's Bench was asserting that the action on the case might be used notwithstanding that the assize might have lain on the same facts.[47]

---

[37] e.g. BL MS Add 25237 f.85ᵛ (*c.*1345), CUL MS Dd 6.89 f.98 (*c.*1350?), BL MS Add 25142 f.97 (*c.*1350?).

[38] e.g. depositing refuse near the plaintiff's land, causing rainwater to splash the plaintiff's house, building a gutter that caused the plaintiff's land to flood when the gutter became blocked: Kiralfy, *Action on the Case*, 62. See too Palmer, *Black Death*, 287–8, 386–8.

[39] Above, p.55.   [40] YB M.2 Hen IV f.11 pl.48 (B&M 581).

[41] YB M.11 Hen IV f.25 pl.48; YB T.33 Hen VI f.26 pl.10.

[42] per Vavasour J. in a moot, *c.*1494, 102 SS 117 (B&M 585).

[43] *Rikhill's Case*, YB M.2 Hen IV f.11 pl.48; YB M.11 Hen IV f.25 pl.48; YB T.11 Hen IV f.82 pl.28.   [44] YB T.33 Hen VI f.26 pl.10.

[45] Baker, *Spelman's Reports, ii* (94 SS), 232–6, esp. 232–3.

[46] *Yevance* v. *Holcombe* (1566) Dyer 250, 3 Leon 13 (B&M 587); *Beswick* v. *Cunden* (1596) Cro El 520; *Crattendon's Case* (1598) BL MS Add 25223 f.86ᵛ.

[47] *Aston's Case* (1585) Dyer 250 in marg; *Anon* (1587) HLS MS 16 ff.355, 401ᵛ (B&M 588); *Leveret* v. *Townsend* (1590) Cro El 198, 3 Leo 263; *Alston* v. *Pamplyn* (1596) Cro El 466*; *Penifield's Case* (1596) IT MS Barr 13 f.171.

The issue was brought to a head in *Cantrell* v. *Church*, argued in the Court of Exchequer Chamber in 1601 on a writ of error from the King's Bench.[48] Here there was an ambiguity in the plaintiff's declaration, so that it did not appear whether or not the assize would have lain. So far as the King's Bench was concerned, this was no matter, for the plaintiff would be entitled to use the action on the case in any event. The Exchequer Chamber, where the Common Pleas judges formed the majority, was more uncertain; at first it inclined to hold that the plaintiff should have shown that the assize could not have lain, so that the ambiguity in the declaration should be resolved against him, but after further argument the majority came down on the side of the plaintiff. In formal terms, there was no relaxation of the rule that the action on the case could not lie where an assize could have been brought, but in practical terms the field in which the assize held exclusive sway was vanishingly small; and, so long as the plaintiff took care not to reveal that the older action might have lain, there was little scope for the defendant to object to the use of the action on the case. The formal separation of the actions was maintained until well into the seventeenth century, but in practice *Cantrell* v. *Church* marked the triumph of the action on the case over the assize of nuisance.[49]

There is a serious point to this formalism. The concentration on the boundary between the action on the case and the assize of nuisance meant that, as the *tort* of nuisance was consolidated, it did not wholly escape the shackles of the old thinking and remained firmly the tort of *nuisance*. So far as private nuisance was concerned it was still primarily concerned with damage to the plaintiff's land and interference with the enjoyment of it,[50] and so far as public nuisance was concerned it was still centred around the blocking of roads and the diversion of watercourses. Just as the assize of nuisance had been (and was) concerned with the protection of the plaintiff's rights, so too in the action on the case there was considerable discussion of which of the plaintiff's interests should be protected. A person claiming damages for the interference with the flow of water to his watermill would have to show a right to the water, whether this be by prescription, prior appropriation, or as a right necessarily appurtenant to the

---

[48] LI MS Misc 492 f.224ᵛ (B&M 588), more accurate than the brief report in Cro El 845.

[49] Though the older actions continued to retain vitality for several centuries in certain situations, such as where the plaintiff wanted a formal order to abate the nuisance and not simply damages (cf. Vin Abr, *Nusance*, I.2 in marg: 'The diversity between a quod permittat, or an assise for a nusance, and an action upon the case for the nusance is, that a quod permittat and a writ of assise are to abate the nusance; but an action on the case is only to recover damages'). It was only in the second half of the nineteenth century, with the convergence of Common law and Equity, that there was power to award an injunction in an action on the case.

[50] Baker, *Spelman's Reports*, ii (94 SS), *235*, citing George Treherne's reading in Lincoln's Inn, 1520.

enjoyment of land;[51] and a person claiming in respect of the stench coming from his neighbour's pigsty had first to show that he had a right to clean air.[52] Not all of the plaintiff's interest in the enjoyment of land was protected, but only those parts that were economically valuable, so that a person might complain of an interference with light but not of the blocking of a view.[53]

At the same time, though, by 1600 nuisance was quintessentially a tort, trespass on the case having to all intents and purposes taken over from the assize of nuisance. This meant that the primary focus of the action was the causation of loss. It was normal to stress this in the pleadings by alleging that the defendant had caused some specific loss to the plaintiff;[54] it was probably necessary to allege that the plaintiff was seised of the injured property at the time when the wrong was committed, not simply at the time when the action was brought;[55] and the time at which the wrong was committed was when the injury was caused to the plaintiff, not when the defendant did the act complained of.[56] It followed from this that no action should have lain for the interference with a right unless the interference had caused loss to the plaintiff.[57] In the same way, the action would lie only against a defendant who had committed the nuisance. In *Moore* v. *Browne*, for example, the defendant's husband had tapped into the main water pipe leading from the fountain at Clerkenwell to the plaintiff's house; after the husband's death the defendant had continued to draw water intermittently, and an action was brought against her; leaving aside certain technical points of pleading, it was held that the action might lie, but only because each turning-on of the tap constituted a separate diversion of the water from the pipe.[58] The result would have been different if the husband had diverted the water into a culvert from which the widow had continued to draw water, for here it would have been said that she was merely taking advantage of the nuisance that had already been committed by her

---

[51] *Russell* v. *Handford* (1583) 1 Leon 273; *Smith* v. *Babb* (1588) 4 Leon 93; *Luttrel's Case* (1601) 4 Co Rep 84b; *Sury* v. *Pigot* (1625) Poph 166, 3 Bulst 339, Jones 145, Latch 153, Noy 84, Palm 444.　　　　　[52] *Aldred's Case* (1610) 9 Co Rep 57b.

[53] *Bland* v. *Moseley* (1587), cited in *Aldred's Case* (1610) 9 Co Rep 57b, 58–58b; *Hales' Case* (c.1570), per Manwood, published as *A Briefe Declaration for what manner of speciall Nusance concerning private dweling Houses, a man may have his remedy by Assise, or other Action as the Case requires* (1636), 20–1.

[54] Cf. e.g. the pleadings in *Luttrel's Case* (1601) 4 Co Rep 84b.

[55] *Moore* v. *Browne* (1572) Dyer 319b, Benl 215, CP 40/1304 m.930. After judgment for the plaintiff a writ of error was brought to the King's Bench, but apparently not proceeded with: KB 27/1249 m.99.　　　　　[56] *Westbourne* v. *Mordaunt* (1590) Cro El 191.

[57] In such a case, if the plaintiff wanted to bring an action (to prevent the defendant establishing a prescriptive right, for example), the appropriate remedy was the avowedly proprietary writ *Quod Permittat*.

[58] (1572) Dyer 319b, Benl 215. See also *Beswick* v. *Cunden* (1595) Cro El 402; *Beswick* v. *Cunden (no 2)* (1596) Cro El 520.

husband.[59] Behind this trespassory dimension of the action lay the analytical assumption that the defendant must have been in breach of some duty, expressed in the Latin maxim *Sic utere tuo ut alienum non laedas*—'So use your own property as not to injure another's'.[60] As a positive test for the scope of liability this was singularly unhelpful: it was far too broad in the suggestion that any interference whatsoever with the neighbour's enjoyment was actionable, but gave no further guidance as to what the correct test should be. It did, however, make the useful negative point that a landowner's right of exploitation of the land was not untrammelled: 'But peradventure it will be sayd, The soyle is his owne, and it is *Damnum absque iniuria*, what then though it be his owne he must so use it, that hee hurt not his neighbour.'[61]

The final question, still not fully resolved today, is whether nuisance constituted a single tort. Although the form of action was the same and the institutional writers treat the tort as an entity, it is difficult to ignore the internal division between private and public nuisances, reflecting their very different antecedents.[62] Most obviously, while private nuisance was always about the interference with the enjoyment of land, public nuisance had no such narrow rule.[63] Unlike private nuisance, public nuisance was concerned with the antisocial nature of the defendant's behaviour; hence it would be relevant to look at the needfulness of the defendant's conduct, or its appropriateness to a particular location.[64] And in private nuisance the plaintiff who had shown actionable damage would be successful; in public nuisance it was necessary to show in addition that the plaintiff's damage was over and above that which was suffered by the generality of people, for otherwise it would have been appropriate to proceed by presentment in the court leet.[65]

---

[59] Thus it could be said that an action on the case lay against the person who continued a nuisance, but continuation involved some positive act (*Rippon* v. *Bowles* (1615) 1 Rolle 221, Cro Jac 373; *Brent* v. *Haddon* (1619) Cro Jac 555). By contrast, the proprietary *Quod Permittat* lay even without a positive act, though here it was necessary to show that the defendant had had notice of the nuisance (*Rolf's Case* (1583) cited at Cro El 402; *Penruddock's Case* (1598) 5 Co Rep 100).

[60] *Aldred's Case* (1610) 9 Co Rep 57b, 59, describes it as a 'rule of law and reason', though its precise source remains obscure. It underpins the arguments for both sides in *Hales' Case* (above, n.53).   [61] *Hales' Case* (above, n.53), 2–3, per Mounson.

[62] e.g. Co Litt 56a; 2 Inst 406: 'Nocumentum est triplex; 1. publicum sive generale. 2. Commune. 3. Privatum sive speciale.' For Common nuisances, see below, n.65.

[63] So in YB M.27 Hen VIII f.27 pl.10 it was said by Fitzherbert J. that, if a man digs a ditch across the highway which I fall into at night, I will have an action on my case against him.

[64] *Rankett's Case* (1605) 2 Ro Abr 139, *Nusans*, F2; *Anon* (1618) 2 Ro Abr 137, *Nusans*, B1–3.

[65] YB M.27 Hen VIII f.27 pl.10; *Fineux* v. *Hovenden* (1599) Cro El 664. There was no such requirement of particular damage in the case of a common nuisance, a public nuisance that was for some reason not prosecutable in the court leet: *Westbury* v. *Powell* (cited in *Fineux* v. *Hovenden*).

TROVER AND CONVERSION

Just as the use of the action on the case translated nuisance into an unequivocally tortious framework, so the development of the action on the case for conversion gave a similarly tortious skeleton to the protection of moveable property.[66] The parallels between the developments of nuisance and conversion are marked: both involved the supersession of older remedies (in the case of conversion the action of detinue) first of all by accretion around the edges of the older action and then by wholesale replacement of it; both pulled the law in the direction of a wrong-based analysis away from a right-based one; but both retained much of the structure of the earlier law.

It has already been noted that the action of detinue took on a more proprietary aspect in the fourteenth century, with considerable consequences for the conceptual structure of contractual liability.[67] Between the middle of the fourteenth century and the middle of the fifteenth, the action underwent an internal division.[68] On the one hand was detinue on a bailment, whose scope was wide enough to include claims for the non-delivery of goods sold. The claim here, although with a strong proprietary aspect, maintained a contractual dimension[69] and it was no defence that the goods did not in fact belong to the plaintiff, nor (without further explanation) that they did not exist.[70] On the other hand, there was the writ of detinue not based on any antecedent transaction; the plaintiff might explain how it was that the goods had come into the defendant's possession, but it was not necessary to do so, and by 1455 this had degenerated into a standard allegation that they had been lost by the plaintiff and found by the defendant.[71] It did not matter what the plaintiff said: no issue could be taken on the accuracy of the story, for the only question was whether the defendant had the plaintiff's thing. This claim, known as 'trover'— finding—in its final form, was substantially more proprietary than the count on a bailment. Here not only was the claim for a specific thing, but it might also be a defence that it was not the plaintiff's thing or that it had been destroyed.

---

[66] Fifoot, *History and Sources of the Common Law*, 102–5; A. W. B. Simpson, 'The Introduction of the Action on the Case for Conversion' (1959) 71 LQR 364; Baker, *Spelman's Reports, ii* (94 SS), *248–53*; J. L. Barton, 'Remedies for Chattels', in E. W. Ives and A. H. Manchester (eds.), *Law, Litigants and the Legal Profession* (London, 1983), 30.

[67] Above, p.34.

[68] See in particular YB T.29 Edw III f.38 and YB T.33 Hen VI f.26 pl.12, well explained by Milsom, *Historical Foundations*, 272–5.

[69] Barton, 'Remedies for Chattels, in Ives and Manchester (eds.), *Law, Litigants and the Legal Profession*, 30, 32.

[70] Above, p.94; YB M.5 Edw III f.38 pl.24 at ff.39–40; YB M.3 Hen VI f.19 pl.31.

[71] YB T.33 Hen VI f.26 pl.12.

The separation off of the trover count from the count on a bailment provided an opportunity for English law to develop detinue as a straightforward proprietary remedy for the recovery of chattels analogous to the Romans' *vindicatio*.[72] The opportunity was not taken. Towards the end of the fifteenth century plaintiffs began to experiment with a new form of trespass on the case, the action of conversion. This had the advantage of forcing the defendant to trial by jury, removing the option of wager of law, which was present in detinue, and could deal with situations that might have been awkward if detinue had been employed: where the goods had been transformed into something else or had otherwise been destroyed, or where the defendant returned the goods in a damaged condition.[73] Instead of basing the action on the defendants' detention of property, plaintiffs complained of the defendants' wrong in 'converting' the goods to their own use. At first the action was used against bailees and sellers of goods;[74] but in the early sixteenth century plaintiffs began to allege that the defendants had found the goods, using exactly the same fiction as had been established in detinue in the fifteenth century.[75]

As had occurred with liability in nuisance, and as was to occur in other areas too, the establishment of the action of conversion as a substitute for the action of detinue was achieved only after considerable hesitation over the permissibility of using an action on the case when another action was available on the same facts. Superficially, the purely formal objection here was relatively easy to dismiss: since detinue was an essentially proprietary remedy, aiming at the recovery of the thing itself, it was possible to distinguish this from the purely personal action for damages for wrongful conduct that was the action of conversion,[76] though, as elsewhere, the Court of Common Pleas was more reluctant to allow the action if detinue would have lain.[77] Plaintiffs in detinue affirmed their property rights; plaintiffs in conversion claimed that they had been deprived of them.[78] The formal problem of keeping the boundary between conversion and trespass *vi et armis* was similarly sidestepped in practice: although in

---

[72] And, apparently, it might have been so described: R. H. Helmholz, 'Canonical Defamation in Medieval England' (1971) 15 Am Jnl Leg Hist 255, 261 n.30.

[73] Simpson, 'Action on the Case for Conversion' (1959) 75 LQR 364, 375.

[74] *Rilston* v. *Holbek*, YB M.12 Edw IV f.13 pl.9 (B&M 524); *Calwodelegh* v. *John*, YB H.18 Edw IV f.23 pl.5 (B&M 526); *Orwell* v. *Mortoft*, YB M.20 Hen VII f.8 pl.18, Keil 69, 77 (B&M 406).   [75] Baker, *Spelman's Reports, ii* (94 SS), 251–3.

[76] *Bourgchier* v. *Cheseman* (1504–8), YB M.20 Hen VII f.4 pl.13, 94 SS *249–50*; *Anon* (1510) Keil 160 pl.2; *Knight* v. *Bourne* (1588) Cro El 116; cf. *Pykeryng* v. *Thurgoode* (1532) 93 SS 4. See Baker, *Spelman's Reports, ii* (94 SS), *248–50*; Simpson, 'Action on the Case for Conversion' (1959) 71 LQR 364, 375.

[77] *Mounteagle* v. *Countess of Worcester* (1555) Dyer 121, 1 And 20, Benl 41 (B&M 531); *Anon* (1579) (B&M 533); *Anon* (1584) Benl 41 in marg.

[78] *Mounteagle* v. *Countess of Worcester* (1555) Dyer 121, 1 And 20, Benl 41 (B&M 531); *Countess of Rutland's Case* (1588) Moo 266; *Gumbleton* v. *Grafton* (1600) Cro El 781.

principle the action of trespass should have lain if the initial taking was wrongful and the action of conversion only if the initial taking was rightful but the subsequent use of the thing wrongful, it was held in the Common Pleas in *Bishop* v. *Viscountess Montague*[79] that the plaintiff was entitled to waive the wrongfulness of the initial taking—impliedly ratifying it—and hence bring the action of conversion for the subsequent misusing of the goods. But these were essentially formal responses to formal objections. The real question was what the plaintiff had to prove. The allegation that the defendant had found the goods—the trover—was easily dismissed as purely a matter of form, expressly by analogy with the action of detinue.[80] The conversion, though, was a different matter. Here there were two distinct lines of argument. The more radical, taken by some judges in the Court of King's Bench, was to assert that the allegation of conversion was only formal too, so that the action would lie whenever detinue would lie whether or not there had in fact been any positive conversion.[81] Less radically, though amounting in practice to the same thing, it was argued that some positive conversion was necessary, but a decidedly broad definition of what constituted a conversion was adopted.[82] Thus, in the leading case of *Easom* v. *Newman*[83] it was held in the King's Bench in 1595 that a 'finder' who had refused to deliver over the plaintiff's property when requested to do so was guilty of a conversion. The line between wrongfully detaining the plaintiff's goods, the cause of action in detinue, and wrongfully refusing to redeliver them, the minimal cause of action in conversion, was a fine one, and Popham C.J. is reported to have insisted on a more positive act of interference than a mere refusal to redeliver.[84] This difference of opinion was effectively laid to rest by the decision in *Isaac* v. *Clark* in 1614–15 that the refusal to redeliver did not in itself constitute a conversion, but that it was evidence from which the jury might infer a conversion.[85] This satisfied the theoretical niceties, maintaining the rule that some positive act of wrongdoing was essential, at the same time as solving the practical problem by leaving it in the hands of the jury.

The action of conversion, therefore, was able to establish its own niche,

---

[79] (1604) Cro El 824, Cro Jac 50 (B&M 540). The waiver of trespass as a justification for shifting to a different form of action or a different substantive legal category was to prove useful in the future: below, p.160.

[80] *Anon* (1579) (B&M 533), following YB P.27 Hen VIII f.13 pl.35.

[81] *Anon* (1579) (B&M 533); *Easom* v. *Newman* (1595) (below, n.83) at BL MS Harg 50 f.205ᵛ, per Clench J.

[82] *Anon* (1579) (B&M 533). Cf. *Anon* (1582) (B&M 534) (Common Pleas).

[83] Cro El 495; Goulds 152; Moo 460; HLS MS 110 f.218ᵛ (B&M 537). There is a version of the manuscript report, in places more comprehensible, in BL MS Harg 50 f.205ᵛ.

[84] Cro El 495.

[85] Moo 841; 1 Ro 59; 2 Bulst 306 (B&M 541). The same point was made in *The Case of the Chancellor of the University of Oxford* (1614) 10 Co Rep 53b, 56b–57a, and *Brook* v. *Miller* (1682) 2 Show 179.

formally independent of the older forms of action. In terms of substantive ideas, though, it was not so independent. Here its development mirrored almost exactly the development of the action on the case for nuisance: the adoption of many of the ideas inherent in the earlier forms of action, coupled with a skewing of them by their incorporation within an explicitly tortious framework.

The proprietary dimension of the action is transparent: the whole point of the action was to compensate for the divestment of property; if the plaintiff sued in conversion but showed merely that the goods had been damaged, the action would fail and a generic action on the case for damaging goods would have to be brought.[86] In order to succeed in the action, the plaintiff had to show 'property' in the goods, though the definition of 'property' retained and intensified the ambiguities of the concept earlier associated with the action of detinue. Whatever chance there might have been for the Common law to develop clear criteria assigning ownership in chattels,[87] the focus on the defendant's wrongdoing that was central to the action of conversion made it absolutely certain that no such development could take place, though it required a long time for these implications to be worked out. This is well revealed by the leading case of *Armory* v. *Delamirie* in 1722.[88] A chimney sweep's boy found a jewel and took it to the defendant goldsmith's shop. The defendant's apprentice removed the jewel from its setting, and told his master that the remaining socket was worth only a trifling sum. The defendant offered the boy this amount, but he refused it and demanded back the jewel. There was no question of the boy 'owning' the jewel, but as between him and the goldsmith the merits were clearly in his favour. A Civil lawyer would have had no difficulty in granting to him a claim *in personam* for damages, but denying him any proprietary claim; but the Common law ran the two together. The boy was entitled to damages; but the justification for this was that he had a 'property' in the goods that entitled him to keep them against anybody who had less right to them than he did. Because of this focus on the defendant's wrong rather than the plaintiff's right, English law has never in practice had to provide answers to many of the proprietary conundra dealt with by civil lawyers. From a purely intellectual point of view, such lack of concern with the taxonomy of legal claims and the identification of the whereabouts of ownership

[86] *Walgrave* v. *Ogden* (1590) Cro El 219, 1 Leon 224, Owen 141.
[87] Above, n.72. We cannot, of course, be sure that any such development would have taken place, but other legal systems did manage to make the transformation from an open-ended 'relative' ownership to a closed 'absolute' one. The best example is provided by Roman law: M. Kaser, 'The Concept of Roman Ownership' (1964) Tydskrif vir Hedendaagse Romeins-Hollandse Reg 5, discussed in G. Dyósdi, *Ownership in Ancient and Preclassical Roman Law* (Budapest, 1970), 94–106.   [88] 1 Str 505.

smacks of a high degree of sloppiness of thought; from a practical point of view, it is beyond reproach.[89]

But if the action of conversion can be seen as a proprietary remedy skewed by its positioning in the law of tort, it can no less be seen as a trespassory—tortious—remedy skewed by its proprietary underpinnings. Its trespassory aspect can be seen in many places. It was an action *in personam* in which the plaintiff claimed damages in respect of a wrong that had been committed: unlike in the action of detinue, the defendant in an action of conversion could not avoid liability by returning the goods to the plaintiff; it was merely a matter to be taken into account in mitigation of damages.[90] Again unlike the practice in the action of detinue, where the measure of damages was the value of the thing detained, damages in conversion were at large and had to be assessed by a jury.[91] If it was found that the defendant had merely failed to hand over goods to the plaintiff when requested to do so, without committing any positive act denying title, no action of conversion would lie.[92] As a trespassory remedy conversion was not passively transmissible—*Actio Personalis moritur cum Persona*—and it followed that it could not lie against an executor for an act of conversion committed by the testator, though an action of detinue (being essentially proprietary in its nature) might lie in appropriate circumstances.[93]

A further consequence of the interplay between ideas of property and ideas of tort can be seen in the place of fault within liability in conversion.[94] There was no difficulty in accepting that a person in possession of property belonging to another might be justified in refusing to deliver it over: the property might have been lawfully seized by a sheriff or distrained by a creditor, or it might be the object of a lien, for example. This had been so in the action of detinue, and the same principles continued in force in the action of conversion. The only difference, a difference in form rather than substance, was that in detinue these reasons were conceived of as justifications entitling the defendant to detain the plaintiff's goods, whereas in conversion they were treated as going to the root of the action and negativing the conversion itself. In practice this did not matter a great deal. More problematic, though, was the case where the defendant had

---

[89] Cf. e.g. the inconclusive mess of the Scots law of *specificatio*: D. J. Osler, 'Specificatio in Scots Law', in R. Evans-Jones (ed.), *The Civil Law Tradition in Scotland* (Edinburgh, 1995), 100–28.

[90] *Countess of Rutland's Case* (1596) Moo 266 pl.416; cf. *Knight* v. *Bourne* (1588) Cro El 116. The fact that the point was worth discussing at all shows just how close to the surface the proprietary dimension of the action was. [91] Baker, *Spelman's Reports, ii* (94 SS), *248.*

[92] *Isaac* v. *Clark* (1614) 1 Ro 59, 60, citing *Thimblethorpe's Case.*

[93] *Baily* v. *Birtles* (1663) T Raym 71.

[94] T. A. Street, *Foundations of Legal Liability* (Northport, NY, 1906), 1.238–9; Fifoot, *History and Sources of the Common Law*, 107–8; J. Oldham, *The Mansfield Manuscripts* (Chapel Hill, NY, 1992), 1171–81.

acted in good faith in refusing to hand over the goods to the plaintiff or in disposing of them. Thus in *Gallyard* v. *Archer* the Court of Common Pleas was divided on the question whether a bona fide purchaser of cloth, who had sold it believing himself to be the true owner, could be liable in conversion.[95] The better view, probably, was that he could not be.[96] By the early years of the seventeenth century, though, it could be said that any unjustifiable intermeddling with another's goods amounted to a conversion.[97] Much depended, of course, on what it was that made a meddling 'unjustifiable', though the standard practice of pleading not guilty rather than raising special justifications resulted in the sidestepping of many potentially revealing discussions of this question. It was, perhaps, not until the decision in *Cooper* v. *Chitty* in 1755[98] that the proprietary aspect of the action finally led to its being explicitly analysed in terms of strict liability:

The plaintiffs here have a right, and must have a remedy against somebody.[99]

A man may, without his own fault, be possessed of a horse which has been stolen; but nevertheless, he is answerable, civiliter to the true owner for it.[100]

The action of trover is in form a fiction, but in fact, and substance, a remedy given the subject, to recover a personal property . . . It is called in our law an action of tort, but the conversion is the whole tort.[101]

TORT AND REPUTATION: DEFAMATION

Just as the action on the case for nuisance and the action of conversion took over much of the structure of the previous law of nuisance and detinue but transformed it into a trespassory mould, so also the action on the case for defamation developed in the sixteenth century by relocating a body of existing law within the action of trespass on the case. Here, though, the

---

[95] (1589) 1 Leon 189 (B&M 535). It is not easy to disentangle the substantive question from the purely formal one whether the defendant was entitled to confess and avoid, pleading that he did not know that the cloth was the plaintiff's, rather than simply pleading the general issue. Cf. *Vandrink* v. *Archer* (1590) 1 Leon 221; *Gybson* v. *Garbyn* (1596) Cro El 480.

[96] This conclusion is strongly supported by the nature of the demurrer in *Gybson* v. *Garbyn* (last note; KB 27/1336 m.1060). Garbyn pleaded, essentially, that he had come into possession of Gybson's cloth in good faith and sold it before he had any notice of his alleged interest. To this Gybson demurred; not on the grounds that the plea was irrelevant and equivalent to an admission of liability, but on the grounds that it amounted to the general issue.

[97] *Gomersall* v. *Medgate* (1610) Yelv 194.

[98] 1 Keny 395, 1 W Bl 65, 1 Burr 20. Cf. the marginally more defendant-conscious approach of *Baily* v. *Bunning* (1665) 1 Sid 271, 1 Keb 932, 2 Keb 32, 1 Lev 173, and *Cole* v. *Davies* (1698) 1 Ld Raym 724. Note especially the remarks of Kelyng C.J. in the former case at 1 Keb 933.

[99] 1 Keny 395, 397 per Norton in argument.

[100] 1 Burr 20, 22 per Norton in argument.

[101] 1 Keny 395, 417 per Lord Mansfield C.J.

earlier law was not to be found in the royal courts at all, but in the ecclesiastical courts.[102]

The ecclesiastical law of defamation had its base in the Constitution *Auctoritate Dei Patris* made at Oxford in 1222, which provided a remedy for the 'malicious' imputation of a crime.[103] The fifteenth-century English canon lawyer William Lyndwood stressed that the law was concerned with allegations of criminality, not of mere 'defects' such as leprosy or bastardy,[104] and there is no doubt that this was the focal case of ecclesiastical defamation even if in practice the ecclesiastical courts might have been willing to push the boundaries of criminality so as to include cases such as these or (from the mid-fifteenth century) to give a remedy in cases of more general abuse.[105] On the complainants' side the whole stress of the action was on loss of credit and good name: they would invariably begin by stating that they were of good fame and reputation, though it does not seem to have been a specific defence that the complainant had no reputation to speak of;[106] the allegedly defamatory words must have lowered the complainant in the eyes of right-thinking people (*apud bonos et graves*); according to the Constitution the complainant must have been injured by the imputation of the crime, though in this context injury rarely meant any more than the loss of the good opinion of one's neighbours; and the whole purpose of the action was the restoration of the lost credit and the punishment of the wrongdoer, not the recovery of damages.[107] The Constitution's stress on the wrongdoer's malice similarly pulled the focus away from any loss suffered by the victim. The core sense of 'malice' was fairly clearly spiteful intent, but its outer boundaries are obscured by the fact that in most situations it would be impossible to discover this intent so that it had

[102] Defamation was also the subject of actions in local courts in the thirteenth and fourteenth centuries, but this jurisdiction had largely died out by 1400. It had, therefore, little if any influence on the development of the tort of defamation in the royal courts. In practice, as well, the law of the local courts seems to have mirrored fairly accurately the law of the ecclesiastical courts. For the local courts, see R. H. Helmholz, *Select Cases on Defamation to 1600* (101 SS), pp.xlviii–lxv.

[103] For what follows, see Helmholz, *Select Cases on Defamation* (101 SS), pp.xiv–xli; and 'Canonical Defamation in Medieval England' (1971) 15 Am Jnl Leg Hist 255.

[104] W. Lyndwood, *Provinciale*, V.17 gl. ad verb. malitiose (1679 edn., p.346).

[105] Helmholz, *Select Cases on Defamation* (101 SS), pp.xxviii–xxx.

[106] Though it may perhaps have been a defence that the complainant had been earlier defamed of the same crime (a view criticized by Lyndwood, *Provinciale*, V.17 gl. ad verb. unde (1679 edn., p.347)) so that a defendant repeating common gossip might be exonerated. Helmholz, *Select Cases on Defamation* (101 SS), pp.xxxv–xxxvi, seems not to draw a sharp enough distinction between prior bad fame generally (which was probably not a defence) and prior bad fame of this offence (which possibly was).

[107] The ecclesiastical courts were forbidden to award damages, but we may suspect that in practice an informal (and hence unrecorded) monetary composition might have been made between the parties in exchange for the malefactor's being released from the canonical penalty: Helmholz, *Select Cases on Defamation* (101 SS), p.xl; 'Canonical Defamation' (1971) 15 Am Jnl Leg Hist 255, 264–8.

to be inferred or presumed from the circumstances, and considerable latitude was given to judges in doing this. All we can do is to indicate a range of situations that were close to the boundary, but probably regarded as outside the range of malicious conduct: words spoken in anger and not repeated; words uttered under provocation; words uttered in judicial pro-ceedings with a view to bringing a wrongdoer to justice; the following-up of the words with an immediate apology; words spoken by way of private reproof.[108]

It was only at the beginning of the sixteenth century that the royal courts began to take jurisdiction over cases of defamation, though the earlier Common law had allowed for defamation-like actions in certain well-defined situations: *scandalum magnatum* (the making of false statements about great men); the publication of false documents with a view to threatening another's title to land; claiming a free man as one's villein; conspiring to indict an innocent person; and false imprisonment.[109] These provided a climate, no doubt, in which actions for defamation might be brought in the royal courts, but the immediate springboard for the accept-ance of a wider jurisdiction was the belief that it was improper for the ecclesiastical courts to take cognisance of defamations involving allega-tions of secular crimes, since it was only the secular courts who could determine whether or not the allegations were true. From the last decades of the fifteenth century writs of prohibition had issued to stop such suits,[110] with the result that there was a perceived gap that had to be filled. Hence, starting in the Common Pleas in 1507, the royal courts came to allow an action on the case to be brought when the defendant had defamed the plaintiff by making an allegation of the commission of a crime.[111]

From the start the contours of the action on the case were closely modelled on the ecclesiastical action, though it was several decades before pleaders ventured confidently far beyond those situations that would have grounded an action in the secular courts in the fifteenth century.[112] The declaration would begin with an allegation that the plaintiff was of good reputation, which had been damaged by the defendant's defamatory words. For some time the allegation was always of the commission of a crime.[113] It

[108] Helmholz, *Select Cases on Defamation* (101 SS), pp.xxxii–xxxiv.
[109] Ibid., pp.lxviii–lxix. The first two categories were provided by Statute (Westminster 1 (1275) c.34 and Stat 1 Hen V c.3 respectively), while the last three could be seen as types of trespasses.
[110] Helmholz, *Select Cases on Defamation* (101 SS), pp.xliii–xlv. An example in the Year Books is YB T.22 Edw IV f.20 pl.47.
[111] *Owughan* v. *Baker* (1507) 101 SS 42; the first case in the King's Bench was *Sparowe* v. *Heygrene* (1508) 101 SS 42.
[112] Helmholz, *Select Cases on Defamation* (101 SS), pp.lxxii–lxiv, lxxvi–lxxix.
[113] Baker, *Spelman's Reports*, ii (94 SS), 242–4; cf. Helmholz, *Select Cases on Defamation* (101 SS), pp.lxxxviii–xcii.

had to have been false. The defendant must have acted maliciously; and, in so far as the boundaries of the concept of malice were defined, they were essentially indistinguishable from those found in the ecclesiastical courts.[114] As with the ecclesiastical action, malice would be presumed if the words complained of were shown to be untrue; it was for the defendant to show that, despite appearances, they had not been uttered maliciously. Although there may have been a tendency for similar cases to be bunched together and take on the appearance of specific defences—no action would lie for otherwise actionable words spoken by a lawyer in the course of legal proceedings, for example[115]—there was no exclusive list of such situations, no restriction on the general right of defendants to deny that they had spoken out of spite or ill-will. Thus in *Grymwood* v. *Prike*[116] a parson (new to the parish) who repeated a story from Fox's *Book of Martyrs*, said to have taken place in the neighbouring town, in his Christmas sermon against perjury was sued by a member of his congregation with the same name as the alleged perjurer; he pleaded that nothing he had said had referred to the plaintiff—nor could it have done so, since, according to the *Book of Martyrs*, the wrath of God had fallen on Grymwood, 'for not long after his bowels gushed out of his belly and so died'—and Anderson C.J. held that no action should lie since the words had not been spoken maliciously. It was equally possible to defend oneself on the grounds that the words had been spoken out of charity to a friend of the plaintiff, or that they had been spoken under provocation.[117]

The move from the ecclesiastical courts to the secular courts, however, did bring with it one substantial new element: since the action was trespassory in nature, it lay for the recovery of damages rather than the punishment of the offender or the clearing of the victim's name. While it would be an exaggeration to regard damage as the gist of the secular action,[118] it was more skewed in this direction than the ecclesiastical action had been. In the sixteenth century the Star Chamber might have been able to take over this palinodial aspect of the ecclesiastical jurisdiction,[119] but after the abolition of that court and the disappearance of the ecclesiastical jurisdiction English law was to be left with no action available to individuals

[114] Helmholz, *Select Cases on Defamation* (101 SS), pp.cx–cxi.
[115] *Nicolas* v. *Badger* (1596) CUL MS Gg 5.3 f.87; *Brook* v. *Montague* (1605) Cro Jac 90.
[116] (1585) Ro Abr 1.87, *Action sur Case* M5; BL MS Add 24845 f.164; KB 27/1291 m.389d. The reports are both brief and confused, and it is possible that there were two separate actions. The version of the case given by Coke in argument in *Brook* v. *Montague* (1605) Cro Jac 90, 91 is inaccurate.   [117] Helmholz, *Select Cases on Defamation* (101 SS), p.cxi.
[118] Holdsworth, *History of English Law*, 8.335.
[119] There is a good description of the mode of apology that might be insisted on by the Star Chamber—with due humility before the judges of assize—in *Acton* v. *Fane* (1598) C2/Eliz1/A7/38 (a Chancery suit arising in the wake of doubts whether the defendant had apologized properly).

who wished simply to clear their names of some defamatory slur rather than to sue for substantial damages.[120] The Common law's stress on damages does not necessarily point to its remedy being purely compensatory: jury awards—then as now—might be so enormous as to leave the reader with the suspicion that they were directed at punishing the defendant as much as compensating the plaintiff.[121] The fact that, until 1622, the judges claimed and exercised an effective power to reduce excessive jury awards points in the same direction.[122]

At a purely formal level all the requirement of damage meant was that it had to be alleged in the plaintiff's declaration that some temporal loss had been suffered, though this was not traversable and rapidly degenerated into a standard-form statement, so that a plaintiff who had in fact suffered no loss might still recover damages at whatever level the jury chose to award them. Nowhere do we find any suggestion that there was anything wrong with the award of an exiguous sum by way of nominal damages: the plaintiff was entitled to judgment, notwithstanding the apparent finding of the jury that no temporal loss had in fact been suffered.[123]

There were, though, substantive consequences too, most importantly the fixing of the requirement that the words should have been published to a third party. Publication had been an essential feature of the ecclesiastical action;[124] and, so far as the secular action was concerned, the requirement of malice was easier to establish where the words had been spoken to somebody other than the plaintiff.[125] The loss-based focus of the action on the case gave added weight to these. At first there was no absolute requirement of publication if loss could be established in some other way: 'If I say to a man that he has robbed me of so much, and it is not so, if no

---

[120] Cf. Zimmermann, *Obligations*, 1072–4, for the way in which continental legal systems were able to develop the *amende honorable* alongside the compensatory action.

[121] e.g. *Lassells* v. *Lassells* (1595) BL MS Add 25198 12ᵛ, 17 (cited by R. H. Helmholz, 'Damages in Actions for Slander at Common Law' (1987) 103 LQR 624, 633 n.46), where £250 was awarded to a father (a Justice of the Peace) whose son had accused him of being an accessory to theft. Later, but yet more striking, is the reported award of £100,000 in an action of *scandalum magnatum* in *Duke of York* v. *Pilkington* (1682) 2 Show KB 246; the fact that the plaintiff was heir apparent to the throne and the defendant Lord Mayor of London may perhaps not have been irrelevant. The award was described by Bishop Burnet as 'the most excessive that had ever been given' (*History of My Own Time* (London, 1724), 1.536). See further *Howell's State Trials*, 9.299.

[122] Helmholz, 'Damages in Actions for Slander' (1987) 103 LQR 624. There was a view that they might increase an inadequate award, though it was not uncontroverted and there is little evidence of its having been exercised. The reversal of the practice of judicial control occurred in *Hawkins* v. *Sciet* (1622) Palmer 314, 2 Rolle 243.

[123] Helmholz, 'Damages in Actions for Slander' (1987) 103 LQR 624, 634.

[124] Helmholz, *Select Cases on Defamation* (101 SS), pp.xxxiv–xxxv.

[125] *Boughton* v. *Bishop of Coventry and Lichfield* (1584) BL MS Harl 4562 f.1, f.2, per Fleetwood Sjt; *Hungerford's Case* (1593) BL MS Lansd 1067 f.181. In the same way defendants sometimes alleged that they had spoken the words out of charity to a friend of the plaintiff, and hence not maliciously: Helmholz, *Select Cases on Defamation* (101 SS), p.cxi.

one hears this he will not have an action, even if he alleges that he was damaged by it. But if he says to him that if he encounters him he will arrest him for the same felony, for which cause he does not dare go about his business, then an action well lies.'[126] Gradually, though, it became a firm requirement. By the end of the sixteenth century, at least where the defamatory words were not written, it had matured into a rule: in the absence of publication, the defendant would not be liable.[127] This took longer to become established in cases where the alleged defamation was in writing than where the words were spoken. In the second half of the sixteenth century it seems to have been accepted that the recipient of a defamatory letter might maintain an action for damages against the writer without any additional publication to a third party.[128] These cases probably proceeded by analogy with the criminal jurisdiction exercised by the Court of Star Chamber, where no publication to a third party was required,[129] for it was argued that in any case where a man could be punished for injuring another the victim might bring an action for damages in his own name.[130] This connection was brought into the open in the early seventeenth century in *Edwards* v. *Wooton*[131] and *Hickes' Case*;[132] in both cases the Star Chamber explicitly stated that its rule was different from that applied in the action on the case. By this time, therefore, we may say that publication to a third party had become fixed as a general requirement of the action on the case for defamation.

A second consequence was that the secular action for defamatory words had a strong potential to expand beyond allegations of the commission of crimes to other situations where the defendant's words had caused loss to the plaintiff.[133] The normally conservative Anderson C.J., at the end of the sixteenth century, got close to formulating this within a general principle of tortious liability: 'it would be against all reason that the party should have loss and damage from such words and no remedy.'[134] Had Anderson's view

---

[126] James Hales' Reading on the Statute of Costs (1537) 101 SS 76 (B&M 345, 348).
[127] *Hall* v. *Hemmsly* (1596) Cro El 486, Noy 57; *Taylor* v. *How* (1601) Cro El 861. Note too the rule that, where the words had been spoken in a foreign language, it was essential that the plaintiff allege and prove that the words had been heard by speakers of that language: *Jones* v. *Davers* (1596) Cro El 496 (Latin), *Price* v. *Jenkins* (1601) Cro El 865 (Welsh).
[128] *Lumley* v. *Ford* (1568) KB 27/1227 m.221, cited Moo 142 (damages of 1,000 marks awarded by the jury); *Bishop of Norwich* v. *Brickhill* (1582), both cited without criticism in *Boughton* v. *Bishop of Coventry and Lichfield* (1584), below, n.140.
[129] *De Famosis Libellis* (1605) 5 Co Rep 125.
[130] W. Hudson, *A Treatise of the Court of Star Chamber*, in F. Hargrave, *Collectanea Juridica* (1792) 2.1, 101–2; *Boughton* v. *Bishop of Coventry and Lichfield* (1584) Bodl MS Rawl C 85 f.52, f.52ᵛ, per Fleetwood Sjt.
[131] (1607) 12 Co Rep 35; J. Hawarde, *Les Reportes del Cases in Camera Stellata* (ed. W. P. Baildon, 1894), 343, 344.   [132] (1618) Poph 139, Hob 215.
[133] The same phenomenon can be seen in medieval local courts: Helmholz, *Select Cases on Defamation* (101 SS), p.lvii.
[134] *Holwood* v. *Hopkins* (1600) 101 SS 89, 91. Cf. the remarks of Littleton J. in *Hulle* v. *Orynge* (*The Case of Thorns*) YB M.6 Edw IV f.7 pl.18, quoted above, p.58.

prevailed, the Common law at the beginning of the seventeenth century might have moved towards the assimilation of liability for words and liability for acts, which has in fact occurred in the second half of the twentieth century.[135]

But Anderson's view did not prevail. Two important factors militated against him. First of all there was the gravitational force exercised by the older ecclesiastical action. Just as the action on the case for nuisance retained the basic structure of the older assize of nuisance and the action on the case for trover and conversion retained the proprietary ideas of the action of detinue, so too the action on the case for defamation did not easily cut loose from its ecclesiastical antecedents.[136] Such extensions as did occur were both tentative and hard won. Secondly, there was the practical problem stemming from the rule that the allegation of damage suffered was not issuable and could not be traversed by the defendant,[137] coupled with the reluctance of the sixteenth-century judges to examine juries to see if the loss alleged by the plaintiff had in fact occurred.[138] This meant that the causation of loss could not be used as the criterion to distinguish between actionable and non-actionable utterances, but was at best a background argument or justification for the existing rules.

The most obvious consequence of the non-traversability of the allegation of damage was that the expansive potential visible in the approach of Anderson C.J. in *Holwood* v. *Hopkins* had to be framed in terms not of the actual causation of loss but of the words' tendency to cause loss. Careful lawyers, or careful reporters, sometimes make this abundantly clear. In *Brook* v. *Watson*, for example, Henry Hobart formulated a principle that, 'whenever any words are maliciously spoken which might be the means to hinder the trade, profession, or preferment of the party against whom they are spoken, this is actionable'.[139] The same thrust is earlier seen

---

[135] Below, p.192.

[136] This is made graphically clear by the argument of Walmsley Sjt in *Boughton* v. *Bishop of Coventry and Lichfield* (1584) as reported in BL MS Add 35943 f.8ᵛ. He defines slander as 'factum vel dictum minus rectum alteri praebens occasionem ruine', a definition taken—as the reporter carefully and accurately notes in the margin of the report—from the fifteenth century canonist Summa Angelica. The reporter notes that the definition was at f.346, though I have not identified an edition with this foliation.

[137] *Russel's Case* (1537) Dyer 26. Cf. Baker, *Spelman's Reports, ii* (94 SS), *240*; James Hales's Reading on Costs (1537) 101 SS 76 (B&M 345, 348). It should be noted that in medieval local courts actual damage might have been necessary, so that plaintiffs who could not prove this would lose their action: Helmholz, *Select Cases on Defamation* (101 SS), p.lvii. A clear example is *Wakefield* v. *Brownsmith* in the Manor Court at Wakefield in 1306–8 (101 SS 31). This rule was general to all actions on the case.

[138] Below, n.164; Helmholz, *Select Cases on Defamation* (101 SS), p.civ.

[139] (1595) HLS MS 110 at f.119ᵛ: 'Quandocunque ascuns parolls sont parle malitiousment queux poient estre meanes de hinder le trade profession ou preferment de le partie vers que ils sont parle ceo est actionable.' Cf. Helmholz, *Select Cases on Defamation* (101 SS), pp.lxxxix–xc.

in the leading case of *Boughton* v. *Bishop of Coventry and Lichfield*.[140] The defendant had written a letter to the Earl of Leicester making allegations about the conduct of the plaintiff. The words used, such as that he was a 'vermin of the common weal' and a 'false and corrupt man', were not obviously actionable, and Sergeants Fleetwood and Gawdy were forced to argue that the court should take a more extensive approach to liability than had previously been done. The defendant was a bishop whose words would be 'credited like the Gospel'; hence words spoken by him had a greater tendency to do harm than words spoken by a common person. The letter had been sent to the Earl of Leicester, a person of influence, so that discredit in his eyes was more likely to be injurious than discredit in the eyes of a meaner subject. Even though the words were too general to bear an action on ordinary principles, here the special circumstances made them tend towards defaming the plaintiff, so an action on the case should lie notwithstanding this. All of these points look to the damaging tendency of the words used; any actual damage suffered could not be brought into issue. The Court of Common Pleas accepted these arguments and gave judgment for the plaintiff. While this was an unusually daring sally—normally they were reluctant to move far from cases in which liability had been recognized already—the arguments that motivated them were not untypical.

If liability were to be determined by looking at the injurious tendency of the words rather than their actual effects, it followed that lists could be made of words that were actionable and words that were not, and from the end of the sixteenth century the courts adopted more or less consistently a canon of construction that required the words to be interpreted in their least defamatory sense—the so-called *mitiori sensu* rule—whatever their natural meaning in the context in which they were uttered.[141] It is probably no accident that it is in defamation cases at this time that we see the first signs of the development of a doctrine of precedent based on the essentially binding authority of previous decisions.[142] Moreover, given the judges' conservative approach in defamation cases, these actionable words could be fitted more or less neatly into a small number of categories. Such categorization was not made explicit until the publication of John March's

---

[140] (1584) 1 And 119; 101 SS 64, 86. There are good manuscript reports in Bodl MS Rawl C 85 f.52; BL MS Harl 4562 f.1; BL MS Add 24845 ff.143, 147ᵛ, 149; BL MS Add 35949 ff.17, 21ᵛ. A writ of error was brought to the King's Bench in 1600: LI MS Misc 492 f.36. The case is discussed by Helmholz, *Select Cases on Defamation* (101 SS), pp.ci–ciii.

[141] Helmholz, *Select Cases on Defamation* (101 SS), pp.xcii–xcv. The rule is found in argument much earlier, but it was only around 1600 that the courts began to apply it consistently.

[142] See e.g. the strongly (and explicitly) precedent-based reasoning of the Common Pleas in *Holwood* v. *Hopkins* (1600) 101 SS 89.

Actions for Slaunder in 1647, but it is easily identifiable in the practice of the courts in the second half of the sixteenth century.

The most obvious of these categories was the allegations of a crime. This was the central case of defamation in the ecclesiastical courts, and it continued to be the most important category in the secular courts. Indeed, in the 1580s it was still worth arguing that words might be defamatory notwithstanding that they did not impute any criminal offence.[143] Not any crime would suffice. True to the pull of the action towards the harmful tendency of the words, it was held that the allegation of a merely regulatory offence, a *malum prohibitum* rather than a *malum in se*, would not ground an action.[144]

The second category to develop was allegations that touched a man in his trade or profession. At first, from the early years of the reign of Queen Elizabeth, there are cases in which lawyers and justices of the peace recovered damages for imputations of professional incompetence[145] and cases in which merchants recovered damages for allegations of bankruptcy, though these latter cases could be explained in terms of the penalties that they might suffer under the Elizabethan bankruptcy legislation.[146] By the 1590s it was argued by extension from these situations that any slander of a man in his trade or profession should be actionable. Thus in *Brook* v. *Watson*[147] the plaintiff, a merchant, complained in respect of the words, 'He is a naughty and false man and keeps a false debt-book and I will prove it.' The action failed, but only on the grounds that, on a technical construction, the words were not a reflection on the plaintiff's credit as a merchant: their falsity might have been the result of error by a servant or by mis-spelling. Similarly, it was said, it would not be actionable to say of a lawyer that he was unlearned, but it would be actionable to say that he had as much law as a jackanapes.[148]

A third category visible by the end of the sixteenth century was where it had been alleged that the plaintiff suffered from leprosy or syphilis (French pox).[149] Actions based on allegations of leprosy are found in the medieval ecclesiastical courts,[150] and it is highly plausible that the appearance of

---

[143] *Boughton* v. *Bishop of Coventry and Lichfield* (1584) Bodl MS Rawl C 85 f.52, f.54, per Gawdy Sjt. [144] *Anon* (1584) Godb 106.
[145] Helmholz, *Select Cases on Defamation* (101 SS), pp.xcvii–xcviii. A good example is *Coke* v. *Baxter* (1585) 101 SS 66.
[146] The Statute of Bankruptcy of 1571 had expressly limited its terms, which included criminal penalties, to merchants. Cf. Helmholz, *Select Cases on Defamation* (101 SS), pp.xcvii n.10, ciii.
[147] (1595) Cro El 403. There are better reports in LI MS Misc 489 f.416, HLS MS 110 f.119ᵛ, and BL MS Harg 7(1) f.96. [148] *Palmer's Case* (1594) Owen 17.
[149] Helmholz, *Select Cases on Defamation* (101 SS), pp.xcvi–xcvii; J. March, *Actions for Slaunder*, 103–4.
[150] Helmholz, *Select Cases on Defamation* (101 SS), p.xxvi. Note Lyndwood, *Provinciale*, V.17 gl. ad verb. malitiose (1679 edn., p.346): allegations of leprosy were not within the

such cases in the royal courts owes something to these medieval precursors. Chroniclers from the beginning of the sixteenth century had put the disease on a par with leprosy, and the connection can only have been strengthened in the contemporary imagination by the frequent use of disused leper houses as hospitals for those suffering from syphilis.[151] Elizabethan lawyers were clearly puzzled by the actionability of such allegations and a number of *ex post facto* justifications are found: the association with unchastity and criminality, the expectation that a person suffering from syphilis would be cut off from society, the tendency of the words to cause genuine loss.[152] The truth of the matter, we may suspect, is that in sixteenth-century terms syphilis was a disease in a class of its own, uniquely the object of opprobrium, shame, and bigotry[153]—the parallel with AIDS in the late twentieth century is often drawn—so that (seriously meant) accusations of it were particularly hurtful. The courts were all too willing to hold such allegations defamatory, no matter if the lawyers could not discern the precise reason for their actionability.

The final category coming to be recognized by the end of the sixteenth century was where it had been alleged that the plaintiff had committed an ecclesiastical offence; given that the definition of an ecclesiastical offence was broad enough to encompass a good deal of sexual impropriety, it is easy to see that this category had the potential to provide a remedy for a huge swathe of offensive language.[154] At first, the secular courts refused to take cognisance of them despite being urged to do so by hopeful plaintiffs, since they would not be in a position to evaluate the truth or falsity of the complaint. Such matters, it was said, were purely for the ecclesiastical courts.[155] There was, however, a difficulty if the victim had genuinely suffered some specific loss as a result of the allegations, since the ecclesiastical courts had no power to award damages.[156] Hence it was argued that in such cases the secular courts should have jurisdiction. This was accepted in the leading case of *Davis* v. *Gardiner* in 1593, where it was held that a woman might have an action against a man who had accused her of having

Constitution *Auctoritate Dei Patris*, for these were merely 'defects' and hence there was no imputation of crime as required by the constitution; they might none the less be punished, since it was in the interests of the state that defects such as these be detected. This no doubt alludes to the medieval practice of excluding lepers from the community.

[151] J. Fabricius, *Syphilis in Shakespeare's England* (London, 1994), 60, 71–2. Leprosy had effectively died out in England by the middle of the fifteenth century.

[152] Helmholz, *Select Cases on Defamation*, p.xcvii.   [153] Fabricius, *Syphilis*, 26–9.

[154] Such allegations were the principal causes of action of defamation in the ecclesiastical courts, particularly in suits brought by women: M. Ingram, *Church Courts, Sex, and Marriage in England, 1570–1640* (Cambridge, 1987), 292–319. For the gender differentiation, see L. Gowing, *Domestic Dangers* (Oxford, 1996).

[155] Baker, *Spelman's Reports, ii* (94 SS), *240–2*; Helmholz, *Select Cases on Defamation* (101 SS), pp.lxxvii–lxxx. Cf. YB T.27 Hen VIII f.14 pl.4 (B&M 626–7).

[156] *Palmer* v. *Thorpe* (1583) 4 Co Rep 20.

122 The Triumph of Trespass on the Case

had a bastard child, as a result of which her prospective husband had withdrawn from their agreed marriage.[157] Nearly all of the early cases involved actions brought by women claiming to have lost marriages—it was not until 1613 that a successful action was brought by a man[158]— though there was no reason why they should be so limited: in *Davis* v. *Gardiner* itself Popham C.J. said that it would be actionable to say a woman innkeeper was a common strumpet as a result of which guests avoided her inn.[159] The judges' first steps were distinctly tentative, with both the majority of the Common Pleas and Popham C.J. and Fenner J. in the King's Bench insisting that in the typical case the action would lie only if the words were spoken to the plaintiff's fiancé with the clear intention of putting a stop to the marriage,[160] but soon it became accepted that all that was required was that the plaintiff should have suffered loss as a result of the words, not that this should have been the narrowly specific intention of the defendant.[161] While the argument for bringing these cases into the secular courts was undoubtedly sound, the rule forbidding the defendant to traverse the allegation of damage[162] meant that in practice it was a rather hollow justification. So long as the loss was alleged with the requisite particularity, even if it was fictional, there was nothing the defendant could do to stop the case going to the jury; and there was nothing to stop the jury giving a verdict for the plaintiff for only nominal damages. Thus in *Matthew* v. *Crass*[163] the plaintiff, who had alleged the loss of his prospective marriage, was awarded only two shillings by the jury. The Court of King's Bench agreed with Fleming C.J. that it would be good practice for the trial judge to get the jury to examine whether or not the allegation of loss was true; though this was at first relevant only to the appropriate level of damages, not to the legitimacy of the plaintiff's claim,[164] it seems soon to have become a substantial check on the success of this type of action.[165]

Within a century the heavily circumscribed form of the tort of defamation was coming to be generalized, though visibly retaining the scars of its sixteenth-century structure. The first, and most important, step in this was the abandonment of the *mitiori sensu* rule.[166] The move away from this began in the King's Bench in the 1660s, when the court began to look to the natural meaning of the words in the context in which they were

---

[157] (1593) 4 Co Rep 16b, Poph 36.
[158] *Matthew* v. *Crass* (1613) Cro Jac 323, 2 Bulst 89.　　　[159] Poph 36, 37.
[160] *Holwood* v. *Hopkins* (1600) Cro El 787, 101 SS 89 (Common Pleas); *Bold* v. *Bacon* (1594) Cro El 346, BL MS Add 35950 f.46, f.47 (King's Bench).
[161] For later cases, see March, *Actions for Slaunder*, 77–87.　　　[162] Above, n.137.
[163] (1613) Cro Jac 323, 2 Bulst 89.
[164] 2 Bulst 89, 90. A contemporary ecclesiastical lawyer commented on the practice of the secular courts to the same effect: Helmholz, 'Damages in Actions for Slander' (1987) 103 LQR 624, 629 n.21, citing BL MS Lansd 253 f.142ᵛ.
[165] *Lowe* v. *Harewood* (1628) Cro Car 140, W Jones 196.　　　[166] Above, n.141.

spoken;[167] and by the beginning of the eighteenth century it had been completely discredited.[168] With the tort no longer bounded by specific categories it was necessary to find some general test of defamatoriness; this was achieved by adopting the approach that had been developed for the crime of libel (which had always been more open-ended than the action on the case), expressed in terms of making the victim the object of contempt or ridicule, in time settling down into the modern formula of 'hatred, ridicule or contempt'.[169]

This was not in itself enough to introduce a general tort of defamation freed from the sixteenth-century categories. Two additional factors brought this about. First was the establishment of the rule that defamatory words otherwise not actionable would become so if they had in fact caused special damage. The old situations of ecclesiastical defamations could be explained on this ground; an action could be given to a tradesman who could point to loss of business as a result of slanderous words falling short of an allegation of professional incompetence; words spoken in anger or otherwise too general to bear an action would be rendered actionable if they had caused some special damage.[170] In combination with the decline of the *mitiori sensu* rule, it provided a potential remedy for cases that might formerly have fallen outside the boundaries of liability: for the schoolmistress alleged to be a hermaphrodite, for the Irish Privy Councillor alleged to be a Roman Catholic, for the Justice of the Peace alleged to be disaffected from the government.[171]

This might have collapsed into a general liability for defamatory words with a potential to cause loss had not the courts of the 1620s been more willing than their predecessors to investigate whether special damage had in fact occurred.[172] By doing so they introduced a distinction between defamations actionable *per se* (the three original categories of the sixteenth century) and statements actionable only on proof of special damage. This distinction was consolidated by two provisions of the Statute of Limitations of 1623 specific to actions for slanderous words: a restriction on the recoverability of costs where damages less than forty shillings were

---

[167] *Lym* v. *Hockley* (1667) 1 Sid 324; *Gaudy* v. *Smyth* (1668) 2 Keb 401; *Kerle* v. *Osgood* (1669) 1 Vent 50, 1 Mod 22; *King* v. *Lake (no. 2)* (1671) 1 Freem 14.

[168] *Harrison* v. *Thornborough* (1714) 10 Mod 196, Gilb 114; *Button* v. *Heyward* (1722) 8 Mod 24.

[169] *Austin* v. *Culpepper* (1683) 2 Shower 314; *Cropp* v. *Tilney* (1693) 3 Salk 226; Hawkins, *Pleas of the Crown*, 1.193. For an alternative formulation—bringing discredit on the plaintiff and depriving him of the conversation of his neighbours—see *Roe* v. *Clarges* (1683) Skinner 88, per North Sjt.; *Duvall* v. *Price* (1694) Shower PC 12.

[170] *Wicks* v. *Shepherd* (1629) Cro Car 155; *Hawes' Case* (1641) March 113; *Dickes* v. *Fenne* (1639) March 59; *Viccarye* v. *Barnes* (1650) Style 217; *Dekin* v. *Turner* (1653) Style 387; *Falkner* v. *Cooper* (1666) Carter 55.

[171] *Wetherhead* v. *Armitage* (1678) 2 Lev 233, 1 Freem 277, 2 Show KB 18; *Roe* v. *Clarges* (1683) Skinner 68, 88; *Duvall* v. *Price* (1694) Shower PC 12.   [172] Above, n.165.

awarded, and the introduction of a limitation period of two years (as opposed to the usual six). The former of these provisions was originally treated as applicable generally to actions for defamation, but at the start of the eighteenth century it was held not to apply to cases where special damage was necessary.[173] This settled down as a formal rule dependent on the category into which the words fell; an action for calling a man a thief could not be taken outside the Act by showing that some special damage had in fact resulted.[174] As such it was embedded in the law, despite judicial discomfiture at applying a more stringent rule to plaintiffs complaining of the more serious defamations.[175] The second provision was interpreted in the same way: if the words were actionable *per se*, the two-year limitation period applied (running from the time when the words were spoken); if they were actionable only with special damage, time began to run only when the damage occurred, and the ordinary six-year period applied.[176] Alongside this, and independent of it, there developed a rule that written words ('libels') might constitute an actionable defamation where spoken words would not do so.[177] At first, probably, this was a facet of the decline of the *mitiori sensu* rule. In *King* v. *Lake* a barrister successfully brought an action where the defendant had published a written response to a parliamentary petition reflecting on his credit and competence. The words were too general to satisfy the stringent requirements of the *mitiori sensu* rule, but it was held by Hale C.B. that 'being writ and published, which contains more malice than if they had been but once spoken, they are actionable'.[178] An alternative reason for the distinction was the parallel with the crime of libel, normally based on written allegations, where there was no limitation to the sixteenth-century categories and no requirement that damage should have been caused. This analogy was consciously drawn in *Austin* v. *Culpepper*,[179] where—following *King* v. *Lake*—it was held that written words might bear an action where spoken words would not. Whatever its basis, the rule was sufficiently well established in the eighteenth century that it no longer needed elaborate explanation.[180] Although doubts were raised at the beginning of the nineteenth century, they were firmly put to

---

[173] *Brown* v. *Gibbons* (1703) 7 Mod 129, 1 Salk 206, 2 Ld Raym 831; *Burry* v. *Perry* (1732) Ld Raym 1588. The earlier approach is clearly visible in *Lowe* v. *Harewood* (1628) Cro Car 140, W Jones 196, and inferentially in *Topsall* v. *Edwards* (1629) Cro Car 163.

[174] *Burry* v. *Perry* (1732) Ld Raym 1588, reversing the effect of *Philips* v. *Fish* (1725) 8 Mod 371 and *Carter* v. *Fish* (1725) 1 Str 645.

[175] *Collier* v. *Gaillard* (1776) 2 Bl 1062, per Blackstone J.

[176] *Saunders* v. *Edwards* (1662) 1 Sid 95, 1 Keb 389, T Raym 61.

[177] J. M. Kaye, 'Libel and Slander: Two Torts or One?' (1975) 91 LQR 524.

[178] (1667) Hardres 470; Kiralfy, *Source Book*, 154. 'Malice' here is ambiguous, but is seemingly used in its primary seventeenth-century sense of 'propensity to do harm'.

[179] (1683) 2 Shower 313, Skinner 123; see too *Bradley* v. *Methwyn* (1736) 1 Selw NP 925 n.2.

[180] *Harman* v. *Delaney* (1738) 1 Barn 438, Fitzg 254, 2 Str 898; *Villers* v. *Monsley* (1769) 2 Wils 403; *Savile* v. *Jardine* (1795) 2 Hy Bl 531.

rest by the judgment of Mansfield C.J. in *Thorley* v. *Lord Kerry*;[181] within weeks it was institutionalized unthinkingly as a fragment of legal dogma wholly dependent on precedent rather than sense.[182]

It required only the slightest reordering of these lines of cases to produce the rule that a successful action in defamation normally required the plaintiff to prove special damage, subject to four exceptions that were actionable *per se*: allegations of a crime; allegations related to a person's fitness for their trade or profession; allegations of certain diseases; and written libels. The modern tort of defamation was lodged in place.[183]

---

[181] (1812) 4 Taunt 355.

[182] F. L. Holt, *Law of Libel* (1812), 198–9 (written after the decision in *Thorley* v. *Lord Kerry* but before the report had appeared in print). Thomas Starkie's *Treatise on the Law of Slander and Libel* (1813) probably has the distinction of being the first printed attack on the irrationality of the distinction.

[183] For the subsequent development of the tort, see below, p.184.

7. *The Rise of the Action of Assumpsit*

If the action of trespass on the case was able to realize its potential to encroach on the sphere formerly occupied by proprietary remedies and largely to take over the formerly ecclesiastical action of defamation, so too in the sixteenth century it became established as the primary, ordinary remedy for the imposition of liability on informal contracts. The route by which this was achieved was the same as that followed in the other situations: first of all the argument that the trespassory remedy was simply supplementing the remedies that were otherwise available, followed by a wholesale expansion into the ground covered by the older remedies. In addition—as had happened with nuisance, conversion, and defamation— the structure of liability that remained after this shift into the trespassory matrix retained much of the framework of the earlier structure of liability but gave a tortious twist to it. In the case of contractual liability, though, this tortious dimension came to lie principally on the surface of the action, whose substance remained firmly defined by pre-existent contractual ideas. Modern law recognizes a tort of nuisance, a tort of conversion, and a tort of defamation. It does not know a tort of breach of contract.

TRESPASS ON THE CASE AND CONTRACTUAL LIABILITY

It has already been seen that the principal thrust of the action of trespass on the case in its earliest manifestations in the middle of the fourteenth century was the provision of a remedy for cases of mis-performance of informal contracts.[1] Such situations had been excluded from the action of covenant as a result of the introduction of the requirement of a deed under seal as an essential of liability in that action, yet they were sufficiently close to the central core of the action of trespass to be reincorporated within it. There was from the start a degree of pressure for the expansion of the remedy to cover cases of contractual non-performance, especially in cases where no other remedy was available, such as cases of non-performance of contracts for services and cases where a vendor of land failed to convey it. The plea rolls show attempts to bring such cases within the action of trespass as early as 1303;[2] by the end of the fourteenth century it is possible to find precedents of actions on the case for contractual non-performance

---

[1] Above, pp.48–56.   [2] Palmer, *Black Death*, 181 n.1.

in Registers of Writs;[3] and attempts to bring such actions are relatively easy to find in the plea rolls of the fifteenth century. None the less, despite this pressure, judicial opinion seems to have been almost uniformly against them until the closing months of the fifteenth century.[4] No doubt some difficulty was seen with the use of a trespassory remedy where the defendant had done nothing, for the courts had always been reluctant to impose liability for mere omissions;[5] no less importantly, though, there was a serious concern that trespass and covenant—tort and contract—should be kept separate. This was explicitly articulated by Martin J. in 1425, where an action on the case was brought for the failure to build a mill: 'If this action should be maintained upon the present facts, then a man would have an action of trespass for every broken covenant in the world.'[6]

The difficulty of imposing trespassory liability for omissions and the perceived problem of compromising the boundary between contract and tort meant that plaintiffs were faced with a near-impossible task when trying to argue that trespass on the case was an appropriate remedy for straightforward cases of not performing contracts. The first successful attempts to circumvent these objections occurred in the first half of the fifteenth century. In *Somerton* v. *Colles*[7] the plaintiff had alleged that he had retained the defendant to be his counsel in the purchasing of a manor; in breach of this the defendant had represented a rival and obtained the land for him instead. The litigation is complicated by a number of highly technical objections; but, cutting through these, it is possible to discern three arguments that pushed the court in the direction of judgment for the plaintiff. First was the fact that he could point to a positive act of wrongdoing on the part of the defendant, acting for the rival rather than for the plaintiff himself. It was not simply that he had failed to do what he had agreed to do, but that he had done something positively inconsistent with it. Secondly, perhaps putting the same point in another way, it could be said that the plaintiff had suffered some genuine loss as a result of the defendant's behaviour; it was not simply that he had failed to labour on his behalf, but that he had made it impossible for somebody else to do so. Thirdly, play was made with the analogy of liability on a warranty, where it was clear that an action on the case would lie. Two further features, neither mentioned in the reports of the case, might have been relevant as well. First was the closeness of this situation to that envisaged by the Statute of

---

[3] Kiralfy, *Action on the Case*, 147.
[4] Simpson, *History of Contract*, 220–7; Baker, *Spelman's Reports, ii* (94 SS), 266-75. See *Watton* v. *Brinth*, YB M.2 Hen IV f.3 pl.9; YB M.11 Hen IV f.33 pl.60; *Watkin's Case*, YB H.3 Hen VI f.36 pl.33; *Tailbois* v. *Sherman*, YB P.21 Hen VI f.55 pl.12; YB H.2 Hen VII f.11 pl.9; YB M.3 Hen VII f.14 pl.20.   [5] Above, p.68.
[6] *Watkin's Case*, YB H.3 Hen VI f.36 pl.33 (B&M 380).
[7] YB T.11 Hen VI f.55 pl.26, YB H.11 Hen VI f.18 pl.10, YB P.11 Hen VI f.24 pl.1 (B&M 385).

Labourers. If the defendant had been retained for a period as a labourer, then an action would have lain against him on the Statute if he had not performed what he had been retained to do. Why should it make a difference in principle if he was a lawyer who had been retained to perform a specific task?[8] Secondly, the defendant's status as a lawyer might have been peculiarly relevant, for the courts claimed some disciplinary jurisdiction and might have been willing to countenance an action here where they would have been more reluctant to intervene in a case involving a different type of defendant.

If we do not know the precise reason for the decision in *Somerton's Case*, the second case, known as *Doige's Case*,[9] is more transparent. The plaintiff brought an action of trespass on the case alleging that the defendant had orally undertaken to sell to him a plot of land in London at a price of £110, but that in spite of the fact that the price had been paid the defendant had in fact conveyed the land to a third party. At first sight it is easy to feel more than a little sympathy with the plaintiff. The defendant was already in the custody of the King's Bench (she was imprisoned in the Court of the Marshalsea), so that there was no other court in which the action could properly have been brought. If the King's Bench gave no remedy, then the plaintiff must remain wholly uncompensated.[10] It is not difficult to follow the reasoning of the judges. They begin in self-evidently contractual terms. Here there was an agreement to buy and sell land, and it was clear that the seller would have an action against the buyer for the price. How could it be, then, that the buyer should have no action against the seller for the land? It would be grotesque—'merveillous Ley'—if there were a contract that bound one party but left the other party wholly free. The difficulty was that there was no action that the plaintiff could obviously bring: not covenant, because there was no deed; not debt or detinue because the action was not for money or chattels, not any real action because no title had yet passed to the plaintiff. The only possibility was the action of trespass on the case. Having essentially decided that the plaintiff was to win, the court was forced to point to some reason why the trespassory remedy was appropriate, notwithstanding its reluctance to encroach on the sphere of contractual liability. This they did by pointing to the fact that the defendant had not simply failed to perform her agreement, but that she had positively broken it by conveying the land to a third party and thereby disabling herself from performance. Judgment was accordingly given for the plaintiff.

The most curious feature of *Doige's Case* is the sum awarded as damages.

[8] Cf. YB M.2 Hen IV f.4 pl.3; YB M.11 Hen IV f.33 pl.60, per Hill J. (B&M 379 (but note 380 n.7)).

[9] *Shipton* v. *Dogge*, YB T.20 Hen VI f.34 pl.4, 51 SS 97 (B&M 391; Kiralfy, *Source Book*, 192).   [10] M. Blatcher, *The Court of King's Bench 1450–1550* (London, 1978), 116–17.

Although the plaintiff had allegedly paid the price of £110, damages were assessed at only £20. Unless something extremely odd was going on, the only plausible explanations are either that the price had not in fact been paid or, more likely, that it had been paid and returned and that we are dealing with a case of fifteenth-century gazumping. Whichever is the true explanation, it seems undeniable that the action was being brought to recover expectation damages, the difference between the price at which the land had been sold and the market value of the land. Despite its trespassory carapace, in substance the action—an action between the parties to an agreement to recover expectation damages—was quintessentially contractual.

The decisions in *Somerton's Case* and *Doige's Case* provided a door through which some cases of contractual non-performance could pass into the action of trespass on the case, and in the half-century after the latter case actions for the failure to convey land, coupled with allegations of disablement, became a routine if not frequent part of the business of the royal courts.[11] More importantly, the arguments rehearsed in those cases provided an armoury that could be used by plaintiffs in a wider range of situations; in particular they might point to the suffering of actual loss irrecoverable in another action or to some positive act on the part of the defendant, or they might simply formulate the defendant's behaviour in terms of the language of wrongdoing rather than the language of rights. The boundary between contract and tort, between covenant and trespass, was not so rigid that it was able to withstand such an assault, and at the very end of the fifteenth century it was breached.

It did not require any court decision to do this. In 1499,[12] speaking in Gray's Inn, Fyneux C.J. said that there was no reason why trespass on the case could not be brought for nonfeasance if (or because) damage flowed from it. No reason in law was given for this volte-face, but the political justification is visible on the surface of his pronouncement: no longer would it be necessary to sue in Chancery.[13] The Common law itself was capable of providing a satisfactory remedy. This breaking-down of the barrier that had for so long marked off the domain of trespass was, so far as we can see, greeted with no great outcry. Well into the sixteenth century lawyers found it still worth saying, perhaps with a hint of incredulity, that trespass on the case could be used in situations of nonfeasance; but none saw fit to deny or doubt the proposition.[14]

The dictum of Fyneux C.J. marked the most important crossroads for

---

[11] Baker and Milsom, *Sources of English Legal History*, 395; Baker, *Spelman's Reports, ii* (94 SS), 266-7.   [12] YB M.21 Hen VII f.41 pl.66.
[13] For the willingness of the Chancery to intervene, cf. YB P.8 Edw IV f.4 pl.11.
[14] Dillon's Reading in Gray's Inn, 1516 (B&M 401); *Anon* (1530) BL MS Harg 388 f.215 (B&M 402); Hales' Reading in Gray's Inn, 1537 (B&M 345).

the law of obligations since the thirteenth century. In one direction, actions for breach of contract could have been reintegrated within the trespassory framework, where they would no doubt have taken their place alongside the newly emergent torts of nuisance, conversion, and defamation. In the other direction lay the retention of the division between contract and tort, though with some redefinition, beneath the formal shell of trespass on the case. By the beginning of the seventeenth century it is clear that the latter of these routes was being taken. An inclination to move in this direction is visible quite early in the sixteenth century, and with hindsight we may see it as having been inevitable; but it might not have been quite so obvious to contemporary lawyers.

CONTRACT AND TORT: THE ACTION OF ASSUMPSIT

From its inception, the emergent action on the case for breach of contract was held in tension between its trespassory and contractual aspects. This tension was not to be fully resolved until the first half of the seventeenth century, and the developed form of the action was never to lose the scars of its passage through the thicket of tort.

On the one hand, its pleadings were firm in their focus on the wrong-doing of the defendant:

Whereas the same John [the defendant] . . . for £5.13s.4d. then and there paid beforehand to the same John by the said Richard [the plaintiff], and for another £5.13s.4d. to be paid to the same John by the said Richard later . . . had bargained and sold to the said Richard forty quarters of malt . . . and the same John had . . . faithfully promised the said Richard and taken upon himself to deliver the forty quarters of malt to the same Richard there in form aforesaid; and the aforesaid Richard, hoping for faithful delivery of the aforesaid malt, had made lesser provision of malt for continuing, perfecting and carrying out his brewings; the aforesaid John Thurgoode, scheming that the aforesaid Richard should sustain and incur loss and detriment in his trade as a brewer for want of malt, has not cared to deliver the aforesaid forty quarters of malt, nor any part thereof . . . so that the same Richard was not only left without any malt to continue and perfect his brewings . . . but also the same Richard was necessarily forced to buy and provide that amount of malt from others, at a much higher price, to continue and perfect his brewings . . . by which the same Richard says he is the worse and has damage to the value of £20.[15]

In pleading terms the assumpsit was only prefatory matter, 'inducement', to the gravamen of the claim, the breach. Invective is heaped on the defendant; and the plaintiff alleges consequential loss. However much we regard these aspects as empty form, and neither the defendant's wickedness

---

[15] *Pykeryng* v. *Thurgoode* (1532) 94 SS 247.

nor the plaintiff's loss was remotely material to the success of the action, they drew attention to the defendant's breach as the basis of the claim. On the other hand, from early in the sixteenth century the action was known as the action of assumpsit, focusing on the central allegation of the action that the defendant 'assumed and faithfully promised'—*assumpsit et fideliter promisit*—to the plaintiff to do something. This naming of the action gave more weight to the original cause of the obligation—the promise or contract—than to its breach.[16] Moreover, it was settled by the 1520s that the proper general issue for the defendant to plead was not 'not guilty', which was otherwise ubiquitous in trespassory claims, but 'non assumpsit'.[17]

On the other hand, from an early date the contractual underpinnings of the action were moulding its substantive nature. This is best illustrated by the question of the measure of damages. However much the action was apparently based on the plaintiff's having suffered some genuine loss, and however much breakdown of the formal bar against the use of a trespassory remedy for cases for nonfeasance was intellectually justified by the argument that it was essential to provide a remedy for such loss, the courts followed the lead given by *Doige's Case* in treating the plaintiff's lost expectations as the 'proper' measure of damages.[18] The assessment of damages was, it is true, purely a matter for the jury, so that we must be careful not to speak too glibly about the criteria by which they were assessed, nor to assume that there were any rigid rules governing the matter, but when the courts did give any opinion on the subject it is clear that they were thinking in terms of compensating plaintiffs for lost expectations. Thus, in *Strete's Case* in 1528, the plaintiff alleged that it had been agreed with the defendant lessee that the latter would (*inter alia*) build a chimney on the demised property, and that the parties would seal indentures embodying their obligations. The plaintiff had performed his side of the agreement, but the defendant, it was alleged, had neither sealed the indenture on his part nor built the chimney. The judges directed the jury that, if they were satisfied that the defendant *assumpsit super se*, the correct measure of damages was the amount that it ought to

---

[16] Cf. the torts of conversion, nuisance, and defamation, with their stress on the nature of the defendant's wrongdoing.

[17] There is no consistency in the defendant's pleas in the first quarter of the sixteenth century, both *non assumpsit* and *non culpabilis* being found. In *Haymond* v. *Lenthorp* (1527; KB 27/1065 m.77d), in a straight action for non-delivery of goods sold, the defendant pleaded the general *non culpabilis* and the plaintiff demurred to the plea. This would have squarely raised the issue of the proper general issue. The case depended until 1531, but no judgment is entered. None the less, subsequent cases are unanimous in holding the appropriateness of *non assumpsit*, and it may be that such doubts as there were had been put to rest by *Haymond* v. *Lenthorp*. Cf. below, n.25.   [18] Baker, *Spelman's Reports, ii* (94 SS), *294–5*.

have cost the defendant to build the chimney.[19] Where a brewer entered
into a contract to buy barley at a fixed price to be delivered at a later date
(a typical futures contract), it seems to have been treated as axiomatic that
the damages should be assessed by reference to the market price on the day
at which delivery should have taken place rather than the contract price.[20]
To the same effect later in the century, where a jury was unsure of how
much to award where an action was brought on a promise to pay a fixed sum
by way of penalty should the defendant not perform an arbitration award, the
King's Bench inclined towards the award of the sum that had been promised,
though holding that the amount was purely a matter for the jury's decision.[21]
None the less, for all this stress on the protection of the plaintiff's expectations, like covenant before it the action of assumpsit was—and was to
remain—an action to recover damages for breach of contract, not an action
to give effect to the plaintiff's contractual entitlement.[22]

A second situation in which the courts looked beyond the surface allegations of the wrongful breach of promise was where the action of assumpsit
was brought to recover a contract debt. Plaintiffs might wish to bring
assumpsit in place of the older action in order to prevent defendants
waging their law or in order to recover consequential damages, and,
although there were difficulties in principle in allowing the action of
assumpsit to be used where an action of debt would have lain, in practice
these difficulties were sidestepped; except for the period between 1595 and
1605, when the judges of the Common Pleas were at their most conservative, it was generally accepted from the early 1530s that assumpsit could be
used in place of debt provided that an appropriate form of pleading was
used.[23] Such actions were generally known as 'indebitatus assumpsit', as
distinguished from 'collateral assumpsit' when the action was brought in a
situation where debt would not have lain. What is particularly revealing is
that in indebitatus assumpsit it came to be established that the pleading
rules appropriate to debt should be applied rather than those otherwise
appropriate to assumpsit. One example will suffice. In an action of debt on
a contract, where the debtor was to pay the sum due on request it was clear
that the liability arose immediately on the contract; the request merely went
to the manner of performance and was not a formal precondition of the

---

[19] BL MS Harg 253 f.19ᵛ. The case was problematic in that the obligation to build the
chimney was not severable from the other obligations of the lessee, so that the value of the
work could not be deduced from the parties' agreement.

[20] *Pykeryng* v. *Thurgoode* (1532) 93 SS 4.

[21] *Coleman* v. *Mowe* (1595) Moo 419, BL MS Harg 7 f.125. The case was eventually
compromised.

[22] M. Rheinstein, *Die Struktur des vertraglichen Schuldverhältnisses im anglo-amerikanischen
Recht* (Berlin, 1932). Below, p.149.

[23] Ibbetson, 'Sixteenth Century Contract Law: *Slade's Case* in Context' (1984) 4 Ox Jnl Leg
Stud 295. For the formal mechanism, see below, p.138.

existence of liability. It followed that, as a matter of pleading, it was sufficient for the plaintiff to allege generally that, 'although often requested' to do so, the defendant had not paid the debt. In assumpsit, on the other hand, where there was a promise to do something on request, it was held that the request was a true precondition of the existence of the defendant's liability, not merely a feature relating to the mode of performance. Hence the request was an essential part of the cause of action and the plaintiff had to allege with precision when and where it had occurred; the general 'although often requested' was insufficient. By contrast with the normal position, when the point arose in indebitatus assumpsit towards the end of the sixteenth century, it was held that the general allegation was all that was needed.[24] In essence this amounted to saying that the liability was the same whether the action was framed in debt or assumpsit. The nature of liability in assumpsit, therefore, was perceived as varying according to the cause of the underlying obligation; it would be wrong for us simply to look to the superficial form of the action as an action for the wrongful breach of a promise and ignore the fact that contemporary lawyers looked below this surface to the substance that lay beneath.

By the beginning of the seventeenth century there was a clear cleavage between situations where the action of assumpsit was brought for mis-performance and situations where it was brought for non-performance. The former, with its roots going back to the 1350s or 1360s, could be treated as a generic action of trespass on the case in which the trespassory 'not guilty' would be the appropriate general issue; in contractual cases this was impermissible.[25] Hence, in an action on the case against a carrier of goods who had allegedly carried them negligently, it was essential to make a sharp distinction between cases where the action was brought on a special term of the contract (where *non assumpsit* alone was appropriate) and cases brought on the general duty of the carrier (where not guilty was acceptable).[26] The same distinction is visible in other areas too. Thus, in *Powtuary* v. *Walton*[27] it was held that, although an allegation that the promise had been made for good consideration was absolutely essential in an action for non-performance, it was unnecessary in an action for mis-performance. In substantive terms this meant that an action could be brought for the negligent performance of a gratuitous undertaking, but not for the mere

---

[24] *Banks* v. *Thwaites* (1586) 3 Leon 73, CUL MS Dd 11.64 f.15; *Estrigge* v. *Owles* (1589) 3 Leon 200, 4 Leon 3, CUL MS Ll 3.8 f.467ᵛ, LI MS Hill 123b f.89ᵛ. 'Assumpsit and Debt in the Early Sixteenth Century: The Origins of the Indebitatus Count' [1982] CLJ 142, 158.

[25] Above, n.17. To the same effect, *Corbyn* v. *Browne* (1596) Cro El 470*, *Turner* v. *Turbervile* (1623) 2 Ro 368.

[26] *Bradley* v. *Tewe* (1606) Noy 114, HLS MS 118c f.147ᵛ. See further Ibbetson, 'Absolute Liability in Contract: The Antecedents of Paradine v. Jayne', in Rose (ed.), *Consensus ad Idem*, 1.23–30. [27] (1598) Ro Abr 1.10, *Action sur Case*, P5.

failure to perform it; two centuries later this would be the springboard from which the tort of negligence took off.

A final situation revealing the extent to which the lawyers of the sixteenth and seventeenth centuries looked beneath the surface of the action of assumpsit was the liability of executors. It had been orthodoxy in the Middle Ages that executors would in principle be liable to pay their testator's contract debts, though this came to be subjected to the countervailing rule that allowed executors to excuse themselves if wager of law would have been open to the testator.[28] In other actions where the plaintiff claimed only unliquidated damages, such as trespass and covenant, the maxim *Actio Personalis Moritur cum Persona*—a Personal Action dies with the Person—held sway. The position in assumpsit was decidedly ambiguous throughout the sixteenth century. The King's Bench, after some vacillation, held in *Norwood* v. *Read* in 1558 that executors would be liable in indebitatus assumpsit but not in collateral assumpsit, mirroring exactly the medieval position.[29] The Common Pleas judges were much more hesitant, shifting from one position to another, until they too came to accept the King's Bench line in 1611.[30] Within little more than a decade of this both courts expanded the scope of the executors' liability to cases of collateral assumpsit. Following the approach typified by *Powtuary* v. *Walton*, they now distinguished between situations where liability was contractual (in the broader sense) and those cases where it was tortious; in the former case the executors would be liable, in the latter they would not. The distinction is absolutely explicit in *Fawcett* v. *Charter*: 'The difference is where the act of the testator includes a wrong (*tort*), where the liability does not extend to the executor, but, being personal, dies with him; just as trover and conversion does not lie against the executor for a trover of the testator; it is otherwise of contracts and promises made on good consideration.'[31]

These situations reveal two phenomena. First of all is the fact that the courts did not treat all actions of assumpsit as equivalent, all based on the wrong of breach of promise. On the contrary, they were willing to look beyond the formal façade of the action at the substance that lay beneath, and they did not baulk at characterizing it as contractual. Secondly, from

[28] Above, p.32.
[29] Plo 180. The argument that the executors should not be liable because they could not wage their law had no bite in the action of assumpsit, for wager of law would not have been available to the testator in the first place.
[30] *Pinchon's Case* (1611) 9 Co Rep 86. The question had been discussed in *Kercher's Case* (1610) Godb 176, BL MS Add 25211 f.191, and *Meane* v. *Peacher* (1610) BL MS Add 35955 f.120, CUL MS Gg 4.9 f.38.
[31] (1624) Palmer 329 (*sub nom Carter* v. *Fossett*), per Jones J. There are earlier hints of the same analysis in *Furnace* v. *Leycaster* (1618) HLS MS 109 f.191; it is repeated in *Mason* v. *Dixon* (1628) Latch 167, Poph 189, W Jones 173, Noy 87.

quite early in the sixteenth century the contractual underpinning of liability in assumpsit was moulding the form that the action was taking, so that by the beginning of the seventeenth it was clear that the action could in fact be divided into two distinct types: a contractual type where the plaintiff complained of non-performance, and a tortious type where the action was grounded on mis-performance.

ASSUMPSIT AND THE THEORY OF CONTRACT

It does not follow from the fact that assumpsit developed as a contractual action rather than a tortious one that the idea of contract that it embodied was the same as that which had been found in medieval law. Indeed, it is all too easy to contrast assumpsit with its precursors.

The medieval notion of contract had been built on two elements. First was the identification of a bilateral agreement as its base, rather than a simple voluntary undertaking of responsibility by one person to another. Second was the restriction of the legal horizon to reciprocal agreements. This is not to say that the law would inevitably ignore arrangements that were unilateral or gratuitous; but it insisted that they should be made under seal and hence marginalized them. On its surface, the action of assumpsit was completely different. The standard-form language of the pleadings, that the defendant *super se assumpsit et fideliter promisit*, proclaims its basis as a unilateral promise or undertaking made *to* the plaintiff rather than a contract or covenant made *with* him. Nor was there anything inherent in the concept of a promise that limited its actionability to situations of reciprocity. This contrast is, however, simply a matter of appearance; by the beginning of the seventeenth century at the latest assumpsit had to all intents and purposes adopted the structure of contractual liability found in the medieval law.

Promise and Agreement

A bewildering diversity of language is used in the early writs and bills of assumpsit, so that we must from the start beware of assuming that the emergent action had any single theoretical base.[32] On the contrary, the diversity suggests that pleaders were exploiting a whole range of elements that might have been thought to have a possibility of success without any coherent idea of what they were doing. Gradually, though, as the action became more popular, a significant degree of uniformity was reached, with the defendant's 'undertaking' and 'faithful promise' as the central elements

---

[32] Baker, *Spelman's Reports, ii* (94 SS), *273-5.*

of the plaintiff's claim. The language of undertaking—*assumpsit*—had been commonly found in the actions on the case for contractual mis-performance from the fourteenth and fifteenth centuries, and its wide-spread use in the sixteenth century may well be no more than the unsurprising continuation of the old form of pleading into the new situa-tion of contractual non-performance. The language of promising, although found in earlier actions on the case, was less typical, and its rise to prominence in the sixteenth-century action of assumpsit is more note-worthy. The very fact that lawyers came to use it so consistently at least raises the possibility that they meant something by it.

It seems highly likely that the model for this formulation is to be found in the ecclesiastical courts' action of *fidei laesio*, which was waning just as the action of assumpsit was beginning to wax.[33] This action, explicitly based on the breach of a 'faithful promise', had been common in the fifteenth century, and it requires little imagination to see some transplantation of language and ideas from the ecclesiastical courts to the secular courts. Of particular value for our purposes, the records of the ecclesiastical courts and the fifteenth-century commentary of William Lyndwood give us a fairly clear indication of what was meant by 'promise', and what was the justification for its enforcement. For these courts, the promise was some-thing very much stronger than a simple voluntary undertaking; it was akin to an oath. The defendant might have 'sworn by his body', 'on a book', or 'by his faith' (equivalent to an oath taken on the Gospels) that he would do something.[34] Nor are these simply *ex parte* statements by plaintiffs forcing their claims into an ecclesiastical mould; they are witnesses' descriptions of what actually happened. Not every contractual obligation would be enforced, therefore; the Church was concerned only with those backed up by oaths or genuine, full-blooded, promises equivalent to oaths. Nor is it difficult to understand the reason for the intervention of the Church, since the promisor's soul was in peril as a result of the breach of the oath or promise. For Lyndwood it was a form of perjury.[35]

It may be, however, that alongside this strong conception of promising allied to oath-taking the fourteenth and fifteenth centuries knew also the weaker version that added little to the notion of a voluntary undertaking. When the language of promising is found in actions in secular courts in this period, it is far more closely identified with the complex of ideas associated with contract than with those of oaths and perjury,[36] though in the absence of witnesses' depositions describing exactly what had happened in these situations we cannot be certain whether or not something additional had

---

[33] R. H. Helmholz, 'Assumpsit and Fidei Laesio' (1975) 91 LQR 406.
[34] Helmholz, 'Assumpsit and Fidei Laesio' (1975) 91 LQR 406, 417–18 nn.55–8.
[35] *Provinciale*, V.15 (1679 edn., p.315), gl. ad verb *Perjurio, Fidei transgressione.*
[36] Above, p.74.

occurred to strengthen the promissory aspect of the case. When the London courts heard an action of covenant in 1486 based on a promise to make a bond, we may question whether this was any more than a way of describing an ordinary commercial transaction;[37] no less commercial was the Chancery action where one of two joint purchasers of a shipload of oil had not carried out his promise to pay the whole price;[38] when a man promised to sell his prospective son-in-law a ship at a favourable price, we seem to be closer to the world of marriage negotiations than to that of formal oath-swearing;[39] or when an action is brought against an apprentice's master who had ignored his 'agreement, promise, and trust' in failing to pay £10 to the apprentice at the age of 21 it is hard to avoid the suspicion that 'agreement', 'promise', and 'trust' are linked together as a way of describing a straightforward apprenticeship agreement.[40] It may be wrong to overstress the contrast between these two conceptions of promising. So far as the participants were concerned, the promise might have had no function other than to intensify the obligation, and we cannot reconstruct their mental world with the degree of precision that would be necessary to know whether or not it was conceived as engendering a duty to God alongside the duty to the promisee. The ambiguity survives to the present day; whereas modern schoolchildren (and others) maintain the strong sense of the idea and require specific words, modern lawyers are happy to refer to any voluntarily assumed obligation as a promise.[41]

It is hardly surprising, therefore, to find an element of ambiguity in the concept of promising as it came to be applied in the action of assumpsit. The first real hint of this is in *Pykeryng v. Thurgoode*.[42] Assumpsit was brought on the breach of a promise to deliver barley to the plaintiff, the price of which had been partly paid in advance. The predictable objection was made that assumpsit, as an action on the case, should not lie because an older action, the action of debt, was appropriate, and it was a rule that the action on the case could not lie in such circumstances. The majority of the King's Bench rejected this:

And although [the plaintiff at bar] could have had an action of debt, this does not matter, for the action of debt is founded on the *debet et detinet*, whereas this action is founded on another wrong, that is, on the breaking of the promise.[43]

---

[37] *Nicholson and Rutter* v. *Parsons* (C1/82/19 (*corpus cum causa*)).
[38] *Banaster* v. *Medcalf* (C1/187/73).   [39] *Harteford* v. *Amadus* (C1/97/32).
[40] *Hort* v. *Pepyr and Claxton* (C1/96/64).
[41] Cf. I. and P. Opie, *The Lore and Language of Schoolchildren* (Oxford, 1967), 141–7, with e.g. P. S. Atiyah, *Promises, Morals, and Law* (Oxford, 1981), 169–76. For a contemporary discussion of the relationship between promises and oaths, see R. Sanderson, *De Iuramenti Promissorii Obligatione* (1647), esp. 121–53.   [42] (1532) 93 SS 4.
[43] per Spelman J.

It is at the election of the plaintiff to take one action or the other, for they are founded upon different points.[44]

Port J., on the other hand, disagreed: 'This promise is part of the contract, and all one. And [there is] no act done by the defendant, but only the non-delivery, for which detinue lies.' In part we should see the argument here as centring around the artificiality of separating the two halves of the bargain and pretending that they were something different from the whole that they comprised; in part, though, there seems to be a difference of opinion about whether the allegation of a promise added anything relevant to the contract that lay behind it.

By the early 1540s a formal mechanism had been invented that separated the promise from the contract, the plaintiff counting that the promise had been made after the contract: the defendant bought a horse on Monday (and hence came under an obligation to pay the price), and on Tuesday—or later on Monday—made a promise to pay for it.[45] In formal terms, therefore, the promise was chronologically and logically distinct from the contract, and transparently added something to it. This was less clear as a matter of substance. Throughout the second half of the sixteenth century the King's Bench held that this subsequent promise might be an empty fiction, and that the plaintiff was entitled to judgment if the jury was satisfied that a contract had been made.[46] More interesting is the opposing position of the Common Pleas, requiring that a genuine promise be proved. This had two elements. First of all was their obvious discomfort with allowing an action to be brought on a wholly fictitious cause of action. Secondly, particularly visible after the mid-1580s (by which time they had ceased to emphasize the requirement that the promise be subsequent to the contract), was the belief that a promise was something different from a contract, so that the fact that a contract had been made did not in any way entail that there had been a promise.[47] After enormous controversy, the position of the King's Bench was finally upheld after (if not in) *Slade's Case* in 1602.[48] From this point on, if the action of assumpsit was an action based on a promise, it was a promise only in the weakest sense of the word, denoting nothing more than a voluntary undertaking.

But it would be misleading crudely to characterize the action as based on a unilateral promise, even in this weak sense. Often, unsurprisingly, the

---

[44] per Fitzjames C.J.

[45] Ibbetson, 'Assumpsit and Debt in the Early Sixteenth Century' [1982] CLJ 142; '*Slade's Case* in Context' (1984) 4 Ox Jnl Leg Stud 295.

[46] *Edwards* v. *Burre* (1573) Dal 104. The point was put pithily in *Norwood* v. *Read* (1558) Plo 180, 182: 'Every contract executory is an assumpsit in itself.'

[47] *Potts* v. *Millworth* (1586) HLS MS 16 f.230, Yale Law School MS G R 29.6 f.9, BL MS Lansd 1068 f.68ᵛ; *Anon* (1588) LI MS Misc 261b f.123ᵛ.

[48] 4 Co Rep 91a; J. H. Baker, 'New Light on Slade's Case' [1971] CLJ 51.

courts do use the language of promising in discussing questions of liability; but it is not uncommon to find the language of agreement used as well, pointing to a link with the contractual structure of the fifteenth century and before. In practice, of course, it would rarely matter whether liability was seen in promise-based or agreement-based terms; it is only when lawyers are concerned to decide when (or perhaps where) the contract was made, rather than whether it was made at all, that the issue becomes serious, and in a period when contracts were typically made between the parties face to face there was little opportunity for these questions to arise. Sometimes, though, they did surface; and when they did the courts showed that it was the two-sided agreement of the parties that mattered, not the one-sided promise.

The point might arise, for example, where the promise was made to a servant or agent acting outside the scope of the master's authority. This was the situation in *Milles* v. *Rainton*,[49] where the defendant had made a promise to pay a certain sum of money if the master would forbear to sue him for a week. It was alleged that the master had in fact forborne for the week, but the defendant had failed to pay. It had clearly been the intention of the promisor to make his promise to the master, albeit through the agency of the servant, and, if liability was conceived in purely promissory terms, there could surely have been no objection to the master bringing the action. The Court of Exchequer Chamber disagreed. Although there had been a communication of the promise to the master and an apparent acceptance of it,[50] evidenced by the fact of his forbearance for a week, this was not sufficient. According to the majority of the court—and we are told that this was the principal reason for their judgment—where a promise was made to an absent plaintiff this was of no effect unless and until there was an express agreement to the promise on the part of the plaintiff himself.

A second situation where the theoretical foundation of the action would have practical implications was where the promisor attempted to withdraw from the arrangement. This arose in the King's Bench in 1618, in *Hurford* v. *Pile*.[51] One Winter had obtained judgment in an action against Foweracres, who had been arrested and imprisoned. Pile, in consideration that Hurford would procure the release of Foweracres, promised to indemnify him for

---

[49] (1600) Yale Law School MS G R 29.14 f.100^v; CUL MS Add 8080 f.107. See too *Holygrave* v. *Knyghtysbrygge*, YB M.27 Hen VIII f.24 pl.3 (husband able to sue on promise to wife only if she acted with his authority or if he subsequently agreed to it); *Mylward* v. *Kymersley* (1598) BL MS Harg 51 f.161^v; *Jordan* v. *Jordan* (1595) Cro El 369.

[50] The language of communication and acceptance is precisely that found in the reports, but we should beware of seeing it in too obviously nineteenth- or twentieth-century terms. It might be preferable to say that the master had acquiesced in the arrangement.

[51] Cro Jac 483; 2 Ro 21, 39 (sub nom *Winter* v. *Foweracres*); HLS MS 105f f.291; LI MS Misc 791d ff.80^v, 85^v.

any costs that he incurred in doing so. Hurford agreed to this, but made no promise on his part to do anything. Subsequently he procured the release of Foweracres and brought an action of assumpsit for his charges. Pile pleaded that before Hurford had done anything towards effecting the release he had revoked his promise. Hurford demurred to this plea, and the King's Bench held that the revocation had not been effective:

A person who promises cannot countermand and recall his own promise, because every assumpsit is made by the mutual agreement of both parties and on reciprocal considerations, and through this creates a contract . . . and because of this the person who assumes cannot make a countermand, for a bargain is a bargain and a contract is a contract and although this was not a complete assumpsit until the consideration was performed, the person who made the promise has nothing more to do, so that his hands are tied and his mouth shut up.[52]

It would be difficult to find a better statement of the classical bargain theory of contractual liability.

Privity of Contract

The formulation of liability in promissory terms provided an opportunity for the law to distance itself from the medieval rules of privity of contract, for it would have been far easier to describe a third-party beneficiary as the recipient of the promise than as a party to the contract. This did not happen. Although there was some shift in the language used and some watering-down of the edges of the doctrine, its central core remained intact. The basic rule, often stated, was that the action had to be brought by the promisee.[53] 'If I make a promise to you to pay £10 to your son, the son is not privy to this, and he will not have an action to demand this, but the father will.'[54] But, conversely, if the promise was made to the son, he was the appropriate person to enforce it. This is straightforwardly illustrated by *Rookwood* v. *Rookwood*.[55] A dying father summoned his sons to his deathbed; in consideration that he allow the lands to pass to the eldest son unencumbered, the eldest son promised to his brothers that he would pay an annuity to each of them. The King's Bench held that an action lay at the suit of the younger sons.[56]

It was one thing to say that the action had to be brought by the promisee,

---

[52] HLS MS 105f f.291. The same issue had been raised, though inconclusively, in *Russel's Case* (1591) CUL MS Ii 5.16 f.85.

[53] *Anon* (1585) CUL MS Ff 5.4 f.149; *Jordan* v. *Jordan* (1595) Cro El 369; *Anon* (1597) CUL MS Dd 8.48 p.1. For the medieval rules of privity, see above, pp.76–80.

[54] *Levett* v. *Hawes* (1599) Yale Law School MS G R 29.10 f.211, per Clench J.

[55] (1589) 1 Leon 192, Cro El 164, Yale Law School MS G R 29.6 f.8ᵛ.

[56] It should be noted that it did not matter that they had given no consideration; all that was important was that the promise had been made to them. Cf. below, p.207.

but quite another to say who the promisee was in any particular fact situation. There was considerable leeway here for the use of ideas of agency. Thus, where a promise was made to a wife acting within the authority of her husband or subsequently ratified by him, the action was properly brought by the husband;[57] and a master might bring assumpsit on a promise made to his servant.[58] This was extended considerably in *Levett* v. *Hawes*[59] at the end of the century. Marriage negotiations had taken place between two fathers, each promising the other that they would pay money to the couple after the marriage had taken place. On the failure of the bride's father to do so, an action of assumpsit was brought by the father of the groom. It was held in the King's Bench that the action should not succeed: the proper plaintiff was not the father, but the groom himself. Popham C.J. argued that this case was different from the ordinary situation where a promise was made to pay money to a third party, for here the son was 'interested in the cause', essentially a party to the arrangement, and not simply the beneficiary of a windfall. Similarly, he said, if one of two joint owners of a horse, acting on the instructions of the other, sold it and provided that the price should be paid to the other, the proper plaintiff was the absentee co-owner. The correct analysis of *Levett* v. *Hawes* was that the promise had been made to the use of the groom; the father was merely acting as his agent.[60] It is worth contrasting this situation with that where *A* had made a bond with *B* to the use of *C*; here there was no leeway to describe *C* as a party to the bond, so the action had to be brought by *B*, though (as in the fifteenth century) *C* would have an action in the Chancery to force *B* to sue.[61]

Contracts, Promises and the Doctrine of Consideration

In medieval law informal contracts were enforceable only if they were reciprocal: the debtor must have received something in exchange, *quid pro quo*.[62] It was a feature of the types of transactions that created debts. In popular etymology this was the very essence of the idea of contract, *actus contra actum*.[63] With the shift towards liability based on promises, at least on the surface, it was by no means obvious that the same theory should apply, and there developed an alternative formulation of the criteria that marked off binding promises from non-binding ones. By the second

---

[57] *Holygrave* v. *Knyghtysbrygge*, YB M.27 Hen VIII f.24 pl.3.
[58] *Cutler* v. *Ward* (1587) Bodl MS Rawl C 647 f.174.
[59] (1598–1599) Cro El 619, Cro El 652, Moo 550, Yale Law School MS G R 29.10 f.211, Yale Law School MS G R 29.12 f.167ᵛ, CUL MS Ll 3.10 ff.33, 58ᵛ.
[60] See too *Rippon* v. *Norton* (1602) Cro El 881, Yale Law School MS G R 29.14 f.283; *Anon* (1609) LI MS Misc 586a f.57ᵛ.   [61] CUL MS Gg 2.31 f.179ᵛ (c.1620). Above, p.80.
[62] Above, pp.80–3.   [63] *Wiseman* v. *Cole* (1585) 2 Co Rep 15a, 15b; Co Litt 47.

half of the sixteenth century this had come to be known as 'consideration'. In order to understand its nature and development, it is essential to look at it on two levels, the formal and the substantial.

In formal terms, it is difficult to talk of any doctrine of 'consideration' before about 1560. While it seems clear that lawyers before this time had the idea that there was some additional factor that was needed to make promises binding, there was no consistent way of describing it. The sources reveal a variety of terms: consideration, *causa*, recompense, *quid pro quo*. As the action of assumpsit became established, consideration emerged as the term that described the necessary feature.[64] At a straightforward linguistic level, 'consideration' meant little more than 'reason' or 'motive', so that the consideration for a promise can be seen as the reason for which it was made.[65] The standard definition of it found by the early seventeenth century underlines this: 'A cause or occasion meritorious requiring mutual recompense, in fact or in law.'[66]

Substantively speaking, though, such a definition of consideration seriously misrepresents its meaning. If it tells us what consideration is, it does not tell us what is consideration. At this level, the primary focus of 'consideration' was the same idea of reciprocity as had lain behind the medieval action of debt.[67] Freed from the constraints of the earlier case law on *quid pro quo*, however, the courts were able to allow consideration to extend into areas that had been problematical for *quid pro quo*. Thus, while *quid pro quo* had been held fairly tightly within the requirement that there must have been some benefit to the debtor, by the 1560s it was recognized that consideration might include situations where the promisee had conferred a benefit on a third party or had acted to his detriment at the request of the promisor without any obvious benefit to anybody. All that was needed was a slightly looser conception of reciprocity.[68] Similarly, in the fifteenth century it had been unclear whether agreements to pay money on a marriage were actionable; such cases were eased into assumpsit by treating marriage as consideration, though precisely how this fitted into the idea of reciprocity remained controversial.[69]

It had never been really necessary for the courts to specify what were the

---

[64] J. H. Baker, 'Origins of the 'Doctrine' of Consideration, 1535–1585', in Arnold *et al.* (eds.), *On the Laws and Customs of England*, 336; Ibbetson, 'Assumpsit and Debt in the Early Sixteenth Century' [1982] CLJ 142, 153–5.   [65] Simpson, *History of Contract*, 318–26.

[66] J. Dodderidge, *The English Lawyer* (1631), 131. The definition is taken from the context of the law of uses, not assumpsit: *Calthorpe's Case* (1572) Dy 334b, 336b. Cf. *Sidenham* v. *Worlington* (1585) 2 Leon 224: 'Some moving cause or consideration precedent for which cause or consideration the promise was made.'

[67] For more detailed discussion of what follows, see Ibbetson, 'Consideration and the Theory of Contract in Sixteenth Century Common Law', in Barton (ed.), *Towards a General Law of Contract*, 67.   [68] Ibbetson, 'Consideration and the Theory of Contract', 68–9.

[69] Ibid., 81–3; above, p.81.

exact boundaries of *quid pro quo*. The defendant could prevent any discussion of difficult points by resorting to wager of law; and in any event the pleadings in the action of debt were sufficiently generalized that there was almost no scope for the discussion of substantive doctrine. The near silence of the fifteenth century contrasts with the near-deafening clamour of cases discussing the meaning of consideration in the second half of the sixteenth. Many of the rules found in the classical model of contract of the nineteenth-century writers were worked out in this period; and nearly all of these were deductions from the general principle of reciprocity.

Forbearance to sue, for example, was generally recognized as good consideration, unless it was for such a minimal period as to be of no value at all. In principle, the forbearance to sue where there was in fact no right in the first place was valueless, and therefore insufficient consideration; but, if the existence of the claim was disputed and the forbearance represented a genuine compromise, then it would be enough, for it was to the advantage of both parties to have their disputes settled without litigation.[70] In principle, a promise to pay money in consideration of the performance of something that the promisee was already bound by law to do would not ground an action, for the promisor was given nothing beyond the original legal entitlement; though it was arguable that the actual receipt of the money without having to sue would be good consideration for it was sufficient additional benefit to the creditor. Hence a promise to discharge a debt in consideration of the payment of less than was due should not be enforced; but the King's Bench was willing to countenance a weakening of this principle where the consideration was the actual payment of the sum rather than the simple promise to pay it, for it could be construed as an advantage to the creditor to have the money in hand rather than having to bring an action for it.[71]

The central concern with reciprocity not only determined what could constitute good consideration, but also determined how the consideration should be related to the promise. Thus it was very early recognized that a counter-promise could constitute good consideration (essentially enabling each party to sue immediately, independently of the performance of his or her own side of the agreement), but only so long as it was legally enforceable.[72] This led to problems with wagering contracts, agreements to observe

---

[70] Ibbetson, 'Consideration and the Theory of Contract', 75–7. See in particular *Lutwich* v. *Hussey* (1582) Cro El 19; *Tooley* v. *Windham* (1590) Cro El 206; *Anon* (1584) LI MS Misc 487 f.192ᵛ.

[71] Ibbetson, 'Consideration and the Theory of Contract', 77–9. See in particular *Hopkin* v. *Thynne* (1596) CUL MS Gg 3.25 f.109ᵛ, BL MS Harl 1697 f.117ᵛ; *Bosome* v. *Paine* (1585) Yale Law School MS G R 29.5 pl.56, CUL MS Ii 5.38 f.5.

[72] Baker, 'Origins of the "Doctrine" of Consideration', 345–50; Ibbetson, 'Consideration and the Theory of Contract', 85–8. See *West* v. *Stowel* (1578) 2 Leon 154; *Butterye* v. *Goodman* (1583) CUL MS Ii 5.38 f.85ᵛ.

arbitration awards, and the like, where an action would accrue to only one of the parties; in such cases it was normal to allege some additional, perhaps nominal, consideration in order to get round the difficulty. It followed too from the principle of reciprocity that the consideration must not have been past, for both the promise had to have been given for the consideration and the consideration for the promise; hence, if there was a chronological separation between consideration and promise, it was essential to link them together, normally by saying that the consideration had been performed at the request of the promisor, so that the later promise was in essence conceived as doing no more than quantifying the amount that was to be paid for the consideration.[73]

It should be stressed that the courts were not concerned with the adequacy of the consideration, except perhaps where there was an objectively determinable relationship between it and the promise (in currency exchanges, for example).[74] Outside this situation it was for the parties to make their own bargain. It was none of the courts' business to determine the fairness of the transaction.[75]

In substance, then, the core of the doctrine of consideration was the same idea of reciprocity that had lain behind the *quid pro quo* of the action of debt, however much its form involved looking at the promisor's reason for making the promise. Occasionally, though, arguments on the formal level infected the substantive issues. The acceptance of marriage consideration is a case in point, though this was more normally analysed in terms of the idea of reciprocity. Such an explanation was not possible where the alleged consideration was the natural love and affection that the promisor had towards the promisee.[76] This would probably have been enough consideration to raise a use in favour of the promisee in the Chancery, and it was argued that the same rules should apply in both contexts. Despite its rejection in the 1560s, the argument was successful in the King's Bench in *Marsh* v. *Rainsford* in 1588.[77] This was very much of an aberration, essentially admitted as such by John Clench, one of the judges in the case, in his report of the decision. One year later it was firmly rejected: 'This is no consideration, for it should exist between every man; and if this

---

[73] Ibbetson, 'Consideration and the Theory of Contract', 88–95. Cf. above, p.82.

[74] Ibbetson, 'Consideration and the Theory of Contract', 72–4. See *Knight* v. *Rushworth* (1596) Cro El 469; *Pillesworth* v. *Feake* (1602) BL MS Add 25203 f.479, Bodl MS Rawl A 415 p.62, p.142. The rule was applied equally in the action of debt: J. Rastell, *Expositiones Terminorum*, sub verb Contract (= 1579 edn., f.48).

[75] *Anon* (1582) BL MS Add 25197 f.13ᵛ. This is not, of course, to deny that the jury and judges might have been able to exercise some discretion when it came to the enforcement of unfair bargains; but there is precious little evidence of their actually having done so. For a rare example, see *Lord Mordaunt's Case* (1602) CUL MS Ee 3.45 f.7ᵛ.

[76] Ibbetson, 'Consideration and the Theory of Contract', 79–81.

[77] 2 Leon 111, Cro El 59, HLS 16 f.393ᵛ (= Simpson, *History of Contract*, 633), Yale Law School MS G R 29.5 pl.134 (Clench's report).

promise was sufficient, every promise would bind every man because this natural love should be between everyone.'[78] The sixteenth-century judges were not willing to resurrect the idea, but it remained beneath the surface to reappear briefly in the later eighteenth century.[79]

The one situation in which arguments from the formal level perhaps did succeed in influencing the substantive rules of liability was where a promise was made to perform an existing duty.[80] The standard form of pleading in 'indebitatus assumpsit' was based upon such a promise to pay an existing debt, and the objection taken by Edmund Plowden around 1567 that there was no consideration in such a situation[81] hence constituted a radical attack on the whole legitimacy of this method of allowing assumpsit to be brought in place of the action of debt. Plowden's objection was based on the premiss that the defendant's promise was the substantive cause of the defendant's liability, and it was undermined by the recognition that in such a situation the promise did nothing to alter the original liability of the defendant, but only provided a new formal shell within which the plaintiff's action might be framed. This would have been a complete answer to Plowden, but it was altogether easier to exploit the ambiguity of the word 'consideration' and simply assert that the existing debt constituted 'consideration in itself' or 'implied consideration', though the lawyers never went so far as to suggest that it was good consideration because the indebtedness was the best possible reason for making the promise.[82] In practice it did not matter a great deal whether it was said that the existing debt was a form of consideration or that in this type of case no consideration was necessary, for either formulation would have given the plaintiff a sufficient cause of action. In the longer term, though, its inclusion in the list of good considerations prevented the articulation of a general theory of consideration in terms of an idea of reciprocity, leaving the way open for future generations of lawyers to argue for a broader conception of the doctrine.

Assumpsit and Contractual Intention

To a large extent, therefore, the introduction of the action of assumpsit did not herald any wholesale shift from the exchange model of contract that had prevailed in the fourteenth and fifteenth centuries, even if the promissory form necessitated some reorientation of that theory. It did, though, bring into sharper relief that the principal basis of liability lay in the will of

[78] *Harford* v. *Gardiner* (1589) LI MS Hill 123b f.85. See too *Breton* v. *Digbye* (1600) Cro El 756 (*sub nom Bret* v. *JS*), BL MS Lansd 1065 f.47.   [79] Below, p.271.
[80] Above, n.45. Ibbetson, 'Assumpsit and Debt in the Early Sixteenth Century' [1982] CLJ 142; 'Consideration and the Theory of Contract', 69–72.
[81] *Anon* (c1567) BL MS Harg 15 f.40.   [82] Cf. Simpson, *History of Contract*, 322–3.

the parties to the agreement. This had been clear when the action of covenant had flourished,[83] but had fallen from view as debt had taken over the ground that had formerly been occupied by covenant; here the prime focus was the indebtedness that had stemmed from the reciprocal transaction of the parties, whose intention was important only when it came to identifying the type of transaction and the precise terms of it.[84] By the middle of the sixteenth century an etymological base was being given for treating 'agreement' as the meeting of the minds of the parties:

Aggreamentum is a word compounded of two words, viz. of *aggregatio* and *mentium*, so that *aggreamentum est aggregatio mentium in re aliqua facta vel facienda.* And so by the contraction of the two words, and by the short pronunciation of them they are made one word, viz. *aggreamentum*, which is no other than a union, collection, copulation, and conjunction of two or more minds in any thing done or to be done.[85]

The building blocks of liability were unchanged as assumpsit replaced debt, but the focus of the action was shifted away from the underlying trans-action to the parties' promise or agreement.

The effect of this was that there was greater scope to answer difficult questions by asking what had been the intention of the parties, though when the words of the agreement were known the court might not look beyond their natural meaning.[86] Thus it was possible to determine whether the obligations of the parties were mutually dependent or independent; in the former case it should be alleged that the consideration for the defen-dant's promise was some act on the part of the plaintiff, which had to have been performed before the defendant's promise was actionable, whereas in the latter case all that was necessary was to specify the consideration as a promise to do something. Which of these was the correct formulation was a question of fact, to be determined by the jury's determination of what the parties had agreed.[87]

This more explicit focus on the will of the parties facilitated the adoption of a truly consensual theory of contract, though this may reflect a change in commercial practice as much as a change in legal theory.[88] It was argued

[83] Above, p.73.
[84] The idea might still have surfaced in the action of debt: YB P.17 Edw IV f.1 pl.2, per Choke J.; above, p.73.
[85] *Reniger* v. *Fogossa* (1550) Plo 1, 17, per Pollard Sjt. This definition was picked up in later editions of Rastell's *Expositiones Terminorum* (1579 edn., f.13ᵛ), from where it found its way into subsequent law dictionaries.
[86] *Anon* (1593) BL MS Add 35950 f.13ᵛ (promise could not bear 'innuendo' alleged by plaintiff).
[87] Baker, 'Origins of the "Doctrine" of Consideration', 345–6; S. J. Stoljar, *The History of Contract at Common Law* (Canberra, 1975), 147–63.
[88] It is noticeable that the same shift towards a purely consensual theory of contract occurred elsewhere in the sixteenth century too: K.-P. Nanz, *Die Entstehung des allgemeinen Vertragsbegriff im 16. bis 18. Jahrhundert* (Munich, 1985).

strenuously as late as 1523 that, while the simple agreement to sell a horse would not be binding (or, which amounts to the same thing, would be subject to a condition that the price be paid immediately), the giving of earnest money was sufficient to make it perfect, seemingly marking a continuation of the medieval requirement of some formality to bind the parties.[89] Allegations of the payment of a small sum of money are found very commonly in actions of assumpsit in the first half of the sixteenth century, but, as the action became established in the 1550s and 1560s, they rapidly disappear. In *Bevalie* v. *Woods*[90] it was assumed in the Chancery that what was necessary for a perfect sale was agreement on all relevant terms, in particular the price; there is no mention of God's penny or earnest. As a matter of law it was the agreement of the parties that created the binding contract, and any formal accompaniment was simply a matter of evidence that might induce the jury to accept that the parties had indeed agreed. No doubt such payments, or handshakes, or shared drinks, continued to be made as a matter of practice,[91] just as a twentieth-century contractor might put down a small sum as a deposit when buying goods or shake hands (or share a bottle of champagne) at the conclusion of a commercial agreement; but no longer would they feature on the legal record.

THE FORMAL STRUCTURE OF CONTRACTUAL LITIGATION

By the beginning of the seventeenth century the action of assumpsit was able to provide a general remedy for informal agreements. The stark medieval distinction between 'contracts', which generated debts, and other types of agreements, whose enforcement was problematical, had disappeared, and with it the formal distinction to claims to entitlements and claims to damages. There were, it is true, very minor differences of procedure within assumpsit, depending on whether the action was brought for non-payment of a debt or for failure to perform some other type of contract,[92] but in so far as there might once have been substantive consequences—essentially the liability of executors—these had effectively disappeared by around 1620.[93] The division between debt-creating contracts

---

[89] YB H.14 Hen VIII f.18 pl.7 at f.22 per Brudenell C.J. Above, pp.75–6.

[90] (1583) Bodl MS Rawl C 647 f.63.

[91] Such practices are visible, for example, in depositions in ecclesiastical courts, where the parties or witnesses simply described what happened, rather than casting it into legally appropriate terminology. In 1629, for example, a man obtained the services of a prostitute on approval, giving a coin to the brothel-keeper as earnest: L. Gowing, *Domestic Dangers* (Oxford, 1996), 68.   [92] Above, pp.132–3.

[93] Above, n.31.

and other forms of agreement, however, did not simply wither away. On the contrary, it was bolted firmly into place by pleading practice.

Already by the middle of the sixteenth century there had developed the form of pleading known as 'indebitatus assumpsit'.[94] This terminology could be used generically to describe any situation in which assumpsit was brought in place of debt, but in the seventeenth century it came to refer more specifically to one particular way of framing a claim. Here the plaintiff alleged that the defendant, being indebted (*indebitatus*) in a certain sum of money, promised to pay that sum, which promise had not been performed. It was held in the first decade of the century that it was necessary to show how the debt had arisen—if it was based on a sealed obligation, for example, the alternative of suing in assumpsit was not available[95]—but it was not necessary to do so with any degree of specificity.[96] There thus developed a small number of standard formulas—the 'common counts'—to cover the most frequently occurring situations. A plaintiff who wanted to bring an action for the price of goods would bring the common count for goods sold and delivered or goods bargained and sold; one suing for wages would bring the common count for work and labour.[97] There was no magic about the common counts: so long as there was a debt for which assumpsit was available, some form of indebitatus assumpsit might be used.[98] If there was no debt due, the plaintiff could not bring indebitatus assumpsit, but instead had to bring an action of 'special assumpsit', the equivalent of the sixteenth-century lawyers' 'collateral assumpsit'. Here the agreement had to be laid out with greater specificity, that the defendant had promised to pay (or to do an act) for some particular consideration to be provided by the plaintiff, which promise the defendant had not performed.[99] Unlike indebitatus assumpsit, special assumpsit carried the risk for the plaintiff that the action would be lost if some material detail of the transaction was not proved as laid out in the declaration, so that it was good practice to join a count in indebitatus

[94] Above, n.23. For a full treatment of the developed form, see E. Lawes, *Practical Treatise on Pleading in Assumpsit* (1810), 418–503.

[95] The main reason for this was that a judgment in assumpsit could not be pleaded in bar in a subsequent action of debt on an obligation. For the same reason assumpsit could not be brought on a promise to pay a judgment debt.

[96] *Woodford* v. *Deacon* (1608) Cro Jac 206.

[97] As well as these there were common counts for money lent, money laid out at the request of the plaintiff, and money had and received to the plaintiff's use.

[98] So indebitatus assumpsit could be brought on a promise to perform the judgment of a foreign court, which did not count as a debt of record in the English courts (*Dupleix* v. *De Roven* (1705) 2 Vern 540; *Crawford* v. *Whittal* (1773) 1 Doug 4 n.); or for customary dues payable by a copyholder (*Shuttleworth* v. *Garnet* (1685) 3 Mod 239); or for a fine payable under a company's by-law (*Barbers* v. *Pelson* (1679) 2 Lev 252); or on a wager (*Leaves* v. *Bernard* (1695) 5 Mod 131).   [99] Lawes, *Pleading in Assumpsit*, 28–417.

assumpsit if at all possible.[100] This continued distinction in pleading meant that, in substance, the old difference between debt-creating transactions and other contracts continued to play its part in the action of assumpsit; and, so long as the possibility of joining alternative counts remained, there was no effective pressure from litigants to break down the barrier between them.

The problems that might arise, and their utter irrelevance in practice, are well illustrated by the forms of pleading known as *quantum meruit* and *quantum valebant*. Here the plaintiff was claiming not a predetermined fixed sum of money, but an assessment of the reasonable value of work done or of goods supplied. The medieval lawyers would not allow debt to be brought on such claims (since there was no sum certain),[101] but they fitted easily into the sixteenth-century action of assumpsit.[102] In the early seventeenth century it began to be said that a form of debt would lie,[103] a view that held until it was finally grubbed out at the beginning of the nineteenth century.[104] So long as debt was available, it followed that indebitatus assumpsit would lie; and, when debt disappeared, indebitatus assumpsit should equally have vanished. However, confusion was introduced by the eighteenth-century procedural rule that a plaintiff who brought indebitatus assumpsit for the failure to pay a fixed sum allegedly due as a debt would be entitled to judgment if the jury found that there had been an agreement to pay a reasonable sum.[105] A plaintiff wanting to claim a *quantum meruit*, therefore, could in practice use indebitatus assumpsit, but only so long as this was done behind the façade of claiming on a contract to pay a fixed sum: the action for a *quantum meruit* was not in itself indebitatus assumpsit, though it was confusingly close to it, an ambiguity waiting to be exploited by later generations of lawyers.[106]

It remained the case, though, that both indebitatus assumpsit and special assumpsit were technically actions for damages, requiring assessment by a jury. It followed that, if the defendant defaulted in appearance, the plaintiff would be entitled only to an interlocutory judgment, expressed to be in such sum as the jury would assess, and not a final judgment for the amount

[100] Ibid. 4; cf. 26–7 for the desirability of joining indebitatus and special counts.
[101] Above, p.31.
[102] J. H. Baker, 'The Use of Assumpsit for Restitutionary Money Claims', in Schrage (ed.), *Unjust Enrichment*, 31, 36. A clear sixteenth-century example is *Fenken* v. *Heywood* (1597) CUL MS Ii 5.16 f.183ᵛ.
[103] *The Six Carpenters Case* (1610) 8 Co Rep 146, 147 (misinterpreting YB P.12 Edw IV f.8 pl.22 at f.9b); *Waring* v. *Perkins* (1621) Cro Jac 626; *Marley* v. *Smith* (1667) 2 Keb 155. But see the doubts in *Mason* v. *Welland* (1688) Skin 238, 242.
[104] J. Chitty, *Treatise on Pleading* (5th edn., 1831), 1.123, differing in this respect from the 4th edn. (1825), 1.97. For late precedents, see J. Wentworth, *Complete System of Pleading* (1794–9), 5.145, 149, 150. Special assumpsit was far commoner: ibid., 1.186–214, 3.54–82.
[105] *Webber* v. *Tivill* (1669) 2 Wms Saund 121 n.2.   [106] Below, p.269.

owing (as was the case in the action of debt).[107] This formal distinction was
rigidly adhered to, though, where the amount due in an action of assumpsit
was a simple matter of arithmetical computation, the common practice by
the end of the eighteenth century was to remit it to an official of the court
rather than requiring the summoning of a jury. This was narrowly interpreted, however, and in practice limited to actions on bills of exchange and
promissory notes.[108] It was not available in normal actions of indebitatus
assumpsit for the price of goods sold or the like, where the principle of
requiring the summoning of a jury was continuously insisted upon.[109] The
principle was important in special assumpsit, but, so far as indebitatus
assumpsit was concerned, it was more a requirement of form than of
substance; here the jury was expected to award the amount of the debt
(together with a sum to represent interest) unless perhaps there had been
some sharp practice on the plaintiff's part.[110]

Assumpsit applied only to actions based on informal contracts. Formal
agreements, normally in the form of conditional bonds, continued to be
widely used well into the eighteenth century.[111] Here the proper remedy
was an action of debt by the creditor to recover the full amount of the
penalty in the bond. In the sixteenth century the Chancery began to
mitigate this by issuing injunctions against the enforcement of penalties
in an initially limited range of situations, and in the seventeenth century it
became ever more routine to issue such an injunction if the debtor had
performed the condition in substance and compensated the creditor for any
additional loss caused by the failure to perform to the letter.[112] This did
not affect the conceptual structure of the law: there was still a debt legally
due to the creditor, and the fact that this debt might not in fact be
recoverable could be concealed within the jurisdictional split between
Common law and Equity. The conceptual structure changed when relief
against penalties was brought within the domain of the Common law
courts by statute in 1697.[113] Now, although the creditor's claim continued
to be framed as an action of debt for the penalty, judgment in this sum
would be given only as security: all that could be enforced was the actual
loss suffered by the creditor as a result of the debtor's non-performance of
the condition. The shift in the real nature of the action on the conditional
bond is brought out by the procedure followed if the plaintiff became
entitled to judgment in default of appearance. Although the normal rule

[107] B. J. Sellon, *Practice of the Courts of King's Bench and Common Pleas* (1796), 2.17–18,
25; W. Tidd, *Practice of the Court of King's Bench* (1790), 313.
[108] *Green* v. *Hearne* (1789) 3 TR 301.
[109] *Anon* (1797) cited in Tidd, *Practice* (9th edn., 1828), 571 note.
[110] *Ramsden's Case* (1640) Clayton 87; *Lowe* v. *Peers* (1768) 4 Burr 2225; J. Sayer, *The Law
of Damages* (1770), 43–7.   [111] Above, p.28.
[112] The details of the history of relief against penalties are dealt with below, p.213.
[113] Stat 8 & 9 Will III c.11 s.8, amended by Stat 4 Anne c.16 s.12, s.13 (1705).

in the action of debt was that the plaintiff was entitled to final judgment for the amount of the debt, in this situation the matter had to be remitted to a jury to assess the amount that the plaintiff had lost through non-performance of the condition.[114] Although in form an action of debt, in substance it was an action for damages.

The potential for confusion was enormous. Indebitatus assumpsit was in substance an action to recover a debt but in form an action for damages; debt on a conditional bond was the reverse, in form an action to recover a debt but in substance an action for damages; and special assumpsit was both in form and substance an action to obtain damages, though it could sometimes masquerade as indebitatus assumpsit to recover a debt. Even at the moment at which the Common law had the potential to recognize a truly general contractual remedy, it was compromised by procedural twisting.

[114] Sellon, *Practice*, 17–18.

Part Three. The Modern Law of Tort and Contract

From the eighteenth century the modern law of tort and the modern law of contract took on their characteristic shape. Athough they differed significantly in points of detail, the dynamics of the development of each of these was essentially the same.

There were three essential preconditions. First was the substantial breakdown of the boundaries between forms of action. So far as contract was concerned, this had largely been achieved by the consolidation of the action of assumpsit in the sixteenth century, though it was not until the division between Common law and Equity was broken down in the middle of the nineteenth century that the unification of the law of contract was complete. The law of tort before the eighteenth century was more deeply fissured, with the fourteenth-century split between trespass and case still unresolved. In the eighteenth century, though perhaps not wholly legitimized until the early nineteenth, there was a wholesale shift of litigation from trespass to case. Just as assumpsit provided the formal framework for the law of contract, trespass on the case provided the frame for the development of the tort of negligence. Secondly, from the eighteenth century there was a shift in the balance of power between judge and jury. A variety of different mechanisms developed to enable judges to minimize the scope of jury discretion, either by controlling jury verdicts or by removing issues from the jury altogether. Matters that would formerly have been allowed to remain ambiguous were perforce made concrete. Thirdly, from towards the end of the eighteenth century there was an efflorescence of legal literature. Fundamental questions that would rarely if ever rise to the surface in legal practice were necessarily elevated to a position of central importance. No less importantly, textbooks that were repeatedly updated allowed both for rules to become fixed and for the law to grow by the continuous accretion of new rules around the old.

Against this backdrop the modern history of both tort and contract can be divided into three stages. Beginning in the eighteenth century there were stirrings of theorization, squeezing English rules into models developed elsewhere. Especially important were the works of the Natural lawyers, and through their influence a range of ideas based in different aspects of Roman law were introduced into England. These stirrings matured into full-blooded theorized structures in the nineteenth century. So far as contract was concerned, there was a further injection of continental ideas based on the works of Pothier, whereas the law of tort was a largely indigenous development from the eighteenth-century Natural law base. The result of this theorization was that both tort and contract became far more sharply delineated. In tort this was accomplished fairly cleanly, for there was little antecedent theory to displace. Contract was more problematic. There were frictions between the emergent model, the Will Theory, and the medieval exchange model that had lain behind the articulation of the sixteenth century, frictions that were resolved largely by ignoring them and—rather unsuccessfully—reorienting pre-existing ideas in line with the newer theory. Finally, largely in the twentieth century, there was a collapse of confidence in the theoretical structures of the nineteenth century; while the language of the nineteenth century (and before) continued to be used, it did so against the background of new theories, against the background of a kaleidoscope of competing theories, or against the background of no theory at all.

8. *Trespass, Case, and the Moral Basis of Liability*

Central to the later medieval law of torts was the division between the action of trespass and the action on the case. The former lay for invasive interferences to land, goods, or the person; the latter covered a range of situations where loss had been caused wrongfully. Liability in the former was on the face of it strict, while in the latter a range of fault-based ideas came into play, though there was no attempt to define further what constituted fault.

Through the seventeenth and eighteenth centuries the division between trespass and case was elided, most notably in cases of injury to the person, as it came to be recognized that liability in both actions was underpinned by similar fault-based ideas. For a variety of procedural reasons, small in themselves but cumulatively significant, the action on the case came to be more advantageous for plaintiffs, and their attempts to frame their actions in case pushed outwards the boundaries of that action; defendants (who were, of course, disadvantaged in equal measure as plaintiffs were advantaged) resisted this; and the courts had to delimit an explicit boundary between the actions. Plaintiffs nagged at this boundary and exploited it, and after a century of struggle the general action of trespass finally gave way. Before 1840 trespass had been essentially marginalized, limited to situations where plaintiffs' rights had been interfered with but no actual loss had been suffered.

At the same time, as a result of extra-legal philosophical speculation, the loose idea of fault became more sharply focused on the specific notion of negligence, the individual's failure to live up to the standard of behaviour of the reasonable person. The way that actions were pleaded meant that this was explicitly applied only in actions on the case, so that before the middle of the nineteenth century the way was clear for the knitting-together of the principal strands of trespass on the case into a unitary tort of negligence.

TRESPASS AND CASE: THE FORMAL DIVISION

Trespass and case had coexisted harmoniously from the middle of the fourteenth century. If there were any doubts as to the formal boundary between the two forms of action they were apparently settled early,[1] and

---

[1] *Berden* v. *Burton* YB T.6 Ric II (AF) 19; YB H.13 Ric II (AF) 103; above, p.55.

there seems to have been little inclination on the part of litigants to try to push the range of case further into the domain of trespass. The reasons for this are not difficult to discern. So far as the procedure of the two actions was concerned, there was at this time little reason to prefer case over trespass—if anything trespass had the marginally more advantageous process[2]—and it would have been far harder for plaintiffs to avoid the formal objection that the action on the case could not apply where some other action was available than it was at other points where there was friction at the boundary with another form of action.[3]

This began to change in the seventeenth century. The initial kick, perhaps, came from the statutory introduction of more stringent rules for the award of costs to the successful plaintiff in a trespass action than in an action on the case;[4] by the end of the century the courts were having to deal with actions on the case brought deliberately to avoid these rules.[5] The effect of these statutes was to make the action of trespass relatively unattractive except where an entry into another's land or a deliberate attack on another's person was involved. Secondly, it was recognized that the bringing of an action of trespass might pass to the defendant the initiative in determining the expenses of the litigation: a defendant who wanted to keep the costs down could plead a general 'not guilty', whereas one who wanted to escalate the costs could plead specially. The action on the case gave no such opportunity to the defendant.[6] Thirdly, and increasingly in the eighteenth century, plaintiffs in actions based on road accidents wanted to join together counts covering a number of possible fact situations where they could not be sure in advance of the trial exactly what would be found to have happened. Counts in trespass and case could not be joined together, so there was considerable pressure to be able to frame all of one's alternative counts in the same form of action. It was generally held that trespass was inappropriate in actions based on vicarious liability, so a count based on a servant's having been at the reins would have to be in case; so too would a count based on the driver having lost control of the horses. It followed that, in order to satisfy the procedural rules, there was equally pressure to use case when the defendant had been at the reins and in full control.[7] Finally, no doubt, there was the relative ease of bringing

---

[2] In trespass the initial process was normally by capias, in case (until 1504) by summons; and in trespass any burden of special pleading fell on the defendant, whereas in case it was the plaintiff who had to define the details of the claim. The main reason for case to take over from other actions, the desire to avoid wager of law, did not operate here, for wager of law would never have been available in trespass.   [3] Above, pp.103, 108, 137.
[4] Stat 43 Eliz c.6; Stat 21 Jac I c.16; Stat 22 & 23 Car II c.9 s.136; Stat 4 & 5 W & M c.23; Stat 8 & 9 Will III c.11. For the effect of these statutes, see Blackstone, *Commentaries*, 3.400.
[5] *Shapcott* v. *Mugford* (1697) 1 Ld Raym 187, 188, citing *Thornton* v. *Austen* (1693).
[6] Cf. J. Morgan, *The Attorney's Vade Mecum* (1787), 1.38.
[7] M. J. Prichard, 'Trespass, Case and the Rule in Williams v. Holland' [1964] CLJ 234, 239–44.

the action on the case in all circumstances: it was inevitably easier not to have to think what the correct form of action was, even if the mental effort involved would not have been great.

These procedural benefits of case might have been counterbalanced by the substantive benefits of an action of trespass, which did not raise any question of the defendant's fault; but in the seventeenth and eighteenth centuries it came to be recognized that there was a substratum of fault in trespass just as much as in case. This occurred in two ways, both within the Common law and at a more intellectual level.

So far as the action of trespass was concerned, on its face liability was no less strict than it had been in the Middle Ages. If the plaintiff's injury had been caused by the defendant, then in the absence of any special justification the defendant would be liable. By the eighteenth century most of the learning in the action of trespass centred around when such a justification could be pleaded.[8] It followed that the principal focus of the action was not so much on the wrongfulness of the defendant's conduct as on its rightfulness: the boundaries of trespassory liability were defined by the absence of right rather than by the presence of wrong.

The alternative to entering a special plea of justification was for the defendant to deny generally having committed the trespass. In essence, as in the thirteenth or fourteenth century, this amounted to a denial that it was the defendant who had caused the plaintiff's injury, though it could be expressed more broadly as a denial that the injury had been caused by the defendant's voluntary act.[9] The notion of voluntariness was rather narrowly construed—so long as the initial act was willed it did not matter that its consequence was not, for example[10]—but there was room within its ambiguities to begin to exploit ideas of fault.[11] Thus it was said that, if a gun went off and injured the plaintiff, the defendant might in some circumstances avoid liability: 'if the defendant had said that the plaintiff ran across his piece when it was discharging, or had set forth the case with the

---

[8] See e.g. J. Wentworth, *Complete System of Pleading* (1799), vol. 9. Trespass to the Person, for example, might be justified by the execution of legal process, extralegal process (as where a churchwarden justified using his cane to knock a man's hat off in church), moderate correction (e.g. a shipmaster ordering a seaman to be moderately flogged and put in irons), protection of property, self-defence, the preservation of the peace, or the prevention of mischief.

[9] *Millen* v. *Hawery* (1625) Lat 13, Lat 119; see esp. the remarks of Dodderidge J. at Lat 13. Cf. above, p.58.

[10] e.g. *Angell* v. *Shatterton* (1663) 1 Sid 108 (B&M 333); *Dickinson* v. *Watson* (1682) T Jones 205 (B&M 335); *Underwood* v. *Hewson* (1724) 1 Str 596.

[11] This was already the case in the early sixteenth century: YB T.13 Hen VIII f.16 pl.1, per Browne Sjt. Cf. the reading on the Statute *De Malefactoribus in Parcis* quoted by Baker, *Spelman's Reports, ii* (94 SS), *223*: 'In the case where a man comes past a park holding his dogs on the leash, and does not intend them to enter the park, yet against his will the dogs break the leash and leave him and enter the park (where perhaps they kill an animal), no action lies against him; for if he were punished it would be against all reason, inasmuch as there was no fault in him.'

circumstances so as it had appeared to the court that it had been inevitable and that the defendant had committed no negligence to give occasion to the hurt.'[12]

The Common law's stuttering recognition of the role of fault in trespass was consolidated by the intellectual climate of the seventeenth and eighteenth centuries. The fault-based nature of liability for wrongs had been a commonplace of Roman law, and from there it had been taken up by the writers of the Natural law school in the seventeenth century. Samuel Pufendorf puts the point quite explicitly: 'Whenever we hurt or endamage another, we do it either out of full purpose and premeditated guilt, or by negligence only and not of design (and this negligence, as it is more or less gross and supine, is more or less culpable). Or lastly we may do it by mere chance, so that the injury cannot rightly be imputed to us . . .'.[13] These writings gained considerable popularity in England around 1700, and they remained important throughout the eighteenth century.[14] In such an atmosphere it is unsurprising that they came to affect the perception of liability in trespass.

Though trespass was coming to be recognized as no less fault-based than case, it was behind the negative proposition that liability would not lie in the absence of fault rather than behind any positive requirement that the plaintiff prove fault. There was a clear potential for an explicitly wrong-based (or fault-based) analysis to develop and to challenge the prevalent right-based approach to trespassory liability. That this did not occur was the consequence of defendants' unwillingness to focus their pleadings on issues of fault; it was dangerous for them to do so, for they might be treated as having admitted the facts alleged by the plaintiff and having failed to justify them.[15] The more prudent course was to plead the general issue and leave the whole matter in the hands of the jury. As a result, at a formal level the action of trespass retained its traditional focus on whether or not the defendant had had a right to do what had been done, though in point of substance the role of fault was clearly recognized.

---

[12] *Weaver* v. *Ward* (1616) Hob 134, Moo 864, HLS MS 112 p.319 (B&M 331); Kiralfy, *Source Book*, 132. The quotation is from Hob 134.
[13] *Of the Law of Nature and Nations*, 3.1.6 ('Caeterum ut aliquis a nobis laedatur, aut damno afficiatur, fieri potest vel dolo malo destinatoque consilio, vel per solam culpam citra propositum quidem, non tamen absque negligentia, eaque vel leviore, vel magis supina; vel denique per casum fortuitum, sic ut ista laesio recte nobis imputari nequeat.')
[14] L. Krieger, *The Politics of Discretion* (Chicago, 1965), esp. 255–69. Blackstone's indebtedness to Grotius, Pufendorf, and Burlamaqui has been very thoroughly examined: see e.g. J. L. Finnis, 'Blackstone's Theoretical Intentions' (1967) 12 Natural Law Forum 163; N. E. Simmonds, 'Reason, History and Privilege: Blackstone's Debt to Natural Law' (1988) 105 ZSS (GA) 200.
[15] As said in *Weaver* v. *Ward* itself, according to Moore's report of the case. See too *Burford* v. *Dadwell* (1669) 1 Sid 433 (B&M 334); *Dickinson* v. *Watson* (1682) T Jones 205 (B&M 335); *Gibbons* v. *Pepper* (1695) 1 Ld Raym 38, 4 Mod 405, 2 Salk 638 (B&M 335).

Once it was seen that the difference between trespass and case was purely formal, the various procedural advantages of case over trespass provided good reason for plaintiffs to try to extend the range of the former action into the domain of the latter; and once plaintiffs began to explore and exploit the boundary between trespass and case it was incumbent on the courts to say what that boundary was. The upshot of this was that by 1700 it was established as a rule, almost certainly introduced by analogy with Roman law, that where the plaintiff had been directly injured by the defendant's act the correct action was trespass, and where the injury was merely consequential case was appropriate.[16] The clearest statement of this rule is found in the well-known illustration of Fortescue J. in *Reynolds* v. *Clarke* in 1725:[17] 'If a man throws a log into the highway, and in that act it hits me; I may maintain trespass, because it is an immediate wrong; but if as it lies there I tumble over it, and receive an injury, I must bring an action on the case; because it is only prejudicial in consequence, for which originally I could have no action at all.'[18] An alternative way of putting the same point was that, if the defendant's act was an invasive interference—a trespass, a wrong—the plaintiff should bring trespass, any consequential loss being recovered in damages; if the act was not in itself a trespass, then the correct form of action was case.[19] This was put slightly differently by Lord Raymond C.J., that if the initial act was unlawful the proper action was trespass but if it was lawful it should be case.[20] Although in substance the same as the distinction of Fortescue J., the slight shift in focus of Lord Raymond's version set it apart as an alternative test, a source of some confusion later in the century.[21]

The concern in *Reynolds* v. *Clarke* was to establish a clear demarcation between the forms of action: until the publication of Blackstone's *Commentaries* nearly half a century later provided a conceptual map, Common-law knowledge was structured firmly around the forms of action, so that any fuzziness in their range of application represented a fuzziness in the law itself. 'We must keep up the boundaries of actions, otherwise we shall introduce the utmost confusion.'[22] So long as the formal boundary between the actions was maintained, the courts were not—for the time being—concerned with how they were mapped by litigants onto the facts of their claims. Thus, if the defendant's wrongful act had injured the plaintiff both directly and consequentially, the latter had the choice of suing in

---

[16] For the Roman law, see Justinian, *Institutes*, 4.3.3. The distinction was found, though less clearly delineated, in medieval law: *Berden* v. *Burton*, YB T.6 Ric II (AF) 19, above, p.55.
[17] 1 Str 634, 2 Ld Raym 1399, 8 Mod 272, Fort 212, (B&M 354).   [18] 1 Str 634, 636.
[19] 1 Str 634, 635. The point was put in precisely this way by Belknap C.J. in *Berden* v. *Burton*, YB T.6 Ric II (AF) 19, 21.
[20] 1 Str 634, 635. See too the pleading manual extracted at B&M 356, 357.
[21] Below, n.35.   [22] 1 Str 634, 635, per Lord Raymond C.J.

trespass (and recovering the whole amount of the loss by way of damages) or waiving the initial trespass and suing in case (recovering only in respect of the consequential loss). This is well illustrated by *Slater's Case*.[23] The plaintiff brought an action on the case for false imprisonment and consequential loss; it was objected that her action ought to have been trespass *vi et armis*, but the King's Bench held that it was open to her to elect between the two actions. Similarly in *Pitts* v. *Gaince*[24] a shipmaster was held entitled to elect between trespass and case when his ship was wrongfully seized, as a result of which he lost the profit of his voyage.

It followed from this that plaintiffs would almost invariably be able to frame their actions in case; this, it seems, is what they did. The only circumstance in which trespass would be obligatory was where there was no consequential injury;[25] in practice, this was limited to cases where the plaintiff was suing to establish the existence of a right rather than to recover damages for loss suffered. Such situations would commonly involve rights over land, and it was at this time that the word 'trespass' began to take on its specific association with going on to the land of another without permission.[26] Where there was both direct interference and consequential injury, plaintiffs might choose to bring trespass; but it seems that they would do so only if they were claiming that the defendant had acted wilfully, for in these circumstances there were no procedural advantages in bringing case.[27] As a matter of practice, therefore, there developed a close association between the action on the case and claims based on the defendant's non-deliberate conduct.

A defendant might legitimately object if sued in trespass when the injury suffered was purely consequential;[28] and by the 1760s it was coming to be said that it was equally improper to bring case where the injury had been directly inflicted.[29] There was still room for some flexibility, though. *Slater* v. *Baker*[30] provides a good example. The plaintiff was being treated for a broken leg. After the joint had begun to knit, the defendant, who had been

---

[23] (1708) Holt KB 22. Cf. *Starr* v. *Rookesby* (1710) 1 Salk 335.

[24] (1700) 1 Salk 10, 1 Ld Raym 558, Holt KB 12.

[25] *Thornton* v. *Austen* (1693), as cited at Holt KB 22 (sub nom *Tonson* v. *Oston*).

[26] S. Johnson, *Dictionary* (1755), *sub verb* 'trespass'; cf. Blackstone, *Commentaries*, 3.209.

[27] Most particularly, the master could not have been liable for the act of a servant (and hence there would have been no problem with the joinder of different forms of action in the same writ), and there would have been no disadvantages from the point of view of costs.

[28] As in *Reynolds* v. *Clarke* itself. Trespass was brought alleging that the defendant had fixed a downspout to the plaintiff's wall, and that the foundations of his buildings had rotted as a result of water collected in his yard. Once it was established that the defendant had had a right to fix the downspout, the plaintiff's claim was doomed to fail.

[29] *Haward* v. *Bankes* (1760) 2 Burr 1113; *Harker* v. *Birkbeck* (1764) 3 Burr 1556; *Tripe and Dyer* v. *Potter* (1767), noted 6 TR 128, 8 TR 191.

[30] (1767) 2 Wils KB 359. Cf. *Annual Register 1767*, 108. Some of the background to the case can be deduced from the news report in the *London Chronicle*, 14–16 July 1767.

surgeon at St Thomas's Hospital since 1739, attached to the leg 'an heavy steel thing with teeth' and once again broke the leg. The plaintiff brought an action on the case; the court received evidence from Percivall Pott, first surgeon at Bart's Hospital and pioneer of the scientific approach to bone-setting, that the defendant's acts were wholly improper,[31] and after lengthy deliberation the jury found for the plaintiff with damages of £500. The defendant argued that the proper form of action should have been trespass rather than case, and that the plaintiff should therefore be required to bring his action afresh. The court seems to have been inclined to accept that trespass was indeed appropriate, but they did not treat this as the end of the matter: 'The court will not look with eagle's eyes to see whether the evidence applies exactly or not to the case, when they can see the plaintiff has obtained a verdict for such damages as he deserves, they will establish such verdict if it be possible.'[32]

Already in *Slater* v. *Baker* there is visible a subtle but crucial change of emphasis. No longer was the court simply looking at the formal propriety of the pleadings; it was going beyond this and considering whether, on the facts revealed by the evidence, the form of action chosen by the plaintiff was correct. This can be associated with an important shift in the balance of power between judge and jury. For most of the previous five centuries the judges had been content to accept the verdict of the jury without looking behind it; indeed, the mechanisms that existed to allow them to do so were almost non-existent. A more critical stance was becoming visible in the early eighteenth century, and by the second half of the century it was becoming more common to reserve points of law from the trial at nisi prius to the court *in banc*. A case stated drawn up by counsel on each side could then be considered by the whole court, who could then decide whether—on these facts—the plaintiff or defendant was entitled to the verdict and judgment.[33] The jury might now become no more than finders of facts; the questions of law, both formal (Is this the correct form of

---

[31] The judicial attitude to expert evidence is described by Pott: 'I remember some years ago to have heard a judge from the bench tell a jury, that he believed a country bone-setter knew full as much, if not more of the matter of his own business, than any, the most eminent surgeon in the kingdom. I will not enter into a disquisition concerning the rightness of the judge's opinion. Perhaps his lordship might very little understand the thing concerning which he decided so peremptorily; without either injustice or partiality, I may certainly suppose him to have been a much more able lawyer than surgeon: and I believe it will also be allowed, that general reflections of this kind are, and must be, the consequences of a petulant attempt to be witty, rather than of conviction; and therefore, at best, are frivolous and idle' (P. Pott, *Some Few General Remarks on Fractures and Dislocations* (2nd edn., 1773), 4).

[32] 2 Wils KB 359, 362.

[33] M. J. Prichard, 'Nonsuit: A Premature Obituary' [1960] CLJ 88, 92–5; Baker, *Introduction to English Legal History*, 160–1. For the earlier development, J. Mitnick, 'From Neighbor-Witness to Judge of Proofs: The Transformation of the English Civil Juror' (1988) 32 Am Jnl Leg Hist 201.

action?) and substantive (On these facts should the plaintiff win?), could be dealt with by the judges.

This mechanism was used in *Scott* v. *Shepherd*.[34] The plaintiff brought trespass alleging that the defendant had put out his eye. The jury found that the defendant had thrown a lighted firework into a market hall, that the person next to whom it landed had immediately picked it up and thrown it away, as had the next person. The plaintiff was not so lucky: he was hit by the firework just as it exploded. It was argued that on these facts the proper action was case, since the injury was consequential rather than direct. The court agreed that the direct/consequential test was the proper one to use, though partially sheltering behind a twisted interpretation of the remarks of Lord Raymond C.J. in *Reynolds* v. *Clarke* that it depended whether or not the initial act was unlawful.[35] The majority of the court, perhaps generously, held that on these facts there was a direct chain of causation; Blackstone J., on the other hand, was inclined to hold that the injury was purely consequential and that case was indeed the appropriate remedy.

If *Scott* v. *Shepherd* was a pointer to the future, it was still rooted in the past: the direct/consequential test may have been ossifying, but it was still accompanied by the rule that where both direct and consequential injury had been suffered the plaintiff might have an election between suing in trespass and suing in case. This is quite explicit in the dissenting judgment of Blackstone J.:

> The same evidence that will maintain trespass, may also frequently maintain Case, but not e converso. Every action of trespass with a per quoad includes an action on the Case. I may bring trespass for the immediate injury, and subjoin a 'per quod' for the consequential damages;—or may bring case for the consequential damages and pass over the immediate injury.[36]

Around 1800 this important qualification disappeared. In *Day* v. *Edwards* it was said in passing by Lord Kenyon C.J. in the King's Bench that, if the plaintiff's injury had been caused directly by the defendant, the action had to be trespass; if it was consequential, the action had to be case.[37] If such a rule were to be enforced, the procedural consequences would be especially catastrophic where the action was brought for injury suffered on the highway or at sea, where the plaintiff could not know in advance whether the action should be trespass (defendant personally

---

[34] (1773) 2 Wm Bl 892, 3 Wils 403.

[35] Above, n.20. It was a statutory offence to throw a squib into a public place: Stat 9 & 10 Will III cap 7, s.1. Blackstone J. explicitly rejected the test: 2 Wm Bl 892, at 894.

[36] 2 Wm Bl 892, at 897.

[37] (1794) 5 TR 648. It should be noted that the point was not specifically in issue in *Day* v. *Edwards*, whose concern was solely with whether the plaintiff's declaration was formally self-consistent (which it transparently was not).

driving and in control of the vehicle) or case (defendant's servant driving, or defendant had lost control of the vehicle), for the rule preventing joinder of counts in trespass and case meant that the plaintiff had to be committed to one form of action or the other.[38] Five years later, in *Ogle* v. *Barnes*, the King's Bench again asserted the rigid direct/consequential test; but its potentially damaging effects were neutralized by equating negligence with nonfeasance and applying the rule that a failure to act could only ground an action on the case.[39] An action based on negligence, therefore, would continue to fit easily into case, since it could not be said that the plaintiff had been directly injured by any act of the defendant. In 1803 this escape route was blocked: in *Leame* v. *Bray*[40] Lord Ellenborough C.J. insisted upon an unqualified application of the test. The decision in *Leame* v. *Bray* was soon criticized by the Court of Common Pleas,[41] and by 1810 Lord Ellenborough C.J. himself was admitting that his earlier decision might have to be reconsidered,[42] perhaps by the reincorporation of the old rule that a plaintiff who had suffered loss consequential upon a direct injury should be entitled to waive the trespass and sue in case.[43] In practice, by the 1820s the courts had moved to this position, though the theoretical aspects of the debate grumbled on until 1833, when it was finally put to rest in *Williams* v. *Holland*.[44] In effect this reinstated the practice of the eighteenth century, though formulating it expressly as a rule of law. If the claim was for a consequential injury, the action had to be case, whether the defendant had acted wilfully or negligently; if the claim was for a direct injury wilfully inflicted, the action had to be trespass; if it was for a direct but negligent injury, the plaintiff had the choice between trespass and case. The only circumstance in which case would not lie, therefore, was where the injury was direct and wilful; but it was peculiarly hazardous for a defendant to argue that the plaintiff's claim fell into this category, since it would amount to an admission of deliberate wrongdoing that he would be estopped from denying in subsequent civil proceedings.[45]

---

[38] The initial response of the King's Bench to this was to hold that cases of vicarious liability based on direct injury should be pleaded in trespass, but they were unable to hold to this position. See *Savignac* v. *Roome* (1794) 6 TR 125; *McManus* v. *Crickett* (1800) 1 East 106.
[39] (1799) 8 TR 188. The equation of negligence and nonfeasance is found in the judgments of Lord Kenyon C.J. (at 188) and Lawrence J. (at 192).   [40] (1803) 3 East 593.
[41] *Rogers* v. *Imbleton* (1806) 2 B & P (NR) 117; *Huggett* v. *Montgomery* (1807) 2 B & P (NR) 446.
[42] *Lotan* v. *Cross* (1810) 2 Camp 464. The pressure is visible two years earlier: *Covell* v. *Laming* (1808) 1 Camp 497.   [43] *Hall* v. *Pickard* (1812) 3 Camp 187.
[44] (1833) 2 LJCP (NS) 190. The settling-down of the practice is best illustrated by *Moreton* v. *Hardern* (1825) 4 B & C 223; but cf. *Lloyd* v. *Needham* (1823) 11 Price 608 and the Third Report of the Parliamentary Commissioners on Courts of Common Law (PP HC 1831, x. 7–8).
[45] *Doe d. Wetherell* v. *Bird* (1835) 7 C & P 6.

THE CRYSTALLIZATION OF NEGLIGENCE

The recognition that tortious liability depended on fault was itself a substantial step. As well, though, in the eighteenth and early nineteenth centuries the Common law began to define what was meant by 'fault' in this context. The term they used was 'negligence'.

Negligence (*negligentia*) was one of the range of terms commonly used since the fourteenth century to designate the basis of liability in trespass on the case.[46] More specifically, it had come to be associated with the liability of the bailee. This association, explicitly borrowing from Roman law, had been firmly put in place by the judgment of Holt C.J. in *Coggs* v. *Barnard* in 1703, reversing the trend of the sixteenth and seventeenth centuries towards strict liability.[47] It was fleshed out and given a solid underpinning of (Roman) learning by Sir William Jones in his *Essay on the Law of Bailments* (1781).[48] Jones was not content simply to say that the bailee should normally be liable for negligence or neglect; this was no more than the corollary of the failure to live up to the appropriate standard of care, which he articulated as normally being the care of 'the generality of rational men', which 'every person of common prudence and capable of governing a family takes of his own concerns'. In appropriate situations either a lower or a higher standard might be demanded; in the former case liability was only for gross negligence, in the latter for slight negligence. This division, he noted, coincided with the Romans' tripartite division into *culpa lata*, *culpa levis*, and *culpa levissima*.[49] The bailee's liability at Common law had its analogue in the liability of the trustee in Chancery, and by the end of the seventeenth century there are echoes of bailment-based reasoning there.[50] In the middle of the eighteenth century the link is explicit; in *Charitable Corporation* v. *Sutton*,[51] for example, Lord Hardwicke moved directly from the liability of the bailee in *Coggs* v. *Barnard* to the liability of the trustee who had mismanaged a fund. And,

---

[46] Above, p.54.
[47] *Coggs* v. *Barnard* (1703) 2 Lord Raym 909, B&M 370. For the sixteenth- and seventeenth-century developments, centring round *Southcote* v. *Bennett* (1601) 4 Co Rep 83, see Ibbetson, 'Absolute Liability in Contract: The Antecedents of Paradine v. Jayne', in F. D. Rose (ed.), *Consensus ad Idem* (London, 1996), 1.23–30.
[48] Ibbetson, '"The Law of Business Rome": Foundations of the Anglo-American Tort of Negligence' [1999] Current Legal Problems, 74, 80–4.   [49] *Essay on Bailments*, esp. 5–9, 21.
[50] *Hussey* v. *Markham* (1676) Rep temp Finch 258; *Morley* v. *Morley* (1679) 2 Ch Cas 2; *Clarke* v. *Perrier* (1679) 2 Freem 48, 79 SS 782 pl.992; *Palmer* v. *Jones* (1682) 1 Vern 144. See generally D.E.C. Yale, *Nottingham's Chancery Cases, ii* (79 SS), *137–41*.
[51] (1742) 2 Atk 400. To similar effect, *Jones* v. *Lewis* (1751) 2 Ves Sen 240. Cf. the generally disapproved view of Lord Northington L.K. in *Harden* v. *Parsons* (1758) 1 Eden 145, 148, that a trustee should be liable only for fraud but that gross negligence was equivalent to fraud.

just as the bailee's liability was consciously rooted in the Roman law, so too was the liability of the trustee.[52]

From the second half of the eighteenth century 'negligence' came more generally to play an increasingly central part in the analysis of tortious liability. Already in 1762 Sir John Comyns, Chief Baron of the Exchequer, could include in his *Digest* a title for the 'Action upon the Case for Negligence',[53] which has a surprisingly modern ring to it, comprised of negligence in a man's trust, negligence in his office, 'neglect in doing that, which by law he ought to do', neglect to do that which he had undertaken, negligence in taking care of animals, and negligence in keeping a fire. Around the same time, perhaps more significantly, Francis Buller went further than this and provided something approaching a general definition: 'Every man ought to take reasonable care that he does not injure his neighbour; therefore when a man receives hurt thro' default of another, tho' the same were not wilful, yet if it be occasioned by negligence or folly the law gives him an action to recover damages for the injury so sustained.'[54] And slightly later he adds a qualification to this: 'However it is proper in such cases to prove the injury was such as would probably follow from the act done.'[55]

Four elements of Buller's statements demand attention. First, as with Jones's *Essay on Bailments*, the primary stress is on the wrongdoer's antecedent duty. Instead of simply saying that there was liability for loss caused by the defendant's fault, or even that there was liability for loss caused by the defendant's failure to take reasonable care, Buller's primary stress is on the duty that has been breached. His starting point is prospective rather than retrospective, what ought to be done rather than what ought not to have been done. Secondly, the duty is expressed as a duty to take care rather than as a crude duty not to cause harm; thirdly, the care that has to be taken is characterized as only 'reasonable' care; and, fourthly, it is only probable harm that can be laid at the charge of the wrongdoer.

---

[52] *Charitable Corporation* v. *Sutton* (1742) 2 Atk 400, 405 (citing Domat's *Civil Laws in their Natural Order*); 1 Eq Cas Abr (1732) 310–11 (citing Vinnius' commentary on Justinian's *Institutes*). Lord Northington's approach in *Harden* v. *Parsons* (above, n.51) seems to be an echo of the classical Roman-law tradition according to which a gratuitous depositee was liable only for *dolus* or *culpa lata*.

[53] Comyns, *Digest*, 1.223–8. 'Negligence' here is closer to the modern 'neglect', with its focus on omissions to act.

[54] *Introduction to the Law of Trials at Nisi Prius*, 35. The text was first published anonymously in 1767; the attribution to Buller appears in the edition of 1772. According to the dedication to the edition of 1772, it was based on manuscript notes of his uncle, Henry (subsequently second Earl) Bathurst, though the nisi prius notes of Bathurst (which were continued by Buller) in LI MS Misc 129 seem to have no connection with the *Law of Nisi Prius*. The section on evidence in the *Law of Nisi Prius* was first published in Bathurst's name (as *The Theory of Evidence*) in 1761.

[55] *Introduction to the Law of Trials at Nisi Prius*, 36.

None of these elements was incompatible with the Common law of the previous four centuries: liability for failing to perform a duty was well known in a number of contexts[56] and it is easy to trace back to the fourteenth century a concern with the defendant's lack of care.[57] On the other hand, there was nothing in the earlier Common law necessitating an analysis of liability in this form. At the most, we could see it as an articulation of ideas that might have been current earlier, which by its very nature imposed a measure of definition and shape on an area of law that had formerly been inherently undefined.[58] Nor were these ideas necessarily indigenous: all of them can be traced into those Natural lawyers of the seventeenth and eighteenth centuries who were particularly influential in England—Grotius, Pufendorf, Burlamaqui, and Barbeyrac.[59]

The Natural lawyers were primarily moral philosophers rather than lawyers, and it was fundamental to their enterprise that they were concerned with the norms of human behaviour. Within the law of contract, for example, the stress was on the responsibility to keep promises rather than the obligation to compensate for their breach. So, too, when looking at wrongs the emphasis fell on the individual's duty, with the obligation to compensate for breach of the duty as a purely secondary matter. This is well brought out by Pufendorf's treatment: 'But those likewise stand responsible who commit an act of trespass, tho' not designedly, yet by such a piece of neglect as they might easily have avoided. For it is no inconsiderable part of Social Duty to manage our conversation with such caution and prudence that it do not become terrible and pernicious to others.'[60] The idea of duty is central to the Natural lawyers' theory of imputation of moral acts. For an act to be imputable to an individual it must have been governed by the will of the actor; for it actually to be imputed there had to be a breach of duty: 'We may impute to a person any action or omission, of which he is the author or cause, and which he could or ought to have done or omitted.'[61] As

---

[56] P. H. Winfield, 'Duty in Tortious Negligence' (1934) 34 Col L R 41, 44–8.
[57] Above, p.54. [58] For the lack of definition of the medieval law, see above, n.14.
[59] Above, p.158. Barbeyrac's influence was principally as editor of other people's writings. For the Natural lawyers' approach to wrongdoing, see H.-P. Benöhr, 'Außervertragliche Schadensersatzpflicht ohne Verschulden? Die Argumente der Naturrechtslehren und-kodifikationen' (1976) 93 ZSS (RA) 208, 208–28, and B. Kupisch, 'La Responsibilità da Atto Illecito nel Diritto Naturale', in L. Vacca (ed.), *La responsibilità civile da atto illecito nella prospettiva storico-comparatistica* (Turin, 1995), 123.
[60] *Law of Nature and Nations*, 3.1.6 ('non minima socialitatis pars sit, ita circumspecte agere, ut nostra conversatio aliis non fiat formidolosa, aut intolerabilis'). Cf. Barbeyrac's pithy note on this: 'Human Society will be happy enough, if every Man carefully abstains from endamaging others, not only out of a formal Design, but thro' the least Negligence.'
[61] J. J. Burlamaqui, *Principes du droit naturel* (1748), 2.193 (I have quoted from the English translation, *Principles of Natural Law* (1817), 148). The idea was taken from Pufendorf's *Elements of the Universal Civil Law*, 3–4; see too *Law of Nature and Nations*, 1.5.3–5, together with Barbeyrac's note to 1.5.3.

with Buller, the starting point is the duty of the alleged wrongdoer, not the suffering of harm by the victim.

The 'Social Duty' described by Pufendorf was not a duty not to injure another, but simply a duty to be careful. Pufendorf's predecessor Hugo Grotius had made essentially the same point; it is well expressed by Thomas Rutherforth, Regius Professor of Divinity at the University of Cambridge, in his course of lectures based on Grotius' work:

Though there is no degree of malice in an action, by which another is injured, yet it might arise from some faulty neglect or imprudence in him, who does it, or is the occasion of its being done: and when any person has suffered damage, for want of his taking such care, as he ought to have taken; the same law, which obliged him, as far as he was able, to avoid doing harm to any man, cannot but oblige him, when he has neglected this duty, to undo, as well as he can, what harm he has been the occasion of; that is, to make amends for the damage, which another has sustained through his neglect.[62]

The third element of Buller's definition was the 'reasonableness' of the defendant's conduct. This again had its basis in the writings of the Natural lawyers' figure of the *diligens homo*, a figure traceable back to the *diligens* (or *bonus*) *paterfamilias* of the Roman law.[63] He was no stranger to English law, having been translated into the guise of the 'reasonable man' in the context of the liability of bailees at the beginning of the eighteenth century,[64] and his integration into the emergent tort of negligence presented no great difficulty.

Finally, Buller had pointed to the propriety of only imposing liability for probable injuries. Again, we may trace here the influence of the Natural lawyers' theory of imputation. If the minimum condition of imputability was a voluntary act, actual imputation following if and only if the voluntary act had been in breach of an antecedent obligation, the imputation would be just only if there was a necessary or accidental connection between the act and the consequences. Moreover, Burlamaqui adds, '. . . the agent must have had some knowledge of this connection, or at least he must have been able to have a probable foresight of the effects of his action . . .'.[65]

It would be premature to see a 'Tort of Negligence' in existence at the end of the eighteenth century. In some fields—notably bailment and the closely allied equitable action for breach of trust—negligence had indeed come to be recognized by the courts as the basis of liability, but outside

---

[62] T. Rutherforth, *Institutes of Natural Law* (1754), 1.415.
[63] A. Berger, *Encyclopedic Dictionary of Roman Law* (Philadelphia, 1953), 377, 437.
[64] *Coggs* v. *Bernard* (1703) 2 Ld Raym 909, 2 Salk 735; above, n.47.
[65] Burlamaqui, *Principles of Natural Law*, 144. Cf. Barbeyrac's note to Pufendorf, *Law of Nature and Nations*, 1.5.3

these its role in legal practice was more peripheral. It did, however, have a more central role in the works of speculative writers and legal scientists. These, building directly or indirectly on ideas found in Roman law, had framed their analysis of liability for causing harm around the failure to take reasonable care; and this in its turn was no more than the corollary of the existence in the first place of a duty to take care not to injure others. It would not have required great foresight to predict that the idea would be taken up by the judges of the succeeding century.

9. The Law of Torts in the Nineteenth Century: The Rise of the Tort of Negligence

The law of torts at the beginning of the nineteenth century was still recognizably medieval. It was characterized by a division between the action of trespass and the action on the case, the latter of which was subdivided into a number of nominate forms and a large residuary group linked together by nothing stronger than that the defendant was alleged to have caused loss to the plaintiff. In the nineteenth century a substantial part of this residuary group coalesced as the tort of negligence. This brought about a wholesale realignment of the law of torts, as this tort, defined by reference to the quality of the defendant's conduct, cut across the previously existing categorization of torts.[1]

THE TORT OF NEGLIGENCE

At the beginning of the nineteenth century there were two competing approaches to negligence. On the one hand, there was the unitary idea that 'Every man ought to take reasonable care that he does not injure his neighbour', concretized in the figure of the reasonable man;[2] on the other was the tripartite division into gross negligence, ordinary negligence, and slight negligence found in Jones's analysis of bailment.[3] Towards the middle of the century the tripartite test came under attack. In *Hinton* v. *Dibbin* in 1842 Denman C.J. professed himself unable to understand it;[4] one year later, in *Wilson* v. *Brett*, Rolfe B. dismissed it cursorily as negligence with a 'vituperative epithet';[5] and in *Ronneberg* v. *Falkland Islands Co*[6] the Court of Common Pleas got very close to holding firmly that a gratuitous bailee was liable for ordinary (non-gross) negligence. Crystallizing the single standard of negligence was the crisp definition of Alderson B. in *Blyth* v. *Birmingham Waterworks* in 1856: 'Negligence is the omission to do something which a reasonable man, guided upon those considerations

---

[1] The material on the history of negligence in this chapter is developed at greater length in my forthcoming article 'The Tort of Negligence in the Common Law in the Nineteenth and Twentieth Centuries', and in '"The Law of Business Rome": Foundations of the Anglo-American Tort of Negligence' [1999] Current Legal Problems, 74.

[2] Buller, *Nisi Prius*, 35 (above, p.165); *Vaughan* v. *Menlove* (1837) 3 Bing NC 468.

[3] Above, p.164.   [4] (1842) 2 QB 646, 661.   [5] (1843) 11 M & W 113, 116.

[6] (1864) 17 CBNS 1.

which ordinarily regulate the conduct of human affairs, would do, or doing something which a prudent and reasonable man would not do.'[7]

From a structural point of view, the developed nineteenth-century tort of negligence had three elements: an antecedent duty to take care owed by the defendant to the plaintiff; a breach of this duty; and resultant loss to the plaintiff.

The Duty of Care

The early stirrings of the use of the duty of care in the analysis of negligence cases occurred towards the beginning of the nineteenth century when plaintiffs who wished to stress that their action was not contractual in its nature began to assert that the defendant's conduct had been such as to impose a duty to take care.[8] The terminology is found in other contexts by the 1830s;[9] but it was in the 1860s that it finally established itself as an organizing device.[10] As late as 1860 the general principle gets only the briefest mention in the first edition of Charles Addison's *The Law of Wrongs and their Remedies*.[11] In 1862 a classic definition was given by Wilde B. in 1862 in *Swan* v. *North British Australasian Co* (not itself a case of negligence): 'The action for negligence proceeds from the idea of an obligation towards the plaintiff to use care, and a breach of that obligation to the plaintiff's injury.'[12] This was rapidly incorporated into Addison's second edition (1864), where the coy prefatory remarks of the first edition were expanded into a full-blooded introductory chapter.[13]

The language of duty had been found in the writings of the seventeenth- and eighteenth-century Natural lawyers, from where it had been taken into Buller's *Nisi Prius*;[14] it would already have been familiar to English lawyers at the beginning of the nineteenth century. Moreover, the tendency to equate 'negligence' with 'neglect' elevated the role of the duty, for just as

[7] (1856) 11 Ex 781, 784. There is good reason to believe that the adoption of a unitary test of negligence in place of the trichotomy of standards of care was directly influenced by changes in continental European practice and theory: Ibbetson, '"The Law of Business Rome"' [1999] Current Legal Problems, 74, 100–9.
[8] *Govett* v. *Radnidge* (1802) 3 East 62; *Ansell* v. *Waterhouse* (1817) 6 M & S 385; M. J. Prichard, 'Scott v. Shepherd (1773) and the Emergence of the Tort of Negligence' (London, 1976), 31–2. For the need to draw a boundary between contract and tort, see below, p.171.
[9] *Bird* v. *Holbrook* (1828) 4 Bing 628; *Daniels* v. *Potter* (1830) 4 C & P 262; *Drew* v. *New River Co* (1834) 6 C & P 754; *Vaughan* v. *Menlove* (1837) 6 Bing NC 468; *Langridge* v. *Levy* (1837) 2 M & W 519, 4 M & W 337.
[10] This is graphically visible from the cases cited by P. H. Winfield, 'The History of Negligence in the Law of Torts' (1926) 42 LQR 184, 199.   [11] Preface, p.v.
[12] (1862) 7 H & N 603, 636. See too the definition of Willes J. in *Grill* v. *General Iron Screw Colliery Co* (1866) LR 1 CP 600, 612: 'the absence of such care as it was the duty of the defendant to use.'
[13] See esp. 13–16. The reference to *Swan* v. *North British Australasian Co* is at p.15.
[14] Above, pp.165–6.

an omission to act would constitute culpable neglect only if there had been a duty to act, culpable negligence could be defined in terms of a failure to observe a duty to take care.[15] It was, too, a convenient way to demarcate those situations in which liability would be imposed from those situations in which it would not. Frederick Pollock made the point briefly; after quoting the definition given by Alderson B. in *Blyth* v. *Birmingham Water-works*, that negligence consisted in the failure to live up to the standards of the prudent and reasonable man, he immediately introduced the qualification, 'provided, of course, that the party whose conduct is in question is *already* in a situation that brings him under a duty of taking care'.[16] Hence it was also possible to say that not every person injured by a negligent act would necessarily be entitled to compensation; liability would arise if and only if a duty were owed *to that person*. Such a qualification was important where the duty was said to have arisen out of a contractual relationship, for here the duty would extend only as far as the parties to the contract.[17] It might equally apply where the defendant was under a statutory duty owed to a person other than the person injured or where the plaintiff was outside the foreseeable range of injury.

It is one thing to say that the idea of the duty of care was part of the conceptual baggage available to nineteenth-century lawyers, but quite another to explain how it came to play a central analytical role in the emergent tort. It would not be an exaggeration to say that the defining feature of the English (and American) tort of negligence, as compared to its continental equivalents, was the separation between the duty of care and the breach of duty. Two factors, specific to the Common-law world, brought this about.

First was the problem of distinguishing between tort and contract. The action on the case straddled a whole range of claims, some of which were clearly contractual, some of which were clearly tortious, and some of which were clearly ambiguous.[18] It was, though, necessary to be able to distinguish between claims in contract and tort for practical reasons. It was possible to join several independent claims in a single action, but contract

[15] See in particular J. Austin, *Lectures on Jurisprudence* (2nd edn. [1st thus], London, 1863), 2.108. Austin's analysis was consciously borrowed by such influential writers as Francis Wharton and Thomas Beven.

[16] *The Law of Torts* (London, 1887), 355 (emphasis added). Cf. F. Wharton, *Treatise on the Tort of Negligence* (Philadelphia, 1874), 1–2.

[17] e.g. *George* v. *Skivington* (1869) LR 5 Ex 1.

[18] C. G. Addison, *The Law of Wrongs and their Remedies* (2nd edn., 1864), 12 (not in 1st edn., 1860); Pollock, *Torts*, 353–4, 429–46; W. Markby, *Elements of Jurisprudence* (Oxford, 1871), 87–91. The ambiguity is marked by references to the middle category as 'Tort founded on Contract' (Addison, *Wrongs* (2nd edn.), 12) or 'Quasi-Torts' (A. Underhill, *Summary of The Law of Torts* (London, 1873), 25), or by analogizing them to the Roman category of Quasi-Delicts (M. de W. Howe (ed.), *The Pollock–Holmes Letters* (Cambridge, 1942), 1.4–5) (Pollock).

claims could be joined only with contract and tort claims only with tort.[19] In contractual actions the limitation period began to run at the moment of breach, in tortious actions from the occurrence of damage.[20] In addition, liability in tort was several, so that an action could be brought against any one of a group of alleged tortfeasors, whereas liability in contract was joint, so that all contracting parties had to be sued together and a verdict in favour of any one of the defendants was fatal to the plaintiff's claim.[21] These issues were particularly acute in actions against carriers of goods and persons.[22] There was no doubt that a carrier might be sued in contract, counting specially on the agreement with the plaintiff. As an alternative, though, there was a standard-form count against a 'common' carrier, and it was not clear whether this should be characterized as contractual or tortious. After some uncertainty, the Court of Exchequer Chamber held in *Bretherton* v. *Wood* (1821)[23] that it was to be regarded as tortious: 'A breach of this duty is a breach of the law, and for this breach an action lies founded on the common law, which action wants not the aid of a contract to support it.'[24] Behind this there lay a general principle that, if the plaintiff's cause of action could be fully stated without reference to any special contract between the parties, then it could properly be regarded as tortious, and the plaintiff was able to take advantage of the favourable rules of joinder. In appropriate cases, therefore, the plaintiff would have the option of suing in either contract or tort.[25]

These practical considerations may have been responsible for the theoretical concern with the boundary between contract and tort. Whatever the explanation, it seems clear that the nineteenth century did witness an increasing recognition that the contract/tort division was the principal analytical division within the law of obligations. In the middle of the century Charles Addison wrote separate treatises on tort and contract, as did Frederick Pollock a generation later; and the near-definition of torts as 'wrongs independent of contract' was well established by the Common Law Procedure Act of 1852.[26] Given this division, some distinguishing

---

[19] *Dickson* v. *Clifton* (1766) 2 Wils 319; Prichard, 'Scott v. Shepherd', 27.

[20] *Battley* v. *Faulkner* (1820) 3 B & Ald 288; *Dyster* v. *Battye* (1820) 3 B & Ald 448; *Fraser* v. *Swansea Canal Navigation Co* (1834) 1 Ad & El 354.

[21] *Ansell* v. *Waterhouse* (1817) 6 M & S 385; *Bretherton* v. *Wood* (1821) 3 Brod & B 54. Equally, joint contractors might have claims for contribution *inter se*, while joint tortfeasors would not: *Merryweather* v. *Nixan* (1799) 8 TR 186; *Powell* v. *Layton* (1806) 2 B & P (NR) 365, 371; *Bretherton* v. *Wood* (1821) 3 Brod & B 54. See Prichard, 'Scott v. Shepherd', 27–8.

[22] Prichard, 'Scott v. Shepherd', 26–8.   [23] 3 Brod & B 54.

[24] 3 Brod & B 54, 62 per Dallas C.J.; cf. *Marzetti* v. *Williams* (1830) 1 B & Ad 415. A curious consequence of this categorization is that the leading case on contract damages, *Hadley* v. *Baxendale*, was in fact technically a case falling within the law of tort: below, p.230.

[25] *Brown* v. *Boorman* (1844) 11 Cl & F 1, 44, per Lord Campbell. The overlapping of remedies is thoroughly explored by Pollock, *Torts*, 429–46.

[26] No less important in locking in place the contract/tort division were the County Courts Acts of 1846 onwards: P. H. Winfield, *The Province of the Law of Tort* (Cambridge, 1931), 76–8.

criterion was essential, but, since it cut across the traditional forms of action, none could be found within the earlier Common law. The most straightforward test was to analyse both contractual and tortious obligations as arising out of breaches of duties, and to say that the duty in contract arose out of the agreement of the parties while the duty in tort arose by operation of law. Whatever the analytical adequacy of this, it provided a rough-and-ready workable distinction, and became entrenched in the literature of the law.

Secondly, and of more fundamental importance, was the division between law and fact. Crudely speaking, the existence of a duty was a question of law, whereas its breach was a question of fact.[27] Unless the matter was dealt with explicitly by statute, the question whether or not there was a duty of care was in principle a matter for the judge, though more sophisticated commentators recognized that it was more complicated than this and that there was an intermingling of the functions of judge and jury.[28] It followed that, the more that issues could be framed in terms of the duty situation, the more they were removed from the sphere of jury discretion. This was no novelty of the nineteenth century, for it was inherent in the action of trespass on the case from its beginnings in the middle of the fourteenth century that its boundaries of application were questions of law rather than questions of fact.[29] At an abstract level the only change in the nineteenth century was the relatively unimportant terminological shift to the use of the language of 'duty of care'; at a concrete level, though, even outside the sphere of statutory duties there was a marked increase in the degree of detail with which duty situations were formulated.[30] The more precisely delineated they became, the more firmly did the incidence of liability fall under the control of the judges. No less importantly, defining them as questions of law rather than of fact meant that they were subject to the operation of the doctrine of precedent, with the result that individuals might more certainly regulate their conduct by reference to them. According to one influential commentator, it was this 'substitution of approximate standards of conduct for the unchecked determination of juries' that brought about the expansion and increasing complexity of the nineteenth-century tort of negligence.[31] In addition, since judges were (reputedly and apparently) less favourably inclined towards injured plaintiffs

---

[27] It is telling that under the heading of 'Duty' in his commonplace book Parke B. notes only that it is a matter of law: Prichard, 'Scott v. Shepherd', 43.

[28] Howe (ed.), *The Pollock–Holmes Letters*, 1.85 (Pollock), 1.92 (Holmes). Particularly penetrating is O. W. Holmes, 'The Theory of Torts', repr. at (1931) 44 Harv L R 773, esp. 779.

[29] Above, pp.48–56.   [30] Below, p.179.

[31] Beven, *Negligence*, 12. See too P. H. Winfield, 'Duty in Tortious Negligence' (1934) 34 Col L R 41, 61 n.92.

than were juries,[32] the increasing judicial control over liability meant that the costs of injuries were to a greater or lesser extent shifted from injurer to injured. Products liability is a fine example. In the seminal case of *Winterbottom* v. *Wright*,[33] where the plaintiff had been injured when a wheel flew off a mail-coach supplied by the defendant to the Postmaster-General, the Court of Exchequer refused to allow an action against the negligent coachmaker. The rules of privity enabled his claim in contract to be blocked; and his claim in tort foundered on the fact that no previous authority could be found in which a contractual duty from *A* to *B* had been held to generate a duty in tort from *A* to *C*;[34] and the court was transparently concerned not to allow an action that might cast what they perceived as an unreasonable burden on manufacturers. As a consequence, judge-made rules, stemming from transparent judicial preferences, meant that negligent manufacturers largely escaped liability for damage caused by their goods.[35]

Breach of Duty

As a counterweight to the judicial determination of the existence of the duty of care, whether there had been a breach of duty was a matter for the jury. It was, in principle, for it to say whether the defendant had taken the care that would have been taken by a reasonable person in the circumstances. In practice, around the middle of the century, the judges began to erode the jury's autonomy. They used two mechanisms to achieve this. Most crude was blatant judicial usurpation. This came to a head in *Bridges* v. *North London Railway Company*,[36] where the House of Lords held that, so long as there was some evidence on which the jury might hold that there had been a breach, it was the duty of the judge to leave the question to them: it was emphatically not his job to replace their judgement with his

---

[32] This was explicitly recognized in *Metropolitan Railway* v. *Jackson* (1877) 3 App Cas 193, 197–8 (Lord Cairns L.C.), 208 (Lord Blackburn). See further Ibbetson, 'The Tort of Negligence in the Common Law', forthcoming.

[33] (1842) 10 M & W 109. For more detail, see Ibbetson, 'The Tort of Negligence in the Common Law', forthcoming.

[34] The only precedent of such a claim (Wentworth, *Complete System of Pleading*, 8.397) was one in which the plaintiff's serjeant had advised that the action should be discontinued as hopeless: the plaintiff, a disappointed legatee, was attempting to sue a solicitor who had been so dilatory in the preparation of a will that the testator had died before he had been able to execute it. *Tempora mutantur.*

[35] Though see the extraordinary case of *George* v. *Skivington* (1869) LR 5 Ex 1, 21 LT (NS) 495, 39 LJ Ex 8 (filled out by the report in *The Times*, 16 Nov. 1869). The court allowed an action against a negligent manufacturer–supplier pleaded in contract by a husband and wife to be treated as if it had been pleaded in tort by the wife alone, and then gave judgment in her favour (equating negligence with fraud) without hearing any argument. The contorted legal background to the case is discussed in Ibbetson, 'The Tort of Negligence in the Common Law', forthcoming.   [36] (1871) LR 6 QB 377; (1874) LR 7 HL 213.

own.[37] *Bridges* v. *North London Railway Company* might have been inter-preted as allowing only a very limited function to the judges, but three years later, in *Metropolitan Railway Company* v. *Jackson*,[38] the House of Lords stressed that they still had the responsibility to remove the case from the jury if there was insufficient evidence of the defendant's negligence.[39] More subtly, the same result could be reached by redefining questions as questions of duty rather than questions of breach. The potential for this was well illustrated by *Blyth* v. *Birmingham Waterworks*[40] in 1856. Unusually severe frosts had caused the defendants' water hydrants to freeze closed; as a result, when the main water pipe ruptured, a large quantity of water seeped into the plaintiff's cellar rather than being released through the hydrant. In an action against the water company, the judge left to the jury the question whether the defendants had acted reasonably, and a verdict was given for the plaintiff. This was overturned by the Court of Exchequer: such a severe frost was unforeseeable, and a reasonable person does not take steps to guard against unforeseeable possibilities.[41] Or, in other words, there was no duty to avoid unforeseeable events.

Remoteness of Damage

The final positive element of negligence liability, the causation of damage, was in principle as much a matter for the jury as was the question of breach. The judges had traditionally been unwilling to interfere with the jury's discretion over the assessment of damages, but there was a long-standing idea that liability would exist only for the 'proximate' conse-quences of the act; 'remote' consequences were too distant.[42] A similar idea had appeared in Buller's *Nisi Prius*, that the wrongdoer should be held liable only for the probable consequences of an act.[43] This was, hesitantly, picked up by Pollock C.B. in the middle of the nineteenth century,[44] and later knitted together masterfully by his grandson Frederick Pollock in the first edition of his text-book on the law of torts:

[T]hose consequences, and those only, are deemed 'immediate', 'proximate', or, to anticipate a little, 'natural and probable', which a person of average competence and knowledge, being in the like case with the person whose conduct is complained

[37] The general principle was established in *Ryder* v. *Wombwell* (1868) LR 4 Ex 32.
[38] (1877) 3 App Cas 193.
[39] See esp. Lord Cairns at 197, and Lord Blackburn at 208.   [40] (1856) 11 Ex 781.
[41] (1856) 11 Ex 781, 784 per Alderson B. The test of foreseeability was already found as a rule of remoteness of damage, and its translation from there marks the first step of its recategorization: below, n.45.   [42] F. Bacon, *Maxims of the Law* (1598), reg.1.
[43] Above, p.165.
[44] *Rigby* v. *Hewitt* (1850) 5 Ex 240; *Greenland* v. *Chaplin* (1850) 5 Ex 243 (dissenting on this point from the other members of the court). Cf. *Hoey* v. *Felton* (1861) 11 CBNS 142, 143.

of, and having the like opportunities of observation, might be expected to foresee as likely to follow upon such conduct.[45]

Foreseeability, therefore, had a dual role to play, determining both whether the damage was too remote and whether there had been a breach of duty.[46] Such a double function entailed a degree of redundancy. The question of breach was more susceptible of judicial control than the question of remoteness, especially when it served as a conduit to reformulate issues in terms of the very existence of the duty, and consequently there was a clear tendency for the question of foreseeability to disappear altogether from the test of remoteness and to be redefined as something determining whether there had been a breach of duty. This was made absolutely explicit by Channell B. in *Smith* v. *London and South Western Railway Co*:

[W]here there is no direct evidence of negligence, the question what a reasonable man might foresee is of importance in considering the question whether there is evidence for the jury of negligence or not . . . but when it has once been determined that there is evidence of negligence, the person guilty of it is equally liable for its consequences, whether he could have foreseen them or not.[47]

Though the view of Pollock C.B., that foreseeability had an independent role as a test of remoteness, was not finally rejected until 1921,[48] in practice the decision in *Smith* v. *London and South Western Railway Co* locked in place the rule that the defendant was liable for all the consequences of the negligent act.

   The combined effect of *Bridges* v. *North London Railway Company* (as explained in *Metropolitan Railway Company* v. *Jackson*) and *Smith* v. *London and South Western Railway Co.* was that the power of the jury had been somewhat abridged, though perhaps not as far as the judges would have liked. Those who wanted to limit the power of the jury further than this were constrained to do so by expanding the role of the duty of care, whose determination was more or less firmly within the judicial domain. It is no accident that it was only a few years after these cases that Brett M.R. began the movement to generalize the duty of care in terms of a requirement to take the care that would be taken by a reasonable man.[49] In this way, the quintessential jury question of breach of duty—had the defendant acted as a reasonable man?—could be transmuted into the judicial question whether there had been a duty in the first place. And, in

[45] *Torts*, 28; cf. the far more sophisticated analysis of Wharton: *Negligence*, 76–152.
[46] *Blyth* v. *Birmingham Waterworks* (1856) 11 Ex 781; above, n.41. The point of the relationship between breach and remoteness appears more strongly in the variant versions of the judgment of Alderson B. (25 L J Ex 212, 213; 2 Jur (NS) 333, 334) and in *Cornman* v. *Eastern Counties Railway Co* (1859) 4 H & N 781, 786.   [47] (1870) LR 6 CP 14, 21.
[48] *re Polemis and Furness, Withy & Co Ltd* [1921] 3 KB 560.
[49] *Heaven* v. *Pender* (1883) 11 QBD 503; below p.189.

the course of this transmutation, foreseeability was further removed from its original home as a rule of remoteness, this time finding its niche in the very heartland of the tort of negligence, whether there was a duty of care in the first place.

Defences

Exactly the same phenomenon occurred in the case of defences to prima facie liability. Contributory negligence, for example, had impeccable medieval antecedents,[50] but in the nineteenth century it took on a far more precisely delineated character. The first steps in this process of articulation were taken by Lord Ellenborough C.J. in *Butterfield* v. *Forrester*;[51] and, after some initial uncertainty whether liability should be negatived in any case where the plaintiff's fault had materially contributed to the injury,[52] the law soon settled down in terms of the 'last-opportunity' test—whether the plaintiff or defendant had had the last opportunity to prevent the occurrence of the injury.[53] Essentially this was a straightforward causal test, different from the medieval rule solely in its relative precision; but it was through this precision that judicial control effectively operated. Judicial preferences come out more clearly in the second principal defence, consent (commonly left in Latin as *volenti non fit iniuria*). In most cases it was no more than a rhetorical flourish accompanying a court's decision that there was no breach of duty (or no evidence of breach to go to the jury),[54] though rhetorical flourishes have an important part to play in justifying decisions made on other grounds. For most of the nineteenth century employers' liability was effectively limited by the rule that employees impliedly consented to run the risks ordinarily incidental to their work;[55] in actions against railway companies this contrasts starkly with the far more plaintiff-oriented approach where injuries to passengers were concerned.[56] A yet clearer example of detailed rules underpinning judicial preferences is the so-called fellow-servant rule—that an employer

---

[50] Above, p.59.   [51] (1809) 11 East 60.

[52] *Bridge* v. *Grand Junction Railway Company* (1838) 3 M & W 244; *Marriott* v. *Stanley* (1840) 1 M & G 568; *Davies* v. *Mann* (1842) 10 M & W 546.

[53] *Tuff* v. *Warman* (1858) 5 CBNS 573.

[54] It was recognized explicitly in the leading case of *Smith* v. *Baker* [1891] AC 325 that it was normally only the correlative of the defendant's not being in breach of any duty. In that case there had been a finding that the defendant had not been negligent, against which no appeal was possible under the terms of the County Courts Act 1888; the defendant was not able to circumvent this procedural rule by recategorizing his argument in terms of *volenti non fit injuria*.

[55] *Clarke* v. *Holmes* (1862) 7 H & N 937. There was a move away from this at the end of the century: *Woodley* v. *Metropolitan District Railway Company* (1877) 2 Ex D 384, 393–4; *Thomas* v. *Quartermaine* (1877) 18 QBD 685; *Smith* v. *Baker* [1891] AC 325.

[56] R. W. Kostal, *Law and English Railway Capitalism* (Oxford, 1994), 279–321.

would not be vicariously liable if one employee negligently injured another employee.[57] This rule first appeared in England in 1850,[58] consciously borrowed from the decision of Shaw C.J. in the Massachusetts case of *Farwell* v. *Boston and Worcester Railroad*,[59] who in his turn claimed to have based his decision on the judgment of Lord Abinger C.B. in *Priestley* v. *Fowler*.[60] English lawyers had not themselves thought to interpret *Priestley* v. *Fowler* in this way; their doing so in 1850 was a transparent judicial choice to adopt the economic liberalism espoused by Shaw C.J. All depended on the 'implied terms' of the contract of employment and on the definition of 'fellow-servant'; both were treated as matters of law for the judges to decide, effectively neutralizing what was perceived to be the pro-employee bias of jurors presented with such cases.[61]

THE FRAGMENTATION OF THE LAW OF TORT

The action of trespass on the case, in its very nature, had always tended to put stress on the individual circumstances of the alleged wrongdoing; but, whereas in continental Europe the nineteenth century had witnessed a generalization of delictal liability, English law remained essentially fragmentary. This fragmentation is visible within the tort of negligence, around the tort of negligence, and outside the tort of negligence.

Duties of Care and the Fragmentation of the Tort of Negligence

The framework of the nineteenth-century tort of negligence was provided by the duties of care. While scholars might disagree as to whether there was a single tort of negligence based on the failure to take care not to injure others, whose precise topography was delineated by the multiplicity of duties of care, or a multiplicity of innominate torts whose common feature was that it was negligence that made the defendant's conduct culpable, there would have been little doubt that a practical understanding of negligence liability required an analysis of the whole range of individual duty situations.[62]

---

[57] Kostal, *Law and English Railway Capitalism*, 254–79.

[58] *Hutchinson* v. *York, Newcastle and Berwick Railway Co.* (1850) 5 Ex 343. See too *Bartonshill Coal Co.* v. *Reid* (1858) 3 Macq 266, where the rule was forced on the unwilling Scots.   [59] (1842) 4 Metc 49.

[60] (1837) 3 M & W 1. See A. W. B. Simpson, 'A Case of First Impression: *Priestley* v. *Fowler*', in *Leading Cases in the Common Law* (Oxford, 1995), 100.

[61] Kostal, *Law and English Railway Capitalism*, 274 n.117. The rule came under attack in the 1870s and its worst effects were removed by the Employers' Liability Act 1880, though it was not until the Workmen's Compensation Act 1948 that it was finally eradicated from the law: P. W. J. Bartrip and S. Burman, *Wounded Soldiers of Industry* (Oxford, 1983), 126–57.

[62] Cf. e.g. Pollock, *Torts*, 22, 352, with Addison, *Wrongs* (2nd edn.), 15.

Bigelow was most explicit: after dealing briefly and generally with the nature of negligence, he admitted that the major part of litigation in negligence revolves around the question whether the facts submitted to the court made a case to be submitted to the jury—that is, whether there was a duty of care; but 'to consider such questions would require a detailed examination of the authorities beyond the scope of this book'.[63] The first edition of Thomas Beven's *Principles of the Law of Negligence* (1889) devoted no less than 700 pages to the subject; and another commentator remarked that 'The Law in regard to Negligence is the most uncultivated part of the "wilderness of single instances" of which our law consists.'[64] This approach to duties of care meant that from the beginning the tort of negligence had a coarse granular quality. The casuistic nature of legal reasoning meant that the grains became ever smaller and the texture of the tort ever finer;[65] but it was only in the twentieth century that it was emulsified into a single duty situation.

Alongside the Common-law action for negligence there were actions in Chancery for breach of trust. Breach of trust might once have been actionable at law, but before the end of the seventeenth century it was a clear rule that trustees were liable only in Equity.[66] Despite the difference in forum, though, the trustee's liability tracked closely the Common-law liability of the bailee.[67] The trustee, who was not permitted by English law to profit from his office, was equivalent to a gratuitous bailee and, it was argued, was consequently required to exercise the standard of care that he showed about his own affairs,[68] the equivalent of the continental lawyers' *diligentia quam in suis rebus*.[69] It was, however, difficult for the courts to know what care the individual trustee normally took, so that this subjective test tended to collapse into a more straightforward objective test of reasonable prudence.[70] In practice the distinction between the two approaches was blurred by the existence of concrete rules governing the duties of trustees (as to permitted investments and such like), and by the inherent flexibility

---

[63] M. M. Bigelow, *Elements of the Law of Torts* (Cambridge, 1889), 283.

[64] 'The Duty of Care towards One's Neighbour' (1883) 18 Law Journal 618, 619.

[65] Although this meant that the books got bigger, it did not mean that the scope of the tort became wider. A beach does not get larger simply because its pebbles are broken down into fine sand.

[66] N. G. Jones, 'Uses, Trusts, and a Path to Privity' [1997] CLJ 174, 189–98; *Sturt* v. *Mellish* (1743) 2 Atk 610, 612. [67] Above p.164.

[68] J. Story, *Equity Jurisprudence* (1st English edn., 1884), §1268 (the earlier American editions are to the same effect); F. A. Lewin, *Law of Trusts* (8th edn., 1885), 294. See *Coggs* v. *Barnard* (1703) 2 Ld Raym 909, 915; *Massey* v. *Banner* (1820) 1 J & W 241, 247, per Lord Eldon.

[69] Zimmermann, *Obligations*, 210–12. This marks a shift from the pure Roman law of Justinian's *Institutes*, 3.14.3; it is significant that the more modern position was followed.

[70] *Pocock* v. *Reddington* (1801) 5 Ves Jun 794; *Caffrey* v. *Darby* (1801) 6 Ves Jun 488; *Clough* v. *Bond* (1838) 3 My & Cr 490 (involving personal representatives rather than trustees). The point was already made by Sir William Jones: *Essay on Bailments*, 30–1, based on Pothier.

of application of equitable rules.[71] The objective test was generally applied in America;[72] and in *Speight* v. *Gaunt*[73] it was treated as axiomatic that the correct test in England too was that of the 'ordinary prudent man of business'. It followed that in this respect the liability of a trustee in Equity was in formal terms no different from the liability of an equivalent person at law; it was only the accident of jurisdiction that prevented its integration into the tort of negligence.

Sometimes Equity and Common law might move independently but in parallel.[74] There was a general principle that a person procuring or assisting in the commission of a tort would be liable as a joint tortfeasor, by analogy with the liability of accomplices in criminal law.[75] The Court of Chancery followed the same line, apparently also by analogy with the criminal law, in determining that a person who knowingly induced or assisted a breach of trust would be required to compensate for any loss suffered.[76] Slightly later the Common law began to apply identical reasoning to impose liability on the person procuring a breach of contract.[77] Both the trust and the contract were underpinned by notions of privity, so that accessory liability could not be dealt with quite as simply as accessory liability in tort, but exactly the same arguments could be employed in all three contexts.

Sometimes Equity might exercise a concurrent jurisdiction with the Common law. Thus liability might be imposed for negligent misrepresentations independent of any antecedent relationship between the parties[78]—as

---

[71] Story, *Equity Jurisprudence*, §1268.

[72] *Harvard College* v. *Amory* (1830) 9 Pick 446, 461; *Lichfield* v. *White* (1852) 7 NY 438, 443–4; *Higgins* v. *Whitson* (1855) 20 Barb 141, 146; *King* v. *Talbot* (1869) 40 NY 76, 85–6. The judgment of Ruggles C.J. in *Lichfield* v. *White* contains an instructive comparison of English law with that of New York.

[73] (1883) 22 Ch D 727; 9 AC 1. cf. PP HC 1895 xiii 450 q.462 (Lindley).

[74] For what follows, see P. Sales, 'The Tort of Conspiracy and Secondary Civil Liability' [1990] CLJ 491, 502–10.

[75] *Barker* v. *Braham* (1773) 2 W Bl 866; *De Crespigny* v. *Wellesley* (1829) 5 Bing 392, 404; *Petrie* v. *Lamont* (1842) Car & M 93, 96; *M'Laughlin* v. *Pryor* (1842) 4 Man & G 48. See generally the discussion in G. L. Williams, *Joint Torts and Contributory Negligence* (London, 1951), 6–16.

[76] *Evans* v. *Bicknell* (1801) 6 Ves Jun 174 (note esp. the citation of Sir Michael Foster's *Crown Law* at 176); *Fyler* v. *Fyler* (1841) 3 Beav 550, 561; *Attorney-General* v. *Corporation of Leicester* (1844) 7 Beav 176; *Barnes* v. *Addy* (1874) LR 9 Ch App 244. This liability is historically and analytically distinct from the liability of the person receiving trust property with actual or constructive notice of the breach of trust.

[77] *Lumley* v. *Gye* (1853) 2 El & Bl 216 (note esp. the dicta of Eyre J. at 232 and Wightman J. at 238). An alternative way of reaching the same result was to argue by analogy with the action for enticing away a servant or interfering with domestic relations (above, p.66). The greater resistance to introducing a form of secondary liability for breach of contract than for breach of trust was that in the latter case the plaintiff could claim that there had been an interference with property whereas contract rights were less easily reified.

[78] *Burrowes* v. *Lock* (1805) 10 Ves Jr 470; *Pulsford* v. *Richards* (1853) 17 Beav 87, 96; *Slim* v. *Croucher* (1860) De G F & J 518. See I. E. Davidson, 'The Equitable Remedy of Compensa-

Lord Campbell pointed out, the Equitable jurisdiction had the advantage of avoiding the uncertainties of jury trial when it came to the assessment of damages[79]—and when the House of Lords put a temporary end to the Common-law action Equity almost immediately followed suit.[80] The trust was not simply a holding of property; it was also a 'fiduciary' relationship, based on dependency or confidence, which placed on the trustee a duty not to take advantage of the beneficiary. This obligation could be extended to other fiduciary relationships, such as principal and agent, solicitor and client, or director and company.[81] Just as a trustee might have to compensate a beneficiary for causing loss in breach of this duty, by the early years of the twentieth century so too might a fiduciary, consciously replicating and complementing Common-law liability.[82]

Vicarious Liability and Non-Personal Fault

The equation of negligence with the actor's failure to live up to the standards reasonably to be expected of individuals in society meant that legal liability was significantly identified with personal moral shortcoming. This moral dimension of the tort was peculiarly problematical for those situations in which one person was made responsible for the wrongful acts of another, cases of vicarious liability. The earlier Common law had dealt with these without any apparent difficulty: so long as the law could reflect popular ascriptions of responsibility, legal liability could straightforwardly be imposed in those cases where it was considered appropriate, and there was no need for any soul-searching analysis to justify this.[83] In so far as lawyers put their minds to it, it could be explained by a theory of identification, treating X's act as Y's in law, or by a notion of agency;[84] behind it,

tion' (1982) 13 Melbourne Univ L R 349. For the commercial background to the intervention of Equity, see M. C. McGaw, 'Travels in Alsatia: "Judges of the Parties' own Choosing", "Monstrous Powers", and the Role of the Courts', in A. Thornton and W. Godwin (eds.), *Construction Law: Themes and Practice* (London, 1998), 131, 170–1.

[79] *Slim* v. *Croucher* (1860) De G F & J 518, 524.
[80] *Derry* v. *Peek* (1889) 14 App Cas 337; *Low* v. *Bouverie* [1891] 3 Ch 82. *Derry* v. *Peek* was generally regarded as wrong by Chancery lawyers, and its slow breakdown fittingly began with the Equitable jurisdiction over fiduciaries (*Nocton* v. *Lord Ashburton* (below, n.82)): W. Gummow, 'Compensation for Breach of Fiduciary Duty', in T. G. Youdan, *Equity, Fiduciaries and Trusts* (Toronto, 1989), 57.
[81] Story, *Equity Jurisprudence*, §§308–27.
[82] *Jacobus Marler Estates Ltd* v. *Marler* (1913) 85 LJ PC 167n (negligent acts); *Nocton* v. *Lord Ashburton* [1914] AC 932 (negligent words). A third example of Equity modelling itself on Common-law remedies is provided by the law of Equitable waste: see esp. *Parrott* v. *Palmer* (1834) 3 My & K 632.
[83] *Hern* v. *Nichols* (1708) 1 Salk 289; *Jones* v. *Hart* (1698) 2 Salk 441; cf. *Kingston* v. *Booth* (1685) Skinner 228. For the medieval law, see above, p.69.
[84] *Middleton* v. *Fowler* (1698) 1 Salk 282; *Turberville* v. *Stampe* (1697) 1 Ld Raym 264.

too, we could perhaps see a skeletal notion of enterprise liability.[85] The shift of emphasis onto personal fault as the grounds of liability put an end to this, and from the 1790s there was an increasing awkwardness in the courts' attitude to such cases.[86] Vicarious liability became an exceptional situation to be justified (if at all) by unprincipled, and relatively feeble, explanations in terms of the maxims *Respondeat Superior* and *Qui facit per alium facit per se*.[87] The truth of the matter was clearly seen by Joseph Story: it was a rule 'founded on public policy and convenience'.[88] Deprived of any principled basis, it rapidly settled down into a set of more or less arbitrary rules. Its essence was seen to be the liability of a 'master' for the torts of a 'servant'; yet the definition of 'servant' clearly owed more to notions of social class than to hard legal analysis,[89] and its application in anomalous cases, such as where a servant was hired out by a general employer to a special employer, was wholly arbitrary.[90] The 'servant' had to be acting 'in the course of employment' rather than 'on a frolic of his own';[91] it was for the jury to decide where employment ended and frolicking began, though in *Limpus* v. *London General Omnibus Company*[92] it was held that acting in breach of the contract of employment did not take the 'servant' out of the course of employment.

The real difficulty with the rules of vicarious liability, though, was not so much that they led to arbitrary decisions as that they excluded liability in some situations where it was thought that liability should lie. There was a clear argument through the first half of the century that special rules applied to occupiers of land, making them liable for the negligent acts of

---

[85] Blackstone, *Commentaries*, 1.417–20; R. Wooddesson, *Systematical View of the Laws of England* (1792) 1.465–6.

[86] e.g. *Stone* v. *Cartwright* (1795) 6 TR 411; *Bush* v. *Steinman* (1799) 1 B & P 404. No less was there a problem with the appropriate form of action. If liability were justified by a theory of identification, then, if the servant's act were a trespass, the master's liability should be in trespass; but if liability were based on the master's employment of an incompetent servant, liability should have been in case. The duality is most clearly seen in argument in *Savignac* v. *Roome* (1794) 6 TR 125, 126–7.

[87] *Weyland* v. *Elkins* (1816) Holt NP 227 and n.; C. M. Smith, *Treatise on the Law of Master and Servant* (1852), 151–2.

[88] J. Story, *Agency* (London, 1839), 404 §452. Not every lawyer was happy with the policy involved: see e.g. the strictures of Joseph Brown Q.C.: PP HC 1876 ix 669, q.942.

[89] Cf. e.g. *Sadler* v. *Henlock* (1855) 4 El & Bl 570 with *Knight* v. *Fox* (1850) 5 Ex 721. In the former a person who gave a 'common labourer' five shillings to clear out a drain was held to be liable for his negligence; in the latter a company employing a surveyor at a salary of £250 per year was held not liable.

[90] *Laugher* v. *Pointer* (1826) 5 B & C 547; *Smith* v. *Lawrence* (1828) 2 Man & Ry 1; *Quarman* v. *Burnett* (1840) 6 M & W 499; *Dalyell* v. *Tyrer* (1858) El Bl & El 899. Cf. *Randleson* v. *Murray* (1838) 8 Ad & El 109.

[91] *Croft* v. *Alison* (1821) 4 B & Ald 590; *Huzzey* v. *Field* (1835) 4 C M & R 432; *Joel* v. *Morison* (1834) 6 C & P 501; *Mitchell* v. *Crassweller* (1853) 13 CB 237.

[92] (1862) 1 H & C 526.

their independent contractors,[93] but this was firmly rejected in *Reedie* v. *London and North Western Railway Co.* in 1849.[94] Shortly after this there was a spate of cases in which the courts made use of a range of strategies to achieve the same result notwithstanding the normal operation of the rules. Occupiers were made liable to (lawful) visitors to their premises injured by the negligence of independent contractors by a subtle reformulation of the duty of care: instead of saying there was a duty to take reasonable care not to injure the visitor, it was said that the occupier had to take reasonable care to ensure that the visitor was not injured.[95] A related strategy, used, for example, in cases of statutory duties, was to say that the duty was non-delegable, so that a person could be held to be in breach of duty through the acts of another.[96] An employer of an independent contractor who had committed a public nuisance, as, for example, by leaving a pile of rubble in the highway, could be held liable as a joint wrongdoer.[97] Liability in private nuisance could be squeezed within the maxim *Sic utere tuo ut alienum non laedas*.[98] In a spectacular example of judicial constructivism, a reservoir-owner was held liable for the negligent conduct of his independent contractor by imposing a form of strict liability for the escape of dangerous things brought onto land.[99] And if all else failed it might still be possible to find personal negligence on the part of the employer.[100] In all of these cases the judges were able to avoid the strictures of the newly developed rules of vicarious liability, but in doing so they added to the fragmentary and atomized nature of the law of tort(s) by setting in place a further set of near-arbitrary rules. The fundamental problem, brought into sharp relief by the problems generated by vicarious liability, was that the moral idea of liability for failing to take reasonable care not to cause foreseeable injury to

---

[93] *Bush* v. *Steinman* (1799) 1 B & P 404; *Sly* v. *Edgeley* (1806) 6 Esp 6; *Laugher* v. *Pointer* (1826) 5 B & C 547; *Rapson* v. *Cubitt* (1842) 9 M & W 710; *Rich* v. *Basterfield* (1847) 4 CB 783.

[94] (1849) 4 Ex 244, 20 LJ Ex 65, 13 Jur 659. The remarks of Parke B, not reported in 4 Ex 244, are briefly eloquent: 'Having an interest in the North-western Railway Company, I decline to take any part in these proceedings unless the counsel allow me. If they do, I must say that I concur in the judgment which has been delivered.' His interest in the company had not prevented him from playing a full part in the argument of the case.

[95] *Pickard* v. *Smith* (1861) 10 CBNS 470; *Indermaur* v. *Dames* (1866) LR 2 CP 311. The passive formulation can be seen earlier, but without anything depending on the shift of voice: *Daniels* v. *Potter* (1830) 4 C & P 262; *Proctor* v. *Harris* (1830) 4 C & P 337.

[96] *Hole* v. *Sittingbourne and Sheerness Railway Company* (1861) 6 H & N 488. The same strategy was used to impose liability in the case of 'hazardous activities': *Woodley* v. *Metropolitan Railway Company* (1877) 36 LTNS 419, 421. See too the judgment of Littledale J. in *Randleson* v. *Murray* as reported in (1838) 7 LJQB 132, 133.

[97] *Ellis* v. *Sheffield Gas Consumers Co* (1853) 2 El & Bl 767 (Queen's Bench); the Common Pleas were less convinced: *Overton* v. *Freeman* (1852) 11 CB 867; *Peachey* v. *Rowland* (1853) 13 CB 182.

[98] *Rich* v. *Basterfield* (1847) 4 CB 783, 802; *Reedie* v. *London and North Western Railway Co* (1849) 4 Ex 244, 257.

[99] *Rylands* v. *Fletcher* (1865) 3 H & C 774, (1866) LR 1 Exch 265, (1868) LR 3 HL 330.

[100] *Wanstall* v. *Pooley* (1841) 6 Cl & F 910 n. (employment of drunken person).

one's neighbour was too narrow a principle to cover even the central core, let alone the whole, of the law of tort; but this was not to be recognized until well into the twentieth century.[101]

Tortious Liability without Negligence

The fragmentary nature of the law was even more marked outside the tort of negligence. Instead of looking at the way in which the defendant's conduct had been wrongful, the non-negligence torts were characterized by reference to the interest of the plaintiff that had been infringed.[102] In this they mimicked the traditional structure of the action of trespass.[103] Since plaintiffs' interests were too multifarious to be reduced to any single test, it followed that each tort had its own particular rules. By contrast to negligence, which did have some structural coherence, the other torts became little more than satellites in orbit around it.

In the action of trespass, so long as some invasive interference was shown it was for the defendant to show some excuse or justification. By the end of the eighteenth century, if not earlier, the action on the case for conversion had taken on this characteristic: a person who meddled with another person's goods would be liable in conversion in the absence of some justification or excuse.[104] Other torts with a strong proprietary dimension took on the same form: private nuisance could be defined as an act done to the hurt or annoyance of another's land (whether a possessory interest, an easement, or a natural right such as a right of support) where there was no justification or excuse;[105] and the new-found strict liability for the escape of dangerous things (based on *Rylands* v. *Fletcher*) was soon qualified by a similar range of defences.[106] In the nineteenth century the action on the case for defamation moved firmly in the same direction. On the face of it, liability was imposed for the 'malicious' publication of untrue statements of a defamatory nature; in the sixteenth and seventeenth centuries the courts had come to recognize a number of situa-

---

[101] Note also the development of no-fault liability for employees' claims in respect of work-related injuries: Workmen's Compensation Act, 1897. Interestingly, only twenty years earlier the secretary of the Trades Union Congress Parliamentary Committee had regarded the possibility of such strict liability as 'preposterous': PP HC 1876 ix 669, q.880. Similar sentiments are expressed by other workers' representatives in PP HC 1877 x 551, q.345, qq.2075–6.

[102] Cf. *Rogers* v. *Rajendro Dutt* (1860) 13 Moo PC 209, 226–7, per Macaulay Q.C.: 'there must have been either a violation by the Appellant of a legal right, or a wrongful act done by him in violation of a legal right or private duty, productive of damage to the Respondents.' See too the opinion of Dr Lushington at 241.   [103] Above, p.58.

[104] Above, p.112. Any residual doubts that there may have been were put to rest by *Hollins* v. *Fowler* (1875) LR 7 HL 757.   [105] Pollock, *Torts*, 329.

[106] Above, n.99. The background role of fault in the principal defences (act of God, act of a stranger, act of the plaintiff) precisely mirrors the situation in the medieval action of trespass: above, p.61.

tions in which it would be presumed that malice had not been present, but this did not detract from the general principle that malice was the root of liability.[107] In the nineteenth century, though, it became established that malice was conclusively presumed if the statement published was untrue unless the defendant could bring the case within one of the narrow and increasingly sharply delineated exceptions—privilege and fair comment— whereupon there would be a burden on the plaintiff to show that there had been express malice.[108] These situations approximated to the commonly occurring situations where malice would be found not to have existed. Crucially, though, there was now no residuary rule that a non-malicious defendant would escape liability: the fault element had ossified into two fixed defences. It followed from this that liability for defamation might arise despite the defendant's having no reason to believe that the words referred to the plaintiff or not having had any reason to believe that the words were defamatory.[109] Around 1900 this infected the closely related actions for slander of title and slander of goods, where again the causation of loss by making an untrue statement was actionable unless some justification or excuse could be shown.[110]

Some of these satellite torts retained a requirement of fault on the defendant's part, though this was never elevated into a uniting feature: malicious prosecution and slander of title, for example, each demanded deliberate wrongdoing, yet there was never any attempt to knit them together into a single tort. More commonly, though, the interest-based approach was reflected in a form of strict liability; this was especially the case if the plaintiff's rights could be expressed in the language of 'property', for the moral view that a person should be liable (only) for failing to take reasonable care was counterbalanced by an equally strong view that property rights should be protected. Conversion was quintessentially an interference with property, and nuisance could easily be characterized in such terms. In *St Helens Smelting Co* v. *Tipping*, for example, the House of

---

[107] Above, p.115.

[108] *Bromage* v. *Prosser* (1825) 4 B & C 247; *Capital and Counties Bank* v. *Henty* (1882) 7 App Cas 741. In some circumstances—where the words were spoken in parliament or in the course of judicial proceedings—even actual malice would not assist the plaintiff; these situations were regulated respectively by parliament and by the disciplinary jurisdiction of the courts. For the withering of malice, see P. P. Mitchell, 'Malice in Defamation' (1998) 114 LQR 639 and 'Duties, Interests, and Motives: Privileged Occasions in Defamation' (1998) 18 Ox Jnl Leg Stud 381.

[109] *Hulton & Co* v. *Jones* [1910] AC 20; *Vizetelly* v. *Mudie's Select Library Ltd* [1900] 2 QB 170. Contrast *Grymwood* v. *Prike* (1585), above, p.115.

[110] See in particular *Royal Baking Powder Company* v. *Wright* (1901) 18 RPC 95, 99, per Lord Davey. The idea had its roots in the judgment of Lord Ellenborough C.J. in *Pitt* v. *Donovan* (1813) 1 M & S 639, 643, but this was not built upon through the nineteenth century: cf. *Wren* v. *Weild* (1869) LR 4 QB 730; *Steward* v. *Young* (1870) LR 5 CP 122.

Lords was tender in its protection of property when it drew the distinction between material injury to property and mere personal discomfort.[111] *Rylands* v. *Fletcher* was consciously argued on property grounds; it seems to have been accepted from the beginning that, had the action been for personal injuries, it would have been essential to have shown negligence.[112] 'Property' might be intellectual as much as physical: there was no question of there being need for any fault element in actions for interferences with patents or for breach of copyright. More hesitantly, in *De Crespigny* v. *Wellesley* strict liability in defamation was justified by saying that the plaintiff had a right in his reputation, Best C.J. going so far as to treat it as equivalent to a property right.[113]

So long as property was involved, the courts of Equity might also intervene; hence situations that might have been described differently at Common law began to be treated in proprietary terms in order to activate the Chancery. Trademarks provide the best example of this.[114] Before the nineteenth century they were protected only by the Common law action for deceit, in which the plaintiff had to prove deliberate wrongdoing; in *Millington* v. *Fox*[115] in 1838 the Chancery accepted the invitation to treat them as a form of property and to issue an injunction protecting them even against innocent borrowing; although there were dissentient voices at first, this analysis was soon accepted.[116] This contrasted with the requirement of fraud at Common law, and from the 1880s the Common-law rule began to be watered down,[117] settling down as a rule that fraud should be inferred from the fact of knowledge that the mark was the plaintiff's.[118] Alongside Law's moving towards Equity, Equity moved

---

[111] (1865) 11 HLC 642.
[112] This is especially clear from the arguments at first instance as reported at (1865) 3 H & C 774; see too the argument in the Exchequer Chamber as reported at (1866) 4 H & C 263 (esp. 266).   [113] (1829) 5 Bing 392.
[114] See in particular *Gee* v. *Pritchard* (1818) 2 Swanst 402 for the exclusive concern of Equity with property rights. The wider ramifications are explored, from a primarily American perspective, by K. J. Vandevelde, 'The New Property of the Nineteenth Century: The Development of the Modern Concept of Property' (1980) 29 Buff L R 325. For trademarks in particular, see F. I. Schechter, *Historical Foundations of Trade Mark Law* (New York, 1925), 122–45.   [115] (1838) 3 My & Cr 338.
[116] *Emperor of Austria* v. *Day and Kossuth* (1861) 3 De G F & J 217 (holding that a sovereign's right to issue banknotes is a property right); *Singer Manufacturing Co* v. *Wilson* (1876) 2 Ch D 434, (1877) 3 App Cas 376. For the earlier doubts, see *Perry* v. *Truefitt* (1842) 6 Beav 66. The transitional state of the law is sharply brought out in E. Lloyd, *The Law of Trade Marks* (1862), 1–8.
[117] In *Singer Manufacturing Co* v. *Loog* (1882) 8 App Cas 15, 32–3, Lord Blackburn left open the question whether fraud was required; and it was argued (L. B. Sebastian, *The Law of Trade Marks* (1878), 96) that the union of law and equity meant that at least nominal damages could be recovered for the inadvertent use of another's mark.
[118] *Pinto* v. *Badman* (1891) 8 RPC 181, 184, per Day J. Cf. *Crawshay* v. *Thompson* (1842) 4 M & G 357, 377.

towards Law, holding that an account of profits would be ordered only if the defendant knew of the plaintiff's rights.[119] Analogous to this, the early stirrings of the equitable tort of breach of confidence were related to ideas of the violation of the plaintiff's intellectual property.[120]

[119] *Edelsten* v. *Edelsten* (1863) 1 De G J & S 185.
[120] *Perceval* v. *Phipps* (1813) 2 Ves & Beames 19; *Gee* v. *Pritchard* (1818) 2 Swanst 402; *Yovatt* v. *Winyard* (1820) 1 Jac & W 394 (equivalent to breach of trust); *Prince Albert* v. *Strange* (1849) 2 De G & S 652; *Morison* v. *Moat* (1851) 9 Hare 241. For the origins of breach of confidence, see F. Gurry, *Breach of Confidence* (Oxford, 1984), 3. As well, though not relevant for present purposes, there was an auxiliary jurisdiction to restrain breaches of confidence arising within contractual relationships. Cf. below, p.208.

10. *The Law of Torts in the Twentieth Century: Expansion and Collapse of the Tort of Negligence*

THE UNITY OF THE TORT OF NEGLIGENCE

However much the nineteenth-century tort of negligence could be expressed in terms of abstract general principles, as a matter of practical reality it was thoroughly fragmented. In the twentieth century, practice moved in the direction of theory as the tendency towards fragmentation was reversed.[1] Detailed duties of care were superseded by a single duty of care. The component parts of the tort—duty, breach, remoteness—increasingly merged into each other. Moreover, it no longer seemed self-evident that there should be a link between legal liability and wrongdoing, with the result that the idea of negligence as the failure to take the care that would have been taken by a reasonable man began to degenerate back into an undifferentiated notion of blameworthiness.

Generalization of the Duty of Care

The characteristic structure of the tort of negligence as it developed in the nineteenth century was largely the result of the tension between judge and jury. The near-total disappearance of the civil jury by the middle of the twentieth century resolved this tension, and with it broke down the fragmentary nature of the tort.

The disappearance of the jury occurred in three stages. First of all, the County Courts Acts provided that trial would be without jury in small cases, and might be without jury in other cases within the jurisdiction of the court (though either party had a right to demand a jury). In practice, jury trials in County Courts were very uncommon in any form of action, including negligence actions; they were abolished in 1934.[2] Secondly, the Common Law Procedure Act of 1854 allowed that the parties might elect not to go to jury trial; and after the Judicature Acts of 1873–5 it was possible for some negligence cases to be assigned to the Chancery Division

---

[1] B. Hepple, 'Negligence: The Search for Coherence' (1997) 50 Current Legal Problems 69.
[2] R. M. Jackson, 'The Incidence of Jury Trial during the Past Century' (1937) 1 MLR 132, 144; (1933) 87 *Hansard* (House of Lords), col.1050; County Courts Act 1934, s.91 (re-enacting County Courts (Amendment) Act 1934, s.17).

of the High Court, where they would be heard by judge alone.[3] Thirdly, and most significantly, after a prolonged stutter, the jury was to all intents and purposes abolished in actions brought in the King's (Queen's) Bench Division: trial by jury was made optional after the Judicature Acts, though in actions sounding in tort the option generally appears to have been exercised;[4] temporary provisions restricting the right to trial by jury to a small number of situations (not including negligence) were in force from 1918 to 1925;[5] new rules of procedure were introduced in 1932;[6] and in 1933 the right to trial by jury in negligence actions was effectively abolished.[7] After this, practically all cases were tried by judge alone.

The most obvious consequence of this was that judicial control over the incidence of negligence liability no longer depended on the precise definition of a multiplicity of duties of care. As early as 1883 Brett M.R. had attempted to formulate a general duty to take care:

Whenever one person is by circumstances placed in such a position with regard to another that every one of ordinary sense who did think would at once recognise that if he did not use ordinary care and skill in his own conduct with regard to those circumstances he would cause danger of injury to the person or property of the other, a duty arises to use ordinary care and skill to avoid such danger.[8]

Although the other two members of the court were unwilling to support such a wide proposition, the same judge (now Lord Esher) restated the proposition in a more limited form a decade later: 'If one man is near to another, or is near to the property of another, a duty lies upon him not to do that which may cause a personal injury to another, or may injure his property.'[9] This time he did receive judicial support,[10] and academic lawyers began to press the case for a generalized test.[11]

---

[3] Common Law Procedure Act 1854, s.1; Rules of the Supreme Court 1883, Order 36 rule 3.

[4] Rules of the Supreme Court 1883, Order 36 rule 6. The graphs printed by Jackson ('Incidence of Jury Trial' (1937) 1 MLR 132, 134–5) conceal the differential incidence of jury trial in contractual and tortious actions. Information given to the Parliamentary Commission on Juries in 1913 suggests that actions in tort were still predominantly tried by jury: PP HC 1913 xxx q.4568.

[5] Juries Act 1918, s.1; Administration of Justice Act 1920 s.2; Jackson, 'Incidence of Jury Trial' (1937) 1 MLR 132, 141.

[6] Rules of the Supreme Court (New Procedure) 1932, introducing new Order 38A.

[7] Administration of Justice (Miscellaneous Provisions) Act, s.6.

[8] *Heaven* v. *Pender* (1883) 11 QBD 503, 509.

[9] *Le Lievre* v. *Gould* [1893] 1 QB 491, 497.

[10] '[A] duty to take due care did arise when the person or property of one was in such proximity to the person or property of another that, if due care was not taken, damage might be done by the one to the other': [1893] 1 QB 491, 504, per A.L. Smith L.J.

[11] See e.g. P. H. Winfield, 'The History of Negligence in the Law of Torts' (1926) 42 LQR 184; F. Pollock, *Torts* (13th edn., 1929), 21; J. Salmond, *Torts* (7th edn., by W. T. S. Stallybrass, 1929), 63–70 (Excursus A).

The turning point came with the well-known decision in *Donoghue* v. *Stevenson*.[12] The plaintiff's friend bought a bottle of ginger beer manufactured by the defendants, and gave it to the plaintiff. When she poured it over her ice cream, she discovered a decomposed snail at the bottom of the bottle, and suffered a strong physical and nervous reaction. She brought an action in negligence, and by a majority of three to two the House of Lords held that it was well founded. In point of detail, this amounted to a reversal of the line of cases stemming from *Winterbottom* v. *Wright*;[13] it was never afterwards doubted that the person injured by a defectively manufactured product might in principle have an action against the negligent manufacturer.

There were three possible routes to this conclusion. Most minimally, it could simply have been said that the cases following *Winterbottom* v. *Wright* had been overruled, and that a duty of care was in fact owed by the manufacturer to the ultimate consumer. This would have been sufficient to explain the decision in the case. It would not, however, have involved any qualification of the traditional analysis in terms of a multiplicity of duties of care; nor would it have involved any qualification of the traditionally conservative 'incremental' approach to liability whereby the plaintiff was expected to demonstrate the existence of a duty of care by showing that the case fell within an already recognized duty situation or was very closely analogous to one. Such a minimalist approach was consistent with the speeches of Lord Thankerton and Lord Macmillan, and was the favoured interpretation of the case by contemporary commentators.[14]

Secondly, *Donoghue* v. *Stevenson* could have been treated as accepting an approach based upon a multiplicity of duty situations, but without any requirement that new duty situations could be recognized only by very close analogy to duty situations that had previously been recognized. This was implicit in Lord Macmillan's speech, and in his central conclusion that 'The categories of negligence are never closed.'[15] Such an approach inevitably involved some element of generalization, though Lord Macmillan himself was diffident about laying down any such principle.[16]

---

[12] [1932] AC 562. The case arose on a preliminary issue, where the facts as alleged were assumed to be true. The facts occurred in Scotland, but the laws of England and Scotland were presumed to be the same. For the factual background of the case, see A. Rodger, 'Mrs Donoghue and Alfenus Varus' [1988] Current Legal Problems 1.

[13] (1842) 10 M & W 109; above, p.174.

[14] See the notes on the case in (1932) 76 Solicitors' Journal 387; [1933] CLJ 116; (1932) 173 Law Times 411 (though even this minimal interpretation was regarded as 'revolutionary'); (1932) 174 Law Times 399; (1932) 74 Law Journal 75; (1932) 10 Canadian Bar Review 478. See too *Farr* v. *Butters Brothers* [1932] 2 KB 606, per Scrutton L.J.

[15] [1932] AC 562, 619. The point was originally made specifically with reference to Scots law: A. Rodger, 'Lord Macmillan's Speech in *Donoghue* v. *Stevenson*' (1992) 108 LQR 236, 242.

[16] [1932] AC 562, 619. The original version is especially explicit: 'There is no absolute standard for determining this question, and no principle of law involved in it other than the principle of reasonableness' (Rodger, 'Lord Macmillan's Speech' (1992) 108 LQR 236, 258).

Finally, and most generally, *Donoghue* v. *Stevenson* might have involved the wholesale rejection of the analysis dependent upon a multiplicity of duties of care in favour of a single requirement of taking reasonable care. This was, famously, the approach of Lord Atkin:

In English law there must be, and is, some general conception of relations giving rise to a duty of care, of which the particular cases found in the books are but instances. The liability for negligence, whether you style it such or treat it as in other systems as a species of 'culpa', is no doubt based upon a general public sentiment of moral wrongdoing for which the offender must pay. But acts or omissions which any moral code would censure cannot in a practical world be treated so as to give a right to every person injured by them to demand relief. In this way rules of law arise which limit the range of complainants and the extent of their remedy. The rule that you are to love your neighbour becomes in law, you must not injure your neighbour; and the lawyer's question, Who is my neighbour? receives a restricted reply. You must take reasonable care to avoid acts or omissions which you can reasonably foresee would be likely to injure your neighbour. Who, then, in law is my neighbour? The answer seems to be—persons who are so closely and directly affected by my act that I ought reasonably to have them in contemplation as being so affected when I am directing my mind to the acts or omissions which are called in question.[17]

In practice there was not a great deal of difference between the approaches of Lord Macmillan and Lord Atkin, for both of them allowed the law considerable flexibility to adapt to new situations. At a rhetorical level Lord Atkin's approach was particularly valuable, for it provided ready support for any conclusion that a judge wished to reach, and it provided a useful starting point for academic analysis. As a matter of reality, though, it was Lord Macmillan's more careful approach that was followed.[18] Textbook writers, while paying lip service to Lord Atkin's statement, still dealt with the law in terms of more or less discrete categories of duty situation, albeit that they were couched at a more general level than they would have been in such a book as Beven's *Negligence in Law*.[19] Judges, too, although less hide-bound by previous precedents, did not expand the law into a whole range of new situations simply on the grounds that the defendant had carelessly caused foreseeable harm to the plaintiff. Two types of case in particular stood in the way of the wholesale recognition of a general duty of care of the sort formulated by Lord Atkin: cases where a trespasser had been injured, and cases where financial loss had been suffered by reliance upon a negligent representation.

It had been accepted since the early nineteenth century that no duty was

---

[17] [1932] AC 562, 580.
[18] R. F. V. Heuston, 'Donoghue v. Stevenson in Retrospect' (1957) 20 MLR 1.
[19] The last edition of Beven was published in 1928: by this time it had swelled to 1,570 pages of text. The table of cases occupied a further 176 pages.

owed by the occupier of land to a trespasser. This was to some extent alleviated by the courts' invention of a number of mechanisms enabling them to treat trespassers in fact as licensees in law,[20] but the frontal attack based on *Donoghue* v. *Stevenson* was more significant. So long as it was foreseeable that someone might trespass and foreseeable that they might be injured, it could be argued that there was a duty of care imposed on the occupier. Such an argument did not meet with a warm reception in the 1950s,[21] but it was regarded more favourably in the 1960s, and was finally accepted by the House of Lords in 1971 when they introduced (or reintroduced) the rule that an occupier of land owed to a trespasser a duty of 'common humanity', no more than a reformulation of the duty to take reasonable (i.e. relatively low) care in the circumstances.[22]

After a brief flirtation in the late nineteenth century, the Common law had turned its face against allowing actions for negligent statements (as opposed to negligent acts or omissions).[23] The wider view of *Donoghue* v. *Stevenson*, though, contained no such limitation, and by the early 1950s it was being argued (unsuccessfully) that liability should be imposed.[24] As in the case of trespassers, this was at first rejected, but in 1963 the House of Lords laid down that there was no relevant difference between causing loss by negligent statement and causing loss in some other way.[25] Thus an action was held to lie in principle (though not on the facts of the case) against a bank that had negligently represented to the plaintiff that its customer was a good credit risk, as a result of which the plaintiff had allowed the customer's order to continue in place and had hence suffered loss.

Hedley Byrne v. *Heller* and *Herrington* v. *British Railways Board* removed the two largest obstacles to the acceptance of Lord Atkin's broad approach. By around 1970 the law of negligence was beginning to be conceptualized in terms of an ocean of liability for carelessly causing

---

[20] e.g. *Lowery* v. *Walker* [1911] AC 10; *Pearson* v. *Coleman Bros* [1948] 2 KB 359; *Phipps* v. *Rochester Corporation* [1955] 1 QB 450.

[21] See e.g. the astonished response of Glyn Jones J. to the suggestion: 'My God!' (*Cairns* v. *St Marylebone Borough Council* (1954) *The Times*, 8 Dec.).

[22] *Videan* v. *British Transport Commission* [1963] 2 QB 650; *Commissioner for Railways* v. *Quinlan* [1964] AC 1054; *Herrington* v. *British Railways Board* [1972] AC 877. See now the Occupiers' Liability Act 1984. Scots law had already taken this step in the Occupiers' Liability (Scotland) Act of 1960; the idea that there was a duty to be commonly humane to trespassers dates back to the spring-gun cases of the early nineteenth century (*Ilott* v. *Wilkes* (1820) 3 B & Ald 304; *Bird* v. *Holbrook* (1828) 4 Bing 628).

[23] *Heaven* v. *Pender* (1883) 11 QBD 503; *Cann* v. *Willson* (1888) 39 Ch D 39. Equity had dealt with such situations earlier, and there is reason to believe that the Common law would have been willing to do so: above, p.180.

[24] *Candler* v. *Crane, Christmas & Co* [1951] 2 KB 164. But see the dissenting judgment of Denning L.J., based on the nineteenth-century cases in the Court of Chancery (above, p.180).

[25] *Hedley Byrne & Co Ltd* v. *Heller & Partners Ltd* [1964] AC 465.

foreseeable harm, dotted with islands of non-liability,[26] rather than as a crowded archipelago of individual duty situations. Such an approach was first articulated by the courts in *Home Office* v. *Dorset Yacht Co,*[27] but its most substantial formulation was by Lord Wilberforce in *Anns* v. *Merton London Borough Council*:

[T]he question has to be approached in two stages. First one has to ask whether, as between the alleged wrongdoer and the person who has suffered damage there is a sufficient relationship of proximity or neighbourhood such that, in the reasonable contemplation of the former, carelessness on his part may be likely to cause damage to the latter—in which case a prima facie duty of care arises. Secondly, if the first question is answered affirmatively, it is necessary to consider whether there are any considerations which ought to negative, or to reduce or limit the scope of the duty or the class of person to whom it is owed or the damages to which a breach of it may give rise.[28]

This approach was subsequently criticized for its excessive generality, especially in the way in which it had opened up the possibility of liability being imposed on public bodies for failing to use their powers of regulation or oversight to prevent banks, builders, and the like causing losses to others.[29] As a response to this the law shifted back to a more conservative approach to liability, favouring the approach associated with Lord Macmillan in *Donoghue* v. *Stevenson* of greater fidelity towards previous decisions than the general approach of Lord Atkin would demand. Thus, it was said, the courts should not recognize whole new areas of liability at a single stroke; rather they should proceed 'incrementally' from previously recognized duty situations.[30] In addition, it was repeatedly stressed that a duty situation arose not merely from the foreseeability of harm, but that there was in addition a requirement of 'proximity',[31] based on the idea of 'neighbourhood' found in Lord Atkin's speech in *Donoghue* v. *Stevenson*, derived from *Heaven* v. *Pender* and *Le Lievre* v. *Gould*.[32] It is doubtful whether this added a great deal to the formulation in terms of prima-facie liability, subject to exceptions grounded in 'policy'.[33] Both had the same

---

[26] For situations of non-liability, see e.g. *Rondel* v. *Worsley* [1969] 1 AC 191 (barrister); *Sirros* v. *Moore* [1975] QB 118 (judge); *Thorne* v. *University of London* [1966] 2 QB 237 (university examiners).　　　　　　　　　　　　　　　　　　　　　　[27] [1970] AC 1004, 1027.

[28] [1978] AC 728, 751.

[29] *Yuen Kun-yeu* v. *Attorney-General of Hong-Kong* [1988] AC 175; *Murphy* v. *Brentwood District Council* [1991] 1 AC 398; *Stovin* v. *Wise* [1996] AC 923.

[30] *Murphy* v. *Brentwood District Council* [1991] 1 AC 398, following dicta in *Sutherland Shire Council* v. *Heyman* (1985) 157 CLR 424, 483.

[31] *Peabody Donation Fund (Governors of)* v. *Sir Lindsay Parkinson & Co* [1985] AC 210; *Caparo Industries plc* v. *Dickman* [1990] 2 AC 605; *Marc Rich & Co A.G.* v. *Bishop Rock Marine Co Ltd* [1996] 1 AC 211.　　　　　　　　　　　　　　　　　　　　　　[32] Above, nn.8, 9.

[33] e.g. M. H. McHugh, 'Neighbourhood, Proximity and Reliance', in P. D. Finn (ed.), *Essays on Torts* (Sydney, 1989), 5. The point is well made by Lord Wilberforce in *McLoughlin* v. *O'Brian* [1983] AC 410, 420 and by McHugh J. in *Hill* v. *van Erp* (1997) 188 CLR 159, 210.

function, the identification of situations where there was no liability in negligence notwithstanding that foreseeable harm had been caused;[34] the only difference seemed to be that, where the requirement of 'proximity' was used, the onus was on the plaintiff to show why liability should arise, while, where 'policy' was used, it was for the defendant to show why it should not.[35]

More substantially, the generalization of liability after *Donoghue* v. *Stevenson* heralded a change in the conceptualization of the tort of negligence. Whereas nineteenth-century lawyers analysed liability in terms of the way in which the plaintiff's loss had occurred, in the second half of the twentieth century there cut across this an analysis by reference to the type of loss suffered.[36] This is particularly visible in two areas, pure economic loss and psychiatric injury. So far as the former is concerned, as late as the 1960s the primary question was whether liability could lie for negligent misstatements, not whether there could be liability for purely economic loss. In *Hedley Byrne* v. *Heller*, for example, the House of Lords hardly addressed itself to the nature of the plaintiff's loss.[37] This had changed within a few years,[38] so much so that it was concern about the extension of liability for purely economic loss that was largely responsible for the backlash against the broad approach of *Anns* v. *Merton*. As a result, there was a tendency to limit the recoverability of pure economic loss to the narrow range of misstatement sanctioned by *Hedley Byrne* v. *Heller*,[39] and the grudging approach to claims to recover in respect of pure economic loss was reflected in cases where a negligent misstatement had led to damage to property.[40] On the other hand, where considerations of 'justice' militated in favour of a remedy, the fact that the loss suffered was purely economic was not an insuperable bar to the granting of a remedy. Hence an action was allowed to the intended beneficiaries under a will when the testator's

---

[34] As well as the 'psychiatric injury' and 'pure economic loss' cases dealt with below, this tool has been particularly important in limiting the private-law liability of public bodies: e.g. *Yuen Kun Yeu* v. *Attorney-General of Hong Kong* [1988] AC 175; *X* v. *Bedfordshire County Council* [1995] 2 AC 633; *Stovin* v. *Wise* [1996] AC 923.

[35] *Stovin* v. *Wise* [1996] AC 923, 949, per Lord Hoffman.

[36] See e.g. *Simpson* v. *Thomson* (1877) 3 App Cas 279, discussed at the time in terms of the insurer's rights of indemnity and only in the later twentieth century reconceptualized in terms of 'economic loss'. Cf. also *Cattle* v. *The Stockton Waterworks Co* (1875) LR 10 QB 453, *Morrison SS Co Ltd* v. *Greystoke Castle* [1947] AC 265.

[37] [1964] AC 465. There are hints that it might be relevant in counsel's argument (at 477), and in the speeches of Lord Hodson (at 509) and Lord Devlin (at 517). In the earlier case of *Candler* v. *Crane, Christmas* only Asquith L.J. animadverted to the problem, and that very much in passing: [1951] 2 KB 164, 189.

[38] *Weller & Co* v. *Foot and Mouth Disease Research Institute* [1966] 1 QB 569; *Spartan Steel & Alloys Ltd* v. *Martin (Contractors) Ltd & Co* [1973] QB 27.

[39] B. J. Stapleton, 'Duty of Care and Economic Loss: A Wider Agenda' (1991) 107 LQR 249. The restrictive position is most clear in *Murphy* v. *Brentwood District Council* [1991] 1 AC 398. [40] *Marc Rich & Co A.G.* v. *Bishop Rock Marine Co Ltd* [1996] 1 AC 211.

solicitor had acted so dilatorily that the testator had died before the will was drawn up.[41] The law's concern with 'psychiatric injury' resulted from a similar skewing. Before the middle of the twentieth century the courts took a restrictive attitude towards liability for 'nervous shock';[42] the focus here was not on the type of injury but on the way in which it had been caused. Gradually this twisted round until 'nervous shock' was identified with 'post-traumatic stress disorder'—a type of harm rather than a mode of causation of harm—from which it shifted yet further into 'psychiatric injury',[43] in the process reinterpreting cases involving palpably physical injuries as cases of psychiatric injury[44] and apparently spawning the paradoxical rule that there should be no recovery for psychiatric injury not resulting from shock.[45]

Reintegration of the Elements of Negligence

The generalization of the duty of care was not the only change in the tort of negligence in the middle of the twentieth century; as well there was a reintegration of the separate elements of duty, breach, and remoteness. Such a tendency was visible in the nineteenth century; it was accentuated by the generalizing approach of *Donoghue* v. *Stevenson*, and with the disappearance of the jury after 1933 any need that had once existed to separate out the various elements of the tort of negligence had disappeared, since all were now equally within the judicial domain. So marked was the quest for homogeneity within the tort that the foreseeability of harm, translated from the question of remoteness of damage into the question of duty in *Smith* v. *London and South Western Railway Co* in

[41] *White* v. *Jones* [1995] AC 207. Contrast the position in the eighteenth century: above, p.174.
[42] *Victorian Railways Commissioners* v. *Coultas* (1888) 13 App Cas 222; *Pugh* v. *London, Brighton and South Coast Railway Co* [1896] 2 QB 248; *Dulieu* v. *White & Sons* [1901] 2 KB 669; *Yates* v. *South Kirkby Collieries Ltd* [1910] 2 KB 538; *Hambrook* v. *Stokes Bros* [1925] 1 KB 150; *Bourhill* v. *Young* [1943] AC 92.
[43] The shift was beginning to be seen in *Owens* v. *Liverpool Corporation* [1939] 1 KB 394 and *King* v. *Philips* [1953] 1 KB 429 (the antinomy physical injury/emotional shock is clearest in the judgment of Denning L.J. at 438–9), and finally occurred in *McLoughlin* v. *O'Brian* [1983] AC 410 and *Alcock* v. *Chief Constable of the South Yorkshire Police* [1992] 1 AC 310. The equivalence of nervous shock and psychiatric illness is treated as axiomatic by the Law Commission (Report no. 249, *Liability for Psychiatric Illness* (1998), esp. 9) and by the House of Lords in *Frost* v. *Chief Constable of the South Yorkshire Police* [1998] 3 WLR 1509; note esp. the speech of Lord Steyn at 1542–3.
[44] In *Dulieu* v. *White*, for example, the shock caused the plaintiff to suffer bodily injury and her child to be born an idiot; in *Hambrook* v. *Stokes* the victim died; and the fishwife in *Bourhill* v. *Young* suffered physical injury (a ricked back) and a miscarriage. Both the Law Commission and the House of Lords blithely describe these injuries as psychiatric.
[45] e.g. *Sion* v. *Hampstead Health Authority* (1994) 5 Med L R 170, based on *Jaensch* v. *Coffey* (1984) 155 CLR 549, 565, per Brennan J. But see *Walker* v. *Northumberland County Council* [1995] 1 All ER 737.

1870, was reintroduced as the test for remoteness in 1961: it would have been irrational to allow foreseeability to determine whether there was a duty without at the same time laying down that only foreseeable damage could be recovered.[46] By the 1970s judges were beginning to admit that the elements of duty, breach, and remoteness were essentially interchangeable:

> The more I think about these cases, the more difficult I find it to put each into its proper pigeon-hole. Sometimes I say: 'There was no duty.' In others I say: 'The damage was too remote.' So much so that I think the time has come to discard those tests which have proved so elusive.[47]

> The truth is that all these three—duty, remoteness and causation—are all devices by which the courts limit the range of liability for negligence.[48]

By 1980 the 'wilderness of single instances' that had characterized the tort of negligence a century earlier[49] had been largely remoulded into the single principle formulated in Buller's *Nisi Prius* a century before that: 'Every man ought to take reasonable care that he does not injure his neighbour.'

Moral Wrongdoing and Fault

A further feature of the fragmented nineteenth-century tort of negligence was its foundation on an over-narrow base linking legal liability with personal moral shortcoming.[50] This made some sense when the person bearing the loss was the person who had caused the harm; but even in the nineteenth century it was clear that liability was commonly imposed on railway companies and other corporate defendants, and in these cases the congruence between legal responsibility and moral wrongdoing was at best difficult to justify. As the corporate defendant became ever more the norm in the twentieth century, so the link between legal liability and moral delinquency became ever more problematic. Added to this, from around the end of the nineteenth century it became possible (sometimes, eventually, compulsory) to insure against legal liability,[51] further weakening the moral explanation of the law.

Parallel to this there occurred an intellectual shift. The acute individualism that had characterized Victorian England began to give way to a

---

[46] *The Wagon Mound (No. 1)* [1961] AC 388; G. L. Williams, 'The Risk Principle' (1961) 77 LQR 179. In practice there was difficulty in holding to this impeccably logical position: *Hughes* v. *Lord Advocate* [1963] AC 837; *Page* v. *Smith* [1996] 1 AC 155.

[47] *Spartan Steel* v. *Martin & Co* [1973] QB 27, 37, per Lord Denning M.R.

[48] *Lamb* v. *Camden London Borough Council* [1981] QB 625, 636, per Lord Denning M.R. (under the subheading 'The Truth').   [49] Above, p.179.

[50] This is still wholly transparent in Lord Atkin's pivotal speech in *Donoghue* v. *Stevenson* (above, n.17).

[51] H. E. Raynes, *History of British Insurance* (2nd edn., London, 1964), 289–308. The first employers' liability policy dates from 1880, the first third-party motor insurance from 1896.

more communitarian approach: no longer was it obvious that an individual who caused harm to another while pursuing economic self-interest
should be liable only for not taking reasonable care. Legal commentators
began to stress that negligence liability depended not on a moral principle
but on a social one; it was based not on something internal to the
defendant but on a failure to live up to an external standard, and that
external standard was something that could be determined by public
policy. The American jurist Oliver Wendell Holmes was the principal
proponent of this view,[52] and even before 1900 it had become so much
part of common learning that it was being misunderstood by examination
candidates.[53] As corporate and insured defendants became the norm,
judges and scholars, especially in America, came to formulate the principles of liability in wholly economic, non-moral, terms.[54] 'There is a
strong and growing tendency,' observed Dean Roscoe Pound in 1914,
'where there is no blame on either side, to ask, in view of the exigencies
of social justice who can best bear the loss, and hence to shift the loss by
creating liability where there has been no fault.'[55]

English law did not discard the evaluative language of the nineteenth
century. Academic writers were slower than their American counterparts to
reveal the hollowness of this, though judges came to recognize that it might
be substantially a mask behind which 'policy' decisions were taken,[56] and it
was questioned whether it was sensible to make the recoverability of
damages for personal injuries dependent on fault at all.[57] This generated
a tension where pragmatism or popular sentiment favoured the imposition
of liability where there could hardly be said to have been a failure to take
reasonable care, or alternatively where the same types of consideration
pointed towards the exoneration of a person who had not in fact taken
reasonable care. Hence, in cases of medical negligence, it was argued by
some that the courts should not be too quick to impose liability for
doctors' mistakes; to do so would create a risk of defensive medicine and
increasingly expensive health care.[58] Orthodoxy demanded the rejection of
these arguments: liability should arise if a failure to take reasonable care

[52] 'Privilege, Malice, and Intent' (1894) 8 Harv L R 1. For the contrary view, see
J. Salmond, *Essays in Jurisprudence and Legal History* (London, 1891), 132.
[53] M. de W. Howe (ed.), *The Pollock-Holmes Letters* (Cambridge, 1942), 1.46 (1893).
[54] See most notably *United States* v. *Carroll Towing* (1947) 159 F.2d 169 (Judge Learned
Hand). This spawned further economic analysis: W. M. Landes and R. A. Posner, *The
Economic Structure of Tort Law* (Cambridge, Mass., 1987), 4–9.
[55] 'The End of Law' (1914) 27 Harv L R 195, 233.
[56] See e.g. the far-sighted remarks of Lord Pearce in *Hedley Byrne* v. *Heller* [1964] AC 465, 536.
[57] See in particular the Report of the Royal Commission on Civil Liability and Compensation for Personal Injury (the Pearson Report) (1978).
[58] The point is made strongly by Lord Denning M.R. in the Court of Appeal in *Whitehouse*
v. *Jordan* [1980] 1 All ER 650, 658.

could be shown.[59] The opposite pressure was at work in road traffic cases, when it could safely be assumed that the defendant was insured. Hence in *Roberts* v. *Ramsbottom*[60] the Court of Appeal held that an action would lie against a driver who had driven into a car after he had suffered from a stroke that had both impaired his capacity to drive and impaired his capacity to recognize his unfitness. This was subsequently disapproved. In *Mansfield* v. *Weetabix*[61] it was stressed that liability was not automatic, so that a driver who was not at fault in failing to recognize the onset of some illness affecting his ability to drive might be exonerated: if no-fault liability were to be imposed on the drivers of motor vehicles, it should be so laid down by parliament rather than the courts. This is precisely what occurred in the case of the liability of manufacturers of defective products. At first, by a mixture of procedural and evaluative factors, the courts weakened the manufacturers' position;[62] and in 1987 parliament, implementing a European Directive, recognized a form of strict liability.[63]

The dissolution of the moral basis of negligence liability washed away the problems of justifying vicarious liability that had dogged the nineteenth century. If liability could be imposed on individuals independently of moral fault, it could equally be imposed on their employers: the only question was whether the (human) wrongdoer was acting as part of the defendant's organization.[64] The disjunction between academic writing and legal reality became very marked here, with much textbook analysis of vicarious liability as an independent topic embalmed in a mid-Victorian timewarp, in which masters (*sic*) carried liability for the torts of their servants (*sic*).[65]

Similar judicial manipulation took place when dealing with defences. A broad discretion to apportion liability in cases of contributory negligence was made available in 1945,[66] though the introduction of this regime removed a tool formerly available when it was thought that the injured party did not deserve any compensation at all. The courts responded to this by using another tool, the defence of consent—*volenti non fit injuria*—in cases where there was in reality no consent (perhaps not even recognition

---

[59] *Whitehouse* v. *Jordan* [1981] 1 WLR 246 (House of Lords). For the more modern position, see M. A. Jones, *Medical Negligence* (London, 1996), esp. 119–21.
[60] [1980] 1 WLR 823. See too *Nettleship* v. *Weston* [1971] 2 QB 691.
[61] [1998] 1 WLR 1263.
[62] e.g. *Grant* v. *Australian Knitting Mills Ltd* [1936] AC 85. See generally C. J. Miller and P. A. Lovell, *Product Liability* (London, 1977), 171–90, 255–60.
[63] Consumer Protection Act 1987.
[64] *Cassidy* v. *Minister of Health* [1951] 2 KB 343; *Roe* v. *Ministry of Health* [1954] 2 QB 66. It is noteworthy how little recent case law there is on the subject.
[65] There are exceptions; e.g. D. Howarth, *Textbook on Tort* (London, 1995), 632–51.
[66] Law Reform (Contributory Negligence) Act, s.1.

of the risk) on the part of the plaintiff, but where the plaintiff had undoubtedly behaved extremely stupidly.[67] In the same vein, where the plaintiff was acting illegally, there began to emerge another public-policy-oriented defence based on the old maxim *ex turpi causa non oritur actio*.[68]

The shift away from the personal moral justification of the tort of negligence to one more firmly rooted in public policy or societal norms moved the main stream of the law of tort back to something like its medieval formlessness. Just as the medieval jury had an almost unlimited flexibility to impose liability where it thought it appropriate, so the judge of the late twentieth century obtained the power to do so. There were still two substantial differences from the medieval position, though: modern law had the encrustation of several centuries' worth of rules, which could at times anchor the law to its past and restrain the courts from exercising a completely free choice;[69] and in modern law it was the judges rather than the jury who exercised the choice, judges constrained in a way that juries were not by the need to give reasons for their decisions and by the require-ment that they take account of previous cases.

NEGLIGENCE AND ITS SATELLITES

The reintegration of the tort of negligence had effects on the other elements of the law of torts.[70] The generalization of the duty of care removed the need to fit a claim into a particular pigeon-hole; and the weakening of the connection between the legal idea of negligence and the moral responsi-bility for failing to take reasonable care meant that the law was more responsive to societal perceptions of where liability ought to lie, indepen-dently of the pigeon-hole in which the plaintiff's action was categorized. The more that 'negligence' was defined simply in terms of the blameworthy causation of loss, the greater the overlap between the tort of negligence and

---

[67] e.g. *I.C.I. Ltd* v. *Shatwell* [1965] AC 656 (inferring consent from act done voluntarily with knowledge of risk); *Morris* v. *Murray* [1991] 2 QB 6 (inferring consent from fact that plaintiff probably knew that defendant was drunk); *O'Reilly* v. *National Rail and Tramway Appliances Ltd* [1966] 1 All ER 499 (inferring consent from fact that plaintiff hit unexploded shell with sledgehammer). The Court of Appeal did, however, baulk when asked to hold that a criminal escaping from the police impliedly consented to being injured by their negligence: *Marshall* v. *Osmond* [1983] QB 1034.

[68] *Pitts* v. *Hunt* [1991] 1 QB 24. The defence is still fairly limited: *Revill* v. *Newbery* [1996] QB 567.

[69] Cf. e.g. the impeccable historical rooting of the majority of the House of Lords in *Hunter* v. *Canary Wharf Ltd.* [1997] AC 655 with the more interventionist line taken by Lord Cooke of Thorndon.

[70] T. Weir, 'The Staggering March of Negligence', in P. Cane and J. Stapleton (eds.), *The Law of Obligations* (Oxford, 1998), 97, 102–18.

the main individual satellite torts: the analysis of liability in terms of the culpability of the defendant's conduct inevitably cut across the analysis in terms of the interest of the plaintiff that had been invaded.

The superimposition of trespass to the person and negligence was made clear in 1959, when it was held that it was essential in both torts to allege that the defendant had acted negligently;[71] and trespass to goods was similarly thought to come within the ambit of negligence, in so far as it had not already been submerged within the tort of conversion.[72] Nuisance, too, moved closer to negligence. Where the defendant was not the immediate cause of the alleged nuisance, the overlap was almost complete;[73] and, even where the nuisance was the result of the defendant's act, it was recognized that it was generally necessary to show fault of some kind, even if not strictly negligence.[74] The assimilation of the two actions was further assisted by the establishment of the same test of remoteness of damage—reasonable foreseeability—in each.[75] The strict liability for the escape of dangerous things based on *Rylands* v. *Fletcher* moved towards a similar fate;[76] fault ideas explicitly suffused the defences arising under it, and, like nuisance, it was held to be subject to the same rule of remoteness of damage as negligence.[77] Defamation began the trek in the same direction. On the one hand, its apparently strict liability started to break down when statutes provided that in some circumstances a non-negligent defendant could avoid liability by the prompt publication of an apology on request and that distributors (as opposed to authors, editors, or publishers) could avoid liability if they had not been negligent;[78] and, on the other hand, the courts started the process of redefining the defences of privilege and the like in terms of the defendant's lack of fault.[79] The law moved slowly towards the position presaged by Anderson C.J. in 1600 that if your words cause me loss through your fault you ought to compensate me.[80]

It is important not to overemphasize the tort of negligence, despite its predominance and its appetite to swallow up its satellites. There remained a myriad of 'torticles', ranging from interference with dead bodies and racial

---

[71] *Fowler* v. *Lanning* [1959] 1 QB 426 (confirming the position arguably reached before 1900 in *Holmes* v. *Mather* (1875) LR 10 Ex 261 and *Stanley* v. *Powell* [1891] 1 QB 86).

[72] For the relationship between trespass and conversion, see above, p.109.

[73] *Sedleigh-Denfield* v. *O'Callaghan* [1940] AC 880; *Goldman* v. *Hargrave* [1967] 1 AC 645; *Leakey* v. *National Trust* [1980] QB 485. The last of these cases introduced a slight qualification to the normal rule in negligence, in that the defendant's resources had to be taken into account in determining whether liability should be imposed.

[74] *Overseas Tankships (UK) Ltd* v. *The Miller Steamship Co Pty (The Wagon Mound (no 2))* [1967] 1 AC 617, 639–40.   [75] *Wagon Mound (no 2)* [1967] 1 AC 617.

[76] Most obviously in Australia: *Burnie Port Authority* v. *General Jones* (1994) 179 CLR 520.

[77] *Cambridge Water Co* v. *Eastern Counties Leather plc* [1994] 2 AC 264.

[78] Defamation Act 1952 s.4; Defamation Act 1996 s.1.

[79] *Spring* v. *Guardian Assurance plc* [1995] 2 AC 296.

[80] *Holwood* v. *Hopkins* (1600) 101 SS 89 (above, p.117).

discrimination to harassment and deceit, each with its own particular rules. Some of these were the product of recent legislation (for example, harassment); others, like malicious prosecution, were of respectable antiquity. Some were separate from negligence in little more than name;[81] some differed only in that the duty of care was fixed by legislation rather than by the courts;[82] some were separate by jurisdictional accident;[83] some were separate because of the type of interest they protect or the fault element they require;[84] and some were separate for a mixture of these.[85] Some, such as the proto-tort of unlawful interference with trade[86] or the embryonic tort of breach of privacy,[87] loosely linked together groups of wrongs; others remained wholly independent: there are no limits to the types of conduct that can be labelled wrongful, and no natural laws determining the ways in which they can be grouped together.

---

[81] e.g. Occupiers' Liability.   [82] e.g. Breach of Statutory Duty.

[83] e.g. Breach of Fiduciary Obligation (founded in Equity rather than Common law), Failure to Implement Community Directive (founded in European Community Law rather than English law).   [84] e.g. Harassment, Malicious Prosecution.

[85] e.g. Breach of Confidence, with Equitable roots and protecting an uncertain range of interests.

[86] *Merkur Island Shipping Corporation* v. *Laughton* [1983] AC 570, 609–10, per Lord Diplock; *Lonrho plc* v. *Fayed* [1989] 2 All ER 65. More generally the 'Economic' or 'Trade' torts, protecting against the deliberate interference with economic interests, could be seen as an amalgam of three classes of 'torticles': (*a*) those where the plaintiff had suffered as a result of a breach of contract brought about by a person not party to the contract and so not liable for breach of contract (inducing breach of contract (above, p.180)); (*b*) those where the defendant had committed or threatened a wrong to a third party, deliberately causing the loss to the plaintiff thereby (indirectly bringing about a breach of contract, three-party intimidation, conspiracy to cause loss by unlawful means); and (*c*) those where the defendant had deliberately caused loss by unfair trade practices (e.g. passing off, conspiracy to cause loss by lawful means, and a ragbag of statutory or regulatory torts). Nearly all of these were substantially developments of the twentieth century.

[87] Perhaps working outwards from the Protection from Harassment Act 1997 or from the liability of fiduciaries for breach of confidence, or building on the dissenting speech of Lord Cooke in *Hunter* v. *Canary Wharf Ltd* [1997] AC 655.

11. *Foundations of the Modern Law of Contract*

The seventeenth and eighteenth centuries marked a period of consolidation of the law of contract, the fleshing-out of the skeletal structure that had been locked in place at the end of the sixteenth century.[1] The Common law courts clearly had some part to play in this, but until the end of the eighteenth century it was all too easy for them to leave difficult issues in the hands of the jury. The more important developments, therefore, occurred in the Chancery, which had begun to operate along clearly defined, rule-based, lines by the time of the Chancellorship of Lord Nottingham (1673–81). For the most part even these developments may well not have been true innovations: there is little in them that cannot plausibly be traced back to the ill-defined practice of the fifteenth-century Chancellors.[2]

In part this conceptual stasis was achieved by sloughing off situations that could not neatly be accommodated within the existing rules. Thus the 'custom of merchants'—i.e. contemporary business practice—was called in aid to justify the enforcement of bills of exchange and the like, which fitted ill with the doctrine of consideration; and the law of trusts came to play a significant part in the enforcement of charitable promises and gratuitous family arrangements. This was not always necessary: lawyers were happy to invent implied contracts and implied terms when it suited their purpose to do so, and the principles themselves were capable of considerable flexibility in their application.

Against this background of legal practice, the eighteenth century saw the first attempts to articulate a theory of contractual liability, largely based on the writings of non-lawyers, at least of non-Common lawyers. These attempts were neither sophisticated nor successful, but they did begin the work of accustoming English lawyers to the fact that there were not several sets of rules applicable to different forms of action in Common law and in Chancery, but a single body of definable rules that could be called 'the law of contract'.

THE MODEL OF CONTRACT

The eighteenth-century lawyers' model of contract owed a great deal to their predecessors. At its heart was the qualified idea of a reciprocal

---

[1] Above, ch. 7.
[2] Above, ch. 5. The one important exception was the Chancery's practice of granting relief against penalties: above, p.150.

agreement, in its essence indistinguishable from the conception formulated before the beginning of the seventeenth century. This was subject to a number of vitiating factors, most clearly visible in the courts of Equity, which went some way to mitigate the rigours of the Common law. In the same way, there was room for some softening of the strict rules otherwise applicable at the remedial level.

Agreement and Reciprocity

In its essentials, the fundamental shape of contractual liability fixed by the beginning of the seventeenth century was little different from the medieval model of exchange: there had to be an agreement; there had to be consideration, in the sense that the transaction had to be broadly reciprocal; and only the parties to the agreement were affected by it.[3] This model underpinned contractual thinking through the seventeenth and eighteenth centuries, though it was only around 1800 that it was given any more detailed articulation.

At points this model had to be qualified. The concern (based on experience) that juries might too easily infer contractual agreements from equivocal evidence led to the incorporation in the Statute of Frauds (1677) of provisions requiring certain types of contracts to be evidenced in writing.[4] The rule that any reciprocal consideration, however trivial, would support a contract had to be restricted so as to exclude considerations that were either illegal or immoral.[5] The definition of the parties to a contract had to take due account of rules of contractual capacity, whose roots were traceable back into the Middle Ages.[6]

---

[3] Above, pp.76–83. Contracts under seal remained different in that their focus was unilateral: there was, therefore, no requirement of consideration, and the requirement of agreement was somewhat attenuated.

[4] *Anon* (1672) MT Treby MS p.747 (B&M 444). By s.4 of the Statute the requirement extended to promises by executors, guarantees, agreements in consideration of marriage, contracts for the sale of interests in land, and agreements not to be performed within a year; s.17 provided that contracts for the sale of goods for more than £10 had to be in writing unless there had been delivery of the goods, payment in whole or of part of the price, or the giving and receiving of something by way of earnest (thereby returning to the position described by Glanvill half a millennium earlier: above, p.74). The qualification in s.4 was itself qualified by the Equitable doctrine of part-performance, the rule that a partly performed contract would be enforced even though lacking some essential form; this rule already existed in Chancery (though with a necessarily limited scope) prior to the Statute of Frauds. See U.-I. A. Stramignoni, 'At the Dawn of Part Performance' (1997) 18(2) Jnl Leg Hist 32, esp. n.2; and more generally E. Rabel, 'The Statute of Frauds and Comparative Legal History' (1947) 63 LQR 174, 178–82.

[5] W. Sheppard, *Actions upon the Case for Deeds* (2nd edn., 1675), 164–5. *Whaley v. Norton* (1687) 1 Vern 483.   [6] Above, p.71.

At the pivot of the model was the reciprocal idea of consideration.[7] Despite broadsides in the second half of the eighteenth century under the Chief Justiceship of Lord Mansfield[8] this remained firmly in place, and so long as this was so the rule that there had to have been an agreement was almost unshakeable: the contract was (invariably) something that bound both parties, so both were required to participate in its formation. This might lead to evidentiary difficulties, but these were overcome in practice by allowing the jury to infer from the conduct of the parties that there had genuinely been an agreement,[9] or by viewing with a more benevolent eye situations where a person offered a reward for some service, which service the plaintiff went on to perform.[10] Moreover, one aspect of the concept of reciprocity was the rule that consideration had to move from the promisee, a rule that could easily meld with the doctrine that non-parties were not affected by the agreement.[11]

There were two principal challenges to the interlocking trinity of doctrines that comprised this stable model of contract: the bill of exchange and other similar documents, originally used primarily in transnational commerce but increasingly found in more domestic inland contexts in the eighteenth century; and the promissory gift, largely the preserve of intra-family settlements and charitable foundations.

Mercantile Documents

The bill of exchange normally arose in the following situation: X owed money to Y; X gave to Y a bill drawn on Z; Y took the bill to Z, who accepted it thereby agreeing that he would pay it. If Z refused subsequently to pay, Y would wish to bring an action against him.[12] So long as X had been acting as Z's agent, this form of transaction created no difficulty: the acceptance of the bill did no more than concretize the obligation that already existed. The problem arose if there was no such agency relationship, for it could be objected that the acceptor, Z, had not received any consideration. From the early years of the seventeenth century actions in assumpsit are found against such acceptors in this type of case, explicitly

[7] The pre-existence of a duty, an important aspect of consideration in the sixteenth century and one that obscured the fundamentally reciprocal nature of the doctrine (above, p.145) was no longer seen in this light in the later seventeenth century, serving simply to revive a cause of action barred by the Statute of Limitations: *Anon* (1674) 1 Vent 258; *Heyling* v. *Hastings* (1698) 1 Salk 29, 1 Ld Raym 421, 1 Com 54; *Dean* v. *Crane* (1704) 6 Mod 309. See the notes to *Hodsden* v. *Harridge* 2 Wms Saund 61, 63 n.6 (at 64a).

[8] *Pillans* v. *van Mierop* (1765) 3 Burr 1663 (below, n.13); *Atkins* v. *Hill* (1775) 1 Cowp 284, *Trueman* v. *Fenton* (1777) 2 Cowp 554.

[9] e.g. *Hutton* v. *Mansell* (1704) 6 Mod 172, 3 Salk 16.

[10] *The Owl's Case* (undated; Bac Abr, *Damages*, D1); below, n.54.

[11] V. V. Palmer, *The Paths to Privity* (San Francisco, 1992), 68–83.

[12] What follows is a (very) condensed account of the development described by J. S. Rogers, *The Early History of the Law of Bills and Notes* (Cambridge, 1995).

based on 'the custom of merchants' that acceptors should be liable on bills; 'the custom of merchants' was similarly used to ground the liability of the drawer of the bill. By the end of the century this rule had been clearly incorporated into the Common law, so that the same rules applied whether or not the parties were technically merchants. The practical consequence of this was that bills of exchange could become near-equivalents of money, a more or less freely negotiable medium of exchange; and individuals could keep their money in (or lend their money to) banks, using cheques to draw on their credit. The legal consequence was that—in this situation—an action of assumpsit could be brought without the need to allege or prove that any consideration had been received.

The bill of exchange was not the only situation in which mercantile practice and the Common-law rules came into collision. In *Pillans* v. *van Mierop*,[13] the plaintiff bank gave credit to one White, who agreed that they should draw on his credit with the defendant bank. The plaintiffs then wrote to the defendants, who wrote back agreeing that they would accept a bill of exchange drawn on them by the plaintiffs. A bill was duly drawn, but the defendants refused to accept it, since, by the time it was presented to them, White had gone bankrupt. The plaintiffs brought an action against them in the King's Bench. It was urged against the action that there was no consideration, the lack of which was fatal to its success, but this was rejected on three grounds. First of all, it was said, there was implied consideration, for the defendants' letter had caused the plaintiffs not to pursue White while he was still solvent.[14] Secondly, more radically, the situation was analogized to the actual acceptance of a bill of exchange, where no consideration was necessary;[15] this could be generalized into a rule that, so far as merchants were concerned, enforceable contracts could be made without consideration.[16] Finally, and most radically, it could be suggested that the doctrine of consideration applied only to oral agreements whether or not the action concerned merchants. This appears most strongly in the judgment of Wilmot J., based on some transparently shoddy reasoning by analogy from Roman law, though it finds echoes in the words of Lord Mansfield C.J. both in argument and in his judgment.[17] Such a general attack on consideration was too much, though, and within little more than a decade it was firmly disapproved by the House of Lords in

---

[13] (1765) 3 Burr 1663.

[14] (1765) 3 Burr 1663, 1672 (Wilmot J.), 1674 (Yates J.), 1675 (Aston J.).

[15] (1765) 3 Burr 1663, 1672–3 (Wilmot J.), 1674 (Yates J., based specifically on Molloy, *De Jure Maritimo*, 2.10.20).

[16] (1765) 3 Burr 1663, 1669 (Lord Mansfield), 1672 (Wilmot J.).

[17] (1765) 3 Burr 1663, 1670–1 (Wilmot J.), 1668, 1669 (Lord Mansfield). But see the opinion of Lord Mansfield on the first argument of the case at 1665–6, where he is at pains to take the instant mercantile situation outside the normal rule requiring consideration without in any way impugning the validity of the general rule.

Rann v. *Hughes.*[18] The result of *Pillans* v. *van Mierop* stood, though, leaving mercantile letters of credit as another special exception to the doctrine of consideration.

The Court of Chancery and the Trust

By the end of the seventeenth century the principles on which the Court of Chancery acted had settled down to a tolerable level of certainty. The efforts of Lord Nottingham in particular had carved out a body of law relating to trusts, and the court routinely supplemented the Common law by offering Equitable remedies where the remedy available at Common law might have been defective. This corpus of Equity jurisprudence could be exploited to mitigate some—but not all—of the rigours of the Common law's contractual doctrines. So long as there was an agreement on good consideration, the Chancery could supply any defect of form,[19] and rectify any document that mis-expressed the agreement.[20] In addition, the discretionary power of the Chancery to grant specific performance and injunctions supplemented the existing Common-law remedy of damages.

While these Equitable interventions merely played around the edges of the Common-law contractual ideas, the trust was able to take some situations outside the domain of contract altogether, redefining them in explicitly proprietary terms. The trust straddled the boundary between right *in rem* and right *in personam*—it could be treated as a personal relationship between trustee and beneficiary or alternatively as a form of property right vested in the beneficiary—but by the late seventeenth century the proprietary dimension was uppermost.[21] So long as there was some specific land or goods, an individual wanting to undertake an obligation to a third party could do so by declaring a trust over the property.[22] This had no effect over the legal title, and possession might remain with the person declaring the trust, but the Court of Chancery treated it as if a shadow property had been created and vested in the beneficiary of the trust. The Chancery would not enforce the declaration of trust unless there was some consideration for it, but 'consideration' here was wider than at Common law: it included not only something given in exchange but also the 'natural love and affection'

[18] (1778) 4 Bro PC 27, 7 TR 350 n. There is a useful manuscript report in LI MS Misc 130 f.74. I am grateful to Mr Warren Swain for this reference.
[19] H. Ballow, *Treatise on Equity* (ed. J. Fonblanque, 1793–4), 1.38–41. Equally it could override restrictive Common-law rules, such as that holding that a contract between a man and woman was avoided by their subsequent intermarriage: *Cannel* v. *Buckle* (1741) 2 P Wms 243.   [20] Below, n.44.
[21] D. E. C. Yale, *Lord Nottingham's Chancery Case, ii* (79 SS), 87–91.
[22] This came to be subject to certain limitations of form. Thus, under s.7 of the Statute of Frauds a declaration of trust of land had to be proved by a signed writing.

presumed to exist between kin,[23] and was therefore of particular use in giving effect to intra-family settlements of property. As well as being based on a weakened notion of consideration, the declaration of trust required less in the way of participation by the beneficiary; no agreement was necessary to make the trust perfect, and, although there was a power to renounce, this operated by nullifying the trust that had come into existence rather than by preventing its coming into existence in the first place.[24]

The availability of these remedies in Chancery took some pressure off the Common-law action of assumpsit. Promises in consideration of marriage,[25] anomalous from the sixteenth century, were still in theory actionable at Common law, though in practice they seem to have fallen increasingly within the domain of the Chancellor, thereby sharpening the edges of the theory of consideration based on reciprocity. More telling was the effect of Chancery intervention on the doctrine of privity of contract.[26] A relatively common situation arose where an eldest son promised his father that he would transfer some property to a sibling in accordance with the father's wishes, as a consequence of which the father refrained from making express provision for the sibling. In the sixteenth century such cases might be brought within assumpsit by treating the sibling as the promisee,[27] but gradually the courts became uncomfortable with such a twisting of the rules. The promise was made to the father, and the only difficulty was that after his death there might commonly be nobody who could (or would) take steps to enforce it. The judges' discomfort is clearly visible in *Dutton* v. *Poole* in 1677–9,[28] though judgment there was eventually given for the plaintiff. So long as the property had come to the promisor, though, the case could be analysed in terms of a trust (provided appropriate language was used) and the privity objections straightforwardly sidestepped. So willing was the Court of Chancery to facilitate this that by the end of the seventeenth century it was allowing the formality rules imposed by the Statute of Frauds to be bypassed: a 'secret trust' did not have to be evidenced in writing and could be asserted in the teeth of an apparently unqualified gift.[29] Similarly the Court of Chancery might in some circumstances allow a third-party beneficiary to bring a bill in Equity to force the

[23] J. Gilbert, *The Law of Uses and Trusts* (1734), 45–52. 'Natural Love and Affection' was easily extended to give effect to trusts in favour of charities: G. H. Jones, *The History of the Law of Charity 1532–1827* (Cambridge, 1969), 62 n.6. The requirement of consideration for a valid declaration of trust continued until the end of the eighteenth century (see e.g. *Colman* v. *Sarell* (1789) 1 Ves Jun 50, 3 Bro CC 12, per Lord Thurlow L.C.), but around the beginning of the nineteenth century it was dropped (*Ellison* v. *Ellison* (1802) 6 Ves Jun 656, per Lord Eldon). See M. Macnair, 'Equity and Volunteers' (1988) 8 Legal Studies 172, esp. 181–2.

[24] e.g. *Dunch* v. *Kent* (1684) 1 Vern 260, 319.   [25] Above, p.142.

[26] Palmer, *Paths to Privity*, 74–83; N. G. Jones, 'Uses, Trusts and a Path to Privity' [1997] LQR 175.   [27] e.g. *Rookwood* v. *Rookwood* (1589) 1 Leon 193, Cro El 164; above, p.140.

[28] 3 Keb 786, 814, 830, 836; Jones T 102; 1 Vent 318, 332; 2 Lev 210; T Raymond 302; 1 Freeman 471.   [29] *Thynn* v. *Thynn* (1685) 1 Vern 296.

contractor to bring an action in law,[30] thereby incidentally allowing the development of the whole law relating to the equitable assignment of choses in action.

Vitiating Factors

At a more general level, contractual liability depended on the voluntary act of the parties, and anything that undermined this voluntariness potentially destroyed the basis of liability.[31] In the seventeenth and eighteenth centuries the courts, especially the Chancery, began to work out a taxonomy of vitiating factors.

The Common law had a relatively small role to play here because of the continuing strength of the jury. So far as the formal rules were concerned, the Common law developed little from its medieval roots: lack of capacity hardly moved beyond married women and infants; duress was restricted to imprisonment; and if there were any question of fraud, it could be raised explicitly only by an action in deceit by the party defrauded. Beyond this juries were in practice allowed to exercise a measure of discretion to mitigate obviously undesirable results—it was clearly recognized that they had an informal power to relieve in cases of fraud, for example—though the evidence suggests that this power was not used heavy-handedly.[32]

The Chancery was more flexible, though in the main operating with the same categories as the Common law. It was here that the rules obtained a measure of definition, though in practice they normally did so in the context of formal agreements under seal rather than purely informal agreements. Central to the Chancery's intervention was the power to relieve against fraud and its close cousin breach of confidence. The most obvious case of this was where one person deliberately made a false statement in order to lure another into a bargain, but it could extend much further than this: a representation by conduct might equally constitute fraud, as might a representation by silence.[33] It had the capacity to embrace negligent representations and even innocent ones where it was the responsibility of the representor to know the truth.[34] In the eyes of Equity, therefore, fraud was a potentially very broad concept, and care is needed not to exaggerate its

---

[30] This possibility was envisaged in *Dutton* v. *Poole* itself: 1 Freeman 471. The practice dated back at least as far as the fifteenth century: above, pp.80, 141.

[31] This was implicit in the medieval law: above, p.71.

[32] M. Lobban, 'Contractual Fraud in Law and Equity' (1997) 17 Ox Jnl Leg Stud 441, 457–65.

[33] See generally *Broderick* v. *Broderick* (1713) 1 P Wms 239 (the court will relieve against *suppressio veri* or *suggestio falsi*); *Chesterfield* v. *Janssen* (1751) 2 Ves Sen 125, 155.

[34] e.g. *Pearson* v. *Morgan* (1788) 2 Bro CC 388. The real extension took place in the nineteenth century: see Story, *Equity Jurisprudence*, §193.

practical role. Except in the most serious cases it was limited to a refusal of specifically equitable relief: a party whose conduct was in some way tainted would commonly be refused an order of specific performance, but the right to sue at law was unaffected.[35]

Chancery's procedures allowed it to look more closely at whether defendants' impaired mental capacity had undermined their voluntariness. Lunatics' contracts would routinely be set aside, for example, though not those of the merely simple-minded.[36] There was some suggestion that more transitory weaknesses such as drunkenness could also nullify contractual intent, but the court was not receptive to such arguments unless clear fraud was also involved.[37] The court was more generous in extending duress from its narrow Common-law base into situations where one party had exercised an undue influence over the other. This was relatively straightforward where there was a relationship of power, trust, or confidence between the parties, such as between trustee and beneficiary, parent and child, or attorney and client;[38] it smacked of fraud for the dominant party to take advantage of the weaker. It was less willing to intervene where there was no prior relationship between the parties: relief was regularly granted where moneylenders and the like had taken advantage of indigent but prodigal expectant heirs,[39] even when they might have been thought old enough to look out for their own interests—a 40-year-old proctor from Doctors' Commons, inaptly named Wiseman, successfully obtained relief[40]—but there was a reluctance to extend it much further than this.[41] The careful approach is well exemplified by the remarks of Lord Thurlow L.C. in *Fox* v. *Mackreth*: 'The Court will not correct a contract, merely because a man of nice honour would not have entered into it; it must fall within some definition of fraud; the rule must be drawn so as not to affect the general transactions of mankind.'[42]

[35] Lobban, 'Contractual Fraud' (1997) 17 Ox Jnl Leg Stud 441, 448–50.

[36] Ballow, *Treatise on Equity* (ed. Fonblanque), 1.46–61.

[37] *Rich* v. *Sydenham* (1671) 1 Ch Cas 202; *Cory* v. *Cory* (1747) 1 Ves Sen 19. The Common-law defence of *non est factum* could be applied to set aside a bond when the obligor was too drunk to know what he was doing: *Cole* v. *Robins* (1704) Bull NP 172. Cf. *Baynard* v. *Haythorne* (undated, but late sixteenth century) C2/Eliz1/B7/1, where a defendant trying to escape liability admitted that the fact that he had sealed the document while drunk would not in itself avail him.

[38] e.g. *Whitackre* v. *Whitackre* (1725) Sel Cas t King 13 (trustee and beneficiary); *Blunden* v. *Barker* (1720) 1 P Wms 634, *Carpenter* v. *Heriot* (1759) 1 Eden 338, *Kinchant* v. *Kinchant* (1784) 1 Bro CC 369 (parent and child); *Walmsley* v. *Booth* (1739–41) 2 Atk 25, *Fox* v. *Mackreth* (1788) 2 Bro CC 400, 420 (attorney and client); *Osmond* v. *Fitzroy* (1731) 3 P Wms 129 (servant and master).

[39] This was based as much on the protection of family property as of the heir himself: Lobban, 'Contractual Fraud' (1997) 17 Ox Jnl Leg Stud 441, 451.

[40] *Wiseman* v. *Beake* (1689) 2 Freem 111, 2 Vern 121.

[41] Extensions were possible, though. Sailors—'a race of men loose and unthinking, who will almost for nothing part with what they have acquired perhaps with their blood'—were analogized to young heirs in *How* v. *Weldon* (1754) 2 Ves Sen 516, 518.

[42] (1788) 2 Bro CC 400, 420.

Occasionally Equity might intervene in cases of mistake.[43] This intervention took two forms. First, there was a general jurisdiction in Chancery to rectify documents that did not reflect the true agreement intended by the parties. Thus, where a bond drafted by a tradesman ignorant of the proper forms provided for joint liability, the court rectified this to give joint and several liability as was (presumably) the parties' intention.[44] Secondly, the court would give relief where one party had entered into the agreement under a misapprehension not shared by the other party, and where there was a suspicion (normally unproved) of sharp practice on the defendant's part.[45] Hence an agreement between a daughter and mother concerning the division of the deceased father's personal estate was set aside at the suit of the daughter when it was revealed that she had agreed to take considerably less than her proper share: there was insufficient proof of undue influence by the mother to justify setting the agreement aside on that ground, so the court took refuge behind the mistake of the daughter who had believed that the agreement quantified her true share.[46] But the court would not normally interfere where the parties shared the same misapprehension, so that there was no hint of imposition by one on the other,[47] nor where the agreement was a speculative one in which a party had misguessed the future value of land.[48]

The courts were concerned to prevent one party taking unfair advantage of another; but not every advantage was unfair. A simple inequality between the two sides of the bargain, or some other evidence of ill-advisedness, was not enough to justify a refusal to enforce the agreement, unless it was so gross as to raise a presumption of fraud.[49] This was explicit in the Chancery,[50] and the only two reported cases give no good reason to believe

---

[43] This is clearly stated as a general principle in e.g. *Gee* v. *Spencer* (1681) 1 Vern 32 and *Morris* v. *Burroughs* (1737) 1 Atk 399, 402.

[44] *Simpson* v. *Vaughan* (1739) 2 Atk 31. See also *Merrick* v. *Harvey* (1649) Nels 48; *Baker* v. *Paine* (1750) 1 Ves Sen 456; *Shelburne* v. *Inchiquin* (1784) 1 Bro CC 338. For the Chancery's concern to establish (rather than rewrite) the agreement of the parties, see Lobban, 'Contractual Fraud' (1997) 17 Ox Jnl Leg Stud 441, 447.

[45] For the limited scope of the defence in the seventeenth century, see Yale, *Lord Nottingham's Chancery Cases, ii* (79 SS), 19.

[46] *Cocking* v. *Pratt* (1750) 1 Ves Sen 400. See too *Turner* v. *Turner* (1680) 2 Ch Rep 154; *Bingham* v. *Bingham* (1748) 1 Ves Sen 126; *Evans* v. *Llewellyn* (1787) 2 Bro CC 150.

[47] *Pullen* v. *Ready* (1743) 2 Atk 587, 592; but note *Lansdown* v. *Lansdown* (1730) Moseley 364, where the court did undo a transaction entered into under a common misapprehension as to legal rights brought about by foolishly consulting the local schoolmaster rather than a professional lawyer. [48] *Mortimer* v. *Capper* (1782) 1 Bro CC 156.

[49] P. S. Atiyah, *The Rise and Fall of Freedom of Contract* (Oxford, 1979), 146–9 (though with a slightly different slant); the evidence is carefully discussed by J. L. Barton, 'The Enforcement of Hard Bargains' (1987) 103 LQR 118.

[50] e.g. *Hobert* v. *Hobert* (1685) 2 Ch Cas 159, *Keen* v. *Stuckeley* (1721) Gilb Rep 155, *Willis* v. *Jernegan* (1741) 2 Atk 251. See J. Newland, *Treatise on Contracts within the Jurisdiction of Courts of Equity* (1806), 65–8.

that juries at Common law operated on different lines.[51] Sharp practice was clearly involved in *James* v. *Morgan*:[52] the defendant bought a horse from the plaintiff promising to give one barleycorn for the first nail in a horse's shoe, two for the second, and so doubling up until the last nail had been counted. There were thirty-two nails. When sued for the barley, amounting to 500 quarters, the court ordered that he should receive no more than £8, the ordinary market price of the horse.[53] Further from simple fraud, but none the less involving the taking of an unfair advantage, was *The Owl's Case*.[54] A pet-owner, no doubt distraught, offered an absurd reward of £1,000 for the return of his lost owl; when the finder brought his action for the £1,000, the jury was told that it might mitigate the damages if it saw fit.

Public Policy

The second group of vitiating factors were those more largely based on public policy. A distinction here could be taken between illegal contracts and those merely contrary to public policy; in the former case neither the Common law nor Equity would countenance any action concerning them, whereas in the latter case the courts would not enforce them but would allow legal processes to be used to undo them.[55]

It is hardly suprising that the courts refused to enforce contracts that were in some way illegal.[56] Even circumstances of collateral illegality, as where a ballet dancer had agreed to perform in an unlicensed theatre, might have sufficed to justify a refusal to enforce a contract.[57] Both the Chancery and the Common-law courts were quick to sniff out any whiff of illegality. In *Morris* v. *Chapman*,[58] for example, an action was brought against a sheriff to execute an unlawful legal process; the defendant entered a technical plea in bar of the action, not mentioning anything of the illegality; this plea was formally defective and the plaintiff demurred to it. In normal circumstances judgment would routinely have been given for the plaintiff, but here the Common Pleas dismissed the case of its own motion. The contract was on its face unlawful, and that was enough to dispose of the case. The same applied in Equity. An action by one highwayman against another to share the profits of their partnership met with predictable

---

[51] Barton, 'Hard Bargains' (1987) 103 LQR 118, 118–23.   [52] (1663) 1 Lev 111.

[53] Cf. *Thornborow* v. *Whitacre* (1705) 2 Ld Raym 1164, a more extreme case of a geometrical progression where the promise was held void since the defendant would have been required to give to the plaintiff a quantity of rye greater than the world could provide.

[54] Undated, but probably early eighteenth century; Bac Abr, *Damages*, D1.

[55] J. Story, *Equity Jurisprudence*, §298, and the references there cited.

[56] Sheppard, *Actions upon the Case for Deeds*, 183–93, with references.

[57] *Gallini* v. *Laborie* (1793) 5 TR 242. The action was brought by the impresario, who was aware of the illegality, against the innocent dancer. For the range of situations encompassed within the idea of illegality, see J. Comyns, *Digest* (5th edn., 1822), 1.322–3.

[58] (1671) T Jones 24.

results: the bill was dismissed, plaintiff's counsel was ordered to pay costs, and his solicitors were fined for contempt.[59] There may have been a feeling that it was harsh to apply the rule to mere *mala prohibita* (essentially regulatory offences) as opposed to *mala in se* (real crimes); but when the point was made it was only to conclude that the rules applied equally to both classes of case.[60]

Behind the prohibition of illegal contracts there was a far wider jurisdiction to refuse to enforce contracts contrary to public policy. There was no predetermined limit to the concept of public policy, and the general principle of not enforcing such contracts is often stated without qualification.[61] Within this broad compass certain categories can be discerned: contracts interfering with freedom of marriage (including marriage brocage contracts and agreements in restraint of marriage),[62] contracts interfering with freedom of trade (agreements in restraint of trade, manipulation of public auctions, and other forms of market),[63] contracts interfering with legal process (such as agreements to suppress criminal prosecutions),[64] and contracts contrary to good government (buying and selling of public offices).[65] Sometimes public policy was reflected in statutes, such as the Gaming Acts or the Statutes of Usury,[66] though the courts exercised a discretion outside the boundaries fixed by these legislative regimes.[67]

By the use of this form of reasoning the judges were able to mould the law of contract around their ideas of social needs and interests. Perceptions of social interests were not constant, however, and the judicial application of the notion of public policy changed substantially through time (and, indeed, from judge to judge). The idea of what constituted an unacceptable

[59] *Everet* v. *Williams* (1725) (Equity Side of the Exchequer), in (1787) 11 European Magazine 360. I have not traced the plaintiff's bill, but the interlocutory proceedings are recorded in PRO E127/34, M.1725 nos.43, 87, 103, 303. The European Magazine notes that the defendant and plaintiff were executed in 1727 and 1730 respectively, and that one of the solicitors was transported for robbery in 1735.

[60] e.g. Sheppard, *Actions upon the Case for Deeds*, 183.

[61] *Osmond* v. *Fitzroy* (1731) 3 P Wms 129; *Collins* v. *Blantern* (1767) 2 Wils 347.

[62] *Hall* v. *Potter* (1695) 1 Shower PC 76 (marriage brocage); *Lowe* v. *Peers* (1768) 4 Burr 2225 (restraint of marriage).

[63] e.g. *Mitchel* v. *Reynolds* (1711) 1 P Wms 181 (with references going as far back as YB P.2 Hen V f.5 pl.26) (restraint of trade); *Bexwell* v. *Christie* (1776) 1 Cowp 395 (manipulating auctions); S. Browne, *The Laws against Ingrossing, Forestalling, Regrating, and Monopolizing* (1765). See also W. Herbruck, 'Forestalling, Regrating and Engrossing' (1929) 27 Mich LR 365 and, more generally J. D. Heydon, *The Restraint of Trade Doctrine* (London, 1971), ch. 1.

[64] *Johnson* v. *Ogilby* (1734) 3 P Wms 277; *Collins* v. *Blantern* (1767) 2 Wils 347.

[65] *Chesterfield* v. *Janssen* (1751) 2 Ves Sen 125.

[66] Stat 16 Car II c.7 s.3; Stat 9 Anne c.14 s.1 (Gaming). Stat 37 Hen VIII c.9; Stat 13 Eliz c.8; Stat 21 Jac I c.17; Stat 12 Anne stat.2 c.16 (Usury).

[67] Ballow, *Treatise on Equity* (ed. Fonblanque), 1.244–7. The Court of King's Bench had refused to enforce a wagering contract, substantially on the grounds that it was contrary to public policy, in *Metcalfe* v. *Ascough* (1599) Moo 549, CUL MS Ii 5.26 f.209, Yale Law School MS G R 29.12 f.162[v].

restraint of trade at the beginning of the seventeenth century was emphatically not the same as that found at the beginning of the eighteenth or at the beginning of the nineteenth.[68] It was, though, this very flexibility of application that enabled the rules to develop as apparently changeless entities, and to become sufficiently firmly established that they could be incorporated into the fabric of the law of contract articulated in the nineteenth century.

Damages and Penalties

By the seventeenth century liability in contract was seen as absolute, in the sense that, once the parties had reached an agreement, they would in principle be held to it unless the defendant could point to duress, fraud, or some other vitiating factor.[69] Consistently with this position, the courts' remedies would normally give effect to the agreement, in Chancery specific performance or injunctions, at Common law damages designed to reflect the parties' lost expectations. Juries may, of course, have gone their own ways; but there is no good reason to believe that they did so, and the expectation-based rule of assessment was clearly established when the judges began to exercise explicit control over damage awards.[70]

This principle was subject to the important qualification that the courts would not enforce penalties.[71] The origins of this lie in the Chancery practice of the late fifteenth century,[72] and by the end of the sixteenth century relief would generally be given if the debtor had blamelessly failed to perform the condition of a bond on time: so long as the condition was performed as soon as possible and the creditor compensated for any additional loss suffered, the Chancery would give an injunction to prevent the debtor enforcing the penalty in the bond at Common law.[73] Though in the years around 1600 Lord Chancellor Ellesmere would grant relief only in cases of genuine misfortune, his successor Francis Bacon was far more generous to debtors; in the common case of the penal money bond, where the penalty was fixed at double the value of the condition, creditors would normally obtain an injunction against enforcement of the penalty so long

---

[68] Cf. *Rogers* v. *Parry* (1614) 2 Bulst 136 and *Jollyfe* v. *Broad* (1620) Cro Jac 596 with *Mitchel* v. *Reynolds* (1711) 1 P Wms 181 and *Hearn* v. *Griffin* (1815) 2 Chit 407. See Atiyah, *Rise and Fall of Freedom of Contract*, esp. at 118–19, 125–7, 408–12.

[69] *Paradine* v. *Jane* (1647) Aleyn 26, Style 47, BL MS Harg 42 f.74ᵛ, HLS MS 145a p.30; Kiralfy, *Source Book of English Law*, 122–5. See Ibbetson, 'Absolute Liability in Contract: the Antecedents of Paradine v. Jayne', in F. D. Rose (ed.), *Consensus ad Idem* (London, 1996), 1, 30–7.   [70] *Lowe* v. *Peers* (1768) 4 Burr 2225.

[71] See esp. Yale, *Lord Nottingham's Chancery Cases, ii* (79 SS), 8–30. Cf. above, p.150. The routine grant of relief against penalties was the most significant factor in the demise of the conditional bond.   [72] *Capell's Case* (1494) 102 SS 13.

[73] E. Henderson, 'Relief from Bonds in the English Chancery' (1974) 18 Am Jnl Leg Hist 298. The point is made explicitly in *Anon* (*c*.1600) Cary 1, and Coke, *Fourth Institute*, 84.

as they paid the principal sum due (the sum named in the condition) together with interest and costs.[74] By the middle of the seventeenth century the granting of relief against the penalty was so routine—if necessary the creditor's actual loss would be determined by a Master in Chancery or by a jury[75]—that creditors unsuccessfully began to try to initiate their actions in Chancery rather than suing at law to get a judgment that would immediately be made the subject of an injunction.[76] The inefficient circuity of actions caused by the superimposition of Chancery remedies on the Common law was removed by statute from 1697. The effect of this was that a defendant who had performed the condition in substance, though not in precise form, would be able to plead this performance in bar of a Common-law action for the contractual penalty; where the condition was the payment of a sum of money, the action for the penalty would be stayed if the debtor paid into court the sum of money due under the condition together with interest to take account of the delayed payment; if neither of these was satisfied, the creditor would obtain judgment for the full amount of the penalty, but execution of this judgment would be stayed if the debtor paid damages to compensate for his breach of the condition.[77] That there was regular relief against the enforcement of penalties says nothing about what constituted a penalty, and on the whole the eighteenth-century judges interpreted this narrowly. At the start of the nineteenth century it was settled that a sum due on the non-performance of a condition would be treated as a penalty only if the condition was itself for the payment of a sum of money or if the condition was multifaceted and capable of being breached in a variety of ways of varying degrees of seriousness. In neither case could it have been pretended that the penal sum due was a genuinely agreed pre-estimate of the plaintiff's loss; in the former the relationship between the value of the condition and the value of the penalty was transparent on the face of the instrument, and in the latter the range of circumstances potentially constituting breaches of the condition made it impossible that the single sum of the penalty represented the true value of any single breach.[78]

---

[74] G. Norbury, 'The Abuses and Remedies of Chancery', in F. Hargrave, *Law Tracts* (1787), 1.425, 431–2.   [75] Yale, *Lord Nottingham's Chancery Cases, ii* (79 SS) *15*.
[76] *Finch* v. *Finch* (1675) 73 SS 403. The routine nature of the Chancery remedy at this time is made quite clear in *Puleston* v. *Puleston* (1675) 73 SS 295.
[77] Stat 8 & 9 Will III c.11 s.8, amended by Stat 4 Anne c.16 s.12, s.13 (1705). There was additional provision to deal with cases where there might subsequently be further breaches of conditions. For the working of the statutes, see *Goodwin* v. *Crowle* (1775) 1 Cowp 357, *Hardy* v. *Bern* (1794) 5 TR 636.   [78] *Astley* v. *Weldon* (1801) 2 B & P 346.

THE THEORY OF CONTRACT

Before 1700 the English law of contract had developed without any articulated theory to support it. The treatment of the subject in Charles Viner's *Abridgement*, published in the middle of the eighteenth century, was typical of the way in which traditional contractual thinking was structured: material relating to contracts is scattered under the headings Action upon the Case upon Assumpsit, Agreement, Baron and Feme, Conditions, Contract, Covenant, Covin, Duress of Imprisonment, Enfants, Executor, Faits or Deeds, Fraud, and so on. Already, though, this lack of theory had begun to be remedied. As occurred with the law of torts at the same time, English lawyers began to use theoretical models to give a structure to contractual liability, and by 1800 the law of contract could be treated as an abstract entity distinct from the forms of action.

Two separate, though related, theoretical positions combined to bring this about. First, and more important for thinking about the structure of the law, was the idea of contract formulated by Thomas Hobbes and used as the basis of his Social Contract theory.[79] Secondly, and central to the way in which detailed legal rules were framed, was the analysis of the Natural lawyers; most notable here at first was Samuel Pufendorf, but by the end of the century his influence was being eclipsed by Robert-Joseph Pothier, whose *Traité des obligations* was first published in 1761. Many, though by no means all, of the elements of these theories could be found in the traditional Common-law model of contract.

Social Contract Theories: Thomas Hobbes

The idea of contract was central to Hobbes's treatment of political society, for it was the agreement between citizens that gave power to the ruler, their mutual act of will transferring authority to him to govern over them.[80] Though ostensibly derived from the Common-law idea of contract,[81] Hobbes's model differed from it in three important respects. To begin with, his approach was more obviously proprietary than was that of the contemporary Common lawyers;[82] 'contract' could be defined as the mutual transfer of rights, in contradistinction to the unilateral transfer of

---

[79] Atiyah, *The Rise and Fall of Freedom of Contract*, 41–4. For the relationship between Hobbes and the Natural lawyers, see N. Bobbio, *Thomas Hobbes and the Natural Law Tradition* (Chicago, 1993), esp. 149–71.

[80] In this Hobbes differed from other social contractarians, for whom the original agreement was between the citizens and the ruler: J. P. Sommerville, *Thomas Hobbes: Political Ideas in Historical Context* (Basingstoke, 1992), 57.

[81] R. A. Grover, 'The Legal Origin of Thomas Hobbes's Doctrine of Contract' (1980) 18 Journal of the History of Philosophy 177.

[82] It was, therefore, closer to the medieval idea behind the word 'contract': above, p.75.

rights that constituted a gift, while 'covenant' designated that species of contract in which rights were to be transferred in the future.[83] This proprietary approach in its turn enabled him to treat the mutual agreement of two or more individuals as generating some new thing, not simply giving the parties rights each against the other.[84] Moreover, it meant that the whole root of contract was to be found in the will of the parties; in this Hobbes went a good deal further than the lawyers of the sixteenth century and before, for whom agreement was already a dominant element in contractual thinking.[85]

The Hobbesian model had two important consequences for the structure of the English law of contract. Most obviously it downplayed the role of consideration, for, if liability was generated by the parties' agreement, then it would not seem to matter whether it was purely gratuitous or had been paid for. The function of consideration is highly ambiguous in Hobbes's sketches of contract—consideration is defined in terms of reciprocity, then treated as no more than evidence of intention to be bound[86]—and this ambiguity was carried forward into the analyses of the nineteenth and twentieth centuries.[87] Its second important consequence was the tendency to treat contracts as something close to property. At a theoretical level this led to the foundation of the model of contract on the paradigm of the purely executory agreement—nothing was needed to create a contract beyond the mutual consent of the parties to it (except, perhaps, consideration)—a model that clearly lies behind all the nineteenth-century analyses of the nature of contract.

The best early example of the framing of contractual thinking on the Hobbesian model is to be found in Sir Jeffrey Gilbert's unprinted treatise on contracts, which has a good claim to be the first serious work on the subject in England.[88] Gilbert defines contract as 'the act of two or more persons concurring, the one in parting with and the other in receiving some property, right or benefit',[89] a position close to that of Hobbes. The contract gains its force from the mutual intention to give and to receive the property or right. Others—presumably the Natural lawyers—argued that a naked declaration of mind is enough to achieve this, since the duty to tell the truth entails a duty to keep faith with words and promises; but this approach, he says, did not accord with English law. The English requirement of reciprocal consideration was more difficult to dispose of,[90] though.

---

[83] *Elements of Law* (ed F. Tönnies, Cambridge, 1928), 1.15.7–10.

[84] Most obviously it was the agreement between citizens that brought about 'the generation of the great LEVIATHAN . . .' (*Leviathan*, 2.17).   [85] Above, p.135.

[86] *Elements of Law*, 1.15.9.   [87] Below, p.238.

[88] BL MS Hargrave 265, 266. The section on oral contracts is in Hargrave MS 265 ff.39–95ᵛ.

[89] BL MS Hargrave 265 f.39. I have throughout tacitly repunctuated Gilbert's text, which is only minimally punctuated in the manuscript.

[90] BL MS Hargrave 265 ff.40ᵛ–58ᵛ. The difficulties of his position are discussed below, p.237.

By the end of the first section of his treatise the theoretical starting point that liability stems from the *mutual* agreement of the parties has been transmuted into the rather different position that it stems from their *reciprocal* agreement; hence a promise to pay for a benefit voluntarily conferred by the promisee is of no effect, not because there is nothing from which the seriousness of the *promisor's* intent can be deduced but because there was no intent to contract on the part of the *promisee* at the time of the original transfer.[91]

The central elements of the Hobbesian theory did not merely migrate into Gilbert's (unprinted) treatise; by the second half of the eighteenth century they were beginning to work their way into legal practice. In the 1760s some judges were willing to think of consideration as no more than evidence of seriousness of intention, so that a seriously intended non-reciprocal agreement should be given full legal force, and, although their position was clearly regarded as too radical at the time, it set the stage for the more wholesale attempts to rationalize consideration in this way in the nineteenth century.[92] The second of the Hobbesian elements, the reification of contracts, was strengthened in practice by the introduction of rules of set-off where the plaintiff was indebted to the defendant,[93] so that the mutual rights and duties arising under the contract could be set against each other so as to produce a composite sum representing the value of the contract-as-thing. Hence contracts were able to move away from being limited to simple exchanges where each party wanted the other's performance; they could now encompass speculative arrangements where the parties were seeking merely to make a marginal profit on a transaction in a volatile market.[94]

Natural-Law Theories: Samuel Pufendorf

The second source of contractual thinking in the eighteenth century was to be found in the writings of the Natural lawyers, especially Samuel Pufendorf. Behind these there was a very substantial body of theory, most sophisticatedly propounded by the Spanish neo-scholastics of the

---

[91] BL MS Hargrave 265 f.41.   [92] Below, pp.239, 240.
[93] Stat 2 Geo II c.22 s.13 (1728), amended and confirmed by Stat 8 Geo II c.24 s.5 (1734). See *Howlet* v. *Strickland* (1774) 1 Cowp 56. The rules of set-off were extended to all liquidated counterclaims by *Morley* v. *Inglis* (1837) 6 Dowl 202.
[94] Atiyah, *Rise and Fall of Freedom of Contract*, 211–12. Cf. *Smee* v. *Huddlestone* (1768), in J. Sayer, *The Law of Damages* (1770), 49–52, where it was held (Wilmot C.J. dissenting) that the correct measure of damages in an action against a buyer who had refused to accept goods was the difference between the contract price and the price at which the seller had been able to resell the goods. This was the corollary of the rule that the appropriate measure of damages in an action against a defaulting seller was the difference between the contract price and the price reigning on the agreed date for delivery: *Cuddee* v. *Rutter* (1720) 2 Eq Cas Abr 16.

sixteenth century, and thence traceable back through Thomas Aquinas to Aristotle.[95] Central to the thinking of the Natural lawyers was the relationship between the obligation to tell the truth and the obligation to keep a promise; the contractual duty stemmed from the unilateral act of the promisor, although it was argued by some that the acceptance by the promisee was a precondition of the concretization of the duty. As with Hobbes's theory, there was little or no room for the Common lawyers' requirement of consideration, though the proprietary dimension that was such an important feature of Hobbes's thought was wholly absent. The theoretical underpinnings of the Natural lawyers' systems were to all intents and purposes totally ignored by the English lawyers; but it was from their works that the conceptual vocabulary of the Common law was culled.

Pufendorf's influence is abundantly visible in the first published English work on contract with any pretension to treat the subject on an abstract basis, a *Treatise on Equity* published anonymously in 1737 but probably the work of Henry Ballow (or Bellewe) of Lincoln's Inn,[96] the first half of which is devoted to a treatment of contract both at Common law and in Equity.[97] For the most part his discussion of contract consists of brief paraphrases of or unattributed quotations from the English translation of Pufendorf's *De iure naturae et gentium*,[98] followed by illustrative material from English case law.

For Pufendorf, contractual obligation derived from the duty to keep one's promise; it followed that the whole focus of his analysis was on the promisor. Ballow picks this up, beginning by examining the nature of assent and contractual capacity.[99] Assent might be vitiated by error,[100] *a fortiori* if brought about by the fraud of the promisee.[101] Behind Pufendorf's theory was Aristotle's theory of justice; in so far as this meant

---

[95] J. Gordley, *The Philosophical Origins of Modern Contract Law* (Oxford, 1991). For the Natural lawyers, see pp. 112–33.

[96] Francis Hargrave's note to the British Library copy of the second edition (BL 510.d.16) explicitly attributes the work to Ballow; see further Holdsworth, *History of English Law*, 12.191–2, with the qualifications of M. Macnair, 'The Conceptual Basis of Trusts in the Later Seventeenth and Early Eighteenth Century', in R. H. Helmholz and R. Zimmermann (eds.), *Itinera Fiduciae: Trust and Treuhand in Historical Perspective* (Berlin, 1999), 207, 211 n.9 (perhaps too doubtful about the attribution of authorship to Ballow). I am very grateful to Dr Macnair for allowing me to see his paper before publication.

[97] That the treatment is found in a book on Equity is eloquent testimony to the role of the Chancery in contractual litigation at this time.

[98] *Of the Law of Nature and Nations*. Ballow appears to have used the translation by Basil Kennett with notes by Jean Barbeyrac, probably in the then-current fourth edition (1729).

[99] *Treatise on Equity*, c.2 s.1–6; c.2 s.1, mirroring Pufendorf, *Law of Nature and Nations*, 3.6.1–5.

[100] *Treatise on Equity*, c.2 s.7, derived from Pufendorf, *Law of Nature and Nations*, 3.6.7. Ballow here gives no English illustration.

[101] *Treatise on Equity*, c.2 s.8, the general part copied word for word from Pufendorf, *Law of Nature and Nations*, 3.6.8.

commutative justice, it followed that inequality of exchange constituted a further vitiating factor. Ballow borrows this too, but provides no English materials to illustrate it.[102] The need for the assent to be properly attested forms Ballow's next chapter. This is largely based on specifically English rules, but where a theoretical slant is needed it is taken from Pufendorf. Thus an agreement must be 'perfect',[103] and there must be an acceptance by the promisee.[104] Agreements must not be impossible or illegal.[105] Contracts requiring the active participation of independent third parties are in some sense impossible if the third party will not agree,[106] as is a promise to do something already promised to another.[107] Ballow's chapter ends with a treatment of the circumstances in which an individual should be entitled to resile from an obligation. Much of this is English law, but beneath it lies the theoretical observation, derived from Cicero via Pufendorf, that the obligation ceases to bind if to perform it would cause some greater harm.[108]

At this point, for the first time, Ballow departs from Pufendorf. He turns to the necessity for reciprocal consideration, a strong requirement in English law but a principle wholly at odds with Pufendorf's theory,[109] and with the mutuality of conditions in the execution of agreements (on which Pufendorf has nothing to say).

Ballow's analysis of contractual liability was a very long way from being a faithful rendition of Pufendorf's. It was little more than a veneer of Natural-law terminology and ideas, the mangled remnants of a once-coherent theory, a skeleton glued together from a selection of bones picked from Pufendorf, with one or two added from elsewhere, on which the rules of Common law and Equity hung loosely and inelegantly. The gulf between the Natural lawyers' model and the practice of English law was so great that it could hardly have been otherwise. It did, however, point the way forward into the nineteenth century, where the terminology and ideas of the Natural lawyers (especially in the Romanized version popularized by Pothier) were freely plundered to give expression to the rules of English law.

---

[102] *Treatise on Equity*, c.2 s.9–12, c.2 s.9, mirroring Pufendorf, *Law of Nature and Nations*, 5.3.1–9. Note c.2 s.10, where he all but admits that it does not represent English law.

[103] *Treatise on Equity*, c.3 s.6, derived from Pufendorf, *Law of Nature and Nations*, 3.5.7–8, and quoting (without attribution) Barbeyrac's note to 3.5.8.

[104] *Treatise on Equity*, c.3 s.12, derived from Pufendorf, *Law of Nature and Nations*, 3.6.15.

[105] *Treatise on Equity*, c.4 s.1–2, s.4, derived from Pufendorf, *Law of Nature and Nations*, 3.7.1–2, 3.7.6. The title of Ballow's fourth chapter, 'Of the Subject Matter of Covenants', is fairly clearly borrowed from Pufendorf's title of 3.7, 'Of the Matter of Promises and Covenants'.

[106] *Treatise on Equity*, c.4 s.17, derived from Pufendorf, *Law of Nature and Nations*, 3.7.10.

[107] *Treatise on Equity*, c.4 s.25, derived from Pufendorf, *Law of Nature and Nations*, 3.7.11.

[108] *Treatise on Equity*, c.4 s.26, derived from Cicero, *De officiis*, 1.10, quoted in *Of the Law of Nature and Nations*, 3.5.9.   [109] *Of the Law of Nature and Nations*, 3.5.9.

12. *The Rise of the Will Theory*

Around 1800, the rather half-hearted tentative sallies in the direction of a theorized law of contract were superseded by more full-blooded attempts to fit the Common law into an apparently rational framework. One reason for this was the increasing need for judges to decide cases themselves rather than leaving them to the jury; in the same way as the judges' control over the jury first brought about a greater degree of definition on the boundary between the action of trespass and the action on the case and later gave shape to the whole of the tort of negligence,[1] so too they were required to articulate contractual ideas whose edges had formerly been allowed to remain fuzzy. Moreover, in the last decade of the eighteenth century there started to appear a steady stream of treatises on the law of contract— Powell (1790), Newland (1806), Comyn (1807), Colebrooke (1818), Chitty (1826), followed by Addison (1847), Leake (1867), Pollock (1876), Anson (1879)[2]—in which the fundamental questions of the nature of contractual liability had to be addressed.[3]

The model from which judges and writers derived their inspiration was the *Traité des obligations* of the French jurist Robert-Joseph Pothier, first published in 1761 and translated into English in 1806.[4] Pothier put forward a version of the Will Theory, loosely based on that of Pufendorf and the Natural lawyers, on the one hand, and the social contractarians, on the other. His central plank was that contractual liability stemmed from the mutual assent of the parties, a shift of perspective from the promise-based standpoint of the Natural lawyers, and the rest of his theory was largely built upon this basic principle. Less popular in England, though exerting considerable influence in the middle of the nineteenth century, was the German Friedrich von Savigny, whose version of the Will Theory (in his

---

[1] Above, pp.161, 173.
[2] J. J. Powell, *Essay upon the Law of Contracts and Agreements* (1790); J. Newland, *Treatise on Contracts within the Jurisdiction of Courts of Equity* (1806); S. Comyn, *The Law of Contracts and Promises* (1807); H. Colebrooke, *Treatise on Obligations and Contracts* (1818); J. Chitty, *Practical Treatise on the Law of Contracts, not under Seal* (1826); C. G. Addison, *Treatise on the Law of Contracts and Liabilities ex Contractu* (1847); S. M. Leake, *The Elements of the Law of Contracts* (1867); F. Pollock, *Principles of Contract at Law and in Equity* (1876); W. Anson, *Principles of the English Law of Contract* (1879).
[3] See A. W. B. Simpson, 'The Rise and Fall of the Legal Treatise' (1981) 48 Univ Chic L R 632.
[4] W. D. Evans, *A Treatise on the Law of Obligations or Contracts, by M. Pothier* (1806). There was an earlier American translation by Francis-Xavier Martin (1802).

System des heutigen römischen Rechts) owed more to German philosophy than had Pothier's.[5]

The great merit of the Will Theory was that it had a measure of intellectual coherence that the traditional Common law wholly lacked, though this coherence had been to some extent bought at the expense of practical common sense. Its greatest demerit was that it was imposed on the Common law from the outside rather than generated from within. It embodied a model of contract significantly different from the traditional English exchange model, and there was considerable friction between the two theories. The Common law did not—of course—simply discard those elements that did not fit neatly into the theory but strained to squeeze them into it. The result was a mess.

The Centrality of Agreement

As an intellectual construct, the idea that contractual liability was based on the meeting of the parties' minds was reasonably satisfactory, but in practical terms it was rather more problematical. All too often it might occur that what appeared to be a perfect agreement concealed a more ragged mixture of things on which the parties agreed, things on which they disagreed, and things to which one or both of them had given no thought. This was early recognized by Joseph Chitty, who borrowed from Archdeacon Paley the theory of objective agreement, conveniently ignoring the fact that Paley's whole theory of liability was completely at odds with the Will Theory derived from Pothier: 'Where the terms of the promise admit of more senses than one, the promise is to be performed in that sense in which the promiser apprehended, at the time that the promisee received it.'[6] So long as trial was by jury, there was little room for the application in practice of this approach,[7] but it came into its own later in the century with the wane of jury trial.[8] The objective theory obviously sat ill with the

---

[5] J. Gordley, *The Philosophical Origins of Modern Contract Doctrine* (Oxford, 1991), 225–6. Savigny's influence on Pollock in particular is marked. See generally M. H. Hoeflich, 'Savigny and his Anglo-American Disciples' (1989) 37 American Journal of Comparative Law 17. For the continental (especially French) background, see V. Ranouil, *L'Autonomie de la volonté* (Paris, 1980).

[6] *The Principles of Moral and Political Philosophy* (1785), 145; Chitty, *Contracts* (2nd edn., 1834), 62 (not in 1st edn.).   [7] *Wood* v. *Scarth* (1858) 1 F & F 293 + n seems to be an example.

[8] *Smith* v. *Hughes* (1871) LR 6 QB 597. See J. Spencer, 'Signature, Consent, and the Rule in *L'Estrange* v. *Graucob*' [1973] CLJ 104; W Howarth, 'The Meaning of Objectivity in Contract' (1984) 100 LQR 265. Jury trial disappeared rapidly in contractual actions after 1854 (above, p.188); after equitable defences came to be pleadable at Common law (by the Common Law Procedure Act 1854, ss.83–6) there was judicial feeling that such cases should be tried by judge alone: *Luce* v. *Izod* (1856) 25 L J Ex 307, 308.

theory that contractual liability stemmed from the meeting of the minds of the parties; the difficulty was explained away by treating it as a rule of evidence rather than a rule of substance, parties being estopped from denying that their words meant what they appeared to mean.[9]

Behind the general requirement of the parties' agreement, there developed a range of specific doctrines and rules of interpretation: offer and acceptance; the nature of contractual terms; the use of implied terms; the doctrine of mistake; and the rules relating to the assessment of damages.

Offer and Acceptance

It was a long-standing question whether it was essential for a promise to be accepted in order to generate a legal obligation.[10] This had been discussed since the sixteenth century, notably by the neo-scholastic writers and the Natural lawyers.[11] The significance of Pothier was that he elevated it to a central position in his theory: a unilateral promise or offer was insufficient in itself to constitute a contract; there had to have been an acceptance by the promisee.[12]

The Natural lawyers' discussions of the need for acceptance had already begun to influence English thinking before Pothier had begun to publish his work, and the use of the language of offer and acceptance (or similar terminology) to formulate the essence of agreement was thoroughly well established in the context of marriage by the time that the *Traité des obligations* was written.[13] It had been touched on in Ballow's treatment of contract in his *Treatise on Equity*,[14] published in 1737, and the allusion in passing to 'offer and assent' in *Payne* v. *Cave*[15] in 1789 suggests that the terminology was already forming part of the vocabulary of the Common law. In the following year it surfaced in Powell's treatise on the law of contract, but—significantly—only as part of his discussion of Roman law,[16] and it received only the most cursory treatment in the writings of the next thirty years. By this time, though, Pothier's work was becoming

---

[9] *Smith* v. *Hughes* (1871) LR 6 QB 597, 607, citing *Freeman* v. *Cooke* (1848) 2 Ex 654, 663 (not itself a contract case). Estoppel-based reasoning might also be used in other situations too: where there was doubt whether a party had contracted at all (*Hammersley* v. *de Biel* (1845) 12 Cl & F 45; *Cornish* v. *Abington* (1859) 4 H & N 549); or where there was in fact no consideration (*Payne* v. *Mortimer* (1859) 1 Giff 118).

[10] A. W. B. Simpson, 'Innovation in Nineteenth Century Contract Law' (1975) 91 LQR 247, 258–62.   [11] Above, p.218.

[12] *Traité des obligations*, 1.1.1 §§1–2, based on the Roman distinction between a *pactum* (requiring the agreement of both parties) and a *pollicitatio*, a one-sided promise (D.50.12.3.pr).

[13] [J. Salmon], *A Critical Essay concerning Marriage* (1724), 180–213, esp. 190–2.

[14] Above, p.219.

[15] (1789) 3 TR 148, 149. See too the hints *Cooke* v. *Oxley* (1790) 3 TR 653 (though, had the idea been dogmatically entrenched by this time, we should have expected a more direct discussion of it).   [16] Powell, *Essay upon the Law of Contracts and Agreements*, 1.334.

well known, and his application of the general principle to the specific case of contracts made by post lay directly, if unacknowledgedly, behind the decision of the Common Pleas in *Adams* v. *Lindsell* in 1818.[17] The next generation of writers made the connection explicit, with both Joseph Chitty and Charles Addison quoting the relevant passage from Pothier in the course of their discussions of the nature of agreement.[18] More generally, the language of offer and acceptance was now firmly established in the cases, too.[19]

Conditions, Warranties, and the Terms of the Contract

Medieval and early-modern Common law knew three different types of action covering what might loosely be described as breach of contract. The simple failure to perform a contractual obligation would give rise to a (contractual) action of assumpsit for damages; if a statement of fact guaranteed to be true turned out to be false, there would be a (tortious) action on the case for breach of warranty; and, if a condition to the whole validity of a contract failed, the innocent party would normally have a right to rescind the contract and to bring an action of indebitatus assumpsit for money had and received to recover back any money that had been paid. Unsurprisingly, such a fragmented remedial structure did not allow the development of any sophisticated approach to the analysis of contractual terms.[20]

In the middle of the eighteenth century the first two situations started to merge together. It was procedurally highly inconvenient for the action for breach of warranty to be categorized as tortious, since it meant that it could not be joined in the same writ with a mainstream action for failure to perform,[21] and around 1750 it began to be reanalysed as contractual.[22] The action for damages for breach of contract and the action for damages for breach of warranty became essentially identical. Conditions, however, were not so easily integrated. The courts adhered firmly to the rule that the action of money had and received would not lie to recover back payments made under a contract while the contract remained in force.[23] It was, therefore, essential to know whether breach of some term of a contract gave the innocent party a right to rescind, and hence to know whether a

---

[17] (1818) 1 B & Ald 681; Pothier's discussion is in his *Traité du contrat de vente*, 1.2.3.1. For the ramifications of the 'postal rule', see S. Gardner, 'Trashing with Trollope: A Deconstruction of the Postal Rules in Contract' (1992) 12 Ox Jnl Leg Stud 170.

[18] Chitty, *Contracts* (2nd edn.), 12 (not in 1st edn.); Addison, *Contracts* (1847), 38.

[19] *Dunlop* v. *Higgins* (1848) 1 HLC 381; *Hebb's Case* (1867) LR 4 Eq 9.

[20] Above, p.83.   [21] For joinder of counts, see above, p.171.

[22] M. Lobban, 'Contractual Fraud in Law and Equity' (1997) 17 Ox Jnl Leg Stud 441, 460 n.116; *Stuart* v. *Wilkins* (1778) 1 Doug 18. Contrast *Beningsage* v. *Ralphson* (1682) 2 Shower KB 250, 1 Vent 365, Skinner 366, where the question was still controversial.

[23] Below, p.279.

term amounted to a condition. By the end of the eighteenth century the Common law was developing rules to determine this. In *Boone* v. *Eyre*[24] Lord Mansfield C.J. held that it was a clear distinction that mutual covenants took effect as conditions precedent if they went to the whole of the consideration, in essence adopting a definition that made a condition a term that was central to the whole contract. This approach was perfectly satisfactory so far as it went; but it did not go very far. In the course of the nineteenth century, especially in the context of the sale of goods, there grew up a considerable volume of highly complex rules of interpretation designed to identify whether a term was a condition or not with a greater degree of specificity than Lord Mansfield's formulation would allow.[25]

Unsurprisingly, as the Will Theory took hold, the question came to be formulated in terms of the intention of the parties.[26] This did not necessarily affect the answer. Behind the veneer of party autonomy the complex rules of construction remained. A representation in a charterparty that a ship was 'A1' amounted to a condition, though a representation that it was 'tight, staunch, and strong' was not; a representation that a ship would sail before an appointed day was a condition; a representation that it would sail directly to the port of loading was not.[27] In practice the rule that it was the intention of the parties that determined whether or not a term was a condition was watered down to a rule that it was open to the parties to depart from the ordinary interpretation, provided that their intention to do so was clearly expressed.[28]

This enabled the nineteenth-century courts to develop rules of law behind a façade of party intention. Thus in *Taylor* v. *Caldwell*[29] it was held that no action would lie for the breach of an agreement to allow the plaintiffs the use of the defendants' music hall when the music hall burned to the ground before the contract fell due to be performed. The analysis of Blackburn J. is revealing. Purporting to follow Roman texts to the effect that there would be no liability on a *stipulatio*[30] to transfer property if it were accidentally destroyed before the due date of transfer, he held that no liability arose in English law either, on the grounds that there was an implied condition that the property should continue to exist; where Roman law had applied a rule, English law construed—or imposed—an intention. Similarly a contract for personal services was subject to an implied condition that the actor should remain alive. The question whether property

---

[24] (1777) 1 Hy Bl 273 n.
[25] J. P. Benjamin, *Treatise on the Law of Sale of Personal Property* (1868), 418–50: 'The rules of law on the subject of conditions in contracts are very subtle and perplexing.'
[26] e.g. Anson, *Contract*, 135: 'Whether or not a term in the contract amounts to a Condition must be a question of construction, to be answered by ascertaining the intention of the parties from the wording of the contract and the circumstances under which it was made.'
[27] Leake, *Contracts*, 342.   [28] Ibid. 349.   [29] (1863) 3 B & S 826.
[30] Above, p.7.

should pass immediately on a contract of sale depended on whether or not this was the intention of the parties; but that intention was ascertained by the application of rules 'which are, perhaps, some of them a little artificial'.[31] In a sale by sample the purchaser could complain if the goods did not match the sample; there was an implied condition to this effect in the contract;[32] but a purchaser in a sale by auction could not escape liability on the grounds that he had not had an opportunity to inspect the lots that he had bought, for here there was no implied condition of inspection.[33] It was an implied condition of a contract between a legal publisher and the barristers producing law reports for it that copyright in the reports would pass to the publisher, an implied condition of the lease of a house that it was not infested with bugs, an implied condition in an agreement to marry that the parties would remain chaste and healthy.[34] When the law of sale of goods was codified in 1893, the language of implied conditions and warranties was the natural way in which the terms of the contract should be defined.

Frequently, no doubt, the implied terms of contracts would genuinely reflect the intention of the parties. So long as the jury was dominant, however, there was a risk that it would interpret the contract differently. Even the use of a special jury—consisting in theory of merchants[35]—would not remove the risk completely. By contrast, judicial determinations were subject to the doctrine of precedent, so that a finding in one case that there was an implied term in a particular class of contract generated a legal rule that would apply in all similar contracts. Just as the imposition of relatively precise duties of care in the early tort of negligence brought about a greater degree of certainty than would have been possible if issues had always been left to the jury, so the device of the contractual implied term brought about a consistency of interpretation (and therefore greater commercial certainty) than would otherwise have been possible. They could, no doubt, have been described more openly as legal rules; the fact that the language of implied terms was used reveals the strength of the Will Theory in the legal consciousness.

Mistake

Though it had been largely ignored in Roman law and earlier English law, the mistake of one or both parties was highly problematic for the Will Theory.[36] For Pothier, mistake was 'the greatest defect that can occur in a

---

[31] C. Blackburn, *Treatise on the Effect of the Contract of Sale* (1845), 147–61, 151.
[32] *Wieler* v. *Schilizzi* (1856) 17 CB 619.
[33] *Pettitt* v. *Mitchell* (1842) 4 Man & Gr 819.
[34] *Sweet* v. *Benning* (1855) 16 CB 459; *Smith* v. *Marrable* (1843) 11 M & W 5; *Hall* v. *Wright* (1858) El Bl & El 746 (cf. *Atchinson* v. *Baker* (1796) Peake Add Cas 103 (rule of law)).
[35] J. Oldham, 'Special Juries in England: Nineteenth Century Usage and Reform' (1987) Jnl Leg Hist 148.
[36] Simpson, 'Innovation in Nineteenth Century Contract Law' (1975) 91 LQR 247, 265–9.

contract, for agreements can only be formed by the consent of the parties, and there can be no consent when the parties are in error respecting the object of their agreement'.[37] Unsurprisingly so: if the parties' agreement was the essence of the contract, then in the absence of agreement it was hard to see that any contract could have been created. In its essence this was a narrow principle, limited to cases where the parties had genuinely been at cross purposes, but Pothier followed the Roman lawyers in giving to it a rather wider scope, covering situations in which the contract had been entered into under some material misapprehension. Cases where this misapprehension was on one side only might conceivably have been characterized as failures of agreement, but he applied exactly the same principle where the misapprehension was shared by both parties to the transaction. All of these could be treated in terms of lack of consent (*consentement*), but only by embracing two logically distinct situations: where mistake brought about a failure of agreement, and where the existence of a material error raised a question about the voluntariness of the act of one or both of the parties.[38] By exploiting the terminological ambiguity, Pothier was able to produce an apparently unified theory.

Pothier's analysis of mistake came rather slowly into English law. The Common law had largely avoided it by not allowing the parties to give evidence and then leaving to the jury the question of what (and whether) they had agreed,[39] by applying to documents a rule of construction that the words had to be given their ordinary meaning,[40] or by implying contractual terms to cover any remaining difficulties.[41] It was almost impossible to envisage a situation in which the court would have to deal with a genuine agreement-mistake.[42] The Chancery was more active, but did little more

---

[37] *Traité des obligations* (trans. Evans), 1.1.3, §1.
[38] In modern English terminology (G. H. Treitel, *The Law of Contract* (9th edn., London, 1995), 262) he included situations both where consent was negatived and where consent was nullified.
[39] *Taylor* v. *Briggs* (1827) 2 C & P 525; *Raffles* v. *Wichelhaus* (1864) 2 H & C 906. On the latter case, see A. W. B. Simpson, 'The Beauty of Obscurity', in *Leading Cases on the Common Law*, 135. Parties were first generally permitted to give evidence in civil suits in 1851: Evidence Act, s.2.
[40] *Robertson* v. *French* (1803) 4 East 130, per Lord Ellenborough C.J.; *Shore* v. *Wilson* (1842) 9 C & F 355, 565, per Tindal C.J.; *Smith* v. *Jeffryes* (1846) 15 M & W 561.
[41] So, in the sale of goods, questions that might have been characterized in terms of errors as to quality or as to the existence of the goods would normally be treated as raising issues of implied warranties or conditions: *Hitchcock* v. *Giddings* (1817) 4 Price 135; *Street* v. *Blay* (1831) 2 B & Ad 456; *Barr* v. *Gibson* (1838) 3 M & W 390; *Couturier* v. *Hastie* (1856) 5 HLC 673; J. L. Barton, 'Redhibition, Error and Implied Warranty in English Law' (1994) 62 Tijdschrift voor Rechtsgeschiedenis 317.
[42] The only clear example is *Thornton* v. *Kempster* (1814) 5 Taunt 786, 1 Marshall 355, where a third party who was acting as agent for both sides told one party one thing and the other another; the court held that in the absence of agreement as to the same thing there could be no contract. Counsel in *Raffles* v. *Wichelhaus* (where there were two ships of the same name, the seller claiming that he intended the goods to be carried on the one, the buyer

than grant relief on the same principles as in the eighteenth century and before:[43] written agreements would be rectified if they did not reflect the true intention of the parties;[44] contracts might be rescinded where one party had been under a mistake, but only where the other party was in some way at fault;[45] and there was a general discretion to refuse to order specific performance against a person who had entered into a contract under a mistake, even where the other party had been in no way to blame.[46] Mistake, as such, was a defence only in relatively rare cases, and its application was largely within the discretion of the court.

The silence of the case law is reflected in the text-writers of the first half of the century: there is no hint of any doctrine of mistake in the leading works of Chitty or Addison.[47] The first treatment of the subject, in which the influence of Pothier can be traced, is William Macpherson's work on the Indian law of contract, which appeared in 1860.[48] In 1861 Macpherson became secretary to the Indian Law Commission, whose 1866 Report on the Law of Contract[49] (largely enacted as the Indian Contract Act 1872) included a clause on mistake inspired by Pothier, in which his hand is plainly visible.[50] The Indian Law Commission report was the first attempt by English-trained lawyers to codify the law of contract, and it excited considerable discussion in England. One year later there appeared the first substantial chapter on mistake in an English textbook, Leake's *Elements of the Law of Contracts*, where agreement-mistakes are grafted onto the end of a more substantial exposition of the effect of mistake in Equity.[51] In the same year Blackburn J. borrowed the general principle, explicitly from Roman law, that a contract would be void if brought about by a mistake

claiming that he thought the other was meant) argued that that too was a case where there was no *consensus ad idem*: (1864) 2 H & C 906, 908. [43] Above, p.210.

[44] *Murray* v. *Parker* (1854) 19 Beav 305; *Sells* v. *Sells* (1860) 1 Drew & Sm 42; *Bentley* v. *Mackay* (1862) 31 L J Ch 697, 709.

[45] *Alvanley* v. *Kinnaird* (1849) 2 Mac & G 1; Story, *Equitable Jurisprudence*, §§147–50. There is a hint of a wider equitable jurisdiction to give relief in *Hitchcock* v. *Giddings* (1817) 4 Price 135, Daniell 1.

[46] *Howell* v. *George* (1817) 1 Madd 1; *Malins* v. *Freeman* (1837) 2 Keen 25; *Manser* v. *Back* (1848) 6 Hare 443; *Swaisland* v. *Dearsley* (1861) 29 Beav 430.

[47] Chitty, *Contracts* (1826); Addison, *Contracts* (1847). The first edition of Chitty to deal fully with mistake is the 20th (1947); Addison never does so. American law was perhaps more forward, though its doctrinal base was hardly developed and it may not in practice have extended far beyond the ill-drawn lines of the English Chancery: V. D. Ricks, 'American Mutual Mistake: Half-Civilian Mongrel, Consideration Reincarnate' (1998) 58 Louisiana L R 663, 715–38.

[48] W. Macpherson, *Outlines of the Law of Contracts as Administered in the Courts of British India* (London and Calcutta, 1860), pp.xi, 2–5. Macpherson seems to have followed Henry Colebrooke, whose *Treatise on Obligations and Contracts* (1818) owed a good deal more to Pothier and the earlier Natural lawyers than it did to contemporary English law.

[49] PP HC 1867–8 xlix. 603.

[50] cl.7 (ultimately s.20 of the Indian Contract Act). See further A. C. Patra, *The Indian Contract Act 1872* (London, 1966), 1.83–8. [51] Leake, *Contracts*, 178–81.

fundamental to the whole agreement.[52] Pothier's influence is yet clearer in Joseph Benjamin's book on the sale of goods, first published one year after Leake, where mistake complements offer and acceptance in his chapter on the need for mutual assent. Twenty years later it was well established, forming the basis of substantial chapters by both Frederick Pollock and William Anson.[53]

Pivotal to this rooting of the law of mistake was the reanalysis of the decision of the House of Lords in *Couturier* v. *Hastie*.[54] Plaintiffs sold to the defendant's principal a cargo of corn, en route from Salonica to England. Unbeknown to the parties, before the contract was made the corn had overheated and begun to ferment, so that it had been necessary to put into Tunis and sell it. The plaintiffs none the less sued for the price. There were a number of peripheral matters, but by the time the case reached the House of Lords the only issue was the legal relevance of the non-existence of the goods at the time of the contract. It was argued on behalf of the defendant either that the contract was wholly void, on the basis that it was a rule of English law that there could be no contract of sale without property existing at the time of the agreement,[55] or alternatively that it was an implied condition of the contract that the corn was still in existence. The House of Lords gave judgment for the defendant on the latter ground. Nowhere in *Couturier* v. *Hastie* was there any attempt to found the case on any doctrine of mistake, but within five years it had begun to be so interpreted by the text-writers.[56] The issue was obviously troublesome, and in the third edition of his textbook Pollock also included reference to the case in his section on initial impossibility. None the less, on this point following Pothier rather than Savigny, he was adamant that it was properly analysed in terms of mistake.[57]

A whole range of situations could be brought under this new-found umbrella. Straightforward agreement-mistakes where there was no *consensus ad idem*, such as *Raffles* v. *Wichelhaus*,[58] were brought in. The centuries-old defence of *non est factum*, denying the efficacy of a purported deed under seal,[59] was generalized to apply to all written documents and interpreted as another example of mistake, shifting the case where a document was made under some misapprehension as to its contents from the margin of the defence to its central core. Unilateral mistakes were consciously recognized

---

[52] *Kennedy* v. *The Panama, New Zealand and Australian Royal Mail Co Ltd* (1867) LR 2 QB 580, 588, citing D.18.1.9, 10, 11; cf. *Cooper* v. *Phibbs* (1867) LR 2 HL 149.
[53] Benjamin, *Sale*, 36–43; Pollock, *Contract* (1876), 355–429; Anson, *Contract* (1879), 116–28.
[54] (1856) 5 HLC 673.
[55] (1856) 5 HLC 673, 677, citing Pothier, *Contrat de vente*, 1.2.1.
[56] Macpherson, *Contracts*, 3 (though the case is not named); Leake, *Contracts*, 176; Pollock, *Contract*, 398; Anson, *Contract*, 121. Benjamin, *Sale*, 57–8, is thoroughly confused.
[57] Pollock, *Contract* (3rd edn., 1881), 386–8.   [58] (1864) 2 H & C 906.
[59] Above, p.20.

as such: a party in error in some fundamental way—as to the person with whom the contract was being made, for example—was able to avoid the whole transaction.[60] For Pollock, even the rule against penalties[61] found its home here. The lumping-together of this disparate range of situations concealed their very distinct sources, both historical and analytical. All were treated in the same way, on the analogy of agreement-mistakes, and all had the effect of making the purported contract void *ab initio*.

Damages

The final area in which Pothier's version of the Will Theory influenced the development of nineteenth-century English contract law was the assessment of damages. Here it did not do so in unalloyed form, but interacted with earlier English and American case law and with the nineteenth-century judges' perceptions of public policy.

The well-established principle that plaintiffs' losses should normally be calculated by reference to their lost expectations[62] was wholly in keeping with Pothier, though its practical application was all too commonly hidden by blank jury verdicts. Where the defendant had defaulted in an obligation to pay money, the plaintiff would recover the sum due together with interest.[63] Where there was an obligation to deliver goods, damages would be assessed as the value of the goods at the date on which they should have been delivered.[64] The difficulty arose where plaintiffs wanted to claim that the defendant's breach of contract had caused some additional loss. As a matter of pleading, the rule was that the plaintiff was entitled to recover only the 'natural' consequences of the breach unless the additional loss had been averred specially, and it was only in the latter situation that evidence of the special loss would have been admissible.[65]

As occurred in the law of torts in the 1850s,[66] the eclipse of the jury was associated with a need to formulate clearer rules about the assessment of damages. This was done in the leading case of *Hadley* v. *Baxendale*.[67] The

---

[60] *Smith* v. *Wheatcroft* (1878) 9 Ch D 223 (quoting Pothier); *Cundy* v. *Lindsay* (1878) 3 App Cas 459; J. C. Smith and J. A. C. Thomas, 'Pothier and the Three Dots' (1957) 20 MLR 38; C. Malecki, 'L'Erreur sur la personne en droit anglais et en droit français de contrats: De l'influence déterminante de Pothier sur la Common Law?' (1995) 72 Revue de Droit International et Droit Comparé 347. The general principle is expressed in *Kennedy* v. *The Panama, New Zealand and Australian Royal Mail Co Ltd* (1867) LR 2 QB 580, 588.
[61] Above, p.213.   [62] Above, p.213; *Alder* v. *Keighley* (1846) 15 M & W 117.
[63] *Fletcher* v. *Tayleur* (1855) 17 CB 21, 29, per Willes J. The power to award interest was based on Stat 3 & 4 Will IV c.42 s.28.
[64] *Gainsford* v. *Carroll* (1824) 2 B & C 624; *Shaw* v. *Holland* (1846) 15 M & W 136.
[65] J. Chitty, *Treatise on Pleading* (5th edn., 1831) 1.371; Leake, *Contract*, 564–5.
[66] Above, p.175.
[67] (1854) 9 Ex 341; 2 CLR 517; 23 L J Ex 179; 18 Jur 358; 2 WR 302; 23 LT 69. For detailed discussion of the case, see in particular R. Danzig, 'Hadley v. Baxendale: A Study in the Industrialization of the Law' (1975) 4 Jnl Leg Stud 249 (= (1976) 6 Ius Commune 234);

plaintiffs, Gloucester mill-owners, needed a new shaft for their mill. They put the broken shaft in the hands of Pickfords, the leading carriers of the time (whose managing partner was the defendant), to deliver to an engineer at Greenwich, who would cast a new shaft on the model of the old. The defendants delayed delivery of the shaft for several days, as a result of which the plaintiffs' mill was idle for longer than necessary. They brought an action for the defendants' breach of contract, claiming damages for loss of profits caused by the delay. The judge directed the jury that the defendants would be liable if they had not delivered the shaft in a reasonable time; and that, if so, damages should be assessed as the 'probable and natural' consequences of the failure; despite objections from the defendants, evidence was admitted of the daily profits of the mill while in full production.[68] The jury (a special jury[69]) found for the plaintiffs and awarded damages of £50. The case was then removed to the full Court of Exchequer, the defendants requesting a new trial.

The case fell in the awkward hinterland of contract and tort. There was clearly a contract between the plaintiffs and the carriers, but the action was brought using the standard form of action against a common carrier.[70] It had been established that, for procedural purposes, these actions were to be categorized as tortious, though it was unclear what consequences followed from this.[71] The whole framework within which the case should be reasoned was therefore ambiguous. A second potential confusion stemmed from the law relating to common carriers, whose operation was regulated at Common law and by statute, for it was arguable that special limitations on the recoverability of damages applied in this situation.[72] Parke B., one of the members of the court in *Hadley* v. *Baxendale*, was something of an expert on carriers' liability: his brother had been Baxendale's predecessor as manager of Pickfords.[73]

J. L. Barton, 'Contractual Danages and the Rise of Industry' (1987) 7 Ox Jnl Leg Stud 40; F. Faust, '*Hadley v. Baxendale*: An Understandable Miscarriage of Justice' (1994) 15 Jnl Leg Hist 41. Most writers on this area have based their conclusions almost exclusively on the report in 9 Ex 341; although the judgment of the court is reported to all intents and purposes identically in the various reports, counsels' arguments can be reconstructed only by using the other available texts too.   [68] Danzig, 'Hadley v. Baxendale' (1975) 4 Jnl Leg Stud 249, 252.

[69] Above, n.35.

[70] An alternative count based on a special contract was abandoned at the trial.

[71] Faust, '*Hadley v. Baxendale*' (1994) 15 Jnl Leg Hist 41, 44–54. The point is explored from a practical point of view in E. Bullen and S. M. Leake, *Precedents of Pleadings* (1860), 72 n.

[72] E. G. M. Fletcher, *The Carrier's Liability* (London, 1932), 174–206; J. N. Adams, 'The Carrier in Legal History', in E. W. Ives and A. H. Manchester (eds.), *Law, Litigants and the Legal Profession* (London, 1983), 39. The Common law had been grappling with the problems of the nature of carriers' liability since the sixteenth century: above, p.164.

[73] Danzig, 'Hadley v. Baxendale' (1975) 4 Jnl Leg Stud 249, 267 n.72, based on PP HC 1844 xi. 249, q.3402. I have not been able to trace any reference to Parke in the surviving records of Pickfords; the earliest journal of the Manchester office (where Parke would have been based) begins in 1817, by which time Baxendale was already in post (PRO RAIL 1133/

The principal question in the Court of Exchequer was whether the jury had correctly taken into account the plaintiffs' loss of profits in their assessment of damages.[74] A series of cases—indiscriminately in contract and in tort—showed that English law recognized such losses[75] It was, therefore, argued that the judge's direction was perfectly adequate, and that it had been properly applied by the jury. The court was clearly inclined against this from the start. Parke B. preferred the limitation found in articles 1149–51 of the French *Code civil*, that in the absence of fraud the defendant should be liable only for harm foreseen (or foreseeable) at the time of entering into the contract, reflecting the test that Pollock C.B. had just begun to apply in straightforwardly tortious actions.[76] Martin and Alderson BB. expressed concern at the possibility of unexpectedly large losses occurring as a result of some relatively trivial breach of contract, again echoing reasoning found in tortious cases.[77] Counsel for the defendant picked up on these judicial concerns, basing their argument in particular on the analysis of the American Theodore Sedgwick, that damages were not really based on a principle of compensation but rather on a more policy-orientated determination of what portion of the loss should be borne by the defendant and what portion by the plaintiff.[78] The appropriate policy was that reflected by the test of foreseeability; damages beyond this should be awarded only in cases of fraud or (relying specifically on carrier cases) where there had been a special contract to this effect.

Given the thrust of judicial interventions in counsels' arguments, it is unsurprising that the court gave judgment for the defendants and ordered a new trial. The true principles, according to Alderson B., were that damages should include those consequences arising naturally from the breach of contract, or those that 'may reasonably be supposed to have been in the contemplation of both parties, at the time they made the contract, as the probable result of the breach of it'.[79] If there were special circumstances

126). Parke B. had also decided two of the leading cases on the liability of carriers: *Wyld* v. *Pickford* (1841) 8 M & W 443 and *Carr* v. *Lancashire and York Railway Co* (1852) 7 Ex 707.

[74] The other point argued, that assessment of damages was so purely a matter for the jury that it was not subject to judicial control, was predictably, and summarily, dismissed as tending to lead manifestly to great injustice.
[75] Most clearly in the plaintiff's favour were *Nurse* v. *Barns* (1662) 1 T Raym 77 (breach of terms of a lease); *Borradaile* v. *Brunton* (1818) 8 Taunt 535, 2 Moo CP 582) (breach of warranty); *Everard* v. *Hopkins* (1615) 2 Bulst 332 (negligent injury to horse); *Ingram* v. *Lawson* (1840) 6 Bing NC 212 (libel); *Bodley* v. *Reynolds* (1846) 8 QB 779 (trover); *Black* v. *Baxendale* (1847) 1 Ex 410 (late delivery of goods by carrier).   [76] Above, p.175.
[77] In particular *Winterbottom* v. *Wright* (1842) 10 M & W 109; above, p.174.
[78] T. Sedgwick, *Treatise on the Measure of Damages* (2nd edn., New York, 1852), 6 (purportedly (though very loosely indeed) following Domat, *Civil Law*, 3.5.2.2), and citing in particular the judgment of Story J. in *The Schooner Lively* (1816) 1 Gall 314, 15 Fed Cas 631 (Massachusetts Circuit Court). English cases in their favour were *Jones* v. *Gooday* (1841) 8 M & W 146; *Walton* v. *Fothergill* (1835) 7 C & P 392; *Archer* v. *Williams* (1846) 2 Car & K 26; and *Boyce* v. *Bayliffe* (1807) 1 Camp 58.   [79] 9 Ex 341, 354.

affecting potential loss known to both parties, then their reasonable contemplation would take into account those circumstances; it would be
unjust to take them into account without such joint knowledge, for that
would be to deprive the ignorant party of the chance of making a special
contract to deal with them. The first of these principles was based on
Pothier, reformulated (following the model of the Louisiana Civil Code)
so as to stress the centrality of the parties' joint state of mind rather than
the more ambiguous idea of foreseeability.[80] The second had no counterpart there; it was substantially derived from the Common law of carriers'
liability, in particular from the cases relating to the effect of notices.

Hadley v. *Baxendale*, therefore, does not represent the unreflecting assimilation into English law of one more aspect of Pothier's Will Theory. It was,
perhaps primarily, the application of a judicial preference for limiting the
scope of legal liability, particularly in entrepreneurial contexts, especially at
a time when the judges were supplanting jury discretion.[81] The fact that the
Will Theory provided the desired answer gave it intellectual respectability,
and no doubt made it easier for the judges to convince themselves and the
rest of the legal profession that it was the 'right' answer. It also meant that
it could fit seamlessly into the intellectual fabric of the Common law of
contract and so take its place as the foundation of the law of damages.[82]

Voluntariness and Contractual Intention

Logically central to the Will Theory was the idea that contractual liability
depended on the voluntary, intentional, act of the parties. There was
nothing new in this; it was an idea that had been familiar to Common
lawyers for at least half a millennium.[83] What was new was the greater
depth given to the idea, and the greater weight placed on it. In the course of
the nineteenth century this came to be formulated in terms of the require-

---

[80] Pothier, *Traité des obligations*, 1.2.3, §161); Louisiana Civil Code (1825) art. 1928, as
applied by Eustis J. in *Williams* v. *Barton* (1839) 13 La 404 (cited in *Hadley* v. *Baxendale* from
the discussion in Sedgwick, *Damages*, 67). Alderson B.'s formulation is sufficiently close to the
Louisiana Code, though not acknowledged as such by him, for us to have no doubt as to his
source. See too the remarks of Parke B. at 2 WR 303.

[81] This is essentially the thesis of Danzig, 'Hadley v. Baxendale' (1975) 4 Jnl Leg Stud 249.
The fact that a judicial choice was involved is well brought out by remarks of Parke B. in
argument, as reported at 23 LJ Ex 179, 181: 'I wish the sensible rule was established, that
damages must be confined to what the parties reasonably anticipated.' For the parallel
situation in the developing tort of negligence, see above, p.176.

[82] It is worth recording that an appeal against the decision was envisaged but not proceeded
with: 23 LT 69, 70. For the establishment of the rule, see *Smeed* v. *Foord* (1859) 1 El & El 602;
Victoria Laundry (Windsor) Ltd v. *Newman Industries Ltd* [1949] 2 KB 528; *The Heron II*
[1969] 1 AC 350 (finally scotching the idea that the rules of remoteness in contract and tort
were identical). Its canonical status was assured by its inclusion in *Smith's Leading Cases*,
whose then editors (Keating and Willes) had been counsel in *Hadley* v. *Baxendale*: Danzig,
'Hadley v. Baxendale' (1975) 4 Jnl Leg Stud 249, 274–6.   [83] Above, p.71.

ment of an intention to create legal relations. In addition, the existing defences of fraud and duress were explicitly conceptualized in terms of the undermining of the defendant's voluntariness.

Intention to Create Legal Relations

By the beginning of the twentieth century it was a commonplace of the law of contract that there had to have been an intention to create legal relations.[84] There are the merest hints of such an idea in the earlier Common law, and its appearance as a central doctrine was substantially an importation from the Will Theory. The Natural lawyers had already insisted on the intention to be bound as the feature that distinguished a genuine promise from a joke,[85] and this was picked up, loosely, by the English writers of the mid-nineteenth century.[86] It did not, however, reach the doctrinal heartland until it was borrowed by Pollock from Savigny and incorporated in his textbook in 1876.[87] Only after this did the disparate body of earlier case law come to be treated as based on the single idea that without an intention to create legal relations there could be no liability.

So long as the law did not require any formal words of promising, cases would inevitably arise in which people would say that they would do things without it being clear whether they had gone so far as to undertake to do them. When issues could be left to the jury, it was possible to conceal this problem behind the 'factual' question whether the defendant had made a 'promise', so that there were very few early examples in the case law.[88] In the nineteenth century the jury was no longer supreme, and the judges had to deal with these cases themselves. They did so more or less fragmentarily, loosely grouping together similar cases. Extravagant claims by advertisers would be dismissed as 'mere puffs' rather than contractual warranties;[89] only in 1893 were these analysed in terms of intention to create legal relations.[90] Whether a timetable constituted a contractual promise was a

---

[84] Simpson, 'Innovation in Nineteenth Century Contract Law' (1975) 91 LQR 249, 263–5; S. Hedley, 'Keeping Contract in its Place: *Balfour* v. *Balfour* and the Enforceability of Informal Agreements' (1985) 5 Ox Jnl Leg Stud 391.

[85] Pufendorf, *On the Law of Nature and Nations*, 3.5.10.

[86] W. Fox, *Treatise on Simple Contracts* (1842), 62–3, Leake, *Contract*, 9–10 (citing Pothier).

[87] *Contract*, 2. Pollock was heavily influenced by Savigny, and it was Savigny who, in his *System des heutigen römischen Rechts*, had stressed this element above others.

[88] Always cited was *Weekes* v. *Tybald* (1605) Noy 11, Ro Abr, *Action sur le Case*, M1, where a father said that he would give £100 to any man who would marry his daughter. The plaintiff married her, and then unsuccessfully sued for the money. The case is ill-reported and may have depended on the point of pleading rather than on high legal theory: it had to be alleged that the defendant had undertaken and promised (*super se assumpsit et fideliter promisit*) and not simply that he had asserted.

[89] *Jones* v. *Bright* (1829) 5 Bing 533, 541; *Dimmock* v. *Hallett* (1867) 2 Ch App 21.

[90] *Carlill* v. *Carbolic Smoke Ball Co* [1893] 1 QB 256 (cf. A. W. B. Simpson, 'Quackery and Contract Law: *Carlill* v. *Carbolic Smoke Ball Company*', in *Leading Cases on the Common Law* (Oxford, 1995), 259); *Heilbut, Symons & Co* v. *Buckleton* [1913] AC 30.

nice question;[91] but it was not answered by using the language of intention to create legal relations. Domestic—as opposed to commercial—
arrangements might be given short shrift. 'Ridiculous', expostulated
Pollock C.B. when asked to enforce a promise by a father to release a
promissory note in exchange for the son's promise to stop pestering him.[92]
But it was only in 1919 that these situations were swept into the more
general principle and explained on the basis that there was no contractual
intention.[93]

Fraud and Duress

Well before the nineteenth century, duress and fraud had been treated as
undermining contractual liability.[94] Both could be treated as situations in
which the promisor's voluntariness was compromised, though in both there
was also a strong element that a promisee who had acted wrongfully should
not be allowed to take advantage of any contract so induced.[95] Those
writing on contract in the first half of the nineteenth century, however,
paid relatively little attention to these, and made no real attempt to explore
their theoretical basis. Comyn, for example, makes no mention of duress
and simply lists fraud at the end of his list of factors making a contract
illegal at Common law;[96] Chitty deals with duress as a factor affecting
contractual capacity and follows Comyn in treating fraud as an offshoot of
illegality;[97] Addison ignores duress, and, although fraud merits a more
substantial treatment than had been given to it by Comyn or Chitty, his
main discussion concerns its effects on contracts of betrothal.[98]

Indian writers in the nineteenth century, more heavily influenced by
Pothier than their English counterparts, stressed the lack of voluntariness.
For Henry Colebrooke, therefore, both duress and fraud vitiated consent,
and so destroyed contractual liability:

---

[91] *Denton* v. *Great Northern Railway Company* (1856) 5 E & B 860; cf. *Harris* v. *Nickerson*
(1873) LR 8 QB 286 (advertised auction not taking place).
[92] *White* v. *Bluett* (1853) 23 L J Ex 36. Cf. the reasoning of Alderson B., that there was no
consideration.
[93] *Balfour* v. *Balfour* [1919] 2 KB 571. There are hints of it earlier, e.g. in *Maddison* v.
Alderson (1883) 8 App Cas 467 and *Canning* v. *Farquhar* (1886) 16 QBD 727.
[94] Above, pp.71–3, 208.
[95] It was generally assumed that duress or fraud by an independent third party would not
avoid the contract; yet, if the only question were of the voluntariness of the promisor's acts,
this case should have been indistinguishable from the case of the wrongdoing promisee. The
confusion is explored by Gordley, *Philosophical Origins of Modern Contract Doctrine*, 183–4.
[96] *Law of Contracts and Promises* (2nd edn.), 58–9. Contrary to the views of other writers,
he states that agreements obtained by fraud are void.
[97] *Contract* 54–6, 222–8. The first move towards a generalized treatment occurs in the
eighteenth edition (1930).
[98] *Contracts*, 580–3. The first real treatment of vitiating factors appears in the ninth edition
(1892).

Consent is excluded by violence, or even by the threat of violence: since force, whether used, or barely threatened, lays a necessity on a man contrary to his will. So that it is in appearance, only, that a man forced or menaced gives assent.[99]

There can be no true consent, when the words or writings, by which the assent is said to be expressed, are drawn from either of the parties by fraud. He has not contracted but been deceived.[100]

The same approach is found in William Macpherson's treatise in 1860[101] and in the Indian Law Commission Report on Contract in 1866 (from where it made its way into the Indian Contract Act of 1872).[102] Hardly coincidentally, one year later Leake's *Elements of the Law of Contracts* was the first English work to deal with the subject in this way,[103] to be followed by the classical textbooks of the 1870s, Pollock and Anson.[104]

This was not simply an intellectual shift. Since 1854 it had been possible to plead Equitable defences in actions at Common law, and the Judicature Act of 1873 had (purportedly) united Law and Equity and provided that in cases of conflict the rules of Equity should prevail.[105] None the less, the rules continued to reflect their origins. This was most transparent in the case of fraud, where the very broad approach of the courts of Equity in treating almost any case of unconscionable conduct as tantamount to fraud was reflected in the development of broad rules as to misrepresentation: even if a contract had been obtained by an innocent misrepresentation, the courts would refuse to enforce it. This was made quite explicit by Jessel M.R. in *Redgrave* v. *Hurd*: 'Even assuming that moral fraud must be shewn in order to set aside a contract, you have it where a man, having obtained a beneficial contract by a statement which he now knows to be false, insists upon keeping that contract. To do so is a moral delinquency: no man ought to seek to take advantage of his own false statements.'[106]

Despite the superficial attractiveness of slipping these defences into a Will Theory based notion of compromised voluntariness, their position here was insecure. On the one hand, in so far as they were treated as defences, there was a tendency, clearly visible in *Redgrave* v. *Hurd* for example, to formulate them in terms of the public policy of not allowing wrongdoers to take advantage of their own wrong. Unless it was to be held that a person could plead fraud or duress by a third party, and nobody argued that this was indeed the law,[107] then the Will Theory could not

---

[99] Colebrooke, *Obligations and Contracts*, 49.   [100] Ibid. 51.
[101] *Contracts*, 5–6.   [102] ss. 14–19.
[103] *Contracts*, 181–205 (fraud), 205–9 (duress).
[104] Pollock, *Contract*, 471–545; Anson, *Contract*, 145–62.
[105] Common Law Procedure Act 1854, ss.83–6; Judicature Act 1873, s.24.
[106] (1881) 20 Ch D 1, 12–13.
[107] See the discussion in *Talbot* v. *von Boris* [1911] 1 KB 854, where it was treated as axiomatic that the promisor must show that the promisee had knowledge of the duress.

adequately account for them. Nor was it easy to explain why they made a contract voidable, while mistake made a contract void.[108] There was, moreover, a very fine boundary between a party claiming to rescind a contract for the other party's fraud or misrepresentation and a party claiming to be entitled to rescission or compensation because the other party's representation had been incorporated as a term in the contract.[109] The latter provided a more flexible range of remedies, and there was consequently a tendency to categorize cases as falling within it rather than squeezing them within one of the available defences.

THE WILL THEORY AND THE MODEL OF EXCHANGE

While the contractual doctrines examined above could not easily have been deduced from the pre-nineteenth-century Common law, they were by and large consistent with it. The need for a voluntary agreement had been an important strut in the exchange model of contract. There were, however, difficulties with the other two principal elements of that model, consideration and privity of contract. A codifying system might legitimately have discarded them as inconsistent with the newly imposed legal model, but this was not an option open to the Common law of the nineteenth century. Instead, through the nineteenth and twentieth centuries, the judges progressively marginalized them by ingenious (and ingenuous) interpretation and undermined them by the use of rival ideas, while legal reformers continued to contemplate the possibility of their abolition.

Consideration

Consideration, in the sense of reciprocity, had been for centuries the linchpin of the English law of contract. The assault on it by Wilmot J. and Lord Mansfield C.J. in *Pillans* v. *van Mierop* had been repulsed by the House of Lords in *Rann* v. *Hughes*,[110] and it was no less strongly entrenched in the courts of Equity. By contrast, it had no part to play in the Will Theory, for, if liability depended exclusively on the union of the parties' wills, there was no reason to impose any additional element of reciprocity; there is hardly a hint of it in Pothier.[111] This was clearly

---

[108] Even in an extreme case, where a party's hand was physically forced to sign a document: Pollock, *Contract*, 500 n.   [109] See e.g. the early discussion in Anson, *Contract*, 267–70.
[110] Above, p.205. It is noticeable that when the case is cited in the nineteenth century it is commonly for the orthodoxy of Yates J.'s judgment, not for the more radical views of Wilmot J. and Lord Mansfield C.J.
[111] The only point at which it surfaces is in his *Traité des obligations*, 1.1.1, §2, where he notes that French law does not normally recognize gratuitous transfers of property without notarization. This is tacked on—irrelevantly—to his discussion of the difference between contracts and pollicitations (above, n.12)

recognized by his translator, W. D. Evans, whose appendix on the nature of consideration in contracts in English law was related back to a single paragraph in which Pothier dealt with the rather different question of the status of an agreement that bound only one of the parties.[112]

The difficulty of incorporating the requirement of reciprocal considera-tion into a contractual model based on the Will Theory is clearly visible in Jeffrey Gilbert's treatise on contract at the beginning of the eighteenth century.[113] Gilbert's starting point was that a naked declaration of promise was insufficient to impose liability; there must be something else to demon-strate that it was seriously intended. This could be inferred if the agreement was under seal, 'for 'tis downright madness to trifle with the solemnitys of law and to pretend after the sealing that there was nothing seriously designed'.[114] Alternatively, there must be consideration:

But if the contract be verball only it binds in respect of the consideration; otherwise a man might be drawn into an obligation without any real intention by random words [and] ludicrous expressions, and from hence there would be a manifest inlet to perjury because nothing were more easy than to turn kindness of expressions into the obligation of a real promise.[115]

Such an analysis would have been wholly stable if 'consideration' had included any factor that evidenced seriousness of intention, but this was not Gilbert's position. He gave 'consideration' its orthodox Common-law meaning of something given in exchange for the promise.[116] Hence a promise in consideration of natural love and affection would be ineffec-tive,[117] though why an intention to be bound could not be inferred is nowhere explained.

The same janus-like explanation, given by the French jurist Franciscus Connanus in the sixteenth century, had been justly mocked by the Natural lawyers.[118] Despite its transparent inadequacy, the writers of the nineteenth century were not able to come up with a better theory. Time and time again it was said, with an almost embarrassed cursoriness, that the law should be concerned only with agreements intended to have legal consequences and that non-reciprocal agreements were not normally so intended.[119] Non-reciprocal agreements that were genuinely intended

---

[112] Evans, *A Treatise on the Law of Obligations or Contracts, by M. Pothier*, 2.19, relating back to 1.29 (where the cross reference is mirrored).
[113] BL MS Harg 265, 266; above, p.216. Gilbert seems to be fleshing out the analysis of Hobbes, *Elements of Law*, 1.15.9.   [114] BL MS Harg 265 ff.39ᵛ–40.
[115] BL MS Harg 265 f.40 (punctuation supplied). Similar sentiments are found at f.43 (effect of error in consideration), f.53ᵛ (words of contracting will normally raise inference of serious intention unless no consideration), and ff.65ᵛ–66 (seriousness of intention manifested from consideration).   [116] BL MS Harg 265 ff.40ᵛ–58ᵛ.
[117] BL MS Harg 265 ff. 41, 41ᵛ.   [118] Pufendorf, *Law of Nature and Nations*, 3.5.10.
[119] Chitty, *Contract* (2nd edn.), 23; Addison, *Contract*, 17–18; Leake, *Contract*, 310. But cf. Pollock's praise of the 'completeness and common sense' of the doctrine: *Contract*, 149.

to have legal consequences were conveniently ignored, as was the apparent redundancy of the doctrine of consideration (if it was indeed no more than a device for taking non-serious contracts out of the legal domain) once the independent requirement of an intention to create legal relations had emerged.[120]

The requirement of reciprocal consideration was so strongly entrenched in the case law of the previous centuries that it could not simply be uprooted on the grounds of inconsistency with the Will Theory. The courts continued to pay unquestioning lip service to it,[121] though there was a clearly visible tendency to discover consideration when none was easily to be found.[122] It was not difficult to insert in a commercial contract a fictitious consideration clause—nobody was fooled by the standard words in a bill of exchange or a promissory note, 'for value received'[123]—and, even if this was not done, the courts were quick to invent nominal considerations in order to give force to commercial agreements intended to be binding. 'I am not ashamed', concluded Willes J. in 1858, 'of having been somewhat astute at the trial to defeat what I conceived to be an unjust and unworthy defence.'[124] The same sharpness lay behind the courts' willingness to get round the rule that past consideration was ineffective. It had been established since the sixteenth century that the rule did not apply where the plaintiff's performance had been at the defendant's request, and it was no great step for the courts to find that there had in fact been a request in order to reach the desired result.[125] There was equally room for generous interpretation of contractual documents. In *Hicks* v. *Gregory*, for example, a written promise by a father to pay £100 per year to the mother of his illegitimate child was interpreted in the teeth of the evidence as a promise in consideration of the mother's behaving herself and bringing up

---

[120] Above, n.87. Cf. Simpson, 'Innovation in Nineteenth Century Contract Law' (1975) 91 LQR 247, 263: 'rather too many doctrines chasing a limited number of problems.'

[121] *Jones* v. *Ashburnham* (1804) 4 East 455; *Eastwood* v. *Kenyon* (1840) 11 Ad & El 438; *Currie* v. *Misa* (1875) LR 10 Ex 153; *Dunlop Pneumatic Tyre Co Ltd* v. *Selfridge & Co Ltd* [1915] AC 847, 855. Even in the late twentieth century: *Midland Bank Trust Co Ltd* v. *Green* [1981] AC 513, 531.

[122] It had already been recognized by Jeffrey Gilbert that the courts would strain to find a consideration, since men were presumed not to have been acting in vain in purporting to enter into a contract: BL MS Harg 265 f.53ᵛ.

[123] *Hatch* v. *Trayes* (1840) 11 Ad & El 702. The Bills of Exchange Act 1882 s.30(1) provided that consideration would be presumed.

[124] *Westlake* v. *Adams* (1858) 5 CBNS 248, 267. Other good early examples are *Bainbridge* v. *Firmstone* (1838) 8 Ad & El 743, *Haigh* v. *Brooks* (1839) 10 Ad & El 309, *Hart* v. *Miles* (1858) 4 CBNS 371. For twentieth-century examples, see Treitel, *Contract*, 80–2.

[125] *Eastwood* v. *Kenyon* (1840) 11 Ad & El 438, 451. This extended to cases where one party had freely accepted a service bestowed by another, where there was in fact no contract at all (e.g. *Taylor* v. *Laird* (1856) 25 L J Ex 329), cases that would subsequently be recognized (or recategorized) as based on a principle of unjust enrichment. See generally T. W. Chitty, A. T. Denning, and C. P. Harvey (eds.), *Smith's Leading Cases* (13th edn., 1929), 1.155–8.

the child properly and not as a simple donative promise.[126] It is all too easy to see the application of the Will Theory behind these cases: if the parties agreed these terms, it was not for the court to decide what benefit the defendant expected to derive; if the promisor had not expected some benefit, he would not have made the contract in the first place.[127]

Where interpretative ingenuousness could not reach the desired result, twentieth-century courts began to use the language of estoppel as a means to avoid the consequences of the traditional doctrine of consideration: thus in *Central London Property Trust Ltd* v. *High Trees House Ltd* Denning J. was able to give effect to a gratuitous agreement to vary the terms of the contract, on the grounds that it would be inequitable to hold the parties to their original terms.[128] Although at first constrained by the requirement that it could be used only by way of defence, the potential of the doctrine increased by its closeness to the rules of 'proprietary estoppel',[129] and in Australia it extended so far as to allow the enforcement of gratuitous promises where the defendant had acted unconscientiously.[130] Alongside this extension by way of estoppel, twentieth-century plaintiffs learned to sidestep the doctrine of consideration completely by formulating their claims in non-contractual terms. Thus the law of torts could be pressed into service when the plaintiff had suffered loss as a result of the defendant's gratuitous but negligent misrepresentation,[131] or more generally where it could be said—uncannily echoing both the reasoning and the language of the lawyers of the fifteenth century—that the defendant had 'assumed responsibility' towards the plaintiff;[132] or the law of trusts might be used if the gratuitous promisor had been careful to use the right language.[133]

---

[126] (1849) 19 LJCP 81. Note in particular the dissenting judgment of Williams J., who was more than content to be overruled by the other two judges so as to enable the plaintiff to get the judgment to which he clearly believed her to be (morally) entitled.

[127] Cf. *Bainbridge* v. *Firmstone* (1838) 8 Ad & El 743, 744; *Haigh* v. *Brooks* (1839) 10 Ad & El 309, 320.

[128] [1947] 1 KB 130. The justification for his decision was transparently based on the Will Theory, the parties having varied the agreement intending it to have legal effects: [1947] 1 KB 130, 134. Commonly such inequity would arise if the representee had suffered some detriment by relying on the representation, but Denning J. (extrajudicially) was clear that this was not essential: 'Recent Developments in the Doctrine of Consideration' (1952) 15 MLR 1, 3–6. For the development of the idea of unconscionability, see below, pp.251–61.

[129] *Crabb* v. *Arun District Council* [1976] Ch 179; below, p.247.

[130] *Waltons Stores (Interstate)* v. *Maher* (1988) 164 CLR 387. The unconscionability might also be relevant in determining the extent of the enforcement.

[131] *Hedley Byrne & Co Ltd* v. *Heller & Partners Ltd* [1964] AC 465 (above, p.192). The reasoning of the House of Lords is shot through with contractual thinking.

[132] *Henderson* v. *Merrett* [1995] 2 AC 145; *Williams* v. *Natural Life Health Foods Ltd* [1998] 1 WLR 830; above, pp.126–30, 135–40.

[133] *Hunter* v. *Moss* [1994] 1 WLR 452 (but see the criticisms of the decision in e.g. A. Underhill and D. J. Hayton, *Law of Trusts and Trustees* (15th edn., London, 1995), 61); cf. above, p.206.

The interplay of these factors is well illustrated by the problem of contractual variation. It had been clear law at least since the sixteenth century
that an informal agreement to vary a contract would not be valid unless the
person against whose interests the variation was to take effect received
some consideration.[134] This was firmly applied in the eighteenth and nineteenth centuries,[135] though with the equally firm proviso that any slight
potential benefit would be treated as good consideration.[136] From 1947 the
High Trees principle provided a defence where the contract price had been
renegotiated downwards, but it did not avail where the price had been
negotiated upwards and the party benefiting was suing to recover the
increased amount. Several centuries of authority held that the absence of
consideration would stand in the way of such a claim; this did not deter the
Court of Appeal in *Williams* v. *Roffey Bros.*[137] The plaintiff had agreed to
carry out building work for the defendants for a fixed price. When it
appeared that he could not carry out the work economically at this rate,
and that there was a risk of his becoming bankrupt, the parties agreed that
a higher sum would be paid if the work was duly done. Without going so
far as to deny the need for consideration altogether, the Court of Appeal
essentially ignored the previous case law[138] and held that the requirement
was satisfied so long as it was of benefit to the defendants that the work
should actually be done. The real test of liability was that provided by the
Will Theory: so long as the parties had freely agreed, without duress, that
the higher sum would be paid, the court would hold them to their agreement.[139] The approach of the Court of Appeal is as revealing as the
decision. No longer is consideration being seen as a positive requirement
of a valid contract. Its relevance, if it is relevant at all, is negative: the
absence of consideration is just another factor among many capable of
undermining prima-facie liability generated by the parties' agreement.

At the same time as the doctrine of consideration was withering away

[134] Above, p.143.
[135] *Cumber* v. *Wane* (1718) 1 Str 426; *Foakes* v. *Beer* (1884) 9 App Cas 605. The rule was
abolished in India in 1872: Indian Contract Act, s.63.
[136] *Sibree* v. *Tripp* (1846) 15 M & W 23 (negotiable securities for lesser sum); *Couldery* v.
Bartrum (1881) 19 Ch D 394, 399–400 ('Canary-bird or tom-tit' sufficient).
[137] [1991] 1 QB 1. See M. Chen-Wishart, 'Consideration, Practical Benefit and the Emperor's
New Clothes', in J. Beatson and D. Friedmann (eds.), *Good Faith and Fault in Contract Law*
(Oxford, 1995), 123.
[138] The only two cases cited for the inadequacy of the consideration, *Harris* v. *Watson*
(1791) Peake 102 and *Stilk* v. *Myrick* (1809) 2 Camp 317, were distinguished on the grounds
that they had involved sailors demanding extra wages at a time when conditions at sea were
dangerous. The actual reasoning in the case might not have been that far removed from that of
the sixteenth-century courts: above, p.143.
[139] Cf. *In re Selectmove* [1995] 1 WLR 474, where the Court of Appeal refused to move any
further along the line away from the traditional rules of consideration. In practice the
enforcement of the agreement may be to some extent counterbalanced by the courts'
unwillingness to award damages in excess of what would be fair: below, p.260.

from inside, it was also being eroded away from without. It had always been the case that, if an undertaking was embodied in a sealed document, the courts would not look beyond this document. The eighteenth-century attempt of Wilmot J. and Lord Mansfield C.J. to extend this principle to unsealed documents was not immediately successful,[140] and in the nineteenth century it was easy enough to say that, if parties really did want to make a binding gratuitous agreement, it was not too much to expect them to reveal their intentions by using a sealed deed. In 1937 the Law Revision Committee recommended that the rule relating to deeds should apply to all contracts in writing, but the recommendation was never implemented.[141] What constituted a seal, though, was progressively attenuated. By the middle of the nineteenth century it was common practice to affix a disc of red gummed paper or simply to touch a document with a moistened forefinger;[142] by the middle of the twentieth it was enough that the parties had indicated on the document an unequivocal intention that it be sealed;[143] and covenants in favour of charitable organizations, made with a view to obtaining tax relief, were commonly and unobjectionably made without any formality other than the completion of a form cut out of a newspaper.

Everybody knows that sealing is now a completely fictitious matter. There may be some noble Dukes, or some old-fashioned people, who get a seal off their watch chain and put down a piece of wax, but normally the sealing consists of either placing a ruler on the piece of paper, or doing nothing at all, or taking a look at a rather scrubby red mark which the Solicitors' Law Stationery Office has put on the document. I would have hoped that we might have got rid of that mumbo-jumbo and aligned ourselves with most other civilised countries.[144]

In 1989 the requirement of a seal was finally eliminated, to be replaced by a formulaic incantation that the document was intended as a deed.[145]

Privity of Contract

The rule that a third party could not enforce rights arising under a contract had been a feature of English law since at least the thirteenth century.[146] It made sense in terms of the exchange model of contract, especially when tied up with the rule that consideration must move from the promisee, but logically had no place in the Will Theory. If rights and liabilities were

---

[140] Above, p.205.
[141] Law Revision Committee, 6th Interim Report, 18–19. Substantial steps in this direction had been taken in the Indian Contract Act 1872, s.25.
[142] *re Sandilands* (1871) LR 6 CP 411; *National Provincial Bank* v. *Jackson* (1886) 33 Ch D 1.
[143] *Stromdale & Ball Ltd* v. *Burden* [1952] Ch 223; *First National Securities Ltd* v. *Jones* [1978] Ch 109.   [144] (1971) 315 Hansard (HL) col.1213, per Lord Wilberforce.
[145] Law of Property (Miscellaneous Provisions) Act 1989, s.1(2).   [146] Above, p.76.

created by the agreement of the parties, there was no compelling reason why those rights could not be generated in favour of others. This was clearly recognized by theoretical purists such as Savigny, though most continental writers retained it, acutely conscious of its centrality in the Roman law that served as their model.[147] Pothier's embarrassed hesitancy is transparent: it is obvious that third parties cannot enforce contracts for their benefit, since this is the rule.[148] English lawyers, with several centuries of history and precedent behind them, shared none of Pothier's doubts. The rule was unabashedly affirmed in *Tweddle* v. *Atkinson*[149] in 1861, it was embraced increasingly dogmatically by doctrinal writers,[150] and by the early years of the twentieth century it was firmly locked in place by the House of Lords as a 'fundamental' principle of law.[151]

Twentieth-century lawyers were less convinced, but—like considera-tion—the doctrine of privity was resilient enough to withstand a barrage of criticism from both academic commentators and judges,[152] and for a long time survived recommendations for more or less comprehensive reform.[153] Only in 1999 were serious moves taken to subject it to a general, though still qualified, principle transparently shaped by the Will Theory: if a contract is made expressly for the benefit of a third party, he or she may have a right to sue on it if this had been the intention of the original parties.[154] Like the doctrine of consideration, its long survival was achieved largely by the invention of a whole range of qualifications and excep-tions.[155] Some of these had been developed by the eighteenth century.[156] Others were more modern legislative introductions, such as the right of non-parties to sue on motor-insurance contracts or contracts for package holidays.[157] Some were the result of judicial manipulation of the law of contract itself: use of the idea of agency enabled third parties to claim the

---

[147] Zimmermann, *Obligations*, 41–5. For the Roman law, see above, p.8.

[148] *Traité des obligations*, 1.1.5, §1.

[149] (1861) 1 B & S 393, 30 LJQB 265, 4 LT 468; V. V. Palmer, *The Paths to Privity* (San Francisco, 1992), 162–71.

[150] Chitty, *Contracts* (2nd edn.), 46–8 (not in 1st edn.); Addison, *Contracts*, 244–54; Leake, *Contracts*, 222–3; Pollock, *Contract*, 190–4; Anson, *Contract*, 199–203. It is noteworthy that those books written before *Tweddle* v. *Atkinson* treat it as the corollary of the consideration rule; those written afterwards deal with it as an independent rule in its own right.

[151] *Dunlop Pneumatic Tyre Co Ltd* v. *Selfridge and Co Ltd* [1915] AC 847.

[152] e.g. *Beswick* v. *Beswick* [1966] Ch 538, 553–4 (Lord Denning M.R.), [1968] AC 58, 72 (Lord Reid); *Darlington B.C.* v. *Wiltshier Northern Ltd* [1995] 1 WLR 68, 76 (Steyn L.J.: 'The autonomy of the will of the parties should be respected').

[153] Law Revision Committee, 6th Interim Report (1937), 31; Law Commission Report 242, *Contracts for the Benefit of Third Parties* (1996).

[154] Contracts (Rights of Third Parties) Bill 1999.

[155] Law Commission Report 242, 9–35.   [156] Above, pp.79–80, 207–8.

[157] Third Parties (Rights against Insurers) Act 1930; Road Traffic Act 1930, s.36(4) (now Road Traffic Act 1988 s.148(4)); Package Travel, Package Holidays and Package Tours Regulations 1992.

benefit of exemption clauses intended to cover them;[158] collateral contracts
could be constructed, giving effect, for example, to manufacturers' guarantees about their products.[159] Some stemmed from the intervention (or
exploitation) of Equity: so long as a requisite intention could be demon-
strated, the intended beneficiary could claim that the contractual claim was
held on trust, so that an action would lie to force the 'trustee' to bring an
action at law;[160] and, more generally, in the nineteenth century it was
argued that Equity might allow the intended beneficiary of a contract to
be joined as co-plaintiff in an action to enforce it.[161] Some took effect
within the law of torts. While a contract breaker's liability was clearly
contractual, a person procuring the breach could be made liable in
tort;[162] and especially in the 1980s the rules of privity could be circum-
vented if the claim could be formulated as the negligent infliction of pure
economic loss.[163] Despite the greater resistance to liability for purely
economic loss in the 1990s, where some additional element made it peculiarly imperative to give a remedy, the courts were not slow to do so by
supposing that the defendant had assumed responsibility towards the third
party.[164]

The strict rule of privity of contract was particularly problematic when
coupled with the rule excluding the award of damages in respect of losses
suffered by third parties, the natural result of the idea that the action for
breach of contract was aiming to compensate for loss, the legacy of its
trespassory origins.[165] Where the action was aimed at the recovery of a
contractual entitlement, as was typically the case in the actions of debt or
indebitatus assumpsit, there was no such restriction: the creditor could
recover the debt, and it was no concern of the court that there might be a

---

[158] *The Eurymedon* [1975] AC 154; *The New York Star* [1981] 1 WLR 138.
[159] *Shanklin Pier Ltd* v. *Detel Products Ltd* [1951] 2 KB 854.
[160] *Fletcher* v. *Fletcher* (1844) 4 Hare 67; *Lloyd's* v. *Harper* (1880) 16 Ch D 290. The exact
scope of this is exceedingly uncertain.
[161] *Gregory* v. *Williams* (1817) 3 Mer 582. The point, made with some diffidence in the first
edition of Anson, *Contract*, 201, is dropped from the second and subsequent editions. Pollock,
no less diffidently, treats *Gregory* v. *Williams* as being really a case where the benefit of the
contract was held on trust for the beneficiary.
[162] *Lumley* v. *Gye* (1853) 2 El & Bl 216; above, p.180.
[163] e.g. *Junior Books Ltd* v. *Veitchi Co Ltd* [1983] 1 AC 520; *Muirhead* v. *Industrial Tank
Specialities Ltd* [1986] QB 507; *Aswan* v. *Lupdine* [1987] 1 WLR 1, 18–24, 27–9. Above, p.194.
[164] Most obviously in *White* v. *Jones* [1995] AC 207, where a solicitor who negligently failed
to draw up a will before the death of the testator was held liable to the disappointed
beneficiaries. Stress was laid on the public responsibility of solicitors, and on the fact that
the person who would have been entitled to sue for breach of contract—the testator's personal
representative—would not have suffered any loss. The pragmatic nature of the reasoning is
clear in the speech of Lord Goff: [1995] AC 207, 254–5.
[165] Doubly so: there was a strong trespassory dimension to the emergent action of covenant
in the thirteenth century (above, p.22) and, more obviously, to the sixteenth-century action of
assumpsit (above, p.130). The rule against the recovery of third-party losses was already
present around 1300: above, p.77.

separate duty to deal in a particular way with the money recovered.[166] In the normal case of special assumpsit, though, not merely could third-party beneficiaries not sue, but the principal contractor could normally not recover damages on their behalf. Practical convenience dictated that there must be qualifications to this: hence the consignor of goods might recover the full value of goods from a defaulting carrier notwithstanding that they were the property of the consignee, a trustee could recover damages in respect of beneficiaries' losses, or a bailee suing on an insurance policy could recover the full value of lost or damaged goods.[167] It was only in the second half of the twentieth century that moves began to be made towards weakening the general principle, first by allowing that the promisee might obtain an order of specific performance despite being unable to claim substantial damages,[168] then by more general application of the Will Theory-based reasoning that substantial damages should be recovered in respect of third-party losses if it could be inferred this was the intention of the contracting parties.[169]

---

[166] Cf. *Tweddle* v. *Atkinson* (1861) 30 LJQB 265, 267, per Blackburn J.

[167] *Dunlop* v. *Lambert* (1839) 6 Cl & F 600; *Tomlinson* v. *Gill* (1756) Amb 330; *Lloyds* v. *Harper* (1880) 16 Ch D; *Waters* v. *Monarch Fire and Life Assurance Co* (1856) 5 El & Bl 870.

[168] *Beswick* v. *Beswick* [1968] AC 58.

[169] *Alfred McAlpine Construction Ltd* v. *Panatown Ltd* (1998) 58 Con LR 46, generalizing from *St Martins Property Corporation* v. *Sir Robert McAlpine Ltd* [1994] 1 AC 85 and *Darlington B.C.* v. *Wiltshier Northern Ltd* [1995] 1 WLR 68.

13. The Decline of the Will Theory: Legal Regulation and Contractual Fairness

Gradually confidence in the Will Theory and the doctrines derived from it began to be sapped. Continental and transatlantic scholars took the lead;[1] it was only in the second half of the twentieth century that writers in England began to voice their doubts.[2] As an intellectual structure the Will Theory was too brittle to bear the weight placed on it, it did not fit easily with commercial practice, and its fundamental idea of party autonomy clashed with widely held principles of social justice. None the less, however much these writings pointed to weaknesses in the traditional theory, they did not displace it from its dominant position in legal thinking. As occurred in the nineteenth century, the judges of the twentieth century showed a greater readiness to adopt new ideas than to discard old ones. Despite tentative attacks, the main doctrines associated with the Will Theory survived; but they were overlaid with new principles, most importantly those generated by considerations of fairness and justice, and in places the older ideas were reinterpreted in the light of the new. As Atiyah points out at the end of his treatment of the failures of the classical model of contract, there is a need for a new theory.[3] No less is there a need to discard something of the old.

INTERNAL WEAKNESS OF THE WILL THEORY

At the heart of the Will Theory of contract was the idea that contractual liability was generated by the voluntary agreement of the parties. Three features in particular embodied this: offer and acceptance; the requirement of an intention to create legal relations; and the rule that a transaction

---

[1] Fundamental was R. Jhering, *Der Zweck im Recht* (Leipzig, 1877–83), trans. I. Husik, *Law as a Means to an End* (New York, 1924), stressing the importance of social interests against individual autonomy; see F. Wieacker, *A History of Private Law in Europe* (trans. T. Weir, Oxford, 1995), 355–7. For the theoretical shift in France, see E. Gounot, *Le Principe de l'autonomie de la volonté en droit privé* (Paris, 1912); V. Ranouil, *L'Autonomie de la volonté* (Paris, 1980), 97 ff.; For America, R. Pound, 'Liberty of Contract' (1909) 18 Yale L J 454.

[2] S. Waddams, 'Unconscionability in Contracts' (1976) 39 MLR 369; and generally P. S. Atiyah, *Essays on Contract* (Oxford, 1986). For an overview of developments in the twentieth century, see E. McKendrick, 'English Contract Law: A Rich Past, an Uncertain Future?' [1997] Current Legal Problems 25.

[3] Atiyah, *Rise and Fall of Freedom of Contract*, 778–9.

induced by mistake was void. Each of these came under attack in the twentieth century.

For Pothier, the analysis of offer and acceptance added little to the notion of agreement—its whole function was to stress that liability stemmed only from bilateral agreements and not from unilateral promises—though it did furnish a framework in which he could deal in principle with situations where the parties' acts were not simultaneous. English writers in the nineteenth century came to recognize the truth of this.[4] It provided the terminology to deal with situations in which negotiations passed between parties, notably with the 'battle of the forms' where each party was endeavouring to finalize the contract on its own standard terms,[5] but without producing any result that would not have been reached as easily by asking simply whether or not they had (yet) agreed. It was of use in determining where, as much as when or whether, the contract was made;[6] but the results reached in all of these cases were little more than arbitrary rules whose function was to give a degree of commercial certainty, not rigorous applications of an abstract theory. The truth of the matter, as was clearly recognized by Pollock in the 1880s,[7] was that the model of offer and acceptance was far too crude a description of commercial practice. Recognition by the courts was less forthcoming; an attempt by Lord Denning M.R. to get beneath the veneer of the doctrine was firmly disapproved by the House of Lords,[8] and it was regularly applied for the benefit of those prosecuted for offering prohibited goods for sale.[9]

It was not merely the analysis of offer and acceptance that came under fire; so too did the whole idea that liability flowed from the agreement of the parties. The general principle that liability stemmed from a meeting of minds was hard to defend in the light of the growth of standard-form contracts that, especially in non-commercial contexts, one (or all too commonly both) of the parties would never have read; ever greater weight had to be placed on Paley's principle of objective interpretation.[10] Even in

---

[4] Pollock, *Contract* (3rd edn., 1881), 1–6 (differing from the earlier editions); Simpson, 'Innovation in Nineteenth Century Contract Law' (1975) 91 LQR 247, 258.

[5] e.g. *Butler Machine Tool Co Ltd* v. *Ex-cell-O Corporation (England) Ltd* [1979] 1 WLR 401.

[6] *Entores Ltd* v. *Miles Far East Corporation* [1955] 2 QB 327; *Brinkibon Ltd* v. *Stahag Stahl und Stahlwarenhandlungsgesellschaft m.b.H.* [1983] 2 AC 34.

[7] 'That particular question seems to me one which might probably be decided by tossing up without any particular harm' (Howe (ed.), *Pollock–Holmes Letters*, 1.17 (Holmes)).

[8] *Gibson* v. *Manchester City Council* [1978] 1 WLR 520, 523 (Lord Denning M.R.) [1979] 1 WLR 294, 297 (Lord Diplock).

[9] *Pharmaceutical Society of Great Britain* v. *Boots Cash Chemists Ltd* [1952] 2 QB 795, [1953] 1 QB 401; *Fisher* v. *Bell* [1961] 1 QB 394; *Partridge* v. *Crittenden* [1968] 1 WLR 1204.

[10] *L'Estrange* v. *Graucob* [1934] 2 KB 394; and see generally the discussion in O. Prausnitz, *The Standardization of Commercial Contracts in English and Continental Law* (London, 1937). Cf. above, p.221.

commercial contexts, the requirement that there should be no liability until the parties had (objectively speaking) agreed diverged from practical reality. As a consequence, in exactly the same way as the doctrines of consideration and privity were shored up,[11] non-contractual remedies grew up around the edges of contractual liability. Actions in tort came to protect those who suffered loss as a result of relying on fraudulent or negligent pre-contractual representations;[12] actions characterized as restitutionary covered the situation where a party incurred expense in good faith in beginning to perform an anticipated contract before negotiations had been completed;[13] and contractual results might be achieved by ostensibly non-contractual means through the unruly device of the proprietary estoppel.[14] In so far as this achieved a measure of practical justice, it did so only at the cost of a breakdown in conceptual coherence.

Nor was the requirement of an intention to create legal relations any more successful as the metwand of contractual liability. It provided a terminological framework within which the refusal to enforce purely domestic arrangements and jokes could be expressed, and allowed parties in apparently commercial contracts to stipulate expressly that they should not have legal force;[15] but beyond this it added little. Too often, it was recognized, parties to agreements had no relevant intention at all. The courts responded to this either by inventing it out of nowhere or by presuming it when it was desired to impose liability, or by holding that despite appearances there was no intention to create legal relations when liability was being denied.[16] Despite the recognition in academic writings that in reality whether or not liability was imposed depended on whether the behaviour of the parties fitted into an institutional mould that the law designated as contractual,[17] the language of intention to create legal relations continued to be used. Collective bargaining agreements were denied legal effects not by the simple imposition of a rule to this effect,

[11]   Above, pp.236–41, 241–4.
[12]   *Esso Petroleum Co Ltd* v. *Mardon* [1976] QB 801; *Howard Marine and Dredging Co Ltd* v. *A. Ogden & Sons (Excavations) Ltd* [1978] QB 574. Cf. the German doctrine of *culpa in contrahendo*: F. Kessler and E. Fine, 'Culpa in Contrahendo, Bargaining in Good Faith, and Freedom of Contract: A Comparative Study' (1964) 77 Harv L R 401.
[13]   *British Steel Corporation* v. *Cleveland Bridge and Engineering Ltd* [1984] 1 All ER 504.
[14]   *Crabb* v. *Arun District Council* [1976] Ch 179 (examined from opposing viewpoints by P. S. Atiyah and P. Millett Q.C. in (1976) 92 LQR 174, 342).
[15]   *Rose & Frank Co* v. *J. R. Crompton & Bros Ltd* [1925] AC 445.
[16]   e.g. *Parker* v. *Clark* [1960] 1 WLR 286 (liability imposed); *Ford Motor Co Ltd* v. *A.E.F.* [1969] 1 WLR 339 (liability denied). Inevitably such findings might easily mask covert value judgements.
[17]   B. A. Hepple, 'Intention to Create Legal Relations' [1970] CLJ 122; S. Hedley, 'Keeping Contract in its Place: *Balfour* v. *Balfour* and the Enforceability of Informal Agreements' (1985) 5 Ox Jnl Leg Stud 391.

for example, but by introducing a statutory presumption that it had not been their intention that they should have been legally enforceable.[18]

The third area in which the strictness of the classical model of liability was qualified was mistake. According to the doctrine developed in the nineteenth century, following the model of Pothier, all kinds of mistake, so long as they were sufficiently fundamental, rendered a contract void.[19] This failed to distinguish between the ill-defined range of situations in which Equity would have treated a contract as voidable (essentially where one party was labouring under a mistake and the other was guilty of a degree of sharp practice) and the situations in which an apparent contract would be void at Common law on the grounds that there had been no consensus between the parties.[20] It was not until 1950, in *Solle* v. *Butcher*,[21] that any attempt was made to rediscover the equitable jurisdiction and to separate cases where there was no agreement between the parties from those where they shared a common misapprehension. Building on the earlier rules of Equity, Denning L.J. argued that common mistake would make a contract voidable if it was unconscionable for a party to insist on its enforcement; this gained acceptance, though the boundaries of the doctrine remained very imprecise. What was not accepted was his more radical suggestion that common mistake could never make a contract void at law, that 'the doctrine of French law as enunciated by Pothier is no part of English law'.[22] Consequently the law relating to mistake became yet more complex as rules generated by the emergent ideas of unconscionability and contractual fairness, sometimes intermeshed with the well-established rules of misrepresentation, were simply overlaid on rules generated by the Will Theory.

UNDERCUTTING THE WILL OF THE PARTIES

The principal cross-current playing against the Will Theory was the idea that the law ought to strive towards a goal of achieving justice or avoiding injustice, rather than simply giving effect to the agreement of the parties. A host of factors lay behind this: the recognition, particularly with the increasingly widespread use of standard-form contracts, that this agreement might be little more than a façade; the rise of social theories within

---

[18] Trade Union and Labour Relations Act 1974 s.18.
[19] Though when a mistake was so fundamental as to have this effect was wholly unclear. The problems are well illustrated by *Bell* v. *Lever Brothers Ltd* [1932] AC 161, and in the conflict between *Ingram* v. *Little* [1961] 1 QB 31 and *Lewis* v. *Averay* [1972] 1 QB 198.
[20] Above, pp.210, 225–9.   [21] [1950] 1 KB 671.
[22] [1950] 1 KB 671, 691–2. Cf. J. C. Smith, 'Contracts—Mistake, Frustration and Implied Terms' (1994) 110 LQR 400.

which individual autonomy no longer held so privileged a position as it once had done; the friction between the Common law and those continental legal systems in which there was a general requirement of good faith between contracting parties; the development of the law of contract by analogy with the newly recognized law of unjust enrichment; the recognition that the law was not value-neutral but might be used proactively to achieve socially desirable ends. It had a similar range of manifestations: the increasing legislative regulation of social and commercial relationships; a greater willingness of judges—no longer operating through or behind juries—to lay down rules of law, to rediscover and develop equitable principles lost in the nineteenth century, or more generally to react against contracting parties thought to be acting unconscionably. Here, although the most wide-ranging interference was the result of legislation, the groundwork was almost exclusively the work of the judges; and, despite the lip service that continued to be paid to the Will Theory, there was clear judicial recognition of what was actually occurring: 'The truth is that the Court, or jury, as a judge of fact, decides this question in accordance with what seems to be just or reasonable in its eyes. The judge finds in himself the criterion of what is reasonable. The Court is in this sense making a contract for the parties—though it is almost blasphemy to say so.[23]

The legal rules giving effect to these aims can be crudely divided into two groups: those that restricted the freedom of contracting parties in the wider public interest; and, more specifically, those that regulated the balance between the parties themselves.

Public Policy and Illegality

As well as refusing to enforce illegal agreements, eighteenth-century lawyers had begun to develop a general category of contracts contrary to public policy that would not be enforced.[24] Nineteenth-century lawyers were less comfortable with this; from the 1820s it became fashionable to liken public policy to an unruly horse that could carry its rider in unpredictable directions.[25] One real difficulty was that it was problematic to give such an uncontrolled power to the judges to determine which contracts should be enforced; judicial legislation was both unpopular and increasingly unnecessary with the growth of parliamentary regulation. In addition, though, it sat ill with the idea of party autonomy inherent in the Will Theory. The gradual shift away from the eighteenth-century approach can be charted through the different approaches taken by the text-writers. For

---

[23] Lord Wright, 'Commercial Law in the Present Century' (1935), in *Legal Essays and Addresses* (Cambridge, 1939), 252, 259.   [24] Above, p.211.
[25] *Richardson* v. *Mellish* (1824) 2 Bing 229, 252; *Newberry* v. *Colvin* (1830) 7 Bing 190, 205; P. H. Winfield, 'Public Policy in the English Common Law' (1928) 42 Harv L R 76, 91.

Chitty (1826) there was a general principle that contracts *expressly* contrary to public policy would not be enforced,[26] the qualification revealing his uneasiness. Addison (1847) expressed no such doubts in his formulation of the general principle, but restricted its operation by treating it as an idea underlying certain specific examples of unenforceability rather than a principle capable of broad application.[27] It was similarly constrained by Leake (1867), essentially indistinguishable from the clear categories of illegality and immorality.[28] By the 1870s Pollock and Anson were at pains to demonstrate that such a principle still existed at all.[29] Pollock gave some shape to this, adopting the French distinction between agreements contrary to morals or good manners and agreements contrary to public policy,[30] and other writers more or less followed his division. Nothing hinged on it, though. More to the point was that, however they were classified, the individual heads were sufficiently fixed for it to be almost impossible to contemplate adding to them. It was recognized that the application of these settled categories would have to change to take account of shifting perceptions of morality or public policy, though in reality it was only in the context of contracts in restraint of trade that there was any evidence of judicial creativity.[31] It was for the legislature, not for the judges, to determine where the public interest lay:

[Public policy] is a vague and unsatisfactory term, and calculated to lead to uncertainty and error, when applied to the decision of legal rights; it is capable of being understood in different senses; it may, and does, in its ordinary sense, mean 'political expedience' or that which is best for the common good of the community; and in that sense there may be every variety of opinion, according to education, habits, talents, and dispositions of each person, who is to decide whether an act is against public policy or not. To allow this to be a ground of judicial decision, would lead to the greatest uncertainty and confusion. It is the province of the statesman, and not the lawyer, to discuss, and of the legislature to determine, what is the best for the public good, and to provide for it by proper enactments. It is the province of the judge to expound the law only; the written from the statutes: the unwritten or common law from the decisions of our predecessors and of our existing courts, from text writers of acknowledged authority, and upon the principles to be clearly deduced from them by sound reason and just inference; not to speculate upon what is the best, in his opinion, for the advantage of the community.[32]

---

[26] Chitty, *Contract*, 217.   [27] Addison, *Contract*, index, 'Illegality', 'Public Policy'.
[28] Leake, *Contract*, 376–412; contracts in restraint of trade, for example, fit awkwardly between champertous contracts and trading with the enemy.
[29] Pollock, *Contract*, 251–92; Anson, *Contract*, 174–80.
[30] Pollock, *Contract*, 242, 251. For the French distinction between agreements *contraire aux bonnes mœurs* and those *contraire à l'ordre public*, see *Code civil*, article 1133). A useful comparative perspective is given by D. Lloyd, *Public Policy* (London, 1953).
[31] Treitel, *Contract*, 412–35.
[32] *Egerton* v. *Earl Brownlow* (1853) 4 HLC 1, 123. This case is pivotal in the development of ideas of public policy in the nineteenth century, and the source of most of the later discussions.

Twentieth-century judges took this warning to heart, making no attempt
to expand the list fixed by the 1870s. Meanwhile, though, there was a huge
increase in the volume of regulatory legislation: by statute, by delegated
legislation, and increasingly by the organs of the European Union. In
addition, as public enterprise was more heavily involved in areas that
would once have been purely a matter of contract—education and health
care are the obvious examples—there was far greater scope for public-law
regulation of what had once been private-law contracts; and even simple
contracts might have a public-law dimension.[33] As well as removing from
the domain of contract law some relationships that would once have been
contractual, those relationships still treated as contractual were inevitably
heavily affected by the regulatory structures. Whether or not the rules
criminalized the mere fact of purporting to make a contract contrary to
them, the long-established principles of illegality would normally lead to
such a contract being unenforceable.

Unconscionability, Fairness, and the Regulation of Contractual Relationships

The control of contracts in the public interest in no way constituted a
challenge to the idea of party autonomy at the heart of the Will Theory;
but this was only one aspect of the twentieth-century development. The
other dimension—holding the balance between the parties—attacked the
very heart of the idea. For much of the century lip service continued to be
paid to the Will Theory at the same time as holes were being shot in it.
From perhaps the 1970s it was recognized that there were certain types of
procedural impropriety, largely associated with taking advantage of
another party's weakness, that vitiated an apparently valid contract.
This, in practice, represented little more than a rearticulation of defences
that had long been recognized by the law, though the process of rearticulation twisted them into a different mould. Rather later, perhaps
only in the 1990s, there began to emerge the more fundamental argument
that there might be principles of substantive fairness underlying contractual liability.[34]

Cf. Winfield's description: 'Up to this point, public policy had suffered nothing more than
some wavering attacks on its character, but in 1853 it had to fight for its life' ('Public Policy in
the English Common Law' (1928) 42 Harv LR 76, 88–9).

[33] J. Beatson, 'Public Law Influences in Contract Law', in J. Beatson and D. Friedmann,
Good Faith and Fault in Contract Law (Oxford, 1995), 263.

[34] S. A. Smith, 'In Defence of Substantive Fairness' (1996) 112 LQR 138. For the distinction between procedural and substantive unconscionability, see A. A. Leff, 'Unconscionability
and the Code—The Emperor's New Clause' (1967) 115 U Pa L R 485, drawing on a distinction
earlier made by the draftsmen of the American Uniform Commercial Code, and *Hart* v.
O'Connor [1985] 1 AC 1000, 1017–18.

Procedural Unconscionability

The two principal vitiating factors in nineteenth-century law were fraud and duress; alongside these there were a number of equitable doctrines that might be used to strike down contracts, but that were in practice of rather less importance.[35]

Whatever its origins, by the end of the nineteenth century the courts of equity had begun to expand the defence of fraud and redefine it in terms of the unconscionability of the defendant's conduct. In the twentieth century the seed planted by Jessel M.R. in *Redgrave* v. *Hurd*[36] that it would be 'moral fraud' to take advantage of an innocent misrepresentation grew into a strong tree; although at first, because of its purely equitable roots, it gave the victim no more than a power to rescind the contract or to resist an application for specific performance, in 1967 the Misrepresentation Act provided an additional remedy in damages, mirroring that already available for fraudulent and (latterly) negligent misrepresentations. The more difficult question was whether an analogous right to rescind should arise where a contracting party had similarly failed to disclose information that would have affected the other party's decision to enter into the contract. English law traditionally allowed no such principle;[37] but there gradually built up a range of specific exceptions, founded both on statute and more generally on principles of equity, in which there was a duty of disclosure.[38] Despite strong dicta by the House of Lords upholding the traditional point of view,[39] academic writers continued to press for some generalization of the circumstances in which such a duty arose,[40] moving towards (though not necessarily reaching) the principles of good faith in negotiations widely recognized by continental legal systems.[41]

The second vitiating factor, duress, was far less developed; indeed, before the middle of the twentieth century it had hardly advanced beyond the threats of violence and imprisonment that were already well established in the thirteenth century.[42] From the mid-1970s, though, it rapidly widened to cover other forms of improper pressure, in particular duress of goods and,

---

[35] Above, pp.208, 234.   [36] (1881) 20 Ch D 1; above, p.235.

[37] B. Nicholas, 'The Obligation to Disclose Information', in D. R. Harris and D. Tallon, *Contract Law Today* (Oxford, 1989), 166.

[38] J. Beatson, *Anson's Law of Contract* (Oxford, 1998), 257–69. Criminal law has gone a long way in the direction of allowing dishonest non-disclosure to be treated as dishonest deception: *R* v. *Lambie* [1982] AC 449.   [39] *Jenkins* v. *Livesey* [1985] AC 424, 439.

[40] J. Beatson, 'Has the Common Law a Future' [1997] CLJ 291, 303–7.

[41] H. Kötz, 'Towards a European Civil Code: The Duty of Good Faith', in P. Cane and J. Stapleton (eds.), *The Law of Obligations* (Oxford, 1988), 243. At the root of this lies Jhering's development of the theory of *culpa in contrahendo*: Kessler and Fine, 'Culpa in Contrahendo' (1964) 77 Harv LR 401.

[42] Above, pp.71, 208, 234. J. Beatson, *The Use and Abuse of Unjust Enrichment* (Oxford, 1991), 95–136 (on which the following paragraph is largely based).

more generally, economic duress;[43] behind this lay the recognition both that there was no sensible reason to distinguish between different forms of improper pressure and that the law of contract should not use a narrower conception of duress than had long been used in the law of unjust enrichment.[44] Nor was it simply that the scope of duress widened; its rationale began to shift, too. The central point, traditionally, was that the coercion of the will prevented a true consent from arising;[45] but gradually emphasis began to be placed more on the impropriety of the plaintiff's conduct than on the overbearing of the defendant's will.[46] Hence it was not necessary that the improper pressure should have been the principal reason for the defendant's having entered into the contract; it was sufficient if it was one factor among others, even if those other factors might themselves have been sufficient to bring about the contract.[47] Alongside this, though, the possibility that a contract induced by duress from a third party might be voidable largely dropped out of sight.[48]

Alongside duress, from the 1970s, the courts began to expand on the earlier equitable defence of undue influence. This had been fairly narrowly conceived, largely limited to cases where there had been abuse of a position of trust or confidence,[49] though there was a strand of authority (typified by the Indian Contract Act of 1872) that extended it to any situation where one person was in a position to exercise domination over another.[50] This more general approach was developed by the House of Lords in a series of cases dealing with the more complex problem of the rights of third parties under contracts procured by undue influence: *National Westminster Bank*

---

[43] *The Siboen and the Sibotre* [1976] 1 Lloyd's Rep 293, 334–5; *North Ocean Shipping Co Ltd v. Hyundai Construction Co Ltd* [1979] QB 705, 715–17; *Pao On v. Lau Yiu Long* [1980] AC 614, 635–6; *Universe Tankships Inc of Monrovia v. International Transport Workers Federation* [1983] 1 AC 366, 383–5; *Williams v. Roffey Bros* [1991] 1 QB 1.

[44] On the latter point, see in particular the judgment of Kerr J. in *The Siboen and the Sibotre* [1976] 1 Lloyd's Rep 293, 335 (based on the arguments of Robert Goff Q.C.), the remarks of Lord Scarman in *Pao On v. Lau Yiu Long* [1980] AC 614, 635, and the observations of Lord Diplock and Lord Scarman in *Universe Tankships Inc of Monrovia v. International Transport Workers Federation* [1983] 1 AC 366, 383–4, 400–1. Cf. below, pp.273, 286.

[45] See e.g. *Pao On v. Lau Yiu Long* [1980] AC 614, 635.

[46] *Universe Tankships Inc of Monrovia v. International Transport Workers Federation* [1983] 1 AC 366, 384, 400.

[47] *Barton v. Armstrong* [1976] AC 104, 118; *Director of Public Prosecutions for Northern Ireland v. Lynch* [1975] AC 653.

[48] The question is considered from the opposite point of view—whether a restitutionary remedy would lie when money was paid under duress from a third party—in Lord Goff and G. H. Jones, *The Law of Restitution* (London, 1998), 308; subject to defences, most importantly change of position, it is argued that a restitutionary remedy should lie.

[49] Above, p.209.

[50] Indian Contract Act 1872, s.16; at the base of this was the argument of Sir Samuel Romilly in *Huguenin v. Baseley* (1807) 14 Ves Jun 273 (substantially based on Pothier's treatment of the subject) and the decision of the Court of Appeal in *Allcard v. Skinner* (1887) 36 Ch D 145.

v. *Morgan, Barclay's Bank* v. *O'Brien*, and *CIBC* v. *Pitt*.[51] At the same time
the focus of the defence was twisted away from the overreaching of the free
consent of the promisor to the impropriety of the conduct of the
promisee.[52] In practical terms, the effects of the shift of focus were to
ensure the exclusion from the scope of the defence of cases of undue
influence by a third party without the knowledge of the promisee, and to
prevent those whose wills had been overborne setting aside transactions
that were not in themselves unfair; the emphasis was on the victimization
of the weaker party rather than on their lack of genuine voluntariness. The
real importance of the shift, though, lay at the theoretical level, in its
weakening of analysis based on the Will Theory of the nineteenth century.

More wide-ranging still, and more threatening to the Will Theory, was
the tentative development of a general defence of unconscionability.
Formally speaking, this had its source in the equitable jurisdiction to
relieve against contracts made by expectant heirs,[53] but with the repeal
of the Statutes of Usury in 1854 it came to have a wider ambit in protecting
indigent borrowers of money from exploitation by moneylenders.[54]
Although relief against unconscionable loans of money was put on a
statutory footing in 1900,[55] the widened equitable jurisdiction remained
in place. Alongside this, in America rather than in England, the doctrine of
unconscionability was given a boost by its incorporation (probably under
German influence) in the Uniform Commercial Code.[56] In the context of
the sale of goods, section 2–302 of the Code provided that unconscionable
bargains should not be enforced, and this was followed by a movement
bringing together traditional cases of undue influence and the like within
the scope of such a general principle.[57] An analogous, though less far-
reaching, process of generalization began to take place in England in the
mid-1970s, indicating the direction in which the law might move in the
future.[58]

---

[51] *National Westminster Bank plc* v. *Morgan* [1985] 1 AC 686; *Barclay's Bank plc* v. *O'Brien*
[1994] 1 AC 180; *CIBC Mortgages plc* v. *Pitt* [1994] AC 200. And see most recently *Royal Bank
of Scotland* v. *Etridge (no 2)* [1998] 4 All ER 705.
[52] See in particular *Barclay's Bank plc* v. *O'Brien* [1994] 1 AC 180, 189–92.
[53] Above, p.209.
[54] *Barrett* v. *Hartley* (1866) LR 2 Eq 789, 794–5. See H. H. Bellot and R. J. Willis, *The Law
Relating to Unconscionable Bargains with Moneylenders* (London, 1897), 45–55.
[55] Moneylenders Act 1900, s.1(1).
[56] J. P. Dawson, 'Unconscionable Coercion: The German Version' (1976) 89 Harv L R 1041.
The German underpinnings of the UCC are explored by S. Herman, 'Llewellyn the Civilian:
Speculations on the Contribution of Continental Experience to the Uniform Commercial Code'
(1982) 56 Tul LR 1125, and J. Whitman, 'Commercial Law and the American *Volk*: A Note on
Llewellyn's German Sources for the Uniform Commercial Code' (1987) 97 Yale L J 156.
[57] See in particular Leff, 'Unconscionability and the Code' (1967) 115 U Pa L R 485;
M. Eisenberg, 'The Bargain Principle and its Limits' (1982) 95 Harv L R 741, 748–85.
[58] Seminal was Waddams, 'Unconscionability in Contracts' (1976) 39 MLR 369.

Substantive Unconscionability

The Will Theory was, perhaps, sufficiently flexible to accommodate the idea of procedural fairness, in that it could be seen as doing no more than assuring that the appearance of party autonomy was not simply a façade.[59] There was, though, a near-irresistible tendency for these considerations to collapse into questions whether the contract was substantively fair, thereby eating away at the Will Theory's core. This tendency was clearly recognized by scholars in the 1980s,[60] and was soon no less visible in the case law. In the absence of direct pressure tantamount to duress, for example, the defence of undue influence was essentially triggered by a finding that the terms of the contract were transparently unfair. If there were not some improper influence at work, why else would the party have entered into a manifestly unfair bargain? In *Credit Lyonnais* v. *Burch*,[61] therefore, where a junior employee had accepted unlimited liability and mortgaged her home as security for the debts of her employer, the Court of Appeal was willing to allow the defence of undue influence. Their real concern, though, was with the substantive unfairness of the transaction, from which the presumption of undue influence arose: 'the transaction . . . shocks the conscience of the court'; it was 'truly astonishing'.[62]

Behind this very tentative generalization there lay a solid core of development stretching back to the beginning of the century. Its first manifestation was in the recharacterization of the rule against contractual penalties, its consolidation in the law's treatment of unfair contract terms.

Although the practice of giving relief against penalties reached back to the beginning of the sixteenth century and had been put on a statutory footing in the seventeenth, it had been emasculated in the nineteenth century when a clause was treated as a penalty clause only if it could not have represented the true intention of the parties.[63] The Indian Contract Act had departed from this, providing that only reasonable compensation for breach of contract could be recovered notwithstanding that a contract had provided for the payment of some specific sum, but this did not herald any change in the English approach.[64] When this change did occur, in the early years of the twentieth century, it was the result of rather different

---

[59] e.g. R. E. Barnett, 'A Consent Theory of Contract' (1986) 86 Col L R 269, 318–19 (contrast the author's approach to ideas of substantive fairness at 283–6).

[60] e.g. Eisenberg, 'The Bargain Principle and its Limits' (1982) 95 Harv LR 741, 752–3; J. Gordley, 'Equality in Exchange' (1981) 69 Cal L R 1587, 1633; M. Chen-Wishart, *Unconscionable Bargains* (Wellington, 1989).

[61] *Credit Lyonnais Bank Nederland NV* v. *Burch* [1997] 1 All ER 144. See M. Chen-Wishart, 'The O'Brien Principle and Substantive Unfairness' [1997] CLJ 60.

[62] [1997] 1 All ER 144, 152, 150, per Millett L.J. and Nourse L.J. respectively. The substantive unconscionability of the bargain could not be raised directly on appeal, since it had not been argued in the court below.   [63] Above, p.214.

[64] Indian Contract Act 1872, s.74.

foreign influences. In *Clydebank Engineering and Shipbuilding Co Ltd* v. *Don José Ramos Yzquierdo y Castaneda*[65] the House of Lords upheld the interpretation of the rule found in Scots law, treating it as a prohibition of the recovery of agreed sums that were intended to be *in terrorem* and not attempts to pre-estimate the party's loss, situations in which it would be 'unconscionable' to enforce the agreement.[66] Though the *Clydebank Engineering* case was itself Scottish, the House of Lords was willing to assume that on this point English law and Scots law were in substance identical. A similar approach was taken in the Privy Council one year later in an appeal from the Cape of Good Hope.[67] South African law had a rule, ultimately traceable back to a text in the Code of Justinian (C.7.47.1) as interpreted by the French and Dutch commentators, that a penalty clause should not be enforced if the penalty greatly exceeded the damage suffered; this was seen as a corollary of the general principle that one person should not be unjustly enriched at the expense of another.[68] Its appearance in the Privy Council so soon after the decision in the *Clydebank Engineering* case inevitably gave added weight to the earlier decision. This was yet further consolidated by the decision of the Privy Council in *Webster* v. *Bosanquet*,[69] where the *Clydebank Engineering* case was expressly followed, producing a congruence between the English law's rule against penalties and the Roman–Dutch law's refusal to award unconscionable damages.[70] Finally, in *Dunlop Pneumatic Tyre Co* v. *New Garage and Motor Co* in 1915,[71] the House of Lords synthesized the two approaches: the rule against penalties was indeed a rule of construction, but—as a matter of construction—a clause would be interpreted as a penalty if it was unconscionable. *Dunlop* v. *New Garage* fixed the rule in the Common law; unlike the earlier decisions of the House of Lords and Privy Council, it could not be ignored as a 'foreign' case and had to take its place in the standard textbooks.[72]

The statutory restrictions on penalty clauses made it easy to incorporate ideas of substantive fairness and unconscionability; it was rather less easy

---

[65] [1905] AC 6. See in particular the remarks of the Earl of Halsbury L.C. at [1905] AC 10–11.

[66] *Forrest & Barr* v. *Henderson, Coulbourn, & Co* (1869) 8 SC (3rd ser.) 187, 193.

[67] *Public Works Commissioner* v. *Hills* [1906] AC 368.

[68] *Hills* v. *Colonial Government* (1904) 21 SCC 59, 78–9, per de Villiers C.J. More accurately the rule was that a liquidated damages clause, where the parties had attempted to preassess the loss that would be suffered, would be enforced unless it was manifestly out of proportion to the loss actually suffered; whereas a penalty clause, where there had been no such attempt at preassessment, would be enforced only if it manifestly did represent the loss actually sustained.

[69] [1912] AC 394 (on appeal from Ceylon).

[70] The difference between the two systems is stressed by Pereira A.J. in the Supreme Court of Ceylon, though glossed over by Middleton A.C.J.: (1911) 13 Ceylon L R 47, 55–6, 50. The case was in fact governed by English law.

[71] *Dunlop Pneumatic Tyre Co Ltd* v. *New Garage and Motor Co Ltd* [1915] AC 79.

[72] Anson, *Contract* (14th edn., 1917), 328; Chitty, *Contract* (17th edn., 1921). The immediately preceding edition of each of these works is impeccably nineteenth century in its tone, giving no hint of the development of any new doctrine.

to do so where there was no such statutory base. The first response of the courts was to take a more critical stance to the question whether a term had in fact been incorporated into the contract. Nineteenth-century lawyers were familiar with the principle that reasonable notice had to be given of a term, and recognized that the more unusual a term the clearer the notice required;[73] but around 1950 the principle began to be used as a means of preventing one party taking unfair advantage of another.[74] Though at first regarded with suspicion, this critical approach gradually came to be accepted as part of the Common law.[75] Similarly the courts, following the crusading zeal of Lord Denning, invented a rule that some terms of a contract were so fundamental that effect would not be given to a clause purporting to exclude liability for their breach.[76] The rule was deliberately introduced as a means of protecting consumers,[77] but was capable of extending far wider than this; three times, therefore, the House of Lords reasserted that it was no more than a rule of construction, which would not normally be used to strike down freely negotiated commercial contracts.[78]

The groundwork done by the courts in the 1950s and 1960s was consolidated by the legislature. Legislative provisions to avoid the exclusion or restriction of liability in certain specific cases could be found much earlier than this,[79] and in the 1960s there was a move to introduce more generally applicable enactments, most notably in transactions between consumers and business organizations.[80] The Misrepresentation Act of 1967 provided that clauses purporting to exclude liability for misrepresentation would be void,[81] and this was soon followed by the entrenchment of unexcludable

---

[73] *Parker* v. *South Eastern Railway Co* (1877) 2 CPD 416; *Crooks & Co* v. *Allan* (1879) 5 QBD 38.

[74] *John Lee & Son (Grantham) Ltd* v. *Railway Executive* [1949] 2 All ER 581, 584, per Denning L.J. Cf. the more formalist reasoning, though reaching the same result, of Sir Raymond Evershed M.R.

[75] *Spurling* v. *Bradshaw* [1956] 1 WLR 461; *Thornton* v. *Shoe Lane Parking Ltd* [1971] 2 QB 163.   [76] *Karsales (Harrow)* v. *Wallis* [1956] 1 WLR 936.

[77] Lord Denning, *The Family Story* (London, 1981), 174. Lord Denning's own approach was rather wider, essentially the application of a general principle that the court should impose a term whenever it was reasonable to do so and reject a clear term that was unreasonable: Lord Denning, *The Discipline of Law* (London, 1979), 36–41; and see the cases cited in Treitel, *Contract*, 224 n.73.

[78] *Suisse Atlantique Société d'Armement Maritime S.A.* v. *NV Rotterdamsche Kolen Centrale* [1967] 1 AC 361; *Photo Production Ltd* v. *Securicor Transport Ltd* [1980] AC 827; *George Mitchell (Chesterhall) Ltd* v. *Finney Lock Seeds Ltd* [1983] 2 AC 803.

[79] e.g. clauses purporting to restrict liability for death or injury of those travelling on public transport (Road Traffic Act 1930 s.97; British Transport Commission (Passengers) Charges Scheme 1959 para. 2(1)); clauses purporting to exclude certain warranties and conditions in hire purchase contracts (Hire Purchase Act 1938 s.5); clauses restricting employers' liability for death or personal injury (Law Reform (Personal Injuries) Act 1947 s.1(3)); clauses excluding solicitors' liability for negligence (Solicitors Act 1957 s.60(4)).

[80] e.g. *Final Report of the Committee on Consumer Protection* (the Molony Committee) (Cmnd 1781, 1962), 137–57.   [81] s.3.

terms in sales of goods where one party was a consumer.[82] Finally, in 1977, the trend indicated by the earlier legislation was generalized: in consumer contracts effect was given to exclusion clauses only in so far as they were reasonable.[83] There was still a degree of disharmony between continental European systems, where the requirements of good faith and fair dealing were far more deeply entrenched, but in 1994 these differences were smoothed out, at least so far as consumer contracts were concerned, by providing that all such contracts should be subject to a general requirement of 'fairness'.[84]

Unconscionability in Enforcement

A third way in which ideas of fairness infiltrated into the law of contract was at the stage of enforcement. In some circumstances the courts would refuse strictly to enforce a contract that was both fairly entered into and fair in itself, on the grounds that circumstances arising or coming to light after it had been made meant that it would be inequitable to hold the parties to it.[85] Alternatively, the remedy awarded might be moulded in order to achieve the ostensibly fair result. These circumstances were never linked together as a general principle, remaining a set of apparently distinct rules and doctrines.

Typical was the doctrine of frustration. In the nineteenth century this had been dealt with by saying that the parties would not have intended their contract to apply had they thought in advance about the changed circumstances;[86] a century later the veneer of the parties' agreement had been cracked to reveal the rule of law underneath:[87] parties would be released from contractual performance if circumstances had made it so radically different from what had been initially agreed that it would be unjust to hold them to their original agreement.[88] Some judges asserted that the courts could exonerate a party whenever it would be just and reasonable to do so, but the majority were unwilling to follow such an ostensibly radical line.[89]

[82] Supply of Goods (Implied Terms) Act 1973, s.4.
[83] Unfair Contract Terms Act 1977, s.3.
[84] Unfair Terms in Consumer Contracts Regulations 1994.
[85] For an early example, see *Redgrave* v. *Hurd* (1881) 20 Ch D 1; above, p.235.
[86] *Taylor* v. *Caldwell* (1863) 3 B & S 826; above, p.224.
[87] *Davis Contractors Ltd* v. *Fareham Urban District Council* [1956] AC 696, 728–9. The shift was presaged by Lord Wright: 'Commercial Law in the Present Century', in *Legal Essays and Addresses*, 252, 258; *Joseph Constantine Steamship Line Ltd* v. *Imperial Smelting Corporation Ltd* [1942] AC 154, 186. The implied-term analysis is still not completely dead: Smith, 'Contracts—Mistake, Frustration and Implied Terms' (1994) 110 LQR 400, 403.
[88] *National Carriers Ltd* v. *Panalpina (Northern) Ltd* [1981] AC 675, 700.
[89] e.g. *British Movietonews Ltd* v. *London and District Cinemas Ltd* [1951] 1 KB 190, 201–2 (Denning L.J.), strongly disapproved in the House of Lords [1952] AC 166, 185; *Staffordshire Area Health Authority* v. *South Staffordshire Waterworks Co* [1978] 1 WLR 1387 (Lord Denning M.R.).

A second mechanism enabling the courts to adjust the remedy with the advantage of hindsight was the classification of contractual terms. By the nineteenth century terms had come to be divided into conditions, whose breach entitled a party to rescind the contract and claim back any money paid under it, and warranties that sounded only in damages. In 1962 the Court of Appeal held, building on the case law of the early nineteenth century and before,[90] that whether or not there was a right to rescind did not depend purely on the classification of the term but also on the nature of its breach.[91] Some terms—'conditions'—might be so central to the contract that a breach would automatically justify rescission; some terms—'warranties'—might be so inevitably peripheral that there could never be more than a right to damages; but many terms could not be so neatly categorized. By thus inventing the category of 'intermediate' terms, the courts rediscovered the power to mould the remedy to the circumstances, thereby escaping the rigidity of the bipartite classification. Even where a statute defined a term as a 'warranty', it was later said, if a breach of it was sufficiently serious, it was open to the courts to allow the innocent party to rescind the contract.[92]

A third example is provided by the use of estoppels, in particular promissory estoppel and estoppel by convention. The former was established by *Central London Property Trust Ltd* v. *High Trees House Ltd,* where it was held that, where one person had led another to believe that existing legal rights would not be enforced, the law would not enforce them if it would be inequitable to do so.[93] In some cases promissory estoppel was relied upon where a later generation might have preferred to use a defence of economic duress or undue influence;[94] but the doctrine might equally apply, as in the *High Trees* case itself, where there had been no improper pressure.[95] The same *ex post facto* reasoning was found in estoppel by convention, a development of the 1980s: where a contract was entered into under a mistaken assumption shared by the parties to it, neither would be allowed to question that assumption if and to the extent that it would be 'unjust and unconscionable' for them to do so.[96]

Equitable considerations had always applied where a party was seeking an order of specific performance. Until the second half of the nineteenth

[90] Above, pp.86, 223.
[91] *Hongkong Fir Shipping Co Ltd* v. *Kawasaki Kisen Kaisha Ltd* [1962] 2 QB 26.
[92] *The Hansa Nord* [1976] QB 44, 83–4.
[93] [1947] 1 KB 130 (Denning J.); above, p.239.
[94] e.g *D & C Builders Ltd* v. *Rees* [1966] 2 QB 617.
[95] *W J Alan & Co Ltd* v. *El Nasr Export & Import Co Ltd* [1972] 2 QB 189; *Maharaj* v. *Chand* [1986] AC 898.
[96] *Taylors Fashions Ltd* v. *Liverpool Victoria Trustees Co Ltd* (1979) [1982] 1 QB 133; *Amalgamated Investment & Property Co Ltd* v. *Texas Commerce International Bank Ltd* [1982] QB 84, 103–4, 122; *Hiscox* v. *Outhwaite* [1992] 1 AC 562, 574–5.

century this was the exclusive preserve of the Court of Chancery, and like all such remedies it was discretionary. This survived the Judicature Acts, so that it was easy to apply principles of *ex post facto* justice and fairness analogous to those found in the context of estoppel and elsewhere. Thus, in *Co-operative Insurance Society* v. *Argyll Stores Ltd*, Millett L.J. (whose dissenting judgment was upheld by the House of Lords) held that it would be wrong to grant an order of specific performance whose effect would be to require the defendant company to keep open a store that was trading at a loss on the grounds that it would be 'oppressive' to do so. Lord Hoffmann agreed with this conclusion: the court should not grant an order that might cause injustice by allowing the plaintiff to be enriched at the defendant's expense.[97] There was no equivalent discretion available in traditional Common-law actions, so the principles of conscience had to creep in more covertly. Some argued that the law should not award expectation damages at all, preferring an award calculated by reference to the party's reliance loss.[98] So far as consequential losses were concerned, the rule in *Hadley* v. *Baxendale* as interpreted in later cases,[99] complemented by the requirement that the defendants take steps to mitigate their losses, was sufficiently formless to provide the courts with adequate flexibility; more ingenuity was needed where damages were sought for the defective performance of a contract, but from the 1960s the courts developed the rule that the plaintiff would be entitled to the full cost of achieving the contracted-for result (the cost of 'reinstatement') only if it would be reasonable to insist on reinstatement.[100] Most difficult of all was where the plaintiff demanded simply the performance due under the contract, a claim that would historically have been categorized as a Common-law action for debt, a remedy that would have been available as a matter of right. None the less, in *White and Carter (Councils) Ltd* v. *McGregor*,[101] an appeal to the House of Lords from Scotland, Lord Reid was willing to countenance the application of equitable intervention in this situation too. The plaintiffs had agreed to erect and maintain litter bins advertising the defendants' products for a term of three years; before anything had been done, the defendants purported to repudiate the contract, but the plaintiffs went ahead with it and brought an action for the agreed contract price. It

---

[97] [1996] Ch 286, 304; [1998] AC 1, 15.

[98] P. S. Atiyah, *An Introduction to the Law of Contract* (5th edn., Oxford, 1995), 444–8. For the classification of damages, see the classic article of L. L. Fuller and W. R. Perdue, 'The Reliance Interest in Contract Damages' (1936–7) 46 Yale L J 52, 373.

[99] Above, p.229. See *Victoria Laundry (Windsor) Ltd* v. *Newman Industries Ltd* [1949] 2 KB 528; *The Heron II* [1969] 1 AC 352.

[100] *East Ham Corporation* v. *Bernard Sunley & Sons Ltd* [1966] AC 406; *Ruxley Electronics Ltd* v. *Forsyth* [1996] AC 344.

[101] [1962] AC 413; followed in *The Puerto Buitrago* [1976] 1 Ll Rep 250, *The Alaskan Trader* [1984] 1 All ER 129.

was held, on the facts, that they should succeed. It would, however, have been different if it had been shown that they had no 'legitimate interest'—though the precise scope of this was not defined—in continuing to perform rather than accepting the repudiation and claiming damages, for here the general equitable jurisdiction of the court would have stepped in to prevent the enforcement of the contract. As with the development of the rule against penalties half a century earlier, the trigger for change was the attempt to harmonize English law and Scots law, where it was established in the nineteenth century that the claimant's prima-facie entitlement was subject to a (limited) range of equitable qualifications.[102]

The combined effect of all these shifts was that by the end of the twentieth century the Will Theory had been severely compromised. No longer could it be said without considerable qualification that contract law was based on the assumption that effect should be given to the agreement of the parties. Yet, just as the Will Theory had itself superseded the older exchange model of contract without discarding those elements that were substantially inconsistent with it, in particular the twin doctrines of consideration and privity of contract, so too the ideas of fairness were simply grafted onto the classical model of contract largely based on the Will Theory. Although the rules of contract law remained tolerably clear, allowing for the open-endedness inevitably generated by the injection of fairness-based standards, there was no doctrinal coherence holding them together. As well as this, the inadequacies of contract law had knock-on effects on the rules of tort and unjust enrichment, as these were pressed into service to achieve results that could not be reached by orthodox contractual routes.

---

[102] *Grahame* v. *Magistrates of Kirkaldy* (1882) 9 SC (4th ser.) (HL) 91; *Stewart* v. *Kennedy* (1890) 17 SC (4th ser.) (HL) 1, 9–10; *Langford & Co Ltd* v. *Dutch* [1952] SC 15.

Part Four. Unjust Enrichment

The two main categories of the law of obligations, contract and tort, were firmly in place by the thirteenth century. Not all situations fitted into them, though, and in the course of the twentieth century a third category, unjust enrichment, coalesced out of the residuary mass. It did not exhaust the field, however; there still remains a residuary group, if a smaller one than before.

Until relatively recently, the ideas of unjust enrichment were far less clearly articulated than those of tort and contract. None the less, with this qualification, its history does reflect that of tort and contract, with a marked time delay. In the Middle Ages it was largely masked by the forms of action; behind these we may identify the operation of notions of unjust enrichment, though they were crystallized around the better-established conceptions of contract and property. In the eighteenth century there were attempts at generalization, as with both tort and contract. These attempts failed: there was no easily accessible theoretical model that had been worked out elsewhere and that furnished a framework that could be borrowed by English law. Unjust enrichment collapsed back into a sterile formalism largely expressed in terms of implied contracts, with a parallel of implied trusts in Equity. It was only at the end of the nineteenth century and the beginning of the twentieth that an intellectually coherent model began to be formed, and only after about 1940 that it came to be applied in practice in the English courts. The interplay between theory and practice has a rather different flavour from that associated with contract and tort in the eighteenth and nineteenth centuries: instead of English law borrowing or half-borrowing a ready-made structure, in terms of which legal rules could be expressed, the scholarly analysis of unjust enrichment has developed hand in hand with its operation in the courts.

14. *Unjust Enrichment*

The conceptual categories of contract and tort cover much of the range of personal obligations but do not exhaust it. Beyond them lies the residuary group characterized by the Roman jurist Gaius as 'obligations arising from various other causes'.[1] Slowly, and tardily, a third category emerged from this group, to be known as 'quasi-contract', 'restitution', or 'unjust enrichment'. The common feature of the cases falling into this category is that the defendant has received money or property that ought in justice to be made over to the plaintiff, or has benefited from the performance of some service that ought in justice to be paid for. Liability arises independently of wrongdoing on the defendant's part, so is distinct from liability in tort. It is independent of any promise or agreement, and so distinct from contract.

The history of this third category of obligations is divided into three phases. The first, the longest, lasted through the Middle Ages until around the middle of the eighteenth century. The second phase, effectively beginning with Lord Mansfield's judgment in *Moses* v. *Macferlan*[2] and the publication of Blackstone's *Commentaries*, lasted from the middle of the eighteenth century to the middle of the twentieth. The common feature of the Common-law remedies was half-recognized, but its nature was twisted and its growth stunted by treating it as an offshoot of contractual liability. The Chancery provided remedies in similar cases to those at law, but a parallel mis-classification in Equity led to their treatment as offshoots of the law of Trusts. The third phase, little more than a half-century old, was brought about by the demise of the implied-contract theory and its gradual replacement by a classification based on Unjust Enrichment, together with a belated attempt to unite legal and equitable remedies within a single theory.

Each of the two nodal points in this history—mid-eighteenth century and mid-twentieth—was accompanied by the injection of a theoretical perspective from outside English law. The first of these was the Roman law of quasi-contract, especially as it was interpreted by those contemporary continental scholars whose work was influential in England. The second was the American law of unjust enrichment or restitution, itself based on the more sophisticated appreciation of Roman law that had begun to take root in continental Europe. Neither of these was simply borrowed, planted in fertile ground cleared of the debris of centuries, but

---

[1] D.44.7.1.pr; above, p.6.   [2] (1760) 2 Burr 1005, 1 W Bl 219.

each provided a fresh abstract framework within which the earlier English law could be understood and developed.

It follows that the history of the third category is more convoluted than the history of contract or tort. Through the Middle Ages and the Early Modern period the latter two had a more or less coherent structure, even if it was largely buried beneath the forms of action. The third category did not. The conscious theorizations of tort and contract from the middle of the eighteenth century were based on models that had genuine explanatory force, the former on the Natural lawyers' analysis of the imputation of responsibility, the latter on the Will Theory.[3] At the same time the third category came to be based on a model superimposing implied contracts and implied trusts, which at its most optimistic could hope to do no more than provide common features linking together the specific instances of liability without ever pretending to provide any explanation why liability was imposed in these cases and not in others. Judicial practice was ineluctably ragged. Any attempt to reduce the case law before the late twentieth century to general principles, therefore, must be accompanied by a recognition that it will not fit neatly into clear-cut pigeon-holes and that apparent rules are riddled with exceptions. More than in any other area, scholarly writers, committed to generalization, have been driven to dismiss judicial pronouncements as simply wrong or not in accordance with true principles.[4]

UNJUST ENRICHMENT BEFORE LORD MANSFIELD

The first period in the history of unjust enrichment lasted until the second half of the eighteenth century. Although there are clear traces of remedies being given in situations that would later coalesce as unjust enrichment, there was no consciousness of any feature linking them to each other. In so far as they were distinct from contract and tort, they were no more than examples of the undifferentiated group of 'obligations arising from various other causes'.

The Medieval Background: Prehistory of a Category

Though the medieval English lawyers knew of no general principle of unjust enrichment, in a number of situations they did give remedies that would later be explicitly categorized in this way.[5] Apart from a small

---

[3] Above, pp.164–8, 221–36.

[4] e.g. W. D. Evans, *Essay on the Action for Money Had and Received* (Liverpool, 1802), 33–4, 45, 47–8, 56–7, 66–8, 91–9 (criticizing *Moses* v. *Macferlan*), 111–12. Evans's essay is conveniently reprinted in [1998] Restitution Law Review 1.

[5] Ibbetson, 'Unjust Enrichment in England before 1600', in Schrage (ed.), *Unjust Enrichment*, 121.

number of statutory writs dealing with very specific cases, the main vehicles for enforcing these claims were the common writs of debt and account. These remedies clustered around the clearly recognized categories of contract and property.

It was a basic prerequisite of contractual liability that the parties had legal capacity. Sometimes, however, an action of debt would lie when this condition was not satisfied. Thus an abbot would be liable on contracts made by a monk if, say, goods had been bought and had come to the use of the monastery;[6] sometimes the contractual dimension was strengthened by alleging something close to agency.[7] In the fifteenth century, it was laid down that an infant, though not normally liable on a contract, would be liable to pay the price of 'necessary' food, clothing, or education.[8] Sophisticated analysis would want to differentiate between liability for the price and liability for the value of the goods, but there is no hint of this before the end of the sixteenth century.[9] Sometimes a person who had discharged legal liability on behalf of another would be able to recover an indemnity or contribution, but the situations in which this occurred were very limited and invariably depended on the payment having been made at the request (or at least with the consent) of the defendant.[10]

Where a person without legal capacity purported to transfer property to another, it would be ineffective and the property could be reclaimed. It was more difficult where it was money that was handed over, since there was no earmarked thing that could be said still to belong to the transferor. None the less, an action—account, or possibly debt—was seemingly allowed to recover the money, based on the same principles as governed specific property.[11] Property ideas were similarly stretched where *A* passed money to *B* to hand on to *C*. In cases involving goods it was easy to identify *C* as the owner (treating *B* as a conduit between *A* and *C*),[12] but money was more problematic, since *C* would not wish to claim the actual coins from *B*. From about 1320 the writ of account was given to allow *C* to claim the

---

[6] YB T.22 Edw III f.8 pl.16. The same applied in the case of loans of money (YB T.7 Edw III f.35 pl.35) or goods (YB T.2 Hen IV f.21 pl.1; YB H.20 Hen VI f.21 pl.19).

[7] But this was not essential: YB 9 Edw II (45 SS) 138; YB 10 Edw II (52 SS) 102 (where the contract was entered into before the monk had entered religion).

[8] YB M.10 Hen VI f.14 pl.46; YB H.21 Hen VI f.31 pl.18; YB P.18 Edw IV f.1 pl.7.

[9] *Stone* v. *Withypole* (1588) 1 Leon 113, 114; J. H. Baker, 'The Use of Assumpsit for Restitutionary Money Claims', in Schrage (ed.), *Unjust Enrichment*, 31, 39.

[10] *Aubrey* v. *Donne* (1374) CP 40/453 m.305 (indemnity: issue taken on whether debt had been paid at defendant's request); *Gillyngham* v. *Watergate* (1380) CP 40/477 m.255d (right to contribution based on defendant's *assensus et voluntas* to expenditure).

[11] *Austen* v. *Gervas* (1615) Hob 77 (account). The lack of early reported cases is very suspicious; it is likely that others are concealed beneath fictitious actions based on alleged loans (e.g. *Thatcher* v. *Hurrell* (1374) CP 40/453 m.472d (debt)).

[12] YB 12 & 13 Edw III (RS) 245.

money from *B* in this situation.[13] Although never quite rationalized, this remedy seems to have been understood in quasi-proprietary terms, depending on a hazy property rationale.[14] *A*'s intention here was crucial, and the courts were exceedingly reluctant to allow any extension to cases where *B* had simply received money (or other property for that matter) that ought in justice to be transferred to *C*.

This proprietary reasoning was paralleled in the Chancery from the fifteenth century. Most obviously the concept of the trust exactly covered the situation where *A* transferred property to *B* for the benefit of *C*. Alongside this, by the middle of the century, the court had laid down the foundations of what would later be called the resulting trust. Where property was transferred by one person to another without its being expressly stated that the beneficial enjoyment was to pass, the transferee would be entitled to retain the property only if such an intention could be inferred from the circumstances—it was said that such an inference could arise, for example, where there was a relationship of natural love and affection between the parties; or where a gift was made to a husband and wife and their heirs, since it could hardly be supposed that the transferor would have enfeoffed a married woman to his own use; or if some value had been given in exchange for the property. If none of these conditions was satisfied, the property would be held to the use of the transferor.[15] This may in principle have been wide enough to embrace the obligation to reverse mistaken transfers, an obligation that came to be enforced by the action of account at Common law only in the last decade of the sixteenth century.[16]

More complex, but still probably conceived in essentially proprietary terms, was the situation where money or other property had been transferred for a purpose that had subsequently failed. Thus a gift given in contemplation of marriage could be recovered if the marriage did not take place,[17] and money transferred to one's factor to trade with could be

---

[13] *Le Taillour* v. *atte Medwe*, YB 14 Edw II (104 SS) 39 (cf. S. J. Stoljar, *Year Books 14 Edw II* (104 SS), pp.xi–xiv); YB P.41 Edw III f.10 pl.5. From the middle of the fifteenth century the action of debt could be used in this situation too: YB 36 Hen VI f.8 pl.5 at ff.9–10.

[14] S. J. Stoljar, 'The Transformations of Account' (1964) 80 LQR 203, 210–12.

[15] F Abr, *Sub Pena*, 23 (1452); Br Abr, *Feoffments al Uses*, 32 (1465) (though the point may be a mid-sixteenth-century interpolation); YB M.20 Hen VII f.10 pl.20. There is a thorough discussion of the subject in Gregory Adgore's Reading on Uses (*c.*1490) LI MS Mayn 3 ff.196–7. For the argument that resulting trusts arose from the presumed intention of the parties, though based on later and rather less secure evidence, see W. J. Swadling, 'A New Role for Resulting Trusts' (1996) 16 Legal Studies 110, 113–15.

[16] *Framson* v. *Delamere* (1595) Cro El 458, Moo 407.

[17] YB 20 & 21 Edw I (RS) 366; R. C. Palmer, 'Marriage in Medieval England: Evidence from the King's Courts circa 1300' (1984) 59 Speculum 42, 44–6. There was a special writ for the recovery of land in this situation, the writ of entry *causa matrimonii prelocuti*, whose proprietary nature was transparent.

reclaimed if it was not used for the intended purpose.[18] Money could be handed over under a contract subject to a condition that it be returned if the defendant's side of the agreement were not performed, or it might be expressed to be a condition in a contract for the sale of goods that the price be repaid if the goods were not of a specified quality,[19] and, even in the absence of a specific agreement where a contract had failed without either party's breach, any money paid under it could be recovered.[20] In the thirteenth century it was not at all uncommon for the same remedy to be given where the defendant was straightforwardly in breach of a contractual obligation.[21] Such actions occur particularly frequently in local courts; thus in the Fair Court of St Ives in 1288 a man who had paid 9d. to have his baldness cured recovered this sum from a barber who left the job unfinished, and in London as late as 1375 a plaintiff recovered 9s.2d. from a necromancer who had received that sum as the price of discovering the thief of certain stolen goods.[22] There may have developed a feeling that this type of case did not properly belong in the Common-law courts, for in the fourteenth century they disappeared. This did not mean that litigants were left remediless, for such claims are a sufficiently common feature of petitions in the fifteenth-century Chancery that we may be fairly confident that they were thought to have some chance of success.[23] This Chancery jurisdiction continued through the sixteenth century,[24] when it was gradually paralleled by a re-emergent Common-law jurisdiction; the King's Bench allowed an action of debt to recover back money paid out on a contract that had wholly failed in *Core* v. *May* in 1536,[25] though it was not until 1598 (in a lawsuit against England's most notorious torturer) that the Common Pleas finally accepted grudgingly that the action might lie.[26]

---

[18] YB P.42 Edw III f.9 pl.7 (debt).

[19] YB P.41 Edw III f.10 pl.5; *de Curtenay* v. *de Elilaund* (Eyre of London, 1276) in M. Weinbaum (ed.), *The London Eyre of 1276* (London Record Society, 12; London, 1976), 103.

[20] *Gaugy* v. *Garton* (Eyre of Yorkshire, 1279) JUST 1/1076 m.58d. Such actions are commoner in local courts than in the royal courts: e.g. *Turk* v. *de Wadencourt* (London Mayor's Court, 1302) *CPMR 1298–1307*, 123 (return of earnest money paid for goods, when goods not delivered as a result of contractually excepted risk).

[21] *Franssey's Case* YB 21 & 22 Edw I (RS) 598 (B&M, 227); *Tichfelde* v. *Trendel* (1292) CP 40/92 m.202.

[22] *de Eltisley* v. *le Barber* (1288) 23 SS 36; *Porter* v. *Chestre* (1375) *CPMR 1364–1381*, 188.

[23] e.g. *Bernard* v. *Tamworth* (c.1400) 10 SS 59 (uncompleted exchange of benefices); *Byflete* v. *Terry* (c.1435) C1/10/263 (money paid for land subsequently conveyed to third party); *Appilgarth* v. *Sergeantson* (1438) 1 Cal Chanc xli (money paid in contemplation of marriage); *Knight* v. *Seman* (c.1475) C1/59/86 (price paid for land that vendor had subsequently failed to deliver).

[24] e.g. *Banaster* v. *Mylward* (1547) C1/1105/6,7; *Anderton* v. *Johnson* (1595) C2/Eliz I/A5/27; *Blount* v. *Quaterman* (1595) C2/Eliz 1/B7/22; *Clopton* v. *Hardinge* (1600) C2/Eliz 1/C5/40.

[25] Dyer 20; 93 SS 132, 327. The situation is discussed in James Hales's Reading on Costs, BL MS Harg 92 ff.35ᵛ–36.   [26] *Earl of Lincoln* v. *Topcliffe* (1598) Cro El 644.

The Action of Assumpsit

The development of the action of assumpsit did not produce any immediate changes in the substance of these rules, though as a matter of form it came to supersede the older remedies of debt and account.[27] Hence one who had discharged another's legal liability might bring assumpsit to obtain an indemnity or a contribution, but only if the payment had genuinely been made at the request of the defendant. In the seventeenth century assumpsit came to be used in the other situations where debt and account had formerly been used: where *A* had given money to *B* for the benefit of *C*, where money had been paid by mistake or under a void contract, or where there had been a failure of consideration.[28] What was important, though, was that the situations in which a remedy lay at Common law were consolidated within a single form of action, an action whose core was commonly associated with contractual liability.

The capacity for assumpsit to slide almost imperceptibly beyond its contractual edges is best seen in the development of the *quantum meruit* count.[29] Here the plaintiff typically alleged that the defendant, in consideration of some service rendered to the plaintiff at his request, promised to pay to the plaintiff the reasonable value of that service. Sometimes, no doubt, there would have been an explicit agreement to this effect, but more commonly it was left to be deduced from the surrounding circumstances. If a man took cloth to a tailor to be made into a robe, for example, it was not difficult to infer from this that he was agreeing to pay for the work even though nothing was said to this effect and no price had been fixed.[30] The tailor's action here could legitimately be said to have been based on an 'implied' promise to pay, but there was no artificiality in classifying it as a mainstream contractual claim. Before the middle of the eighteenth century, *quantum meruit* claims were being allowed where the inference of a genuine agreement to pay a reasonable sum was far less secure. In *Keck's Case*[31] the plaintiff, for an agreed sum, had undertaken to build a house of certain dimensions for the defendant; the building was completed, but the plaintiff was unable to claim the contractual price, since the house did not fully

---

[27] Above, ch. 7.

[28] Baker, 'The Use of Assumpsit for Restitutionary Money Claims', in Schrage (ed.), *Unjust Enrichment*, 31, 41–2, 47–50. See *West* v. *West* (1613) Ro Abr, *Action sur Case*, Q1; *Gilbert* v. *Ruddeard* (1607) HLS MS 105 f.88, Dyer 272 in marg; *Beckingham and Lambert* v. *Vaughan* (1616) Moo 584, 1 Rolle 391 (B&M, 465); *Bonnell* v. *Fowke* (1657) 2 Sid 4; *Martin* v. *Sitwell* (1691) 1 Show KB 156, Holt KB 25 (B&M, 467); *Holmes* v. *Hall* (1704) 6 Mod 161.

[29] Baker, 'The Use of Assumpsit for Restitutionary Money Claims', in Schrage (ed.), *Unjust Enrichment*, 31, 35–41. Other counts in special assumpsit might follow the same model.

[30] *The Six Carpenters' Case* (1610) 8 Co Rep 146, 147, per Coke C.J.

[31] (1744), in Buller, *Introduction to the Law Relative to Trials at Nisi Prius* (1768), 196; J. L. Barton, 'Contract and Quantum Meruit: The Antecedents of Cutter v. Powell' (1987) 8 Jnl Leg Hist 48, 53–5.

match the contractual specifications. It would clearly have been unjust to have allowed the defendant to keep the house without paying anything, and the court allowed a *quantum meruit*, leaving it to the jury to take into account that he had not matched the agreed specifications in determining what a reasonable payment was. We have now crossed into fiction, though the line between this case and the case where a builder built a house without having agreed any price was a fine one. Though legal writers continued to speak of inferring agreements from the circumstances,[32] there was an awareness that *quantum meruit* actions might be different from ordinary contractual claims. Borrowing the language of Roman law, they were coming to be known as quasi-contractual,[33] a term that could be used indiscriminately to designate any situation in which an action of debt, account, or assumpsit was brought to enforce a non-contractual liability.[34] While from an analytical point of view the basis of liability in these cases was wholly distinct from contract, its characterization as 'quasi-contractual' was not completely inapt. As a matter of pleading the *quantum meruit* action was unequivocally contractual. Sometimes there had been an explicit agreement, sometimes an agreement inferable from the circumstances, sometimes an agreement erected by the law in order to reach a desired result. It was only when the lawyers treated the third of these as genuinely contractual, losing sight of the fact that the contract was a fictitious construct of their own making, that problems arose.[35]

The same slipperiness can be seen in the analogous situation where the plaintiff had incurred expenditure that would otherwise have had to be incurred by the defendant.[36] As a matter of form, this might be pleaded as indebitatus assumpsit (for money laid out at the request of the defendant), though as a matter of substance its only difference from *quantum meruit* was that the claim was for a fixed sum. Just as they had done with the *quantum meruit* action, early seventeenth-century lawyers analysed the situation in essentially contractual terms, plausibly inferring an agreement

---

[32] Baker, 'The Use of Assumpsit for Restitutionary Money Claims', in Schrage (ed.), *Unjust Enrichment*, 31, 38, citing Jeffrey Gilbert's treatise on contracts and Robert Chambers's Vinerian lectures of 1767.   [33] *Cock* v. *Vivian* (1734) W Kel 203, 205.

[34] Thus in *Hosdell* v. *Harris* (1669) 2 Keb 462, 536, 2 Wms Saund 64, 67, the language of quasi-contract was used to designate an action of debt to enforce an arbitration award, and, in *City of London* v. *Goray* (1676) 3 Keb 677, 684 (B&M 476), it described an action to enforce a fine. It was still used in this wide sense by Blackstone, and retained conservative adherents in England until the middle of the twentieth century (below, nn.145, 183). The language had earlier been used to cover situations not in themselves contractual but having some relation to a contract, notably where liability was transferred from a contracting party to another (e.g. *Mason* v. *Dixon* (1628) W Jones 173; J. Cowell, *Institutiones Iuris Anglicani* (1605) 3.28 (= 193–5)).   [35] Below, p.279.

[36] Baker, 'The Use of Assumpsit for Restitutionary Money Claims', in Schrage (ed.), *Unjust Enrichment*, 31, 41–5.

from the defendant's request or subsequent promise to pay,[37] but gradually the contractual veneer got thinner and thinner. In the second half of the eighteenth century Lord Mansfield introduced the principle that in some cases the action would be allowed where both the request and the promise were fictitious. Thus an action would lie for contribution from a co-surety whether or not there had been any request that the plaintiff should pay the guaranteed debt,[38] and more generally an indemnity could be claimed where one person had been forced to discharge another's legal liability.[39] There were even moves in the direction of allowing the action to be brought where the plaintiff had discharged another's moral responsibility, but this was associated with an ultimately unsuccessful attempt by Lord Mansfield to treat an antecedent moral duty as good consideration for an action of assumpsit[40] and in the event it came to be limited to the single case of the recovery of funeral expenses from the head of a family when a wife or child had died in his absence.[41]

The *quantum meruit* action and indebitatus assumpsit for money laid out essentially took over and expanded those situations that in medieval law had clustered around the central core of contractual liability. Alongside these, taking over and expanding those situations clustering around proprietary notions in the Middle Ages, was the action of indebitatus assumpsit for money had and received.[42] This action started to emerge at the beginning of the seventeenth century,[43] but it was in the eighteenth century that it really came into its own.[44] Its foundation was the allegation that the defendant had received a sum of money to the use of the plaintiff, which sum of money he had subsequently promised to pay. The promise to pay here was wholly fictitious, using the device originating in the sixteenth century to enable assumpsit to be used in place of some other form of action,[45] and there was no intelligible sense in which liability could have been said to be contractual at all. None the less, by

---

[37] *Anon* (1626) in W. Sheppard, *The Faithful Councellor: Or the Marrow of the Law in English* (1651) 1.13, quoted by Baker, 'The Use of Assumpsit for Restitutionary Money Claims', in Schrage (ed.), *Unjust Enrichment*, 31, 42; *Widdrington v. Goddard* (1664) B&M 472.

[38] *Decker v. Pope* (1757) Selw NP (1812 edn.), 1.71–2; L1 MS Misc 129 (unfol.).

[39] *Exall v. Partridge* (1799) 8 TR 308, 3 Esp 8.

[40] *Atkins v. Hill* (1775) 1 Cowp 284; *Trueman v. Fenton* (1777) 2 Cowp 554. Doubts were expressed in the notes to *Wennall v. Adney* (1802) 3 B & P 247, and the idea was firmly banished in *Eastwood v. Kenyon* (1840) 11 Ad & El 438.

[41] *Jenkins v. Tucker* (1788) 1 Hy Bl 90; *Ambrose v. Kerrison* (1851) 10 CB 776.

[42] *United Australia Ltd v. Barclays Bank Ltd* [1941] AC 1, 7, per Denning K.C., based on *Foster v. Stewart* (1814) 3 M & S 191, 200.

[43] *Beckingham and Lambert v. Vaughan* (1616) Moo 584, 1 Rolle 391 (B&M 465).

[44] Evans, *Essay on the Action for Money Had and Received*, 6–7.

[45] Above, p.138. It is sometimes said that the non-contractual use of assumpsit stemmed from the decision in *Slade's Case* (1602) 4 Co Rep 92, but examples of its use can be found earlier in the sixteenth century (e.g. *Ireland v. Higgins* (1588) Cro El 125, *Lord North's Case* (1588) 2 Leon 179).

the early years of the eighteenth century the courts had moved from the wholly accurate proposition that these actions were based on implied promises to the wholly inaccurate proposition that they were based on implied contracts.[46]

Unlike *quantum meruit* and the action for money laid out, the action for money had and received did not develop by moving very slowly outwards from a genuinely contractual core. Lord Mansfield, who professed himself a 'great friend to the action',[47] analogized it to a bill in equity that would lie when the defendant could not in conscience retain money that had come into his hands.[48] The most influential statement of his opinion was found in *Moses v. Macferlan*:[49]

If the defendant be under an obligation, from the ties of natural justice, to refund; the law implies a debt, and gives this action, founded in the equity of the plaintiff's case, as it were upon a contract ('quasi ex contractu' as the Roman law expresses it). This species of assumpsit ('for money had and received to the plaintiff's use,') lies in numberless instances, for money the defendant has received from a third person, which he claims title to, in opposition to the plaintiff's right; and which he had, by law, authority to receive from such third person.[50]

The gist of this kind of action is, that the defendant, upon the circumstances of the case, is obliged by the ties of natural justice and equity to refund the money.[51]

Despite his obvious attempt to generalize the basis of the action, Lord Mansfield himself later recognized the difficulty and danger of doing so.[52] While the reason for imposing liability might have been that the defendant ought equitably to hand over money to the plaintiff, there was a list—if not a closed list—of circumstances in which that liability arose. Around 1800 this list was articulated by William Evans:[53] money paid by mistake;

---

[46] *Jacob* v. *Allen* (1703) 1 Salk 27; *Cock* v. *Vivian* (1734) W Kel 203, 205.

[47] *Weston* v. *Downes* (1778) 1 Doug 23, 24; *Longchamp* v. *Kenny* (1778) 1 Doug 137.

[48] *Clarke* v. *Shee* (1774) 1 Cowp 197, 199, Lofft 756, 758.

[49] (1760) 2 Burr 1005, 1 W Bl 219.

[50] 2 Burr 1005, 1008–9. For the Roman-law context of Mansfield's judgment, see P. B. H. Birks, 'English and Roman Learning in *Moses* v. *Macferlan*' [1984] Current Legal Problems 1. It has been suggested (H. L. MacQueen and W. D. H. Sellar, 'Unjust Enrichment in Scots Law', in Schrage (ed.), *Unjust Enrichment*, 289, 314–16) that this might have been the result of Scots influence on Lord Mansfield, especially from Lord Kames' *Principles of Equity*. This is possible, though the evidence is not compelling. The treatment of the subject in the first edition (1760) of the *Principles of Equity* (pp.90–2) is unsophisticated (it is substantially altered in later editions); and Blackstone's report of *Moses* v. *Macferlan* suggests that the Roman learning may have been more the work of Wilmot J. than of Lord Mansfield, and that it was derived directly from the Digest and the Code. In addition, if there was any Scots influence, it may have been present in English law well before *Moses* v. *Macferlan*: below, nn.72, 76.   [51] 2 Burr 1005, 1012.

[52] e.g. *Weston* v. *Downes* (1778) 1 Doug 23. Contrast his earlier, more expansionist, approach in *Decker* v. *Pope* (1757) L1 MS Misc 129 (unfol.).

[53] *Essay on the Action for Money Had and Received*, 1.

money paid on a consideration that has (totally[54]) failed; money paid through imposition or extortion; and money paid on illegal contracts—to which should be added the simple situation of *A* paying money to *B* to hand on to *C* and the complex situation of waiver of tort.[55] In practice, it was through the elaboration of these categories that most of the later development of the law occurred.

More importantly at a classificatory level, Lord Mansfield's generalization in terms of natural justice and equity came just a few years too late. Already by this time William Blackstone was dealing with quasi-contract in his lectures at Oxford, including under his rubric of implied contracts the diverse range of situations in which debt, account, or assumpsit would lie despite the absence of any genuine contractual relationship: the payment of taxes; the performance of a judgment of an inferior or foreign court; *quantum meruit*; *quantum valebat*; money had and received; account stated; and some cases of mis-performance of office, as where a sheriff made a false return or a gaoler allowed a prisoner to escape.[56] The decision in *Moses* v. *Macferlan* was incorporated into this framework some time after 1760 (and thence into the published *Commentaries*), but only by way of elaboration of the subcategory of the action for money had and received.[57] It would take a century and a half to backtrack from this disastrous false step—though how many lecturers today rewrite their lectures from scratch to take account of some new development?—dropping the obligation to pay taxes and the like from the domain of implied contract and identifying the reversal of unjust enrichment as the single guiding principle behind what remained of the category of quasi-contract.[58]

The Courts of Equity

Covering much the same ground as the Common-law action for money had and received, by the eighteenth century the courts of Equity exercised a general jurisdiction to grant relief where it would be unjust for a recipient of property to retain it for himself.[59] Thus there was an equitable jurisdiction

---

[54] The requirement that the consideration must have failed totally was not fixed until *Hunt* v. *Silk* (1804) East 449 (cf. S. J. Stoljar, 'The Doctrine of Failure of Consideration' (1959) 75 LQR 53, 71–4); but it is strongly implicit in Evans's treatment of the subject: *Essay on the Action for Money Had and Received*, 25–34.

[55] On which see P. B. H. Birks, 'Restitution for Wrongs', in Schrage (ed.), *Unjust Enrichment*, 171, 182–6.

[56] University College London MS 210 f.105 (notes taken at the lectures in 1758).

[57] 3 Comm 162; Birks, 'English and Roman Learning in Moses v. Macferlan' [1984] Current Legal Problems 1, esp. 13–14. Interestingly, there is no allusion to the case in All Souls College Oxford MS 300, vol. 18 (unfoliated) (notes taken in 1761).

[58] And in America rather than in England: F. C. Woodward, *The Law of Quasi-Contracts* (below, n.136).

[59] This was the precise corollary of their general jurisdiction to rescind contracts: above, p.208.

to order the reconveyance of property conveyed by mistake, mirroring the Common law's jurisdiction;[60] there was an equitable jurisdiction to order the return of property obtained by fraud;[61] there was an equitable jurisdiction over property obtained by duress, extortion, or other forms of oppression.[62] In practice, the equitable jurisdiction was normally called into play in respect of land, but this was not the consequence of any formal limitation. *Colt* v. *Woollaston*, for example, involved a claim to money, a claim that could easily have been brought at Common law. The defendants had obtained a patent for the extraction of oil from radishes, and had sold shares to the value of £100,000 in a project to exploit this. The whole scheme was fraudulent. No radishes were sown, no oil extracted. The plaintiffs brought a bill in Chancery for the return of their investment. Despite an objection that they had a perfectly good remedy by the action for money had and received, the Master of the Rolls decreed for the return of the money together with interest and costs: in cases of fraud the Chancery had a concurrent jurisdiction with the courts of Common law.[63] Similarly, in *Attorney-General ex rel Ethery* v. *Hunton*[64] it was decreed that a Chief Constable who had received more than was due to him from local ratepayers should disgorge the overpayment; the legal action for money had and received would undoubtedly have lain, but it would have been inconvenient to have required a separate action by each ratepayer.

Secondly, harking back to the fifteenth century, there was the Chancery's category of resulting trusts.[65] These were imposed whenever one person purchased property with money provided by another, where property (including money) was conveyed without consideration, or more generally where a person had disposed of the legal interest without fully disposing of the equitable interest: the person holding the legal title would be treated as trustee for the transferor.[66] It was a commonplace that these resulting trusts arose by operation of law, but it was open to the transferee of the legal title to adduce evidence that the intention of the transferor had been to pass the full beneficial title, either for the benefit of the transferor absolutely or on trust for some third party.[67]

---

[60] *Pusey* v. *Desbouverie* (1734) 3 P Wms 216; *Bingham* v. *Bingham* (1748) 1 Ves Sen 126; *Evans* v. *Llewellyn* (1787) 2 Bro CC 150, 1 Cox CC 333.

[61] *Colt* v. *Woollaston* (1723) 2 P Wms 154; *Chesterfield* v. *Janssen* (1751) 2 Ves 125.

[62] *Clarkson* v. *Hanway* (1723) 2 P Wms 203; *Nicholls* v. *Nicholls* (1737) 1 Atk 409; *Evans* v. *Llewellyn* (1787) 2 Bro CC 150, 1 Cox CC 333. All of these cases could be categorized under the very broad equitable heading of fraud.

[63] (1723) 2 P Wms 154; see too *Sowerby* v. *Warder* (1791) 2 Cox CC 268.

[64] (1739) West t. Hardwicke 703.

[65] Above, n.15. The terminology was in common use by the end of the seventeenth century.

[66] *Pool* v. *Walton* (1592) BL MS Harl 1576 f.148 ('He that cometh in without consideration is to be bound by a trust'); *Kirk* v. *Webb* (1698) 2 Freeman 229; *Lloyd* v. *Spillet* (1740) 2 Atk 148.

[67] e.g. *Riddle* v. *Emerson* (1682) 1 Vern 348; *Gascoigne* v. *Thwing* (1685) 1 Vern 526; *Mumma* v. *Mumma* (1687) 2 Vern 19. This was particularly important after the Statute of Frauds 1677,

The third substantial head of Chancery jurisdiction overlapping with the action for money had and received was breach of confidence. This was of particular importance where the defendant was a trustee, attorney, or the like; here it was clear law that he could not retain any money that came to him in that capacity, but must hold it on trust for the beneficiary or client. This rule was firmly locked in place by the decision of Lord King L.C. in *Keech* v. *Sanford*.[68] The defendant held the lease of a market on trust for an infant. The lessor refused to renew the lease in favour of the infant, but would do so in favour of the trustee personally, and this was duly done. It was held that, even though there was no evidence of fraud on his part, he could not take the benefit of the transaction, but must hold the renewed lease on trust for the infant.

Finally, there was a jurisdiction in Equity to order the restoration of property where the purpose behind its transfer had failed, shadowing the Common-law action for money had and received based on failure of consideration. Hence a settlement of land made in consideration of an impending marriage would be treated as ineffective if the marriage did not take place, so that the recipient of the land would be required to return it and account for all the profits received from it;[69] a master who dismissed an apprentice before the completion of the term would be required to return part of the premium;[70] a man who gave substantial gifts to a woman in the reasonable hope that she might marry him could recover them (or their value) should the woman subsequently 'deceive' him.[71] Analogously, if money or other property was given to a person for one purpose but used for a different purpose, Equity had a jurisdiction to decree the return of its value.[72]

There was a strong temptation to analyse the claims in these situations as based on trusts. This was the characteristic device used by the Chancery to give effect to rights, and already in the 1670s it had been recognized that there was a class, known as 'constructive trusts', that arose by operation of

since the normal requirement of writing to give effect to a trust applied neither to the imposition of resulting trusts nor to their rebuttal. The older view, that the resulting trust arose to give effect to the presumed intention of the parties, is no longer reflected in the cases (cf. R. Chambers, *Resulting Trusts* (Oxford, 1996), 33–5).

[68] (1726) Sel Cas t. King 61.   [69] *Hamond* v. *Hicks* (1686) 1 Vern 432.

[70] *Therman* v. *Abell* (1688) 2 Vern 64; similarly *Newton* v. *Rowse* (1684) 1 Vern 460 (master died shortly after beginning of term). The principle behind these cases was strongly criticized by the end of the eighteenth century: Evans, *Essay on the Action for Money Had and Received*, 33–4 (below, n.94).

[71] *Robinson* v. *Cumming* (1742) 2 Atk 409. It would be different if the man was an 'adventurer', for then the risk of rejection would be on him.

[72] *Sturt* v. *Mellish* (1743) 2 Atk 610 (decree not awarded); *Gage* v. *Bulkeley* (1745) Ridg t. Hardwicke 278. Cf. *Attorney-General* v. *Stevens* (1737) West t. Hardwicke 50, 1 Atk 358 (decree not awarded), explicitly drawing the analogy with Scots law's action based on the Roman *conditio causa data causa non secuta*.

law rather than by the will of the parties.[73] It did not follow that they had all the qualities of express trusts, though: when, for example, plaintiffs argued that their claims did not fall within the Statute of Limitations (which, though not strictly applicable, was applied by analogy in Equity to cases other than actions for breach of trust), they were invariably given short shrift by the courts.[74] It was only when the analogy was pushed too strongly and the interest of the claimant analysed in the proprietary terms appropriate to express trusts that it became possible to draw a substantive wedge between the nature of equitable relief and relief at Common law.

IMPLIED TRUSTS AND IMPLIED CONTRACTS

Beginning in the mid-eighteenth century, and increasingly rapidly in the nineteenth century, the law of torts and the law of contract were each structured around a theoretical framework, the former around the Natural lawyers' theory of imputation and the latter around the Will Theory. whatever the merits and demerits of these, they did provide an abstract general framework for contract and tort that both held them together and provided some sort of moral justification for them. By contrast, the third category, despite the foundations laid down by Lord Mansfield and others in the later eighteenth century, got lost in an orgy of fictions. Instead of seeking to identify an abstract basis for liability, the Common lawyers talked about implied promises, implied requests, and implied contracts. It would perhaps be too harsh on Lord Mansfield's successors to blame them entirely for this. The continental sources that had furnished their conceptual frameworks of contract and tort were themselves deficient when it came to the third category, increasingly toying with the language of the implied contract.[75] The trap had been avoided by Scots law, which had several times been cited as a model in English cases in the eighteenth century,[76] and by Grotius; but Pufendorf brought it all too close to the surface. Pothier, whose influence on the law of contract was so powerful,

[73] *Cook* v. *Fountain* (1676) 3 Swanst 585, 591 ('implied trusts' arising by 'construction of law'); *Grey* v. *Grey* (1677) 2 Swanst 594, 597 ('constructive trusts'). See D. E. C. Yale, *Lord Nottingham's Chancery Cases, ii* (79 SS), *101–12*.
[74] *Llewellyn* v. *Mackworth* (1740) Barn 445; *Sturt* v. *Mellish* (1743) 2 Atk 610; *Gage* v. *Bulkeley* (1745) Ridg t. Hardwicke 278; *Townshend* v. *Townshend* (1781) 1 Bro CC 550. But cf. *Hamond* v. *Hicks* (1686) 1 Vern 432.
[75] P. Birks and G. McLeod, 'The Implied Contract Theory of Quasi-Contract: Civilian Opinion Current in the Century before Blackstone' (1986) 6 Ox Jnl Leg Stud 46.
[76] *King* v. *Withers* (1735) Cas t. Talbot 117, 122; *Attorney-General* v. *Stevens* (1737) West t. Hardwicke 50, 53, 1 Atk 358, 360; *Langley* v. *Brown* (1741) 2 Atk 195, 202. For the Scots law, see MacQueen and Sellar, 'Unjust Enrichment in Scots Law', in Schrage (ed.), *Unjust Enrichment*, 289.

railed against it;[77] but his principal discussions were not translated into English and the brief remarks in the *Traité des obligations* were accompanied by a note by his translator minimizing their relevance to English law.[78] And, just as the Common lawyers gravitated to the language of implied contracts, the Court of Chancery locked itself in the language of implied trusts. Apart from concealing any common threads that there might have been in Common law and Equity, this effectively prevented any principled development of the third category of obligations.

Quasi-Contracts and Implied Contracts

By the beginning of the nineteenth century the Common-law analysis in terms of implied contracts was clear orthodoxy:

We have no term in the English law strictly corresponding with that of quasi contracts in the civil law: many of the cases falling within the definition of that term, may be ranked under the denomination of implied contracts, but that denomination is applicable rather to the evidence than to the nature or quality of the obligation, as in judgment of law an actual promise is deemed to have taken place, and the consequences are the same as if such promise had been declared by the most express and positive language.[79]

Throughout the century judges and legal writers continued to reproduce statements of the same sort, though commonly revealing a degree of schizophrenia as to how far liability was genuinely contractual. Leake, for example, followed dicta of Maule J. in *Lewis* v. *Campbell*[80] to the effect that liability arose from the existence of some pecuniary inequality between the parties that the law recognized as requiring compensation on equitable principles, but at the same time fitted it into a framework of implied requests, implied promises, and implied contracts redolent of the judgment of Wilde C.J. in the same case.[81] Even the clearest-minded of the commentators at the end of the nineteenth century, Anson and Pollock, give space to the subject in their books on contract at the same time as stressing that the liability was not in fact contractual at all.[82] This schizophrenia reached its high point in Oxford in the early 1930s, where the annual course of

---

[77] *Du Quasi-contrat appelé Promutuum; et de l'Action Condictio Indebiti* (known as the *Traité de l'Action Condictio Indebiti*), in *Traités des contrats de bienfaisance* (1766), 1.283–332; *Traité des obligations* 1.2, §114. See too his *Du Quasi-Contrat Negotiorum Gestorum*, in *Traités des contrats de bienfaisance*, 2.334–402.   [78] *Traité des obligations* (trans. Evans), 69.
[79] Evans, *A Treatise on the Law of Obligations or Contracts, by M. Pothier*, 1.69 n.
[80] (1842) 8 CB 541, 545. Other cases adopting analyses without reference to implied contracts are *Pownal* v. *Ferrand* (1827) 6 B & C 439, per Lord Tenderden C.J.; *Kelly* v. *Solari* (1841) 9 M & W 54.   [81] Leake, *The Elements of the Law of Contracts*, 38–9.
[82] Pollock, *Principles of Contract at Law and in Equity*, 28–30; Anson, *Principles of the English Law of Contract*, 321–7.

lectures on quasi-contract was given by P. A. Landon, who proclaimed with passionate fervour that the subject did not exist.[83]

The implied contract analysis was indubitably inelegant. Nowhere was its ugliness more mercilessly exposed than in actions for contribution between co-sureties. That a surety who paid a debt in full could claim contribution from co-sureties was clear by the middle of the eighteenth century. In *Deering* v. *Earl of Winchelsea* this was explained as being based on 'fixed principles of justice' rather than on any form of contract,[84] but by the middle of the nineteenth century the courts had shifted to the terminology of implied contracts.[85] The rule at Common law was that each contributing surety was severally liable for his own aliquot share, so that if there were originally, say, six sureties each would be liable for one-sixth of the debt; by contrast the courts of Equity calculated the shares by reference to the number of solvent sureties remaining when contribution was sought.[86] It was no mean feat to formulate this rule in terms of implied contract. Since liability was several rather than joint (which would have been the normal contractual rule), it was necessary to imply individual contracts between each pair of co-sureties. Hence in *Batard* v. *Hawes*,[87] where there were twelve original co-contractors, it followed that there might have been sixty-six implied contracts of contribution between the parties. Since they were separate contracts, they could be made the subject of separate lawsuits—*Batard* v. *Hawes* itself originated as four distinct actions—which did not have to be heard together, with the result that there was a severe risk of inconsistent decisions if there was any doubt about how many co-sureties there were. And why should it be assumed that the parties had impliedly chosen to contract on the basis of the Common-law rule rather than the rule of Equity? The English judges were unconcerned by these problems, though outsiders were not slow to point out the absurd inconveniences that they entailed.[88]

If the point was simply one of elegance of classification, it would perhaps not have mattered unduly. But it was not: all too frequently substantive consequences flowed from it.

Some of these consequences were procedural. It was necessary, for example, to determine the proper limitation period within which actions

---

[83] See his review of Winfield's *Province of the Law of Tort* in (1931) 8 Bell Yard 19, together with the comments of W. T. S. Stallybrass, (1932) 10 Bell Yard 18, 23.

[84] (1787) 2 B & P 270, 272, per Eyre C.B. To the same effect are *Craythorne* v. *Swinburne* (1807) 14 Ves 160, 164, *Stirling* v. *Forrester* (1821) 3 Bligh 575, 590, and *Browne* v. *Lee* (1827) 6 B & C 689.

[85] *Kemp* v. *Finden* (1844) 12 M & W 421; *Batard* v. *Hawes* (1853) 2 El & Bl 287.

[86] *Cowell* v. *Edwards* (1800) 2 B & P 268; *Browne* v. *Lee* (1827) 6 B & C 689. After 1873 the equitable rule was made generally applicable: Judicature Act, s.25(11).

[87] (1853) 2 El & Bl 287.

[88] *Rambux Chittangeo* v. *Modhoosoodun Paul Chawdhry* (1867) 7 WR (India) 377.

had to be brought. The Statute of Limitations of 1623 had introduced a six-year period for, *inter alia*, 'actions of debt based upon any lending or contract without specialty', and by the end of the nineteenth century it was held that this might apply to a quasi-contractual action.[89] Hence an action for a penalty imposed by a chartered corporation on one of its members was brought within the Statute, backed up by the spurious justification that the member had consented to become a member of the corporation,[90] as was a claim by local justices to recoup overpaid charges.[91]

Equally 'contractual' was the courts' approach to the subsidiary nature of quasi-contract.[92] It was a clear—and wholly sensible—rule that a party to an express contract could not simply discard it and sue on an implied contract:[93] a man who agreed to build a house for £100 could not bring a *quantum meruit* simply because he thought his labour had been worth more than that, any more than he could bring an action for £200. It was only a short step from this to the proposition that, so long as an express contract remained on foot, it was not open to a party to it to bring a *quantum meruit* or an action for money had and received.[94] What this meant in practice was that, once a contract was in place, a party could not bring a quasi-contractual action until the first contract was rescinded, either because of the operation of some term within it, because of duress or some similar vitiating factor, or because of the other party's breach: where a contract simply stalled, no action would lie for the value of any services that had already been performed. Hence in *Cutter* v. *Powell*,[95] it was held that, where a sailor who had been contracted to serve for a whole voyage died in the course of it, no action would lie for unpaid wages for the period for which he had worked. Similarly in *Appleby* v. *Myers*,[96] where a contract to erect machinery was prematurely terminated because of the accidental destruction of the premises on which the machinery was to be built, the Exchequer Chamber held that the builders could have no claim for the value of the work that they had already done.

The relationship between this rule and the operation of the Statute of

[89] Cf. the position in the seventeenth century, where these actions were explicitly treated as non-contractual: *Hosdell* v. *Harris* (1669) 2 Keb 462, 536, 2 Wms Saund 64; *Cockram* v. *Welby* (1677) 1 Mod 245, 2 Mod 212.
[90] *Tobacco Pipe Makers Co* v. *Loder* (1851) 16 QB 765. So far as the court was concerned, the choice was between saying that liability was based on a contract or that it was based on a specialty. Cf. *Cork and Bandon Railway Company* v. *Goode* (1853) 13 CB 826, where it was held that a statutory penalty was a debt due on a specialty.
[91] *Mayor of Salford* v. *Lancashire County Council* (1890) 25 QBD 384.
[92] Below, n.184.
[93] *Duncomb* v. *Tickridge* (1648) Aleyn 94; *Jacob* v. *Allen* (1703) 1 Salk 27 (principle inapplicable on facts); *Weaver* v. *Boroughs* (1725) 1 Str 648. Barton, 'Contract and Quantum Meruit: The Antecedents of Cutter v. Powell' (1987) 8 Jnl Leg Hist 48, 54–5.
[94] *Power* v. *Wells* (1778) 2 Cowp 818; *Weston* v. *Downes* (1778) 1 Doug 25.
[95] (1795) 6 TR 320.   [96] (1867) LR 2 CP 651.

Frauds reveals the courts' schizophrenia. Where a contract had been terminated, or was void or unenforceable from the start, there was no objection to the use of a *quantum meruit* claim. If this claim was indeed contractual, then it should have been subject to the requirement of writing imposed by the Statute on contracts for the sale of interests in land, sales of goods for more than £10, and contracts that were not to be completed within one year.[97] 'Interests in land' was wide enough to embrace crops that had not been severed from the soil; yet in *Earl of Falmouth* v. *Thomas*[98] it was said that, although such an express contract of sale would fall within the Statute and be unenforceable, if the buyer had actually taken the crops it was only right that he should be forced to pay for them. So too, where a man had worked under an oral agreement for three years, it was held that he could not sue on the contract but that he might bring a *quantum meruit* on the implied contract and produce the oral agreement as evidence of what a reasonable wage would have been.[99]

Sometimes the schizophrenia was visible in the way that different judges adopted different analyses of similar situations. It was, for example, a question whether a quasi-contractual action could be brought against a defendant who did not have contractual capacity. If the claim was indeed genuinely contractual, then no action should lie either to recover back money paid or to obtain the reasonable value of services provided. It was held in 1849 that no *quantum meruit* action would lie against a corporation that had no power to enter into an oral contract;[100] but in 1862 an action was allowed to recover back money that had been lent to a corporation acting *ultra vires*;[101] in 1899 it was said that such a loan could be recovered so long as the money had not been spent;[102] and finally in 1914 the House of Lords, treating the action as contractual, held that money so paid could not be recovered.[103] A contractual analysis was applied when the defendant was a minor: where one had sold non-necessary goods to an infant, the vendor would have neither a contractual action for the price nor an action for the value of the goods,[104] and on the

---

[97] Statute of Frauds 1677, s.4, s.17.

[98] (1832) 1 Cr & M 89; cf. *Mayfield* v. *Wadsley* (1824) 3 B & C 357. Later dicta, perhaps, hint that this was not because the claim was non-contractual, but because it was possible to imply a contract for the sale of the crops after severance, by which time they would no longer be classifiable as interests in land: *Harman* v. *Reeve* (1856) 18 CB 587.

[99] *Scarisbrick* v. *Parkinson* (1869) 20 LT 175.

[100] *Lamprell* v. *Billericay Union* (1849) 3 Ex 283, 306.

[101] *re Phoenix Life Assurance Company* (1862) 2 J & H 441, 448 (though it is possible that it was only the purpose for which it was received, not the receipt of the money itself, that was *ultra vires*).

[102] *re Wrexham, Mold and Connah's Quay Railway Co* [1899] 1 Ch 440, 456–7.

[103] *Sinclair* v. *Brougham* [1914] AC 398. A parallel claim for equitable relief did succeed, however.

[104] *Re Jones* (1881) 18 Ch D 109, 120; *Cowern* v. *Nield* [1912] 2 KB 419. The rule that the infant was liable to pay only the reasonable value of necessaries sold (and not the contract price) was enshrined in the Sale of Goods Act 1893, s.2.

same principle it came to be held that no action would lie to recover money lent.[105] Where necessary goods or services were supplied to a lunatic, Mellish L.J. was happy to allow a *quantum meruit* on an implied contract at the same time as accepting that the lunatic's lack of capacity would have prevented an action being brought on the express contract;[106] ten years later this was denied by Jessel M.R., though the point was left open;[107] but Kay J. and the Court of Appeal subsequently took the opposite point of view and held that there would be liability.[108]

Implied, Resulting, and Constructive Trusts

It is hard to avoid the conclusion that the judges had little clear idea what they were doing. Common law, undoubtedly, was in a mess. So too was Equity. At the beginning of the nineteenth century there was reason to believe that the Court of Chancery would develop a jurisdiction over-lapping significantly with that at Common law, if it had not done so already.[109] These claims were coming to be accommodated within the language of trusts: all equitable claims relating to property, other than those based on express trusts, could be brought together under the blanket heading of constructive trusts.[110] This was expanded into a principle of general application by James Hill in his *Law of Trustees* in 1845, using language strongly reminiscent of that of Lord Mansfield in *Moses* v. *Macferlan*:

Wherever the circumstances of a transaction are such, that the person, who takes the legal estate in property, cannot also enjoy the beneficial interest, without necessarily violating some established principle of equity; the court will immedi-ately raise a constructive trust, and fasten it upon the conscience of the legal owner, so as to convert him into a trustee for the parties, who in equity are entitled to the beneficial enjoyment.[111]

In contrast with this, other writers adopted rather different terminology. In the standard work on trusts by Thomas Lewin, the constructive trust was limited to situations where an express trust was extended by operation of law either to property not originally forming part of the trust or to a

---

[105] *R Leslie Ltd* v. *Sheill* [1914] 3 KB 607.
[106] *re Gibson* (1871) LR 7 Ch App 52, 53–4.   [107] *re Weaver* (1881) 21 Ch D 615, 619.
[108] *re Rhodes* (1890) 44 Ch D 94.   [109] Above, p.273.
[110] e.g. *Beckford* v. *Wade* (1805) 17 Ves Jun 87, 96, per Grant M.R.
[111] J. Hill, *Practical Treatise on the Law Relating to Trustees* (1845), 116. See too A. Underhill, *Concise Manual of the Law Relating to Private Trusts and Trustees* (1878), 79 n.(a): 'It would be a quite endless task to enumerate every kind of constructive trust, for they are, as has been said, coterminous with equity jurisprudence.' It is noteworthy that this formulation survived into the twelfth edition of the work (1970).

person not originally constituted trustee.[112] These were to all intents and purposes the circumstances in which a person holding property for another would be treated as an express trustee for the purposes of the operation of the Statutes of Limitations and the rules of equity derived from them.[113] At the risk of terminological extravagance, perhaps, they might more accurately have been called 'constructive express trusts'.[114] Though the broad terminology of the constructive trust continued to be used,[115] it was gradually supplanted by the narrower usage popularized by Lewin, and by the end of the nineteenth century it had substantially disappeared.[116] With such a narrow scope given to the 'constructive trust', other Equitable remedies existed in a more fragmentary form. Where the legal interest in property had been transferred to another without fully specifying what was to happen to the beneficial interest, or where one person had provided all or part of the purchase price of property bought in the name of another, a 'resulting trust' might arise, and it did not matter a great deal whether or not this was treated as a subspecies of the constructive trust.[117] Other situations

---

[112] T. Lewin, *Practical Treatise on the Law of Trusts* (1837), 201–24. Later editions adopt slightly different terminology, but without affecting the substance of the analysis. George Spence, in his magisterial and near-authoritative *Equitable Jurisdiction of the Court of Chancery* (1846), 1.511–12, alluded to the wide ambit afforded by Hill to the constructive trust but restricted his own discussion to the range of situations treated by Lewin.

[113] *Soar* v. *Ashwell* [1893] 2 QB 390. The general practice of the Chancery, subject to a discretion to act differently if justice so demanded, was to treat equitable claims as subject to the same rules as would have applied to the equivalent claim at Common law; except that there was no strict limitation period in cases of actual fraud or where the beneficiary of an express trust sued a trustee. This was put on a statutory footing by s.25 of the Real Property Limitation Act 1833 (land) and s.25(2) of the Judicature Act 1873 (other property). See generally G. N. Darby and F. A. Bosanquet, *Practical Treatise on the Statutes of Limitations* (1867), 172–200; R. A. Brunyate, *Limitation of Action in Equity* (London, 1932), 50–112. The relevance of the rules relating to limitation periods is hinted at by G. H. Jones, 'The Role of Equity in the English Law of Restitution', in Schrage (ed.), *Unjust Enrichment*, 149, 153; a markedly high proportion of the nineteenth-century cases discussing constructive trusts revolve round these rules.

[114] Similarly, in late-twentieth-century England, the 'constructive trust' is narrowly interpreted as arising from the inferred intention of the parties: *Gissing* v. *Gissing* [1971] AC 886.

[115] e.g. *Petre* v. *Petre* (1853) 1 Drewry 371; *Soar* v. *Ashwell* [1893] 2 QB 390, 393, 396, 400. But cf. *McCormick* v. *Grogan* (1869) LR 4 HL 82, 97, per Lord Westbury (person taking property by fraud converted by equity into trustee for the person injured by the fraud) with the same judge's remarks in *Phillips* v. *Phillips* (1861) 4 De G F & J 208, 218 (property held under conveyance liable to be set aside for fraud said to be subject to an equity rather than an equitable estate, and so not binding on subsequent purchaser for value without notice of the interest). For the nineteenth-century development, see D. Waters, *The Constructive Trust* (London, 1964), 7–73.

[116] 'Constructive Trusts' (1894) 38 Sol Jnl 212; F. W. Maitland, *Lectures on Equity* (Cambridge, 1910), 82–5. The only situation generally referred to as a constructive trust that fell outside this classification was the estate contract (where there had been a sale of land but no effective conveyance to the purchaser); the precise nature of this relationship was highly controversial thoughout the nineteenth century: Waters, *The Constructive Trust*, 74–143.

[117] Lewin, *Practical Treatise on the Law of Trusts*, 168–201. On the terminological difficulty see Chambers, *Resulting Trusts*, 2–5.

fell outside the language of trusts, though without generating significantly different substantive results. Hence an action to recover land from a fraudulent purchaser might not be described as based on any form of trust, but the vendor's rights were none the less substantially identical to those of a beneficiary against a trustee: rescission of the contract would lead not merely to the recovery of the land plus an account of profits actually received, but also an account of profits that would have been received were it not for the purchaser's wilful default.[118] Sometimes, however, the courts might have reached different substantive results from those that would have stemmed from a trust-based analysis. Thus a person who had freely accepted the benefit of improvements to his or her property done by another might be estopped from taking the benefit without compensation, but the precise status of the rights might not have been wholly clear.[119] The unpaid vendor of land could claim an equitable lien on the land for the amount owing, but could not claim the return of the land;[120] by contrast, where land was conveyed for a purpose that did not eventuate, the transferor could (probably) reclaim the land itself.[121]

The difference between Lewin's approach and that of Hill was threefold. Most obvious was the terminological difference: the 'constructive trust' had a far greater role to play for Hill than it did for Lewin. Secondly, and more importantly, whereas Hill's formulation was expressed in terms of a general principle, Lewin's could not be. Thirdly, whereas it was a clear corollary of Hill's analysis that the plaintiff had a proprietary claim and not merely a personal one, for Lewin this was not in the least clear: the resulting trust was clearly proprietary in its effects (so that the plaintiff was entitled to any increase in the value of the property claimed, for example), but there was room for debate about the proper analysis of the other equitable claims. Given that the situations in which remedies were given remained isolated from each other, this was not a debate that had to take place. Moreover, the fragmentation of the remedies meant that any common underpinnings linking together the situations in which a remedy was granted remained hidden. Whereas American lawyers at the start of the twentieth century, brought up on the broad principles of Joseph Story's *Equitable Jurisprudence* rather than Lewin's *Law of Trusts*, were able to manipulate the constructive trust into a remedial device to reverse unjust

---

[118] *Murray* v. *Palmer* (1805) 2 Sch & Lef 474; *Edwards* v. *M'leay* (1818) 2 Swanst 287; *Gibson* v. *D'Este* (1843) 2 Y & C 542, 580.
[119] *Dillwyn* v. *Llewellyn* (1862) 4 De G F & J 517; *Ramsden* v. *Dyson* (1868) LR 1 HL 129. It is still controversial today: R. J. Smith, 'How Proprietary is Proprietary Estoppel?', in F. D. Rose (ed.), *Consensus ad Idem* (London, 1996), 235 and the references there cited.
[120] *Chapman* v. *Tanner* (1684) 1 Vern 267; *Mackreth* v. *Symmons* (1808) 15 Ves Jun 329; *Winter* v. *Lord Anson* (1827) 3 Russ 488; *Nives* v. *Nives* (1880) 15 Ch D 649.
[121] Though not so held explicitly until *re Ames' Settlement* [1946] Ch 217.

enrichment,[122] contemporary English lawyers were straitjacketed by the nineteenth-century break-up of equitable remedies and left with the constructive trust as a tightly bounded proprietary institution treated as an express trust in all but name.

QUASI-CONTRACT, RESTITUTION, AND UNJUST ENRICHMENT

The first, faltering steps away from the implied contract theory were taken—in India—in the 1860s. In *Rambux Chittangeo* v. *Modhoosoodun Paul Chawdhry*[123] it was held, with references to Pothier and Austin's *Jurisprudence*, that a claim for contribution from a co-surety was not a contractual claim, that the use of the language of implied contracts was something forced on the Common law by the purely fortuitous fact that the remedy was framed in assumpsit, and that a system like the Indian that was not dependent on the forms of action could profitably abandon all talk of implied contracts. The Indian Contract Act of 1872 followed this line: under the heading 'Of Certain Relations Resembling those Created by Contract' it included claims for necessaries supplied to those without contractual capacity, claims for indemnity or contribution, claims to be paid for the value of beneficial services provided without the intention of making a gift, claims against the finder of goods, and claims for the reimbursement of money paid by mistake.[124] It is tempting to see in this the hand of Sir Henry Maine, the legal member of the Governor's Council in India at the time of the Law Commission's Contract Report, for already in 1861 he had included in his *Ancient Law* an attack on the idea that quasi-contract was anything to do with contract:

It has been usual with English critics to identify the Quasi-Contracts with *implied* contracts, but this is an error, for implied contracts are true contracts, which quasi-contracts are not. In implied contracts, act and circumstances are the symbols of the same ingredients which are symbolised, in express contracts, by words; and whether a man employs one set of symbols or the other must be a matter of indifference so far as concerns the theory of agreement. But a Quasi-Contract is not a contract at all.[125]

'This gets rid of the English fiction of an implied contract and promise to pay',[126] was the unequivocal comment of Maine's pupil Whitley Stokes in

---

[122] R. Pound, 'The Progress of the Law—Equity' (1920) 33 Harv L R 420; A. Scott, *The Law of Trusts* (Boston,1939), 2307–602.   [123] (1867) 7 WR (India) 377.
[124] Indian Contract Act 1872, ss.68–72. The draft bill of the Indian Law Commission also included its provisions on misrepresentation under this heading: PP HC 1867/8 xlix 622, 665.
[125] *Ancient Law* (1861), 343–4. He continues by drawing attention to the close link between implied-contract thinking in private law and in political theory.
[126] W. Stokes, *The Anglo-Indian Codes* (Oxford, 1887), 1.586 n.7; *Badr-un-Nisa* v. *Muhammad Jan* (1880) 2 All 669, 674 per Straight and Spankie JJ.

his commentary on this part of the Contract Act. None the less, other lawyers were more wedded to the English forms. Markby J. (whose extra-judicial *Elements of Law* steadfastly ignored the problem[127]), for example, talked of the practice of joining a count on an implied contract to cover the possibility that evidentiary difficulties might prevent recovery on an express contract.[128] Within a decade of the passing of the Act it was held that the co-surety's claim for contribution was in fact a contractual claim after all: the earlier cases discussing its contractual nature, it was said, were delivered before the passage of the Act, 'when legislation had not stepped in with plain language to give distinct vitality and effect to certain relations between parties out of whose moral obligations one to another a legal fiction had grown up for implying a contract, and while, as learned expositions of law, they may be read with interest and advantage, for practical purposes to the point under consideration they are obsolete and irrelevant'.[129] No claim for an indemnity would lie at the suit of a person who had paid another's liability without being interested in the payment (the language used by the Act), hence 'the fiction of an implied request . . . cannot properly be imported into the case'.[130]

The seeds of clear analysis may have fallen on parched ground in India, but their shoots did not all wither away. Maine's influence transplanted the idea into more fertile transatlantic soil. From the middle of the nineteenth century courts in America had been moving away from the implied-contract theory of liability,[131] and in 1893 William Keener brought out the first substantial treatise on quasi-contract as an independent subject, with Maine's brief analysis at its theoretical heart;[132] within weeks it was being cited in the American courts.[133] Keener's structure still owed something to Blackstone's, in that the common feature of quasi-contract was that a contractual remedy was used although liability was non-contractual. It had three species: the obligation to perform a legal judgment; the obligation to perform a duty imposed by statute, custom, or office; and,

---

[127] There is the briefest of references to it in the first edition (1871), s.186, but even this was soon to disappear.

[128] *Oomabutty Debia* v. *Pureshnath Pandey* (1869) 12 WR (India) 521.

[129] *Nath Prassad* v. *Baij Nath* (1880) 3 All 66, 71, per Straight J.; approved in *Krishno Kamini Chowdhrani* v. *Gopi Molun Ghose Hazra* (1888) 15 Cal 652.

[130] *Chedi Lal* v. *Bhagwan Das* (1888) 11 All 234, 242.

[131] *Hertzog* v. *Hertzog* (1857) 29 Pa 465; *Bixby* v. *Moor* (1871) 51 NH 402; *Sceva* v. *True* (1873) 53 NH 627 (note the reference to Maine at 633); *Woods* v. *Ayres* (1878) 39 Mich 345.

[132] W. Keener, *Treatise on the Law of Quasi-Contracts* (New York, 1893). The quotation from Maine is at p.6. The first chapter (on the theoretical basis of liability) appeared separately as 'Quasi-Contract, its Nature and Scope' (1893) 7 Harv L R 57. Behind Keener's work was James Barr Ames: below, n.137.

[133] *Robinson* v. *Turrentine* (1894) 59 F. 554, 558–9 (North Carolina Circuit Court); *Merriam* v. *United States* (1894) 29 Ct Cl 250, 252 (Court of Claims). See too *Ingram* v. *United States* (1897) 32 Ct Cl 147, 149–50 (Court of Claims), where Keener's analysis was the catalyst for an argument based on Pothier and on contemporary commentaries on Gaius' *Institutes*.

most importantly, obligations arising out of 'unjust enrichment'.[134] Once mentioned, though, the first two categories were ignored; the rest of his book was concerned with the subspecies of liability based on unjust enrichment.[135] By the time that the next treatise on quasi-contract came to be published—by Frederic Campbell Woodward in 1913—the first two categories had been silently dropped: the American law of quasi-contract had finally become co-extensive with the law of unjust enrichment.[136]

The source of this language is easy to discern. Keener's category of obligations based on unjust enrichment is explicitly derived from James Barr Ames's 'fundamental principle of justice that no one ought unjustly to enrich himself at the expense of another'.[137] This in its turn is to all intents and purposes a direct translation of a text of the Roman jurist Pomponius,[138] perhaps (though not necessarily) transmitted via the works of Pothier. The precise language used here is crucial. Elsewhere in Europe the focus was not on the injustice of the enrichment, but on its justifiability. Hence French law knew a principle of 'enrichissement sans cause' and German law 'ungerechtfertigte Bereicherung',[139] both of these in their turn deriving from the third category of personal obligations identified by Grotius in his *Introduction to the Jurisprudence of Holland*.[140] At the very moment at which the Common law (in America if not yet in England) came to adopt ideas derived from the Civil law, it did so in a way subtly but importantly different from the way in which those ideas had been received into modern European systems; consequently, as the twentieth-century

---

[134] *Quasi-Contracts*, 16.

[135] Money paid by mistake; waiver of tort; rights of plaintiff in default under a contract; obligations of defendant in default under a contract; recovery for benefits conferred at request but without a contract; recovery for benefits intentionally conferred without request; recovery for improvements made upon the land of another without request; recovery of money paid to the use of the defendant; recovery of money paid under compulsion of law; recovery of money paid to the defendant under duress, legal or equitable.

[136] F. C. Woodward, *The Law of Quasi Contracts* (Boston, 1913).

[137] 'The History of Assumpsit: Implied Assumpsit' (1888) 2 Harv L R 53, acknowledged by Keener, *Quasi-Contracts*, 16. More important, perhaps, was the apparently far more sophisticated analysis essayed by Ames in his lectures in the Harvard Law School: E. V. Abbot, 'Keener on Quasi-Contracts' (1897) 10 Harv L R 479 n.

[138] D.50.17.206: 'Jure naturae aequum est, neminem cum alterius detrimento et injuria fieri locupletiorem.' Cf. D.12.6.14, identical apart from the omission of 'et injuria'. Similar is the rule of Canon law, 'Locupletari non debet aliquis, cum alterius injuria vel jactura' (Liber Sextus, De Regulis Juris, reg.48), the important background and context of which are discussed by J. Hallebeek, *The Concept of Unjust Enrichment in Late Scholasticism* (Nijmegen, 1996).

[139] J. P. Dawson, *Unjust Enrichment, a Comparative Analysis* (Boston, 1951); B. Nicholas, 'Unjustified Enrichment in the Civil Law and Louisiana Law' (1962) 36 Tul L R 619; Zimmermann, *Obligations*, 887–91. Scots law, true to its mixed heritage, appears to use the terminology of 'unjust' and 'unjustified' enrichment interchangeably.

[140] *Inleidinge tot de Hollandsche Rechts-Geleerdheid*, 3.30 (= R. W. Lee (ed.), *The Jurisprudence of Holland* (Oxford, 1926), 448–55). See R. Feenstra, 'Grotius' Doctrine of Unjust Enrichment as a Source of Obligation', in Schrage (ed.), *Unjust Enrichment*, 197.

Common-law and Civil-law systems began to move in parallel tracks, they carried with them two quite distinct sets of preconceptions about the underlying nature of the liability.[141]

It took some time for the English courts to escape from the shackles of the old forms of action. If anything, the implied-contract analysis gained a stronger grip, with the decision of the House of Lords in *Sinclair* v. *Brougham*[142] that lack of contractual capacity undermined quasi-contractual liability too, so that money paid by mistake to a company acting wholly *ultra vires* was as irrecoverable as a loan would have been. The point was made no less forcibly at a general level. Even a judge as clear-sighted as Scrutton L.J. curtly dismissed the Common law's attempts to formulate liability in abstract terms as 'well-meaning sloppiness of thought'.[143] The turning point occurred in the 1930s. In 1931 there appeared Winfield's *Province of the Law of Tort*, which devoted a very substantial chapter to quasi-contractual liability, treating it as based on unjust enrichment.[144] Though Winfield's argument was not universally accepted,[145] it familiarized English lawyers with the principles coming to be accepted in the United States. Further impetus was given by the appearance in 1937 of the American *Restatement of the Law of Restitution*, and by Lord Wright's reanalysis of *Sinclair* v. *Brougham*, published in 1938.[146] Scholars began to observe that English law might reach the same results as were reached under the continental regimes of unjustified enrichment.[147] No less important were the historical writings of Sir William Holdsworth and R. M. Jackson, building on the earlier American work of Ames;[148] by exposing the way in which the implied-contract analysis had grown up as the chance consequence of the use of indebitatus assumpsit, these writers made it possible for the courts to begin to sweep away the detritus left by the forms of action and to rebuild the law on a more rational basis. The case law of the late 1930s began to show an awareness of the unsatisfactoriness of the implied-contract analysis,[149] and in *United Australia Ltd* v.

---

[141] Below, n.181.   [142] [1914] AC 398; above, n.103.

[143] *Holt* v. *Markham* [1923] 1 KB 504, 513. To the same effect *Baylis* v. *Bishop of London* 1 Ch 127, 138 per Hamilton L.J.

[144] P. Winfield, *The Province of the Law of Tort* (Cambridge, 1931), 116–89.

[145] Most memorably by Landon: (1931) 8 Bell Yard 19; see too W. S. Holdsworth, 'Unjustifiable Enrichment' (1939) 55 LQR 37.

[146] Lord Wright, 'Sinclair v. Brougham' [1938] CLJ 305. Lord Wright also published a lengthy, and high-profile, review of the American Restatement in (1937) 51 Harv L R 369.

[147] H. C. Gutteridge and R. J. A. David, 'The Doctrine of Unjustified Enrichment' [1934] CLJ 204; W. Friedmann, 'The Principle of Unjust Enrichment in English Law' (1938) 16 Can Bar Rev 243, 365.

[148] Holdsworth, *History of English Law*, 8.88–98; R. M. Jackson, *The History of Quasi-Contract* (Cambridge, 1936). For Ames, see above, n.137.

[149] *Craven-Ellis* v. *Canons Ltd* [1936] 2 KB 403, 410; *Brook's Wharf and Bull Wharf Ltd* v. *Goodman Bros* [1937] 1 KB 534, 545; *Morgan* v. *Ashcroft* [1938] 1 KB 49, 74–5; *re Cleadon Trust Ltd* [1939] Ch 286, 312.

Barclays Bank Ltd[150] the House of Lords finally took the decisive step and abandoned it:

These fantastic resemblances of contracts invented in order to meet requirements of the law as to forms of action which have now disappeared should not in these days be allowed to affect actual rights. When these ghosts of the past stand in the path of justice clanking their mediæval chains the proper course for the judge is to pass through them undeterred.[151]

Replacing the creaky reasoning on the basis of the implied contract was an analysis more or less directly derived from the American Restatement of Restitution.

The approach of the House of Lords in *United Australia Ltd* v. *Barclays Bank Ltd* was consolidated two years later in *Fibrosa Spolka Akcyjna* v. *Fairbairn, Lawson, Combe Barbour Ltd.*[152] The defendants had agreed to build machinery for the defendant company in Poland, receiving part of the price in advance, but before the contract could be completed war broke out and it had to be abandoned. The plaintiffs brought an action to recover the money they had paid. It had earlier been held, in *Chandler* v. *Webster*,[153] that in these circumstances no claim would lie; and behind this lay the earlier rule that where there was an express contract there could not simultaneously be an implied contract.[154] The House of Lords overruled *Chandler*, neutralizing the earlier line of authorities. That the basis of the action was the reversal of unjust enrichment, or restitution, is brought to the fore in the speech of Lord Wright, where the historical fallacy at the heart of the implied-contract analysis was once again exposed.[155]

The combined effect of *United Australia* and *Fibrosa* was to fix in English law the third category of obligations, neither contractual nor tortious, identifiably based on the principle of unjust enrichment. Though the idea still had its doubters and detractors[156]—it was perhaps not until 1991 that it was finally put beyond question[157]—within a few years academic lawyers had become accustomed to the language of 'restitution', following the American model, and 'quasi-contract' and 'contracts imposed by law' disappeared from textbook treatments of the law of contract. In their place,

---

[150] [1941] AC 1.
[151] [1941] AC 1, 29, per Lord Atkin; at the base of his debunking of implied contracts lie the historical critiques of Ames, Holdsworth, and Jackson. It is easy to see the roots of Lord Atkin's speech in the argument of Denning K.C. [1941] AC 1, 5–6, 7.
[152] [1943] AC 32.   [153] [1904] 1 KB 493.   [154] Above, n.94.
[155] [1943] AC 32, 61–4.
[156] e.g. *Reading* v. *Attorney-General* [1951] AC 507, 513–14; *Orakpo* v. *Manson Investments Ltd* [1978] AC 95, 104. Academic criticism continues: see in particular S. Hedley, 'Unjust Enrichment as the Basis of Restitution—an Overworked Concept' (1985) 5 Legal Studies 56; '"Unjust Enrichment"' [1995] CLJ 578.
[157] *Lipkin Gorman (a firm)* v. *Karpnale Ltd* [1991] 2 AC 548.

from 1966, there appeared independent text books on restitution.[158] The time had come to begin to clear up the debris of two centuries of mis-analysis (both at Common law and in Equity) and to impose some structural coherence on the law.

The most straightforward debris-clearing brought about by the identification of unjust enrichment as the foundation of liability was the clarification of the basis of liability and the consequent reversal of earlier decisions grounded too literally on implied contracts. Just as the rejection of the implied-contract reasoning in the *Fibrosa* case[159] enabled the House of Lords to provide a remedy where contracts were frustrated, so, in *Westdeutsche Landesbank Girozentrale* v. *Islington Borough Council*, the House of Lords departed from its own previous decision in *Sinclair* v. *Brougham* and held that in an action for repayment of money it was not relevant that the defendant had been acting *ultra vires* and so could not have been held liable in a contractual action.[160] More radically, the generalizing effect of unjust-enrichment analysis played its part in the reversal of the rule that money paid under a mistake of law (as opposed to a mistake of fact) could not be recovered back. This rule, traceable back to a cursorily reasoned decision of Lord Ellenborough C.J.,[161] had been in place since the beginning of the nineteenth century; except in India (where it was arguably abolished in 1872),[162] it survived in Common-law systems until lawyers began to discover that it did not sit easily with a theory of unjust enrichment. Canadian law departed from it in 1989, Australian law in 1992; and, after a preliminary sally in 1993, the House of Lords finally decided in 1998 that it should be finally and firmly expunged from the law of England.[163]

Secondly, the analysis of liability in terms of unjust enrichment enabled judges and academic commentators to begin to re-examine the foundations

---

[158] The ground-breaking work was R. Goff and G. H. Jones, *The Law of Restitution* (1st edn., London, 1966).

[159] *Fibrosa Spolka Akcyjna* v. *Fairbairn, Lawson, Combe Barbour Ltd* [1943] AC 32 (above, n.152).

[160] [1996] AC 669, followed in *Guinness Mahon & Co Ltd* v. *Kensington and Chelsea Royal London Borough* [1998] 3 WLR 829. For the decision in *Sinclair* v. *Brougham*, see above, n.103.

[161] *Bilbie* v. *Lumley* (1802) 2 East 469, following dicta of Buller J. in *Lowry* v. *Bourdieu* (1767) Dougl 467; earlier dicta can be found in *Munt* v. *Stokes* (1792) 4 TR 561 (which would seem to favour Lord Ellenborough's position) and *Farmer* v. *Arundel* (1772) 2 W Bl 824, 825 (which would seem to be against it). Lord Kenyon C.J. is said to have allowed recovery for mistake of law: Evans, *Essay on the Action for Money Had and Received*, 21–2, citing J. Chitty, *Bills of Exchange* (1799), 102. See generally the discussion of Evans, *Essay on the Action for Money Had and Received*, 19–22 (written before *Bilbie* v. *Lumley*).

[162] Indian Contract Act 1872, s.72, as interpreted by the Privy Council in *Sir Shiba Prasad Singh* v. *Maharaja Srish Chandra Nandi* (1949) 76 IA 244 (note especially Lord Reid's distinction between the rules for vitiating contracts and the rules providing for restitution).

[163] *Air Canada* v. *British Columbia* [1989] 59 DLR (4th ser.) 161; *David Securities Pty Ltd* v. *Commonwealth Bank of Australia* (1992) 175 CLR 353; *Woolwich Equitable Building Society* v. *Inland Revenue Commissioners* [1993] AC 70; *Kleinwort Benson* v. *Lincoln City Council* [1998] 3 WLR 1095 (note especially the historical analysis in the speech of Lord Goff at 1109–13).

and boundaries of liability in problematic areas. Claims for indemnity or contribution from those who discharged another's legal liability, for example, could be reformulated in terms of unjust enrichment, abandoning the contorted nineteenth-century language of implied contracts in favour of the more open-ended language that had preceded it.[164] This involved no more than a terminological scouring; but sometimes the shift had a substantive dimension. It might involve a process of generalization, as where the House of Lords (picking up on academics' arguments) recognized a general defence of change of position in claims based on unjust enrichment, or where the Privy Council moved in the direction of allowing restitutionary claims for non-total failures of consideration.[165] Alternatively, it might involve the smoothing-down of apparently arbitrary inconsistencies between legal and equitable rules, such as those dealing with the situation where the plaintiffs' property had, without their knowledge, been transferred to the defendants. By the Common-law rules the defendants were strictly liable to return the property (subject to the existence of a range of defences), whereas in Equity it was essential to prove fault, perhaps even dishonesty, on the part of the defendants.[166] Once the inconsistency was revealed[167]—and only then—was it possible to sweep away the baggage of two centuries of independent developments in Equity and Common law and to begin the process of reasoned analysis to achieve a substantial assimilation of the two systems.[168]

Perhaps the most difficult debris-clearing arose from the possibility of deconstructing the old division between claims at Common law and claims in Equity, the former being exclusively claims *in personam*, the latter commonly operating *in rem*.[169] Once the common foundation in unjust enrichment was exposed, it ceased to be obvious why the court in which a claim would (probably) have been heard in the nineteenth century should determine whether, for example, the plaintiff should have a preferential claim on the defendant's insolvency.[170] Thus, in *Chase Manhattan Bank* v.

---

[164] *Brook's Wharf and Bull Wharf Ltd* v. *Goodman Bros* [1937] 1 KB 534; *Owen* v. *Tate* [1976] QB 402. See Goff and Jones, *Law of Restitution* (5th edn., London, 1998). 437–56. For the eighteenth- and nineteenth-century law, see above, p.271.

[165] *Lipkin Gorman (a firm)* v. *Karpnale Ltd* [1991] 2 AC 548; *Goss* v. *Chilcott* [1996] AC 788, 798.

[166] Cf. *Lipkin Gorman (a firm)* v. *Karpnale Ltd* [1991] 2 AC 548 with *Carl Zeiss Stiftung* v. *Herbert Smith & Co (no. 2)* [1969] 2 Ch 276.

[167] For which the credit belongs to P. Birks, 'Misdirected Funds: Restitution from the Recipient' [1989] Lloyds Maritime and Commercial Law Quarterly 296.

[168] This has perhaps begun to be achieved by the decision in *Lipkin Gorman (a firm)* v. *Karpnale Ltd* [1991] 2 AC 548: C. Harpum, 'The Basis of Equitable Liability', in P Birks (ed.), *The Frontiers of Liability* (Oxford, 1994), 9, 25.   [169] Above, p.283.

[170] Cf. R. M. Goode, 'Proprietary Restitutionary Claims', in W. Cornish (ed.), *Restitution: Past, Present and Future* (Oxford, 1998), 63.

Israel–British Bank[171] it was held that a claim to recover money paid under a mistake, which would typically have grounded an action for money had and received, might equally found an equitable claim, thereby enabling the plaintiffs to rank ahead of general creditors on the defendants' insolvency. Similarly, in *Barclays Bank* v. *Quistclose*,[172] it was held that money paid over for a particular purpose, in this case the payment of dividends to shareholders, should be treated as belonging (in Equity) to the lenders if that purpose failed. There was a resulting trust for the lenders, whose proprietary nature meant that their rights prevailed over the rights of other creditors of the borrowing company when it went into liquidation.[173] In *Attorney-General for Hong Kong* v. *Reid*[174] the Privy Council determined that bribes received by an employee acting in breach of trust belonged (in Equity) to the employer, departing from previous authority, which would have allowed only a personal claim.[175] In other situations the courts were less willing to extend proprietary remedies. In *re Goldcorp*,[176] for example, it was held that buyers of goods who had paid the price were limited to their (personal) claim for damages for non-delivery when the sellers went bankrupt, and could not choose to claim back the sum paid. More far-reachingly, the speech of Lord Browne-Wilkinson in *Westdeutsche Landesbank Girozentrale* v. *Islington Borough Council* pointed towards a very substantial restriction on the range of proprietary restitutionary claims.[177]

A good deal of the credit for the re-examination of these points is due to—and duly given to—academic lawyers. No less important is their role in mapping out the whole field of unjust enrichment.[178] The Natural lawyers of the seventeenth century played a crucial part in the history of the tort of negligence by articulating a framework within which it could develop in the eighteenth and nineteenth centuries; by providing a skeletal structure that appeared to be both rational and self-consistent, Pothier's version of the Will Theory, itself with roots in the Natural lawyers' writings, played a crucial part in the emergent contract law of the nineteenth century; so too

---

[171] *Chase Manhattan Bank N.A. Ltd* v. *Israel–British Bank (London) Ltd* [1981] Ch 105.
[172] *Barclays Bank Ltd* v. *Quistclose Investments Ltd* [1970] AC 567.
[173] The precise nature of the trust created is a matter of terminological controversy. I follow the analysis of Chambers, *Resulting Trusts*, 68–89.   [174] [1994] 1 AC 324.
[175] *Metropolitan Bank* v. *Heiron* (1880) 5 Ex D 319; *Lister* v. *Stubbs* (1890) 45 Ch D 1.
[176] [1995] AC 74; P. Birks, 'Establishing a Proprietary Base' (1995) 3 Restitution Law Review 83.
[177] [1996] AC 669; P. Birks, 'Trusts Raised to Reverse Unjust Enrichment: The *Westdeutsche* Case' (1996) 4 Restitution Law Review 4.
[178] The path-breaking work here was P. Birks, *Introduction to the Law of Restitution* (Oxford, 1985), followed by a series of exploratory articles by the same author, most recently 'Misnomer', in Cornish (ed.), *Restitution: Past, Present and Future*, 1. Behind these lie the writings of Keener and others in the United States, and of von Caemmerer and others in Germany.

the writings of Birks and others will prove to have been crucial in moulding the law of unjust enrichment in the twentieth and twenty-first centuries. And, just as the writings of the Natural lawyers and Pothier had their roots sunk deep in the heritage of classical Roman law, so too the modern framework of unjust enrichment can be traced back to the pregnant principle of the Roman jurist Pomponius that 'no one ought unjustly to enrich himself at the expense of another'.[179] The listing of the situations in which liability arises is replaced by an extended commentary on the meaning of 'unjust', 'enrichment', and 'at the expense of another', together with a consideration of whether liability should be *in personam* or *in rem*.

Just as the broad notion of fault-based liability was too general to provide a reliable determinant of the precise scope of tortious liability in the nineteenth century,[180] so the language of 'unjust enrichment' is insufficiently focused to indicate precisely when liability should be imposed. Academic writers have, therefore, argued for the adoption of a conservative approach to liability in unjust enrichment, requiring that the legal remedy should be activated only if there is some definable 'unjust factor', the functional equivalent of the nineteenth-century law of tort's duty of care.[181] Just as the law of tort was able to expand gently by the incremental development of new duties of care, so the law of unjust enrichment can identify new 'unjust factors'; and, just as the law of tort in the later nineteenth century witnessed a tension between the incremental approach and a broad generalized approach to liability (running from *Heaven* v. *Pender* to *Donoghue* v. *Stevenson*), so too the incremental approach to unjust enrichment exists in tension with a tendency to generalize.[182] In addition, the potential breadth inherent in the general terminology of unjust enrichment creates the possibility of its expansion into areas traditionally dealt with in different legal categories. As one early writer, critical of the explosive potential of such an unbounded legal category, hinted, it was powerful enough to take over the whole of the law of personal property;[183] and a more modern commentator has warned of the dangers of 'unnecessary

---

[179] D.50.17.206; above, n.138.   [180] Above, p.178.

[181] Cf. the approach of continental lawyers, working outwards from the requirement that the enrichment be unjustified: R. Zimmermann, 'Unjustified Enrichment: The Modern Civil Law Approach' (1995) 15 Ox Jnl Leg Stud 403. The tension between generality and specificity in continental law is explored by E. von Caemmerer, 'Problèmes fondamentaux de l'enrichissement sans cause' (1966) 18 Revue International de Droit Comparé 573.

[182] Visible, for example, in the speech of Lord Browne-Wilkinson in *Westdeutsche Landesbank Girozentrale* v. *Islington London Borough Council* [1996] AC 669, discussed by Birks, 'Trusts Raised to Reverse Unjust Enrichment' (1996) 4 Restitution Law Review 4, 19–23.

[183] Landon, (1931) 8 Bell Yard, 19, 22. The connection between property and unjust enrichment was already well explored by Grotius: Hallebeek, *The Concept of Unjust Enrichment in Late Scholasticism*, 87–103.

empire-building'.[184] On the other hand, the creation of a transparent law of unjust enrichment has produced opportunities as well as dangers, in its opening-up of the possibility of recategorizing situations that might once have been seen as parts of the law of quasi-contract, constructive trusts, or unjust enrichment. Thus, it has been argued, where wrongdoers are required to disgorge the profits of their wrongs, it might be desirable from the point of view of legal taxonomy to characterize the action against them as tortious, notwithstanding that in the eighteenth century such a claim would have fallen under indebitatus assumpsit for money had and received, just as other forms of wrongdoing historically remediable in the courts of Equity, such as breach of confidence, may too be redefinable as part of the law of torts;[185] in the same way the award of restitutionary damages for breach of contract[186] can be seen as properly belonging to the law of contract. Liability for knowingly assisting in a breach of trust, once clearly part of the law of constructive trusts and the preserve of the courts of Equity, is perhaps in the process of joining with the tort of inducing breach of contract and with the rules relating to joint tortfeasors, generating thereby a uniform approach to civil secondary liability.[187]

---

[184] P. Birks, 'The Independence of Restitutionary Causes of Action' (1990) 16 University of Queensland Law Journal 1, 2. Cf. *Weston* v. *Downes* (1778) 1 Doug 23, 24, per Lord Mansfield C.J. The same goal is achieved, albeit with greater rigour, in those continental systems derived from French law by the more or less well-developed principle of 'subsidiarity', according to which an action based on unjust enrichment will not lie where there is already a claim in contract or tort: B. Nicholas, 'Unjust Enrichment and Subsidiarity', in *Scintillae Iuris: Studi in Memoria di Gino Gorla* (Milan, 1994), 2037.

[185] Birks, 'Misnomer', in Cornish (ed.), *Restitution: Past, Present and Future*, 1.

[186] Cf. *Attorney-General* v. *Blake* [1998] Ch 439.

[187] C. Harpum, (1995) 111 LQR 545, 546, noting *Royal Brunei Airlines Sdn. Bhd.* v. *Tan* [1995] 2 AC 378.

15. *Legal Change and Legal Continuity*

The Common law has many virtues; tidiness is not among them. It could hardly be otherwise when for the last seven or more centuries legal decision-making has been based on a model of judicial consistency. As far back as we can see, judges have been expected to apply the law rather than invent it afresh from case to case; and formal legal arguments have invariably been couched in such a way as to show that, properly understood, the existing law favours the client in the instant case. Legal change occurs through filling in gaps between rules in the way that seems most convenient or most just at the time; through twisting existing rules, or rediscovering old ones, to give the impression that a change in the law is no more than the application of the law that was already in place; through reformulating claims into a different conceptual category, normally one less encumbered by restrictive rules; through inventing new rules that get tacked onto the existing ones; through borrowing rules from outside the Common law; through injecting shifting ideas of fairness or justice; and, very occasionally, through adopting wholesale procrustean theoretical frameworks into which the existing law can be squeezed.

In the absence of large-scale codification or substantial legislative change, and the law of obligations has seen neither, the inventing of the new is rarely combined with the discarding of the old. However inconvenient or inconsistent, centuries-old rules, principles, and doctrines can remain in place, as quaint survivals from the past or as traps for the unwary in the future, sometimes encrusted by so many exceptions that their original functions are wholly undermined. Invariably, of course, there is sufficient flexibility in the application of the law to ensure that it does not routinely produce injustice; and the use of open-ended standards of 'reasonableness' and the like allows the law to adapt continuously and painlessly to shifting social standards. The real cost is an ever-increasing, and unnecessary, complexity.

Whatever changes have occurred on the surface of the law, and whatever accretions have been incorporated into its fabric, at a deep level the structure of the Common law of obligations has remained remarkably slow-moving. With the exception of the coalescing category of unjust enrichment, the basic divisions of the law found in the twelfth or thirteenth century are reflected in the structure of the law at the end of the twentieth: the uneasy division between contract and tort (or covenant and trespass); the division within the law of contract between actions to vindicate entitlements and actions claiming damages or penalties; the distinction within the law of tort(s) between actions dependent on the causation of economic loss and actions to give effect to rights. Like an ancient building in continual use for centuries but readapted to satisfy the needs of each generation, the medieval ground plan of the Common law of obligations remains visible through all the reordering of its internal features and the change of use of its component rooms.

A principal motor for legal change has been the need to articulate formerly ambiguous rules. This was particularly marked in the Chancery, both in the way in which it softened Common-law rules and in the way in which questions that would have been left to the jury at Common law became matters for formal determination. Within the Common law it was especially important in the period after 1750 when the balance between judge and jury shifted: points that could once have been loosely formulated as issues for the jury to decide became more clearly delineated as their discretion was increasingly constrained. The process of articulation was inevitably not arbitrary, but might be influenced by considerations of justice and fairness in the instant case, by wider conceptions of social policy, or by the desire to mould the law in accordance with a set of theoretical preconceptions about the nature of legal liability. Because of the nature of Common-law reasoning, such decisions once taken were incorporated into the law and might themselves influence future developments.

Decisions in the seventeenth-century Court of Chancery setting aside contracts in which advantage was taken of expectant heirs, therefore, formed a seed from which a doctrine of substantive unconscionability in contract could grow centuries later, first by striking down unfair bargains by moneylenders, then (perhaps) by allowing the courts to create from this a general doctrine of unconscionability. The eighteenth-century Chancery refused to enforce contracts where there was a suggestion of sharp practice; if this could not be proved, their refusal might be justified on the grounds of mistake; and two centuries later these decisions could be disinterred to provide the foundation for a doctrine of equitable mistake. It was a terrible thing in the sixteenth century to allege that a person was suffering from syphilis; after a few twistings and turnings, this was eventually transmuted into the rule that a false allegation that a person is suffering from a communicable disease should be actionable without proof of special damage.

Nineteenth-century judges were concerned not to impose what was conceived of as excessive liability on commercial enterprises. The articulation of a narrow rule of manufacturers' liability in tort in 1842 fixed the law for the next century; it required more than one wave of legislation to remove the fellow-servant rule, exonerating employers from vicarious liability for injuries caused by one employee to another; the differential treatment of 'sensible property damage' and 'mere personal discomfort' deriving from mid-Victorian case law on the tort of nuisance remains firmly in place almost one and a half centuries later. Similarly explicit considerations of policy lay behind the decision in 1854 that consequential damages in actions in contract should ordinarily be limited to that which the parties to the contract might reasonably have foreseen; the same rule, though subject to exceptions and qualifications, prevails today.

Most important of all was the fitting of the law into a theoretical model. Both the classical forms of the tort of negligence and of contractual liability developed in the nineteenth century under the influence of the models of the Natural lawyers of the seventeenth and eighteenth centuries and their successors. Specific doctrines of the law of contract in particular were derived explicitly from the works of Pothier and Savigny: offer and acceptance, mistake, the requirement of an intention to create legal relations. All of the principal elements of the tort of negligence can be found in the writings of Pufendorf and his followers, and it may well be that nineteenth-century Common lawyers consciously replicated shifts in continental theory in Common-law contexts. There is good reason to believe that a similar process is at work in the modern-day development of the law of unjust enrichment.

The need to give greater definition to ambiguous legal rules was not the only force for change, nor even the most important. Really significant shifts in the law commonly resulted from the conceptual recharacterization of claims by litigants (or their lawyers) trying to avoid some irksome procedural rule or to take advantage of some more favourable legal process available elsewhere. The emergence of the action of trespass on the case in the middle of the fourteenth century seems to have been brought about at least in part by the desire of plaintiffs to avoid being wrong-footed in the context of the mechanisms of the contemporary jury trial; probably the principal reason for the establishment in the sixteenth century of the action of assumpsit as a general remedy for informal contracts was the desire to use a form of action in which the defendant was not given the option of wager of law as a means of avoiding liability; and the pressures that brought about the triumph of the action on the case over the general action of trespass in personal injury claims in the eighteenth century were the desire to take advantage of more favourable rules for the recovery of costs, the wish to retain the initiative over the expense of the lawsuit, and the need to join together multiple counts in the same action in order to retain maximum flexibility in the formulation of the claim. In none of them, so far as we know, was there the slightest suggestion that any change in substantive rights or duties was contemplated; yet each brought about centrally important movements in the whole structure of the law of obligations. The legacy of each of these has survived into the modern law. The central feature of trespass on the case was that liability was imposed where wrongful conduct had caused loss; though the contours of 'wrongful' were almost infinitely flexible, the rule that loss must have been caused was more tenacious. The modern law of torts, except for those parts that can claim kinship with trespass rather than case, is consequently strongly focused on the causation of loss and there is difficulty in adapting it to cover wrongful conduct that does not cause loss, such as interferences with privacy. The action of assumpsit was, in form, an action of trespass on the case, and so carried through into the law of contract the basic idea that damages were awarded to compensate for loss suffered, albeit loss of expectations. The modern law of contract, except in so far as actions can properly be characterized as debt, still largely takes the form of claims for unliquidated damages for breach of contract rather than actions to give effect to contractual entitlements. Finally, the triumph of case over trespass in the eighteenth century prepared the ground for the emergence of a tort of negligence in which the focus was on the way in which the defendant had acted wrongfully rather than on the way in which the plaintiff's right had been compromised.

The influence of procedural factors is no less visible at a more detailed level. The basic division of contractual terms into conditions and warranties replicates the framework imposed by the medieval rules of pleading; the fixing of the division between contract and tort in the middle of the action on the case resulted from the desire to avoid the strict rules relating to the joinder of parties in contractual actions. Much of the contorted structure of the modern tort of defamation stems from procedural factors: the classification of claims by reference to the words used rather than the damage caused flowed from the difficulty in taking issue on the occurrence of loss in the sixteenth century; the irrational distinction between defamations actionable *per se* and those actionable only on proof of special damage, for example, was fixed in place by manœuvres designed to exploit ambiguities in the interpretation of the Limitation Act of 1623; and the structure of liability in terms of strict liability subject to a limited range of defences (essentially privilege and fair comment) can be understood only as a response to the plaintiff's problem of proving that the defendant was actuated by malice and the defendant's problem of disproving it.

Most noteworthy is the potentially very long-term effect of these relatively minor procedural changes. Like the shifting of tectonic plates, a small disturbance in one area can—very slowly—bring about large-scale changes in the conceptual organization of the Common law. The point is well illustrated by looking at the effects of three small fourteenth-century alterations in particular rules of pleading and proof.

In the early years of the century there was introduced the rule that an action of covenant would lie only on a contract under seal. The effect of this was to force actions for contractual mis-performance into the formal shell of the action of trespass, soon splitting off as trespass on the case, bringing it about that a significant group of actions arising out of contracts became characterized as tortious. Some centuries later, it was these actions that were to form the main core of the Common-law tort of negligence. Actions for contractual non-performance were fragmented; the clear potential that the action of covenant had to develop into a general contractual remedy was dashed, and the appearance of such a general remedy was delayed for a quarter of a millennium. When it did appear, described as an action for breach of promise, it was skewed by its being framed within a tortious form of action, the action of assumpsit, and by overtones of ecclesiastical penalties for oath-breaking and perjury. After another quarter of a millennium, it was this general form of contractual remedy that was refashioned in the wake of the Will Theory, picking up fragments of terminology from the Natural lawyers' theories of (genuinely) promissory liability. Little more than a century later the law of contract was recognized as an unsurprisingly confused mess.

Slightly later in the fourteenth century, the writ of detinue was allowed to divide into two subforms with slightly different rules as to the type of defence that might be pleaded. On the one hand, there was the action based on a bailment; on the other, the action based on a finding. The former was used where there was any sort of contractual relationship between plaintiff and defendant, not necessarily a bailment, the latter whenever there was no contract between them. By this time the action of detinue was being characterized in explicitly proprietary terms, and the shaping of the defences made it possible for the bailment-based actions to fit into this mould, thereby masking their contractual aspect. Six hundred years later the Common law still struggles to categorize bailments. Meanwhile the non-contractual part of detinue was superseded by the action on the case for conversion, borrowing not merely the proprietary skeleton of detinue but also its fiction of a finding. Hence the Common law's treatment of moveable property developed behind a façade of fictitious finding and fanciful conversion whose main effect was to prevent any real consideration of the very concepts underlying the formal rules.

A couple of decades after the division of detinue, the requirement that a trespass be alleged to have been committed by force of arms in breach of the king's peace, *vi et armis contra pacem domini regis*, was near-silently dropped. This could have been achieved straightforwardly; but the only circumstance in which there was strong pressure for the change was where the plaintiff wanted to tell a story of contractual mis-performance, and the removal of the allegation of force and arms was bundled together with the question of the legitimacy of the plaintiff's telling the story. Hence, the action of trespass sheared into two parts: the general action of trespass, within which the allegations of force, arms, and breach of the king's peace continued to be used, and the action on the case, in which the story was told and the common-form words were unnecessary. This was no doubt the line of least resistance—a small change is easier to accomplish than a large one—but it had the effect of locking in place the division of the law of torts into actions based on allegedly forcible invasive interferences (to land, to goods, or to the person) and actions based on other forms of wrongdoing. Four centuries later the boundary between trespass and case became a pressing issue as litigants tried to join together different types of count in the same action; the question that had remained dormant for generations had at last to be resolved. A century and a half after this had been done it was established that, so far as injuries to the person were concerned, trespass and case were governed by the same rules as to fault. Whether the same applies to actions for damage to goods remains unclear, and may perhaps continue unclear for another century or two; and trespass to land will remain different—which it undoubtedly is—until English law comes to terms with the general problem of establishing liability in tort in the absence of the causation of actual damage or loss.

Given the tiny amount of legislative intervention suffered by the law of obligations, none should be surprised that the shape of the modern law is strongly determined by its history. In a system so heavily dependent upon case law, it is change that needs to be explained, not continuity. The belated recognition of the category of unjust enrichment—so belated that it was substantially the work of historians—reveals better than anything the near-inevitable truth that, in the absence of sufficient pressure for change, things will remain largely the same. It is not enough that the current state of the law is recognized to be generally over-complex, dependent on fictions, or otherwise unsatisfactory. In a case-law system the initiative rests with the litigants, and it is only when the advantage to be gained in the instant case by doing something different is large enough to outweigh the chance of loss that the well-advised litigant will take the risk and depart from the well-trodden path. Hence, for several centuries, claims that would later be categorized in terms of unjust enrichment were massaged into other legal categories. By the seventeenth century this had settled down into two focal situations: the implied contract in the courts of Common law, and its shadow, the implied trust, in the courts of Equity. Although the unsatisfactory nature of this was recognized by lawyers as clear-sighted as Lord Mansfield, the pressure to move away from it was not so great that it could overcome the inertia of what had become a well-established way of doing things. It was only when highly placed judges willing to countenance change could broadcast this in academic journals and elsewhere that barristers could safely take the hint and begin to argue cases on the newer basis.

Structural continuity is most clearly visible in the law of contract. Just as for Glanvill there was a basic distinction between contracts proved by witnesses and contracts proved by charter, the modern law recognizes the division between contracts made by deed and contracts without such form; only in 1989 did the legal definition of 'deed' shift noticeably from Glanvill's conception of a charter. In addition, running through the twentieth-century law of contract like an ill-sewn scar, is the fundamental thirteenth-century distinction between a claim to a contractual entitlement and a claim to damages for breach of contract. In an action for a debt the claim may be expressed in foreign currency; a claim to damages has to be in sterling.[1] In an action for breach of contract damages will be reduced to take into account any failure on the part of the plaintiff to mitigate the loss; in an action for an entitlement there is no duty to mitigate. In an action for damages the plaintiff must in principle show that loss has been suffered, though the courts are slowly coming to terms with the possibility that damages may be recovered for the benefit of a third party; in an action to recover a contractual entitlement loss is wholly irrelevant. And, until the wholesale reform introduced by the new Civil Procedure Rules of 1999, different procedural mechanisms might apply: different forms of writ of summons, different rules for the recovery of interest, different rules for the entry of judgment on the defendant's failure to enter an appearance.[2]

The main stock of the medieval law of torts was characterized by its lack of internal structure. 'Trespass' meant nothing more than 'wrong'. As the failure of the nineteenth-century attempts to give the law greater definition comes to be recognized, the modern law appears little different, substituting 'tort' for 'trespass'. Outside this central core there are the principal satellites protecting particular interests. The medieval lawyers knew the separate wrong of nuisance where the plaintiff complained of an interference with the enjoyment of land, and awkwardly straddling the boundary between the law of torts and administrative regulation was what was known by the sixteenth century as public nuisance; the same remains true today. By the end of the thirteenth century lawyers would have recognized a separate wrong of defamation actionable in the ecclesiastical courts rather than at Common law; despite the breakdown of the jurisdictional barrier in the seventeenth century and some twisting of its rules, the modern lawyer's tort of defamation is structurally identical. Although new satellites unknown in the Middle Ages have sprung up—principally conversion around 1500 and the economic torts in the twentieth century—they have remained as satellites and had no real effect on the core of tortious liability. And beyond these there is the little-noticed and ill-defined dust of legal wrongs that can be catalogued but which for the time being defy any larger-scale categorization.

---

[1] *Miliangos* v. *George Frank (Textiles) Ltd* [1976] AC 443; *Practice Direction (Judgment: Foreign Currency)* [1976] 1 WLR 83, [1977] 1 WLR 197.
[2] *Supreme Court Practice 1999*, Order 6, Rule 2(1)(b); para. 42/1/17; para. 14/4/37.

This type of structural continuity is perhaps typical of any legal system that has not undergone codification or other revolutionary change. Since it affects only the legal skeleton, the way in which questions are raised or the way in which concepts are related to each other, it has relatively little effect on the substance of the law. More problematic is the legal hangover: although the Common law is capable of sloughing off outdated rules that have become inconvenient, it is less successful at losing doctrines or whole bodies of ideas. Once established, these obtain a degree of fixity that makes them difficult to dislodge. They can become hedged round with exceptions that undermine much of their substance; they can be given functions radically different from their original purposes; but their essence survives. When they are restrictive doctrines, sets of rules that have to be satisfied before a certain type of claim can be allowed, their negative consequences can be marked. The law of contract is riddled with these. The doctrines of consideration and privity are throwbacks to the medieval exchange model of contractual liability, despite consideration having been given its characteristic shape only in the sixteenth century; offer and acceptance, intention to create legal relations, and the rules of mistake are offshoots of the nineteenth-century Will Theory. All of these stand in the way of the elaboration of a satisfactory modern theory of contract, however much commercial practice has managed to manœuvre around them. Their main effect is to clog up the law, spawning rules that cannot safely be ignored, bypasses that have to be remembered in order to activate them, and a multiplicity of exceptions that add to the complexity of the law.

Hangovers are less obviously dangerous when they are concerned with the consequences of legal acts, but they may still lead to difficulties that are at best unnecessary. It took English lawyers centuries to escape from the problems thrown up by the rule that a contract for the sale of specific goods automatically passed property, hedging it around with exceptions and presumptions, and still longer to escape from the problems generated by the rule that contracts for the sale of non-specific goods did not. The situation arises most frequently with claims historically rooted in the equitable jurisdiction of the Court of Chancery, whose typical mode of intervention was to attach a trust to money or property in issue. Thus, because of its split derivation from both Common law and Equity, the modern law of unjust enrichment is shot through with both a degree of ambiguity in determining whether or not a claim is a proprietary claim or not and a degree of capriciousness in the results reached. Yet, where the defendant is insolvent, or where third parties are concerned, the distinction is of crucial importance.

Hangovers are least dangerous when they are facilitative rather than restrictive, when they provide an additional, if unnecessary, means to achieve some end. Within the law of torts, for example, it is not obvious that a separate tort of nuisance protecting the enjoyment of land is essential nor that its results differ in any significant way from the results that are achieved by the tort of negligence. The special rules relating to the escape of fire, dating back to the fifteenth century and before, and their nineteenth-century analogue, the imposition of strict liability for the escape of dangerous things under the rule in *Rylands* v *Fletcher*, can—as the High Court of Australia has shown—be reformulated within the tort of negligence without excessive difficulty. The principal consequence of all of these is, as more generally, to clog up the law by allowing several parallel routes, each with its own pitfalls, to the same end result. Sometimes, indeed, they can be pressed into service in beneficent ways: trespass to land can be used as an efficient mechanism to assert property rights even when there is no injury to the plaintiff; in nuisance an injunction against future conduct can be obtained; and an action in defamation can be used to clear the victim's name. Sometimes they can be overstretched, as with the stillborn attempt to create a tort of harassment in the shell of the action of private nuisance. Sometimes they can lead to unexpected results, as in the different compensatory consequences of the torts of negligence and trespass. Negligence is all-or-nothing, and, so long as the plaintiff shows on balance of probabilities that the defendant's act caused the injury, full compensation can be recovered.[3] But where the causation of loss is not technically part of the cause of action, as, for example, in trespass, the assessment of damages is geared to the probabilities; hence a plaintiff who cannot show that the defendant probably caused the injury complained of may still recover some damages, while one who can satisfy the balance-of-probabilities test may still not recover full compensation.[4] This perhaps crucial distinction is the legacy of the initial division between trespass and case, as skewed by the nineteenth-century realignment within the law of torts.

[3] *Hotson* v. *East Berkshire Area Health Authority* [1987] AC 750; *Wilsher* v. *Essex Area Health Authority* [1988] AC 1074.

[4] As recognized in argument in *Hotson* v. *East Berkshire Area Health Authority* [1987] AC 750, 778. The distinction between negligence and trespass may also have implications for the operation of limitation periods, though the courts have minimized these: *Stubbings* v. *Webb* [1993] AC 498. All these difficulties were recognized by Lord Denning M.R. in *Letang* v. *Cooper* [1965] 1 QB 232, 238–40.

Index

Gaius 6 n., 264, 285 n.
Gilbert, Sir Jeffrey 216–17, 237–8
Glanvill 11, 13, 17–21, 74
God's penny 74–6
  see also Earnest money
Good faith in contracts 252, 258
  in Roman law 8
Grotius, Hugo 158, 166, 167, 276, 286

Handshake 2, 5
Heirs, liability in contract 78
Highwaymen, partnership between 211–12
Hobbes, Thomas 215–17
Holmes, Oliver Wendell 197

Illegality in contracts 211–12
Indemnity 266
Indian law:
  Indian Contract Act 227, 235, 253, 255
  Recovery for mistake of law 289
  Rejection of theory of implied contract
    284–5
Inducing breach of contract 180, 243
Inequality in bargains 210, 277
Iniuria:
  in Bracton 16, 100
  in Roman Law 6, 7, 16
Innkeepers, liability to guests 42, 53, 62
Innominate contracts, in Roman law 9
Insurance 196, 197
Intention to Create Legal Relations 233–4,
  247–8

Jones, Sir William 164, 165, 169
Judge and jury 63–4, 116 n., 161–2, 173–4,
  188–9, 233
Judicial proceedings, no liability for
  misconduct in 65 n., 193 n.
Jury:
  disappearance of 188–9, 221
  and fault 58, 158
  and medieval civil procedure 49–51, 64–5
  see also Judge and jury
Justinian, Institutes of 6, 19, 74, 99, 165 n.

Keener, William 285
King's Peace, breach of 3, 13, 39–40
Kiss 5

Labourers, Statute and Ordinance of 31, 38,
  66, 75, 127–8
Leake, S. M. 227, 250, 277
Lease 75, 94
  and covenant 21, 26–7, 37
  and trespassory remedies 37–8
Leprosy, *see* Syphilis
Letters of credit 205–6

lex Aquilia 7, 16, 159
Libel, *see* Defamation
Loss, wrongful:
  in assumpsit 130–1
  as basis of liability in nuisance 105
  as basis of liability in trespass 14–15

Macmillan, Lord 190–1
Macpherson, William 227, 235
Maine, Sir Henry 284–5
Malice in defamation 113–14, 115, 124, 184–5
Mansfield, Lord 204, 205, 224, 236, 264, 271,
  272, 276, 281
Marriage:
  allegation of 47
  contracts in restraint of 212
  loss of 122
  offer and acceptance 222
  promises on 81, 82, 142, 144, 207
Misrepresentation 257
  fraudulent 181; *see also* fraud
  innocent 208, 235, 252
  negligent 180–1, 192, 208, 247, 252
Mistake 73, 210, 225–9, 274, 290–1
  of law 289

Natural law:
  contract 217–19, 237
  liability and fault 158, 166–8
Negligence:
  definition 169–70
  emergence as tort 164–8
  in nineteenth century 169–84
  and nuisance 200
  and trespass 200, 302
  in trespass on the case 54, 134
  in twentieth century 188–201
Non est factum, defence of 20, 72, 228
Nottingham, Lord 202
Novel disseisin, assize of 13, 98, 100
  see also Nuisance
Nuisance 13, 69, 98–106
  action on the case 103–6
  assize of 98–100, 103–4
  in Bracton 99
  common 106 n.
  injunction 99, 101, 104 n.
  in London 101
  need for damage 105
  and negligence 200
  in nineteenth century 183, 185–6
  public 101–3, 106
  remoteness of damage 200
  and trespass 101–3
  viscontiel 100–1

Oath 4, 5, 136, 137 n.